U.S. PRESIDENTS AND
FOREIGN POLICY MISTAKES

U.S. PRESIDENTS AND FOREIGN POLICY MISTAKES

Stephen G. Walker
and Akan Malici

STANFORD SECURITY SERIES

An Imprint of Stanford University Press

Stanford, California

Stanford University Press
Stanford, California

Special discounts for bulk quantities of Stanford Security Series are
available to corporations, professional associations, and other
organizations. For details and discount information, contact the special
sales department of Stanford University Press. Tel: (650) 736-1782,
Fax: (650) 736-1784

Printed in the United States of America on acid-free,
archival-quality paper

Library of Congress Cataloging-in-Publication Data

Walker, Stephen G., 1942– author.
U.S. presidents and foreign policy mistakes / Stephen G. Walker
and Akan Malici.
pages cm
Includes bibliographical references and index.
ISBN 978-0-8047-7498-7 (cloth : alk. paper)—
ISBN 978-0-8047-7499-4 (pbk. : alk. paper)
1. United States—Foreign relations—Decision making. 2. National
security—United States—Decision making. 3. Presidents—United
States—Decision making. I. Malici, Akan, 1974– author. II. Title.
JZ1480.W33 2011
327.73—dc22   2011004620

Typeset by Westchester Book Composition in 10/15 Sabon

Contents

CONTENTS

Preface

IN THIS BOOK we undertake a critical examination of U.S. foreign policy by focusing on foreign policy mistakes made by U.S. presidents in the exercise of power. Our goals are to understand how mistakes occur and how to avoid or fix them. These goals have led us inevitably to consider why mistakes happen, a task that can be approached on a case-by-case basis or within the framework of a general theory of mistakes. Our approach is the latter one, which has led us to incorporate into our analysis insights from several theories of action and interaction in the academic literature on foreign policy and international relations. However, we envision our audience as broader than the academic community, extending into the ranks of both ordinary citizens and political leaders. It is tough to write for all three of these audiences, which bring different perspectives and degrees of interest to bear on our topic. Since the main thrust of our analysis is to provide both a map and a compass for avoiding foreign policy mistakes, therefore, we think it is appropriate here to provide similar guidance to the readers of this book who may want to find their way to some parts of our analysis and avoid other areas.

Parts I, II, and III of the book address questions that ordinary citizens and students are likely to raise about foreign policy mistakes: What are they? How many kinds are there? How do you tell one kind from another? What causes them? What are some examples of each kind of mistake in the history of U.S. foreign policy over the last 100 years or so up to the present? We answer these questions with a relatively simple classification scheme for distinguishing different kinds of foreign policy mistakes, based on ordinary usage of the word "mistake," which differentiates between mistakes of omission and commission. We take this distinction and use it to identify mistakes regarding how to recognize and exercise social power in world politics. Then we show how various episodes in U.S. diplomatic and military history illustrate these different kinds of mistakes.

Parts IV and V of the book address questions that directly interest academic policy analysts and political leaders: How does one avoid foreign policy mistakes and fix them if they occur? What are optimum strategies for making foreign policy decisions? How and why do these strategies insure against mistakes and failures and raise the chances for successful outcomes? We answer these questions with the assistance of an array of theoretical and methodological tools, including game theory, role theory, exchange theory, social network theory, and signed graph theory. We also examine evidence from computer simulations by social scientists and philosophers and from extensive reviews of world politics compiled by historians and other social scientists. We use this information to construct a general argument on behalf of certain foreign policy strategies while being more critical of others. Instead of historical case studies, the analytical narratives in these chapters are told with tables and figures adorned by mathematical symbols and statistics.

We end the book with a summary of the whole argument and a list of ten precepts that attempt to capture its main elements. A casual reader may want to begin there and then select chapters of personal interest from this menu. We expect a more specialized reader will probably want to start at the beginning and follow the entire argument in detail. In our efforts to make this argument and to receive helpful feedback, we have presented aspects of it to audiences at Arizona State University, Baker University, Furman University, the University of Kansas, the University of Missouri, the University of North Texas, Texas Christian University, Zirve University (Turkey), Sabanci University (Turkey), and Trinity College (Dublin), and at annual meetings of the American Political Science Association and the International Studies Association.

We are grateful for the comments from colleagues in these venues and for the careful reviews of the entire manuscript by Yaacov Vertzberger and Patrick James. We are indebted as well to Steven Brams, Robert Axelrod, and Robert Jervis, whose collective scholarship on agent strategies and system effects in world politics informed and inspired much of the theoretical analysis in this book. Any errors that remain are our own. It is our pleasure to acknowledge the assistance and enthusiasm of Geoffrey Burn and Jessica Walsh at Stanford University Press, John

Donohue at Westchester Book Services, and the institutional support from the School of Politics and Global Studies at Arizona State University and the Department of Political Science at Furman University.

We dedicate this book to our respective wives, Jacqueline Dierks-Walker and Johnna Malici, who have believed in the project and its authors throughout its gestation from notes scribbled on the back of an envelope outside a classroom in Dublin to publication as a book several years later.

Stephen G. Walker	Akan Malici
Flagstaff, Arizona	Greenville, South Carolina

U.S. PRESIDENTS AND FOREIGN POLICY MISTAKES

PART I

The Anatomy of Foreign Policy Mistakes

CHAPTER 1

Mistakes as a Feature of
Everyday Political Life

INTRODUCTION

In the *Apology*, Plato recounts Socrates' inquiry into human wisdom. The story begins with the journey of Socrates' pupil, Chaerephon, to the Oracle in Delphi where he asks the question, "Who is the wisest of all men?" The Oracle responds, "No one is wiser than Socrates." The pupil reports this to Socrates who, knowing that he himself is not wise, subsequently seeks out a politician reputed for his wisdom and aims to demonstrate the fallibility of the Oracle. To his disappointment, Socrates finds that the politician has no wisdom either, although the politician thinks of himself as wise. Socrates concludes, "Well, although I do not suppose that either of us knows anything really beautiful and good, I am better off than he is—for he knows nothing, and thinks that he knows. I neither know nor think I know" (Plato 1892, 21). In the end it is this recognition, Socrates' self-awareness, that vindicates the Oracle.

Philosophers from Socrates through Michel de Montaigne, Baruch Spinoza, Immanuel Kant, and Isaiah Berlin remind us that true wisdom and full knowledge may be a utopian fantasy. They instead argue that uncertainty is an inescapable fact of human life. They stress that any action, however carefully undertaken, involves the risk of error and potentially disastrous consequences. Indeed, uncertainty may be one of only two certainties in life. The other is that humans will go on making statements and engaging in risky action even in a world of uncertainty. The obvious implication is the need to develop a calculus of action under the condition of uncertainty. The philosophers' answer to this need is rather simple. The desired calculus is an ethic of humility and modesty.

The governance of a state requires more. In *The Republic*, Plato (2000, 191) likens this task to the command of a ship sailing an ocean of uncertainty:

Imagine . . . one ship and a state of affairs on board something like this. There's the shipowner, larger and stronger than everyone in the ship, but deaf and rather short-sighted, with a knowledge of sailing to match his eyesight. The sailors are quarrelling among themselves over captaincy of the ship, each one thinking that he ought to be the captain, though he has never learned the skill, nor can he point to the person who taught him or a time when he was learning.

The combination of an ocean of relative uncertainty sailed by a ship of human beings with significantly limited powers of navigation is clearly a recipe for the inevitable making of mistakes. Indeed, in much of what humans set out to undertake, they are surrounded by uncertainty and bounded in skills or otherwise. Such is the human condition. Some of these human shortcomings are identified in contemporary terms by Robyn Dawes (1976), who describes how cognitive and motivated biases lead to limitations of the human mind in processing information from the environment without distortions (see also Kahneman, Slovic, and Tversky 1982; Bell, Raiffa, and Tversky 1988). These biases appear in the form of ideologies, self-convictions, emotions, memories, misperceptions, and other contingent elements of the human mind that make us apt to make mistakes. They affect ordinary people and, of course, also leaders as they steer the ship of state. The tragedy is that neither ordinary people nor state leaders are always aware of their biases or their mistakes, and the latter are only discovered with the benefit of hindsight.

An exchange in the aftermath of 9/11 and following the U.S. invasion of Iraq underlines the importance of the insights of Plato and Dawes. It has also served as the immediate catalyst for this book about foreign policy mistakes. In a news conference on April 13, 2004, President George W. Bush was asked to name his biggest mistake since 9/11 and what lessons he had learned since then. In his response Bush joked, "I wish you'd have given me this written question ahead of time so I could plan for it." He then took a longer pause before adding, "I am sure something will pop into my head here in the midst of this press conference, with all the pressure of trying to come up with an answer, but it hadn't [sic] yet." Ultimately, the president wandered in his meandering style from affirming his decisions to invade Afghanistan and Iraq to stating his unshaken belief that the former Iraqi president Saddam Hussein possessed weapons of mass destruction and would be inclined to put them to use. In the end, President Bush could not identify any mistakes he had made since 9/11.

One may wonder whether the president's remarks were simply ingenuous, a reflection of his character, or an indication of a real puzzle that needs to be investigated. In this book we assume the third possibility, that foreign policy mistakes pose a real puzzle. One can be confident that presidential historians, political scientists, and commentators will judge President Bush to have made genuine mistakes. This assertion follows from recognizing that mistakes are unavoidable facts of daily life for citizens and politicians alike. This inescapable fact plagued the first U.S. president and every one of his successors, and will also befall every future president of the country. Given the ubiquity of this problem, we ask a series of fundamental questions in this book: What are foreign policy mistakes? How and why do they occur? What can be done to avoid them?

It may come as no surprise that scholars have focused on mistakes in the past. What distinguishes this book from some previous efforts is that our answers to these questions center on a single concept—that of *power*. Power has more than one meaning, including the manifestation of physical power in the form of force or energy in physics, the actual exercise of social power in the form of control by an agent over a patient in social systems, and the capacity of an agent to exercise either social or physical power in politics (McClelland 1966). The ambiguity in the meaning of power leads analysts to discount or qualify its use for explaining human behavior (Haas 1953; Claude 1962; Brams 1994, 121). Others emphasize that the exercise of power is at the core of human interactions and, specified properly, offers important insights into human behavior (Dahl 1957; French and Raven 1959; Bachrach and Baratz 1962; Emerson 1962, 1976; McClelland 1966; Lukes 1974; Baldwin 1979; Morgenthau 1985; Gelb 2009). We shall take the latter position and apply these conceptualizations of power at some length throughout this book to explain foreign policy mistakes.

At the core of our book is Vladimir Lenin's famous question, "kto-kovo?" regarding the exercise of power, translated literally as "who-whom?" and understood as "who (can destroy, control, utilize) whom?"

(Leites 1953, 27–29). Our general argument is that improper, inaccurate, or misinformed answers to this question specify and explain mistakes by the makers of policy. Conversely, we claim that correct answers can avoid mistakes and reduce policy failures. Although all politics requires policy makers to answer correctly Lenin's question in order to avoid mistakes, our specific concern in this book is with U.S. presidents and foreign policy mistakes.

When presidents commit mistakes, they are costly regardless of whether they occur in the arena of domestic politics or international politics. Presidential mistakes in the domain of international politics, however, can be, and often are, more costly and deadly than in any other policy area. The U.S. wars in Korea and Vietnam, and the ongoing wars in Afghanistan and Iraq, are cases in point. Good judgment can avoid wars or win them while poor judgment can start wars or lose them (Renshon and Larson 2003, vii). International political history is full of disastrous decisions and avoidable mistakes by leaders who have put not only the country's troops in harm's way but also the safety and well-being of the entire nation.

The study of questions about foreign policy mistakes is perhaps more pressing than ever. The bipolar cold war order, with its rather well-defined rules, is passé for two decades. The events of 9/11 have introduced us to a world in which the ancient Chinese curse, "may you live in interesting times," would seem to condemn us to a life of uncertainty, flux, and danger. Following 9/11 and the wars in Afghanistan and Iraq, new challenges are emerging. U.S. relations with Syria and Iran are troublesome. Generally, the situation in the Middle East continues to deteriorate and could easily lead to another full-scale war with U.S. involvement. Also of concern are the tensions between nuclear powers Pakistan and India, which may compel the United States to get involved. Analysts also have imagined scenarios with heavy U.S. military engagement as a response to the acquisition of nuclear weapons by North Korea. The United States' future may well depend on whether and how U.S. presidents make or avoid mistakes in the face of these and many other challenges.

In the remainder of this chapter we review the academic scholarship on mistakes. Our hope is that by the end of this exercise we will have established a general understanding of what foreign mistakes are and why they occur. While insights from past scholarship on foreign policy mistakes will help guide our inquiry, we hope in the next chapter to provide a more systematic, rigorous, and policy-relevant framework for foreign policy analysis and evaluation.

WHAT ARE FOREIGN POLICY MISTAKES?

It might at first seem unnecessary to define what constitutes a mistake. Indeed, it is tempting to simply borrow from Justice Potter Stewart's assessment of pornography and accept that we will know a mistake when we see it. However, in a way this approach is too simple and, moreover, it is not true. If what counts (or should count) as a mistake is only in the eye of the beholder, then serious analysis may degenerate quickly into partisan debate and an inability or unwillingness to recognize a mistake—witness President Bush's inability to name a single mistake and the partisan divide over his decision to invade Iraq on March 20, 2003. What we seek is a more objective standard from which one can judge mistakes more reliably.

According to the *American Heritage Dictionary* (1994, 534), the word "mistake" means "an error or fault" or "a misconception or misunderstanding" and comes from the old Norse *mistaka*, "take in error." The same source (p. 288) defines "error" as derived from the Latin *errare*, "wander," and offers three definitions: "1. An unintentional deviation from is [*sic*] what is correct, right, or true. 2. The condition of being incorrect or wrong. 3. Baseball. A defensive misplay." These definitions highlight important similarities and differences in mistakes. They share the common feature of "wandering," that is, deviating from some standard of "rectitude" (error) or "truth" (understanding), which implies a standard or context (e.g., a baseball game) in which to identify the nature of the deviation. Two different dimensions of mistakes are also implied: behavioral (misplay) and cognitive (misconception).

Underlying all of these features is the assumption that all mistakes are *procedural* (i.e., they are cognitive or behavioral phenomena that should not be confused with their consequences or outcomes). The importance of a given mistake in thought or action is often judged by its effects. If a baseball player makes a defensive misplay that costs his team a victory, it carries greater weight in human affairs. It is important to remember that although a procedural mistake may lead to a substantive failure, a causal connection is not always present. Sometimes failures occur despite the absence of mistakes, and even when mistakes occur, they do not necessarily affect the outcome. The occurrence of a misplay in baseball that yields an unearned run does not affect the outcome of the game when the score is already so lopsided in favor of one team that the outcome is not in doubt. It is also possible for mistakes to follow failure—a team that is behind may try too hard and make a misplay.

It is also important to realize that other causes besides mistakes influence success or failure in both sports and politics. It is wise as well to remember that sometimes there is a tension between avoiding mistakes and avoiding defeat. The well-known sportswriter Grantland Rice made the famous observation, "It's not whether you win or lose, but how you play the game." A lesser-known baseball manager, Leo ("the Lip") Durocher, is also famous for his brash comment, "Nice guys finish last." Together they remind us that in baseball the players are goal oriented and sometimes forget or ignore the rules of the game in order to achieve those goals. More generally, failures in everyday life come in two forms: mistakes are procedural failures whereas outcomes are substantive failures. And sometimes it is possible to achieve substantive successes at the price of procedural failures.

These insights apply to political life. When Germany attacked Poland in 1939, Hitler and Stalin divided Poland between them according to the terms of the Nazi-Soviet Non-Aggression Pact signed a couple of weeks before the outbreak of war. Although this agreement called for the two dictators to settle disputes between them without the use of force, Germany invaded the Soviet Union almost two years later and forced the Red Army out of its part of occupied Poland. This reversal of relationships between the two totalitarian regimes also brought Russia into World War II on the side of Britain and the exiled government of Poland in London. London Poles pressed immediately to learn more about the whereabouts and welfare of Polish prisoners of war captured earlier by Soviet forces in 1939 (Herz 1966).

Previous inquiries had yielded vague reports of their hasty evacuation from Poland far behind the lines into Russia ahead of the invading Nazi forces. When Nazi forces near Smolensk discovered the graves of these prisoners in 1943, the Soviet Union attempted to blame the Germans. However, forensic evidence at the site in the Katyn Forest pointed toward the Russians as their executioners in 1939 (Herz 1966, 45–46, 66–67). It was also a decision recognized as an error of some kind by Lavrenti Beria, the Soviet secret police chief, who reportedly declared to some Polish members of the London exile government as early as the spring of 1940 that "a great mistake had been made" with respect to the then-missing Polish prisoners of war (Herz 1966, 45).

What exactly was the Soviet mistake associated with this decision? At the time of their capture in 1939, the Soviet Union and Germany were fighting the Poles as a common foe. In addition to the moral mistake of violating the rules of international law for the treatment of prisoners of war (POWs), the Soviets were guided by Stalinist ideology that diagnosed the POWs as class enemies and potential counterrevolutionaries in territory that had been part of the old tsarist empire. The prisoners were reserve officers in the Polish army who occupied elite civilian positions in Polish society when they were not mobilized for active duty. When the Soviet Union executed these soldiers, they were also purging the potential leaders of an opposition movement to the partition of Poland between Russia and Germany (Herz 1966).

The "great mistake" of execution rather than imprisonment prevented the Soviet Union from repatriating these officers when the Soviet Union and Poland became de facto allies against Germany after the Nazis invaded Russia in June 1941. When the truth came out about their fate, it became an important local cause of the cold war's beginnings between the United States and the Soviet Union following World War II. The Katyn Forest massacre alienated Russia from Poland's exile government in London. In turn, this estrangement contributed significantly to a breakdown in the implementation of the Declaration on Poland signed by Russia, Britain, and the United States at the Yalta conference in 1945, which called for free elections and a democratic government in Poland. Ultimately, this failure was one of the issues that converted the two superpowers from peaceful partners to cold warriors following the end of World War II (Herz 1966, 76–112).

CONCEPTUALIZING FOREIGN POLICY MISTAKES

We infer from the distinctions made in ordinary language about the common invocation of a standard of truth or rectitude to identify different kinds of mistakes that the Soviet foreign policy mistake in this example falls into one or more of three general domains: (1) *morality*, in which a moral rule or law is violated; (2) *intelligence*, in which a cognitive judgment is blinded by ignorance, bias, or passion; and (3) *policy*, in which a prescription for behavior is costly and results in unanticipated and undesirable effects. A foreign policy mistake may involve all three domains insofar as a foreign policy decision is evaluated as (1) right or wrong, (2) informed or misinformed, and (3) effective or ineffective. The Soviet decision to execute Polish POWs and bury them in the Katyn Forest is a foreign policy decision that falls into all three domains. It was a violation of international law, based on a diagnostic judgment blinded by ignorance of the future and by communist ideology, which led to a prescription for a policy action that alienated future allies.

If we consider the Katyn Forest case more carefully, it suggests some other features of mistakes. Moral, intelligence, and policy errors may be mistakes of *omission* or *commission* (i.e., each kind of error may be an error in two opposite directions). Leaving moral mistakes aside and crossing these possibilities with the categories of *diagnosis* and *prescription* creates the general typology of mistakes in Figure 1.1. The Katyn Forest episode appears to fall under the Commission column as a case in which Soviet decision makers diagnosed the Polish POWs as a class enemy. This ideological diagnosis of the situation led them to prescribe the preemptive action of executing the POWs soon after their capture by Soviet troops in the fall of 1939. The Katyn Forest case appears to fit the "Too Much/Too Soon" pattern of commission associated in Figure 1.1 with more dogmatic decision makers.

Although the ideological filter of Stalinist ideology probably blinded the Soviets into misperceiving the situation and prescribing an erroneous

FIGURE 1.1   *General Typology of Foreign Policy Mistakes*

	TYPES OF MISTAKES	
	OMISSION (Pragmatic)	COMMISSION (Dogmatic)
INTELLIGENCE (Diagnosis)	Detection (Too Little)	Misperception (Too Much)
DECISION-MAKING PROCESSES		
FOREIGN POLICY (Prescription)	Hesitation (Too Late)	Preemption (Too Soon)

preemptive response in this case, the lack of such a filter can lead to the opposite pattern of mistakes. Without such an organized belief system to guide diagnosis and prescription, a decision maker may detect too little relevant information and hesitate too late in responding to a situation. The result may be the "Too Little/Too Late" pattern of omission associated in Figure 1.1 with more pragmatic decision makers. Generally, decision makers can engage in mistakes of omission or commission regarding an *opportunity* or a *threat*. The former is a cooperative situation in which gains are likely, whereas the latter is a conflict situation in which losses are likely (Lebow and Stein 1987; Herrmann 1988). These different consequences are associated with possibilities for different kinds of substantive failures (outcomes), which follow from different kinds of procedural failures (mistakes).

One can distinguish among four types of substantive failures that may result from procedural failures, as shown in Figure 1.2. For threat situations there are deterrence failures and false alarm failures. A deterrence failure may be the result when a decision maker does not detect an existing threat of losses or else hesitates too long and thereby does not take action sufficient to deter the threat. A false alarm failure may be the result when a decision maker misperceives a threat of losses that does not exist or initiates action that creates a threat. For opportunity situations there are reassurance failures and false hope failures. A reassurance failure may be the result when a decision maker does not detect an existing opportunity for gains or else hesitates too long and thereby misses the opportunity for making gains. A false hope failure may be the result

FIGURE 1.2 *Types of Situations and Types of Foreign Policy Consequences*

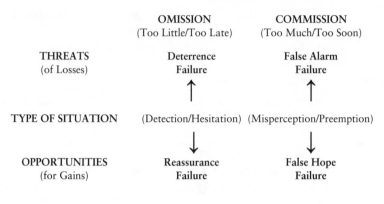

when a decision maker misperceives an opportunity for gains that does not exist or initiates action that does not increase gains.

Mistakes of omission (too little/too late) leading to substantive outcomes of deterrence failure or reassurance failure were common in British relations with Germany in the late 1930s (Taylor 1962). A deterrence failure occurred in 1938 when Britain's "keep Germany guessing" strategy of hesitation failed to deter Germany's occupation of the Sudetenland in Czechoslovakia (Colvin 1971; Middlemas 1972). Belated British efforts to negotiate an alliance with Russia against Germany in 1939 resulted in a reassurance failure. Joseph Stalin elected instead to sign a nonaggression pact with Hitler after Britain had rebuffed Soviet offers of support the previous year against Germany during the Sudeten crisis (Colvin 1971). The disastrous consequences are well known. Finally, the Katyn Forest massacre was also based on the Soviet misperception of gains in cooperating with Germany in the removal of Poland from the map of Europe. A mistake of commission (too much/too soon) and a moral failure, it was also a false hope failure.

The taxonomies and the illustrative typologies of mistakes and examples presented so far are heuristics (i.e., suggestive ways of thinking about mistakes and cases). It rarely happens that actual empirical cases will neatly fit a particular cell of these typologies. Although reality is too complex and defies such rigorous categorization, typologies nevertheless fulfill two important functions. First, they allow a more systematic approach to the identification of foreign policy mistakes. Second, they provide an appropriate vocabulary for the understanding and analysis of foreign policy mistakes.

To sum up, foreign policy mistakes fall broadly into two general categories of omission and commission regarding either threats or opportunities. Each kind of mistake may occur at two different stages of the decision-making process: diagnosing a foreign policy situation or prescribing a foreign policy response. A third possibility is that a mistake occurs at both stages of the decision-making process. Having elaborated how foreign policy mistakes can be classified, what is missing is an explanation for why they occur. We find that this question is best answered by first examining in more detail the processes of diagnosis and prescription in making or avoiding foreign policy mistakes.

AVOIDING OR MAKING FOREIGN POLICY MISTAKES

Avoiding political mistakes ideally requires from the decision maker certain qualities and skills or, in the words of philosopher Isaiah Berlin (1996, 46), "a capacity for integrating a vast amalgam of constantly changing, multicolored, evanescent, perpetually overlapping data." By "integrating" Berlin means "to see the data as elements in a single pattern, with their implications, to see them as symptoms of past and future possibilities, to see them pragmatically, that is in terms of *what you or others can or will do to them,* and *what they can or will do to others or to you*" (Ibid.; emphasis added). Berlin's description of the necessary qualities of leadership reflects our understanding of mistakes as incorrect answers to Lenin's Question. In the absence of these qualities, incorrect answers to the *kto-kovo* (who-whom) question become likely and result in mistakes.

We have already stated that identifying and assessing foreign policy mistakes requires a standard of truth or rectitude from which to make analytical judgments. A first approximation of such a standard is that mistakes manifest themselves as the pursuit of policy contrary to the self-interest of the decision maker or the interests of his constituency (Wriggins 1969; Bueno de Mesquita et al. 2003). For such a mistake to qualify and be recognized as a public folly, it must meet two criteria. First, the policy undertaken "must have been perceived as counterproductive in its own time, not merely by hindsight." Second, "a feasible alternative course of action must have been available" (Tuchman 1984, 5). The feasible alternative course of action must also be understood as a *rational* course of action (Bueno de Mesquita and Lalman 1992).

An emphasis on rationality leads to a formalization of our effort to conceptualize foreign policy mistakes. The rational actor model can be traced back to the work of Von Neumann and Morgenstern (1953) in the early 1940s. In their expected utility theory, decision makers engage in calculations about the outcomes "that could result from the available choices as well as the chances of those outcomes occurring, and then choose the alternative that seems in some rough way to offer the best potential" (Beach and Mitchell 1978, 441). Rational choice theorist Mancur Olson (1965, 65; emphasis added) explains that an individual's actions are rational when her objectives are "pursued by means that are *efficient* and *effective* for achieving these objectives." This means that the evaluation of whether any particular action is rational or not must be considered not only in terms of the *benefits*, that is, whether the policy goals will be achieved, but also in terms of the *cost* that it would bring (Baldwin 2000).

In their classic work *Politics, Economics, and Welfare*, Dahl and Lindblom (1953, 38–39) explain why both aspects are important considerations in conceptualizing mistakes:

An action is rational to the extent that it is "correctly" designed to maximize goal achievement. . . . Given more than one goal (the usual human condition), an action is rational to the extent that it is correctly designed to maximize net goal achievement. . . . An action is "correctly" designed to maximize goal satisfaction to the extent that it is efficient, or in other words to the extent that goal satisfaction exceeds goal cost.

The need for comparative evaluation of both the costs and the benefits of policy alternatives in the decision-making process is also argued by Simon (1976, 179):

An administrative choice is incorrectly posed, then, when it is posed as a choice between possibility A, with low costs and small results, and possibility B, with high costs and large results. For A should be substituted a third possibility C, which would include A plus the alternative activities made possible by the cost difference between A and B. If this is done, the choice resolves itself into a comparison of the results obtainable by the application of fixed resources to the alternative activities B and C.

Applying the argument specifically to the area of foreign and security policy, Bueno de Mesquita (1981, 183) suggests a similar logic with respect to choosing between force and diplomacy as two alternatives of statecraft:

Leaders expecting a larger net gain through diplomacy than through war . . . should rationally elect to pursue their goals through diplomatic bargaining and negotiating. This is true even if the expected gross gain from war is larger than the gross gain from diplomacy, provided that the cost differential is large enough (as it frequently is) to make the net effect of diplomacy preferable to war.

The identification of opportunity costs as an important calculation also allows us to specify more precisely an important distinction made earlier in this chapter between procedural policy *mistakes* and substantive policy *failures*. Mistakes do not always produce failures, nor are mistakes always equivalent to policy failures. It is possible for a policy to realize its goals and still be a mistake, because of the costs of success. As we have suggested earlier, it may also be the case that a policy will not achieve its goals through no fault of the decision maker, because of the efforts of others to thwart their achievement. A policy may conversely achieve its goals because of the mistakes of others rather than one's own efforts and skill (Baldwin 2000).

We contend that these rational actor calculations represent a standard of truth, and deviations from this standard constitute foreign policy mistakes. Two factors may contribute to deviations from this standard, and they are reflected in Isaiah Berlin's quote above. The first factor is a miscalculation of what others can or will do to self. The second factor is a miscalculation of what self can or should do to others. In either case, a less-than-optimal calculation of cost–benefit ratios can cause potentially inaccurate or improper answers to Lenin's *kto-kovo* question regarding power politics and subsequently to a mistaken decision.

If avoiding mistakes is equal to making rational decisions and making foreign policy mistakes is equal to making irrational choices, this conceptualization still begs the question: why do decision makers fail to engage in rational decision making? The decision-making literature identifies an abundance of factors that may cause deviations from a rational course of action. In the next section we provide an illustrative list of the kinds of such factors and show that explanations for foreign policy mistakes can be couched at different levels of analysis and different levels of generalization. All of them constitute possible causal mechanisms that limit the capacity to make rational choices among alternative courses of action and thereby lead to foreign policy mistakes.

EXPLAINING FOREIGN POLICY MISTAKES

The analysis of foreign policy decision making has long been dominated by rational choice approaches. Decisions can be understood as the product of a calculated process of problem solving by key actors pursuing well-specified interests. Ideally, the process encompasses several demanding tasks, including comprehensive problem diagnosis, holistic information search, assessing the consequences of alternatives, cost–benefit computations, and choice. Built on deductive logic, in these models

one does not need to make elaborate, highly speculative inferences concerning what was going on inside the minds of particular policy makers at particular times. One simply posits that governments respond in a rational . . . manner to the reward and punishment contingencies of the international environment. (Tetlock 1991, 24)

Decisions made this way constitute good judgment. In effect, this process can also be understood as equal to the avoidance of mistakes through purposeful action (Lake and Powell 1999).

A key premise of political psychologists is that these assumptions and the qualities this type of decision-making process requires are unrealistic.

Vertzberger (1990, 144) contends that foreign policy problems are generally "ill-structured" and that decision makers "grope in a maze of uncertainty as to the meaning of the past, the nature of the present, and the shape of the future" (see also Steinbrunner 1974). Political psychologists argue that "policy-makers, like ordinary mortals, see the world through a glass darkly—through the simplified images that they create of the international scene" (Tetlock 1998, 376). In short, ill-structured foreign policy problems can hinder proper diagnosis of a situation and the proper prescription of a response. Therefore, they obstruct effective and efficient (i.e., rational) cost–benefit calculations and lead to mistakes.

In addition to "ill-structured" problems, these scholars also argue that the decision maker's actual decision-making capacities are often far from optimal, and therefore foreign policy choices cannot be understood by the deductive logic of rational choice approaches. Instead, one needs to study the processes by which they are made. A linear model of information processing and choice fails because it misses a host of agential and structural contingencies that occur during the decision-making process and bias the decision maker's diagnostic and prescriptive propensities (Dawes 1976; Slovic, Fischoff, and Lichtenstein 1977; Betts 1978; Nisbett and Ross 1980). These contingencies can be located at individual, group, or organizational levels of analysis, and they can have the potential to steer the decision away from a rational course. A brief review below provides examples of various antecedent conditions that result in either diagnostic or prescriptive mistakes, or both. Because any factor at the group or organizational level of analysis is ultimately translated to the individual level for executive decision, we focus mostly on the latter.

Scholars analyzing agential contingencies subscribe to an ecological approach introduced to the study of foreign policy decision making in the 1950s and 1960s (Sprout and Sprout, 1956, 1965). The ecological approach contends that the connection between the environment and a decision is not direct but is mediated by the subjective perceptual representation or the psychological climate of leaders and the construction of the environment in their minds (Snyder, Bruck, and Sapin 1962; Brecher, Steinberg, and Stein 1969, 48, 77, 81). In turn, the psychological climate is shaped by a leader's belief system, personal motivations, personality traits, and similar factors.

Robert Axelrod's *Structure of Decision* (1976) and Robert Jervis's classic *Perception and Misperception in International Politics* (1976) are among the seminal works in this area. Beyond the factors already mentioned, Axelrod and Jervis draw attention to sources of mistakes such as subjective cognitive maps, heuristics, attribution errors, desires to maintain cognitive consistency and avoid cognitive dissonance, selective attention, and other warm emotional or cold cognitive biases that lead to policy distortions. These "contingent elements of personality, prejudice, and subjective preference, and all of the weaknesses of intellect and will which flesh is heir to," as Hans Morgenthau put it, are likely "to deflect foreign policies from their rational course" and subsequently result in mistakes (Morgenthau 1985, 7–8).

Beliefs have been recognized as central in any decision-making process, and they make a leader susceptible to mistakes. Belief systems, as Philip Tetlock (1998, 876) points out, are of "enormous cognitive utility" because they "provide ready answers to fundamental questions about the political world." What is the essential nature of political life? Is the political universe essentially one of harmony or conflict? What is the fundamental character of one's political opponents? What is the best approach for selecting goals or objectives for political action (George 1969)? Because belief systems constitute subjective representations of self and others in the environment, they may distort reality and any decision-making calculations about this reality, resulting in potential foreign policy mistakes.

Beliefs are often the result of past experiences. In his classic work *Lessons of the Past,* Ernest May (1973, ix) argues that "framers of foreign policy are often influenced by beliefs about what history teaches or portends." A glance at twentieth-century U.S. history illustrates the point. The Munich crisis in 1938 led to the "lessons of Munich," which were invoked subsequently by Truman in 1947 in his decision to aid Greece and Turkey and then again in intervening in Korea in 1950. The Munich analogy also influenced the decisions of John F. Kennedy in the Cuban Missile Crisis in 1962, Lyndon B. Johnson in Vietnam in 1965, Ronald Reagan in Nicaragua in the early 1980s, and George H.W. Bush in the

Persian Gulf War in 1990. In turn, each of these crises has acquired its own historical status and led to new lessons or modified previously held beliefs. The "lessons of Korea" influenced U.S. political discourse about Indochina, and the "lessons of Vietnam" were brought forth in debates about crises in the Persian Gulf and in Bosnia.

In a subsequent collaborative work with May, *Thinking in Time* (1986), Richard Neustadt explored further the actual applicability of these analogies. The basic premise of the book is reminiscent of George Santayana's classic aphorism, "Those who cannot remember the past are condemned to repetition" (quoted in Bennett 1999, 1). Neustadt and May (1986, xi, 38) argue that many policy makers do "not know any history to speak of and [are] unaware of suffering any lack." As these authors see it, "usual" decision-making practice is flawed in several ways. Two of these stand out. First is the proposition that decision making is plagued by a tendency toward hasty action, that is, responding to a challenge with the question "what do we do?" rather that "what is the problem?" Second is the failure to question key assumptions, especially about desirable goals and likely consequences.

Neustadt and May (1986) caution that decision makers should focus on explaining why a decision seems to be called for and on identifying the objectives they hope to achieve. The first step in making foreign policy decisions should involve discriminating the "known" from the "unclear" from the "presumed." History then can become useful in determining what the nature of the issue is, whether and how the situation has changed from the status quo ante, and what action has been taken in similar situations, in pursuit of what objectives, and to what effect. The odds for mistakes can be minimized further by subsequently asking "What new Knowns would bring you to change items Presumed? When? And Why?" (Neustadt and May 1986, 152–156). However, there is no guarantee for avoiding mistakes. As Jervis (1976, 275) argues, with a twist on Santayana's aphorism, "Those who remember the past are condemned to make the opposite mistakes."

In *Analogies at War* (1992), Khong shares the assumption that leaders frequently turn to historical analogies for guidance when confronted with novel foreign policy challenges. His efforts are concentrated toward identifying the actual cognitive mechanisms leading to faulty analogical reasoning. At the center of Khong's analysis is the fundamental recognition that human beings are "creatures with limited cognitive capacities." They tend to rely on analogies understood as cognitively stored knowledge structures. These structures help leaders "order, interpret and simplify, in a word, to make sense of the world" (Khong 1992, 12). The dilemma is that people tend to "access analogies on the basis of surface similarities," leading to inferential steps that may, in turn, lead to simplistic and often incorrect interpretations of incoming stimuli (Khong 1992, 14). The result is often a foreign policy mistake.

In addition to beliefs and knowledge structures, scholars have also researched motives as variables influencing decision making. Psychologists have developed a list of twenty motives or "needs" that fall into two fundamental categories—interpersonal harmony seeking and individual assertive striving (Winter 2003a, 23). Applying them to the realm of politics, Winter (2003b, 155) identifies three key motives as a leader's affiliation, power, and achievement motives. The affiliation motive is defined as a concern over establishing, maintaining, or restoring a positive affective relationship with another person or group of persons. The power motivation is a concern over establishing, maintaining, or restoring one's power, that is, one's impact, control, or influence over others. The achievement motivation is a striving for excellence and accomplishment. Winter's review of this literature concludes that these motivations bias the decision-making process in various ways. For example, leaders with a high need for power are higher risk takers than are leaders with a high need for achievement; leaders with a high need for affiliation are more peaceful, whereas leaders with a high need for power are more war prone (Winter 2003b).

A somewhat different focus is given by scholars engaged in personality analysis, although the list of variables here also includes power and affiliation motives. Margaret Hermann (1980, 2003), for example, extends the analysis to the traits of ethnocentricity, suspiciousness, self-confidence, and cognitive complexity. She argues (2003, 186) that "traits provide information that is relevant to assessing how political leaders respond to the constraints in their environment, how they process information, and what motivates them to action." Any one personality trait can lead to a mistake. Overconfidence can lead decision makers to "dismiss opposing views out of hand" and to "assimilate incoming information to their existing beliefs" (Tetlock 1998, 878). High levels of suspiciousness can lead decision makers to exaggerate the value of information fitting their predispositions.

Personality traits have also been shown to play a role in risk-taking behavior. Individual risk orientation is commonly associated with prospect theory (Kahneman and Tversky 1979; Tversky and Kahneman 1986, 1992; Levy 1997). The chief differences between the personality approaches and prospect theory is that the latter focuses on the situational context and not individual differences. Prospect theory asserts that subjects think in terms of gains and losses and that their risk propensities vary from one kind of situation to the next. When decision situations are "framed" as a loss in relation to a subjective reference point, individuals tend to be risk acceptant; when these situations are framed as a gain regarding the same reference point, individuals tend to be risk averse.

A concern with prospect theory by personality theorists is that it "depersonalizes" the actual decision-making situation. Contrary to the prediction of prospect theory, Kowert and Hermann (1997, 623) find that open and intuitive individuals "prefer risk more strongly when problems were framed as gains." In contrast to expectations from prospect theory, they also find that individuals who are low in anxiety and self-consciousness "preferred risky options to certain ones regardless of the frame." To widen prospect theory's explanatory space, the authors suggest that scholars must consider not only how leaders frame situations but also the character and personality traits of leaders themselves as these sources may potentially exacerbate foreign policy mistakes.

Such a model is at the center of Boettcher's (2005) study *Presidential Risk Behavior in Foreign Policy*. Boetcher develops a risk explanation framework that adopts the notion of reference dependence but also incorporates factors of personal predisposition as well as uncertainty and information accuracy. Similar to Kowert and Hermann, he argues that the interplay of these variables determines risky behavior. Vertzberger (1998, 111) notes, "the description and explanation of risk assessment and the formation of risk-taking preference defy parsimony. . . . No single cause effectively explains either risk assessment or the formation of a risk-taking preference; instead, explanations require a broad socio-cognitive approach." He thus moves toward a multipath model and argues that cultural, organizational, and small group dynamics are equally as important as personality traits in explaining risky behavior.

The inclusion of group dynamics and advisory groups with the psychology of the individual leader stands at the center of a second strand of research focusing on presidential decision making. Intuitively, advisory groups are thought to help leaders avoid mistakes and enable good decision making. However, this assumption is not necessarily the case. As President Dwight Eisenhower (1965, 630) put it, "Organization cannot of course make a successful leader out of a dunce, any more than it should make a decision for its chief." Similar to the individual level, a host of factors can interfere to produce diagnostic and prescriptive errors, thereby biasing a decision toward a mistake on the group level.

The most influential study on group dynamics is Janis's classic 1972 work *Victims of Groupthink*, as well as well as some of his subsequent works (1982, 1989; Janis and Mann 1977). Janis defines groupthink as a "mode of thinking that people engage in when they are deeply involved in a cohesive in-group, when their members' striving for unanimity override their motivations to realistically appraise alternative courses of action" (Janis 1982, 9). Such concurrence seeking results in a distorted view of reality, excessive and unwarranted optimism, and hasty decisions leading to policy "fiascos." Ironically, rather than simply balancing these effects of concurrence seeking, more heterogeneous groups may also choose relatively extreme behavior by exhibiting a "risky shift" syndrome in which the polarizing processes associated with conflicting points of view lead to an aggregate decision that is more extreme than the average preference of members of the group (Moscovici and Zavalloni 1969).

Another important work is Alexander George's (1980) *Presidential Decisionmaking in Foreign Policy*. According to George, the viability and effectiveness of decision-making groups is a result of group structures constituted through group size, composition, role distribution, decision rules, and leadership on group decisions. Like Johnson (1974) some years earlier, George distinguishes between formal, competitive, and collegial groups, with each of these group structures having advantages and disadvantages. Collegial groups, for example, may prove to be more efficient in reaching decisions. However, this efficiency can come at a price of insufficient attention to alternative courses of action resulting in ineffective decision making and ultimately in foreign policy mistakes.

More recently, Schafer and Crichlow (2010) have conducted a quantitative study of antecedent conditions resulting in group pathologies such as groupthink. Among these conditions are group insulation (decision makers' tendencies to isolate themselves from others not in the immediate decision-making circle), lack of impartial group leadership, lack of methodical procedures, group homogeneity, closed-mindedness, and pressure toward uniformity. In their analysis the authors find that group insulation is too rare a phenomenon for drawing any inferences. However, they also assert that factors related to leadership style, group procedures, and patterns of group behavior are indeed strong predictors not only for different types of information-processing errors but also for unfavorable outcomes.

Other studies examining the nexus between the leader and the advisory group can be found in Preston's (2001) *The President and His Inner Circle* and Kowert's (2002) *Groupthink or Deadlock?* Preston advances a model with three dimensions: a leader's need for power, cognitive complexity, and policy experience or expertise. He combines policy expertise with each of the other two qualities to produce various leadership styles and the effects these have on the advisory process. Presidents with extensive policy experience and a high need for power are, for example, "Directors" and allow only limited opposition. Similarly, Kowert distinguishes between leaders with open and closed learning styles within open or closed advisory group structures. If these characteristics of leaders and groups are matched properly, information gathering is effective. In the case of a mismatch, groupthink (premature convergence on an agreed decision) or deadlock (divergence and deferral on an agreed decision) become likely outcomes of the policy process.

Beyond the analysis of individual leaders and advisory groups, a third research strand focuses on two related yet distinct aspects of a government's decision-making process—bureaucratic politics and organizational behavior. In their classic works, Graham Allison (1971) and Morton Halperin (1974) consider policy decisions as the end result of competing bureaucratic interests and preferences. Bureaucratic organizations are carried by autonomous interests and preferences beyond the common interest that they would serve exclusively in an ideal world. The approach thus emphasizes the politicized nature of bureaucratic life and the impact that bureaucratic parochialism and inter- and intra-agency rivalry and competition can have on information processing, decision making, and policy outputs (Parker and Stern 2002, 609). The net effect is for politics to be defined as a strategic interaction process rather than as a problem-solving process (Sylvan and Voss 1998; Lake and Powell 1999).

While the bureaucratic politics approach focuses primarily on the processes among intragovernmental agencies, the emphasis of the organizational behavior approach is on structural features of organizational life (Steinbrunner 1974; March and Olsen 1989). Governmental decision making is considered as "organizational output, highly dependent on the structure, goals, preferences, priorities, rules, norms, roles and routines in question." Moreover, "experiences from previous problems become embedded in dominant analogies and practices, which in turn color perceptions and suggest solutions to current problems" (Parker and Stern 2002, 609). As in the bureaucratic politics model, these structural factors can hinder the rational course of a decision-making process and bias it toward a mistake.

This brief literature review illustrates some of the most prominent factors that contribute to diagnostic mistakes, prescriptive mistakes, or both. Our list is not exhaustive. Ultimately, at each level of analysis a myriad of factors can intervene in the decision-making process. But regardless of how far one extends the list, such factors share in common a role as antecedent conditions for diagnostic and prescriptive errors. The processes identified by these studies illustrate particular configurations of the causal mechanisms associated with general decision-making theory. The effects of these configurations are labeled as "mistakes" when they deviate from the norms of rational choice.

Missing from this scholarship is the identification of a single theoretical construct around which arguments and insights can be organized to make this normative judgment of rationality and offer a parsimonious explanation for mistakes. Our contention is that a focus on power serves this function. An emphasis on power is not new to political analysis, as realist scholars from Niccolo Machiavelli to Hans Morgenthau and their descendents will quickly point out. We agree with this point and respond that "the devil is in the details" (i.e., that our actual application of a focus on power must be evaluated in order to judge its contribution to solving the research puzzles associated with foreign policy mistakes). We shall argue theoretically and attempt to demonstrate empirically that the immediate cause for a mistake is a leader's misperceptions of the power relationship between self and other, in the form of an incorrect answer to Lenin's question "kto-kovo?"—who is able to destroy, control, utilize, help whom? We contend that a misunderstanding of power relationships between self and others leads to mistaken calculations of costs and benefits regarding alternative strategies of statecraft and thereby to policy failures.

CHAPTER 2

Foreign Policy Mistakes and the Exercise of Power

INTRODUCTION

In 2006 the McConnell Center at the University of Louisville organized the "Political Moments" conference. It featured the results of an expert survey looking at some of the most significant mistakes made by U.S. presidents throughout the history of the country. Some of the country's preeminent scholars in the study of the U.S. presidency and U.S. politics ranked these mistakes and analyzed the impact they had on the office of the presidency, the nation, and the world. The result of the survey is a list of the "Top Ten Greatest Presidential Mistakes." These specialists agreed that President James Buchanan committed the greatest blunder in U.S. history by failing to oppose the secession of the southern states from the Union.

Historian Elbert Smith (1975, 1) wrote about the pre-secession period, "The America that elected Buchanan president in November, 1856, was already painfully divided by sectional differences, animosities, and fears." Buchanan, however, proved unable, and perhaps unwilling, to grasp adequately the political realities of the time, which rapidly divided the nation ever further. Ignorant of the fact that the North would not accept constitutional arguments favoring the South, he colluded with Supreme Court justices. In his inaugural address the president referred to the territorial North-South question as "happily, a matter of but little practical importance," because the Supreme Court was about to settle it "speedily and finally." When the Court indeed decided in favor of the southern states, furor broke out in the North, where the ruling was perceived as paving the way for a complete disintegration of the country. As matters worsened, Buchanan did nothing to stop it. On the Web site of the McConnell Center, presidential scholar Michael Genovese concluded, "Buchanan fiddled while Rome burned. He saw the breakup of the republic but believed his hands were tied and thus watched the union break," resulting in the devastating Civil War that ensued from 1861 to 1865.

According to the scholars at the conference, President Andrew Johnson's reconstruction policies in the immediate aftermath of the Civil War constituted the second greatest blunder in U.S. history. The nation faced two fundamental questions in 1865: First, under what conditions should the North readmit southern Confederacy states into the Union? Second, what status and rights should the former slaves have? Johnson engaged the first question in ways favorable to the South. Regarding the second question, he rejected any further improvements in justice for southern blacks beyond abolishing slavery. In doing so, the president defied public opinion in the North as well as the Republican majorities in Congress. He vetoed several bills that would have given former slaves legal status as citizens with a right to vote. The ultimate consequence for Johnson was impeachment. The consequence for the country was decades of officially sanctioned racial politics. As a country, "We continue to pay," concluded presidential historian Michael Les Benedict on the McConnell Center Web site.

Another prominent case on the list is President Thomas Jefferson's Embargo Act of 1807. Designed to force Britain to lift its restrictions on American trade, the act prohibited all export of goods and cargo from U.S. harbors. The act failed in its goal and almost completely destroyed the American economy. It was repealed in 1809, but its failure precipitated yet another mistake on the list of presidential mistakes, one made only three years later. Motivated seemingly by the same goal as his predecessor, President James Madison declared war on Britain in 1812, even as Britain was reforming its trade policy toward the United States. Historians have argued that Madison's ulterior motivation was actually territorial gain in Canada rather than removal of British trade restrictions and that therefore his decision was a war of choice. The war concluded with the establishment of the status quo antebellum. Once again, much was paid and nothing was gained.

Presidential mistakes have also occurred in modern times. Mistakes of the twentieth century on the "Greatest Presidential Mistakes" list are

President Woodrow Wilson's refusal to compromise on the Versailles Treaty, leading to the failure of the League of Nations and subsequently to World War II. In the post–World War II era, well-known mistakes include President Kennedy's Bay of Pigs invasion, which ultimately led to the Cuban Missile Crisis. President Lyndon Johnson's escalation of the Vietnam War resulted in tens of thousands of U.S. casualties. Aside from making the list of top ten presidential blunders, what do these cases and others of lesser notoriety share as mistakes in the exercise of power?

In this chapter we address this question by developing and illustrating a general theory for diagnosing and explaining mistakes in the exercise of power. This theory supplies the context necessary for identifying a mistake as diagnostic or prescriptive and whether its pattern is a mistake of omission (too little/too late) or commission (too much/too soon). As in the case of the baseball mistakes that we mentioned in Chapter 1, we define foreign policy mistakes as deviations from a standard of truth or rectitude within the context of a game. Instead of a baseball game, however, we substitute a power politics game as the context for play. We will elaborate our theoretical framework in two steps. The first step covers the basic elements of our theory; the second step addresses its dynamism. We also illustrate some of our theoretical points with historical examples. In subsequent chapters we shall employ this theory to identify and analyze different kinds of foreign policy mistakes made by U.S. presidents.

FOREIGN POLICY MISTAKES AND THE EXERCISE OF POWER

As we have seen in Chapter 1, the causes of foreign policy mistakes are many and varied. Individual beliefs and personality traits, group dynamics, and institutional processes separately and together can contribute to mistakes of omission and commission regarding opportunities for cooperation and threats of conflict. But what do we mean when we say "cooperation" and "conflict"? Both terms suggest a social process—it takes at least two participants to make peace and to make war. Peace and war are possible outcomes of cooperation and conflict, respectively, but they are not the processes themselves that we conceptualize here as involving the *exercise of power* between the participants. This conceptualization excludes mistakes in other domains of human affairs, such as an engineer's diagnostic error in designing a building that does not withstand shocks without collapsing or a carpenter's prescriptive error in using inadequate materials to build it. These errors may be mistakes of commission or omission, but they do not fall within the domain of *social acts*—an individual may construct buildings and bridges for his/her own use without involving another human being (Hewitt 1994). The point is that both cooperation and conflict processes as exercises of social power require a human subject (agent) and a human object (patient) in order to be complete while these other examples of physical power do not.

Within the domain of social acts we focus on the subset of *political acts*, which are characterized by the exercise of sanctions by an agent toward a patient. By sanctions we mean various actions (words or deeds) by the agent (Actor A) designed to get the patient (Actor B) to do something that s/he would not otherwise do (Dahl 1957). Collectively, these actions are forms of the exercise of control (power) by the former over the latter. Social power theorists distinguish between positive (P) sanctions and negative (N) sanctions, depending on whether a sanction is based on rewards or punishments for its control effects (Baldwin 1971, 1978). From this focus on the exercise of power as its defining characteristic, it follows that politics as a process can assume just four logical forms between at least two actors A and B: cooperation {A(P), B(P)}, conflict {A(N), B(N)}, exploitation {A(N), B(P)}, or appeasement {A(P), B(N)}. The outcomes (effects) of the cooperation and conflict processes are settlement (exchange of rewards) and deadlock (exchange of punishments); the exploitation and appeasement processes result in the outcomes of domination (punishments in exchange for rewards) and submission (rewards in exchange for punishments).

The relationship among these forms of the exercise of power between two actors (A & B) is portrayed visually in Figure 2.1 as a game in which each player has two choices: positive (P) or negative (N) sanctions. The intersection of their respective choices defines the status quo between them and the "initial state" of their game (Brams 1994, 23–24). By their subsequent choices either they can choose "move" and change the status quo, or both players can choose "stay" and make the status quo the final

FIGURE 2.1   *Basic Who-Whom Power Game*

PLAYER B (Whom)

		P	N
	P	A & B Settle	A Submits/ B Dominates
PLAYER A (Who)			
	N	A Dominates/ B Submits	A & B Deadlock

outcome of the game. P and N for each player become strategies that each may choose to influence the final outcome and which each player may decide to play either unconditionally (e.g., "Player A always chooses P") or conditionally (e.g., "if Player B chooses P, then Player A chooses P, but if Player B chooses N, then Player A chooses N"). An unconditional strategy is called a dominant strategy in game theory if it "leads to outcomes at least as good as any other strategy in all contingencies, and a better outcome in at least one contingency" (Brams 1994, 222).

Steven Brams in *Theory of Moves* (1994) has devised the "correct" theoretical strategy for each player to follow in each of the seventy-eight possible 2×2 games (two players with two choices) governed by rules of play and by the two-sided information assumption that *each* player knows the rank order of preferences for *both* players regarding the four possible outcomes (cells) in the game. According to Brams (1994, 138–148), if the game allows for pre-play communication between the players, alternating moves by each player, and repeated plays of the game, then these rules permit the players to calculate four moves ahead before choosing to "move" or "stay" and also to exchange credible threats and promises before each player chooses a strategy. By extension if a player does not follow the "correct" strategy, then it is a "mistake" (i.e., a misplay in the context of the game). In other words, it is possible to assess how well they play it within the rules of play defined by Brams's theory of moves (TOM).

These rules of play also appear to be realistic approximations of the conditions under which states make foreign policy decisions toward one another. It is the case as well that the basic who-whom power game does not expand into all seventy-eight possible variations of the 2×2 game in our own theory of power politics (Marfleet and Walker 2006; Walker and Schafer 2007). There are only a relatively small number of such power games, defined by the answers to two questions, and which we identify in parentheses with the game (G) numbers assigned by Brams (1994, 215).[1]

- Do the two players (A & B) believe that each one is friendly (+) or hostile (–) toward the other? The possible answers to this question are (A,B=+,+), (A,B=–,+), (A,B=+,–); (A,B=–,–).
- Do the two players (A & B) believe that the power relationship between them is symmetrical (A=B) or asymmetrical (A≠B)? The possible answers to this question are (A=B and B=A), (A>B and B<A), (A<B and B>A).

The answers to both questions, together with our theory of inferences about preferences (TIP) regarding the exercise of power prescribe a rank order for each player's preferences regarding the final outcomes of settlement, deadlock, domination, and submission.[2] TIP is a series of rules for how to rank preferences based on the assumptions that the achievement of these outcomes depends on the orientations (friendly/hostile intentions) of each player and their power relationships (symmetrical/asymmetrical relations). The rules also imply a third assumption, namely, that they apply to both players: when the positions of A and B in these statements are reversed, they remain true and explain B's preference rankings as well as A's (Marfleet and Walker 2006). These rules are as follows, where A is one of the players in a dyad and B is the other player:

> Proposition 1. If Player A is friendly toward Player B and if Player A is inferior in power to Player B, then Player A ranks Settle > Deadlock > Submit > Dominate.
>
> Proposition 2. If Player A is friendly toward Player B and if Player A is equal in power to Player B, then Player A ranks Settle > Deadlock > Dominate > Submit.
>
> Proposition 3. If Player A is friendly toward Player B and if Player A is superior in power to Player B, then Player A ranks Settle > Dominate > Deadlock > Submit.

Proposition 4. If Player A is hostile toward Player B and if Player A is inferior in power to Player B, then Player A ranks Dominate > Settle > Submit > Deadlock.

Proposition 5. If Player A is hostile toward Player B and if Player A is equal in power to Player B, then Player A ranks Dominate > Settle > Deadlock > Submit.

Proposition 6. If Player A is hostile toward Player B and if Player A is superior in power to Player B, then Player A ranks Dominate > Deadlock > Settle > Submit.

While these rules make ontological (descriptive) claims about friendly/hostile intentions and inferior/equal/superior power relations, they make normative claims about the rank order of preferences. The underlying norms are that players ought to base their rank order of political outcomes on what they are able to do in exercising control over others and on how the two players are oriented toward one another. These norms are both *kto-kovo* (power) norms in that friendly/hostile orientations are signaled by the exercise of positive (P) and negative (N) sanctions toward one another, and these power relations specify whether one player is able to dominate the other. Although this theory takes the form of a universal normative theory, it is only a probabilistic empirical theory. It is possible for players to violate these norms and the inferences in TIP derived from them. Leaders follow these rules most (but not all) of the time; therefore, the propositions in TIP are not equivalent to the universal laws of a theory in classical physics that predict the behavior of physical objects. They do conform to rules of rationality that make human behavior calculated and therefore predictable, allowing the observer to identify deviations as mistakes of one kind or another (Ball 1987; J. Snyder 2003; Glaser 2010).

Foreign policy mistakes can occur at different levels in a political universe defined primarily as a strategic interaction game and characterized by the exercise of power. Players make diagnostic mistakes when they are wrong regarding the friendly/hostile orientations of self and other or the symmetrical/asymmetrical power relations between self and other. Players who do not follow TIP's rules of inference from each player's rank order of preferences make prescriptive mistakes in miscalculating whether it is better to choose "stay" or "move" by not thinking ahead beyond the next move in the game. These calculations are governed by the rules of play in TOM for 2×2 games. The rules of play assume that each player can and will "think ahead" four moves before choosing whether to "stay" or "move." The underlying goal in these calculations is to figure out the "nonmyopic equilibrium" (NME) for the game, given the initial state (cell) from which play commences (Brams 1994, 2002). An NME is the final state from which "neither player, anticipating all possible rational moves and countermoves from the initial state, would have an incentive to depart unilaterally because the departure would eventually lead to a worse, or at least not a better, state" (Brams 1994, 224).

To illustrate some implications of this theoretical discussion, we use these new tools to reanalyze the Katyn Forest massacre decision by the Soviet Union. We know already that this case is a mistake of commission (too much/too soon), which the Soviet leadership even admitted was a "great mistake" in addition to an unacknowledged moral failure. But why was it a mistake in the exercise of power by the Soviet Union? What kind of game was occurring between *who* and *whom*? Did the Russians commit a strategic diagnostic mistake either about the intentions of the other player or about the power relationship between the players? A strategic prescriptive mistake in the exercise of power? Or all three?

WHY WAS THE KATYN FOREST MASSACRE A FOREIGN POLICY MISTAKE?

The elements of the decision to execute the Polish officer corps are more complex than it seems at first glance. What appears superficially to be a simple decision by the Soviet Union to execute members of a defeated Polish army ignores a deeper look at the "who-whom" issues raised by the basic power game. The Polish officers were part of the Polish government that went into exile in London. In turn, the London exile government was allied with Britain via the latter's guarantee of Polish territorial integrity. This unilateral guarantee was formalized by the 1939 Anglo-Polish Agreement signed on August 25, two days after the announcement of the Nazi-Soviet Non-Aggression Pact. The latter agreement contained a secret protocol that called for Germany and Russia to partition Poland in the event that Poland and Germany went to war. When the two dictator-ships carved up Poland, Britain as a Polish ally declared war on Germany. British relations with Russia became somewhat ambiguous, as Poland fought both invaders, but Britain did not declare war on Russia. Up almost to the date of the pre-war Non-Aggression Pact, Britain and Russia had also conducted talks to see whether the two governments could reach a military alliance agreement. When Russia chose to execute the Polish officers, therefore, Moscow was acting as well against Britain by virtue of the latter's alliance with Poland.

What were the answers to the two questions that specified the basic power game between Britain and Russia at that point? Since Britain had not declared war on Russia following the German invasion of Poland, the formal relations between the two states were neutral (i.e., nominally friendly) (Russia, Britain = +,+). What was the power relationship between the two states? The relationship between them was generally symmetrical (Russia = Britain), as both were great powers: one a major land power and the other a major sea power. Neither posed an asymmetrical threat to the other because their potential military power was not fungible (i.e., Britain's navy could not invade the Russian land mass and Russia's army could not invade the British Isles). According to TIP, these characteristics of the two actors A and B define the following no-conflict game in Figure 2.2 with symmetrical preference rankings of settle > deadlock > domination > submit.

The two games in Figure 2.2 represent two different definitions of the strategic situation for Russia. Russia was playing a nominal, no-conflict game with Britain while engaging simultaneously in a mixed-motive game with Poland. This kind of complex situation is not unusual in world politics where third parties are often connected by alliances or other diplo-matic agreements to a strategic interaction situation between two other parties. In deciding whether Russia's decision to execute the Polish officer corps was a mistake, our conclusion depends on how these complexities are analyzed. It is possible to keep the two games separate and analyze them in isolation. It is also possible to combine the two games.

The two games in Figure 2.2 represent the first possibility. In this case, the Russian decision to choose "stay" by executing the Polish POWs is a

FIGURE 2.2   *Russia's Basic Power Games with Britain and Poland*

	Britain			Poland	
	Coop P	Conf N		Coop P	Conf N
Coop P	4,4*	1,2	Coop P	2,4	1,1
Russia			**Russia**		
Conf N	2,1	3,3*	Conf N	4,2	3,3*
	No-Conflict Game			**Mixed-Motive Game (G41)**	
	Intentions: Rus, Bri = +,+			Intentions: Rus, Pol = −, +	
	Power: Rus = Bri			Power: Rus > Pol	

Brams nonmyopic equilibria are in bold, and Nash myopic equilibria are asterisked.

rational calculation and not a strategic mistake by Moscow. The mixed-motive game between Russia and Poland has two nonmyopic equilibria: (4,2) domination by the USSR and (3,3) deadlock. Russia preferred the former and sought to make it permanent by decapitating Poland's elite, thereby taking the Polish player out of the game. However, this strategic move was based on a diagnostic mistake in identifying the power of their opponent. Relations with Britain were not incorporated into this myopic definition of the situation. The Polish exile government in London had a powerful ally in Britain, which alters a rational diagnosis of the who-whom power relations between Russia and Poland from (Rus > Pol) to (Rus = Pol/Bri) and implies that the other game in Figure 2.2 is also important.

How should analysts and decision makers combine the two games in order to make a rational choice? One way is to subordinate one game and argue that the other game takes precedence. The subordination path conforms to the existing alliance agreement between Britain and Poland, which gives precedence to the game with Britain in Figure 2.2. This game calls for both players to move to (4,4) as the final outcome from any other cell in the game. The domination outcome represented by Russia's military victory over Poland is (2,1) in the Russo-British game, which calls for Russia to move to settlement (4,4) as an NME for the Russo-Polish game. With hostilities between Russia and Poland leading to a Soviet military victory and the capture of Polish soldiers, therefore, it would be a mistake to stay at (4,2) domination in the Russo-Polish game and execute

FIGURE 2.3 *Alternative Russo-British Power Games*

	Britain				Britain	
	Coop P	Conf N			Coop P	Conf N
Coop P	3,4	1,2		Coop P	3,3	1,4
Russia				Russia		
Conf N	4,1	2,3*		Conf N	4,1	2,2*

Mixed-Motive Game (G27)   Conflict Game (G32)
Intentions: Rus, Bri = –, +   Intentions: Rus, Bri = –,–
Power: Rus = Bri   Power: Rus = Bri

Brams nonmyopic equilibria in bold. Nash myopic equilibria are asterisked.

the prisoners. This move would alienate the Polish government in exile allied with Britain and thereby worsen Anglo-Russian relations. If Russia chooses "stay" in either game, Britain will choose "move" to (3,3) deadlock as the likely final outcome.

Another way to combine the two games is to map one set of Russian preferences on to both games in Figure 2.2. Although Anglo-Russian relations were nominally friendly, the hostile actions of Russia against Poland could be construed as also directed against Britain as the guarantor of Polish territory. In this interpretation the answer to the two questions defining the game between Russian and Britain shift to a mixed pattern (Rus, Bri = –,+) regarding their orientations toward one another while their power relationship remains equal (Rus = Bri). According to TIP, this definition of Russo-British relations produces the mixed-motive game in Figure 2.3. Britain still prefers mutual cooperation as its highest-ranked outcome preference while Russia now ranks domination highest in this game, which makes it a mixed-motive game.

According to TOM, the rational choice for Russia in the mixed-motive game is to move to (3,4) settlement rather than to stay at domination (4,1) following their military victory over Poland. If they choose "stay" and execute the POWs, then in order to avoid its worst outcome (4,1), Britain will move to (2,3) deadlock, which is an inferior final outcome for both players compared with the Pareto-superior outcome of (3,4).[3] The same logic holds true even if Russia defines the game as a conflict game, in which each player ranks domination of the other player as its highest outcome. This game in Figure 2.3 is the famous prisoner's dilemma conflict game (Rapoport and Chammah 1970). TOM prescribes that in a prisoner's dilemma game Russia should choose "move" from (4,1) domination to (3,3) mutual cooperation, in order to avoid a British move to (2,2) deadlock as the inferior NME (Brams 1994, 78–79, 138–140).

So even in the worst case, when Russia assumes Britain is hostile (Russia, Britain =–,–), their equal power relations in the conflict game still dictate that Russia should avoid a deadlock with Britain over the fate of the British POWs. Even if the Russian decision makers made a categorical error in wrongly diagnosing Anglo-Russian relations in terms of their hostile or friendly relations, it does not excuse them from the strategic mistake of executing the POWs. Our analysis of the Katyn Forest massacre and Anglo-Russian relations has illustrated the basics of our power game. Next we address the dynamic nature of our theoretical framework before applying it in subsequent chapters to the analysis of U.S. presidents and foreign policy mistakes after World War II.

TRANSITIONING OUTCOMES AND GAMES

As opposed to conventional game theory, which has been described as "thoroughly static" (von Neumann and Morgenstern 1953, 44), TOM is dynamic. To make this point, we shall give first the conventional analysis of the famous prisoner's dilemma game in Figure 2.4. In this game if we take (1,4) as the initial state, Player A ranks this outcome lowest (1) and therefore has an incentive to choose "move" from P to N. Player B has an incentive to choose "stay" at N rather than "move" to P, because s/he ranks this outcome highest (4). Choosing "N" is not only the choice of

FIGURE 2.4   *Prisoner's Dilemma Game*

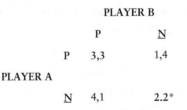

PLAYER B

		P	<u>N</u>
	P	3,3	1,4
PLAYER A			
	<u>N</u>	4,1	2.2*

Brams nonmyopic equilibria are in bold. Nash myopic equilibrium is asterisked. Dominant strategies are underlined.

both players in this initial state; it is also the dominant strategy for both players. The "dilemma" in the game is that in the absence of communication, coordination, and reciprocation, both players follow their dominant strategy, thereby also avoiding their second-best, Pareto-superior outcome (3,3) and end up worse off at (2,2) as the final outcome for the game (Rapoport and Chammah 1970; Axelrod 1984; Brams 1994).

Although this outcome may be likely, it is not certain. Early conventional game-theoretic analyses exclude player communication from the game. States can and do communicate, however, and this communication is an important part of the game (Milner 1991). In contrast to conventional game theory, TOM explicitly incorporates prior (pre-play) communication, alternating (sequential) moves and repeated (more than one) plays of the game as dynamic features. Each of these features merits further discussion with the prisoner's dilemma game, as shown in Figure 2.4 and employed as a good example.

As Brams (2002) points out, starting play at one cell of a game (the initial state) and having each player choose to "stay" or "move" until both choose to "stay" in a cell (the final state) is a more realistic way to depict the actual exchange of moves between states in international relations to reach an equilibrium as the end of the game.[4] It is also not unusual for such strategic interaction episodes to be repeated, with the final state becoming the new initial state in a replay of the game between the players during a protracted conflict, such as an enduring rivalry characteristic of the cold war between the United States and the Soviet Union. The representation of this process of interaction in game theory can be in the "extended" form of a decision tree rather than the "normal" form of a matrix such as the one in Figure 2.4 (Morrow 1994).

In this book we shall use the normal form matrix along with a convention developed by Brams to "extend" the matrix by representing a player's decision to choose "stay" or "move" from one cell to another with an arrow ($\rightarrow$) indicating "move" and a blocked arrow ($\rightarrow|$) indicating "stay." The initial state of a game will be marked with quotation marks, and the final state of a game (a Brams NME) will be in bold. Some games may have more than one NME and other relevant characteristics that may influence the decisions of players to choose "stay" or "move." These include whether one or both players have an "always choose P" dominant strategy or a "choose P or N" contingent strategy depending on the other player's choice, and whether an NME is also a Pareto-optimum and/or a Nash myopic equilibrium. The prisoner's dilemma game in Figure 2.4 has all of these characteristics. As already noted, the dominant strategy for both players is "always choose N," which leads to (2,2) as the final outcome under the rules of play in which each player chooses simultaneously from "outside" the game rather than alternates choices from an initial state "within" the game and no pre-play communication or repeated plays of the game are allowed.

However, an inspection of this game reveals that (3,3) is a superior outcome for both players and attainable with different rules of play that provide for alternative moves from an initial state, prior communication, and repeated play. Under these conditions (2,2) is an NME only when (2,2) is also the initial state from which decisions to "stay" or "move" commence. If any of the other cells is the initial state, then (3,3) becomes the NME under the rules of play just specified and the assumptions that both players agree on the game that they are playing (the two-sided information assumption) and that both players will act so as to reach an NME (the rational actor assumption). An illustration of these points and the method of "backward induction" (thinking ahead in extended form) in the prisoner's dilemma game appear in Figure 2.5.[5]

If both players have the capacity to communicate from an initial state of (1,4), they can reach (3,3) as the final outcome. This requires both players to "think ahead" and recognize that with myopic players, the absence of pre-play communication, alternating moves as rules of play, and two-sided information as an assumption, (a) if Player B has the next move from (1,4), s/he should choose "stay"; (b) if Player A has the next move, s/he should choose "move." These calculations are relatively straightforward for myopic players: Player B should choose "stay" because to choose "move" would lead immediately to an inferior (lower-ranked) outcome (4 to 3); Player A should choose "move" because it will lead to a superior (higher-ranked) outcome (1 to 2). If A moves to (2,2), then neither player has an incentive to move from this new initial state. Thinking ahead, a decision by either player to move leads immediately to a worse outcome

FIGURE 2.5   *Different Solutions to the Prisoner's Dilemma Game*

	PLAYER B				PLAYER B	
	Coop Deeds	Conf Deeds			Coop Words	Conf Words
						(A's threat or promise)
Coop Deeds	3,3 →	"1,4"		Coop Words	3,3 |←	"1,4"
PLAYER A	↑̄	↓		PLAYER A	↓_	↑̄
Conf Deeds	4,1 |←	2,2*		Conf Words	4,1 →	2,2*

Myopia and No Prior Communication
Player A's Strategy: Move

Nonmyopia and Prior Communication
Player B's Strategy: Move

Initial state is in quotation marks, and final outcomes are underlined. Brams nonmyopic equilibria are in bold. Nash myopic equilibria are asterisked. The arrows indicate thinking ahead via backward induction by each player about whether to move (→) or not move (→|).

for that player (2 to 1), and the other player would then choose "stay" at its highest-ranked outcome (4).

However, if one assumes a nonmyopic capacity to think ahead more than one move, the calculations leading to choices become more complex. Player B may realize that a magnanimous choice for him would be to move from (1,4) to a Pareto-superior (3,3) outcome, thereby avoiding a stable and Pareto-inferior (2,2) outcome. Player A may also induce Player B to move to (3,3) by exercising credible threat power in pre-play communication to move to (2,2) and thereby deter a decision by B to "stay" at (1,4).

The arrows in Figure 2.5 chart the process for each player of thinking ahead by reasoning backward from the last possible move to the initial state in quotation marks (1,4). The reasoning process for Player A's strategy is to reason backward counterclockwise from (1,4) that B will move from (3,3) to (1,4), A will not move from (4,1) to (3,3), B will not move from (2,2) to (4,1), and A will move from (1,4) to (2,2). Therefore, A should choose to move from an initial state of (1,4). The reasoning process for Player B's strategy is to reason backward clockwise from (1,4) that A will not choose to move from (2,2) to (1,4), B will move from (4,1) to (2,2), A will not move from (3,3) to (4,1), and B will not move from (1,4) to (3,3). Therefore, B shouldn't choose to move from (1,4) to (3,3). If each player engages in a "one-sided" analysis of the game, then the outcome of their choices will be for B to choose "stay" ($|\leftarrow$) while A chooses "move" ($\downarrow$) from (1,4). The final outcome will be (2,2), because the next choice by B is "stay" ($\leftarrow$) at (2,2). However, if each player engages in a "two-sided" analysis of the game and calculates what *both* players' rational choices are, then B may magnanimously choose "move" to (3,3) as a Pareto-superior outcome for both of them and A may employ threat power to encourage B to choose "move." If B chooses "move" ($\leftarrow$), then the final outcome will be (3,3) because A's next choice is "stay"($\downarrow$) at (3,3) (Brams 1994, 67–70).

In order for magnanimity by B or threats by A to result in a choice by B to move from (1,4) to (3,3) as a *stable* final outcome, both A and B must have credible threat power. A must be willing and able to punish B in case B chooses "stay" at (1,4), and B must be willing and able to punish A for defecting from (3,3) in the event A chooses "move" to (4,1) after B moves magnanimously to (3,3). In order for the (3,3) outcome to be stable (endure), therefore, both players have to exercise mutual "threat power" in prior communication, that is, threaten each other credibly with a subsequent punishing move to (2,2), if either one moves away from (3,3) (Brams 1994, 138–148). Repeated plays of the game are necessary to ensure such credibility.[6]

The exercise of promises is an amendment to TOM, yet it represents a logical counterpart to threat power. Whereas the latter threatens punishments following a move by the other player, the former promises benefits following a move by the other player. As in the exercise of threat power, the use of promise power is intended via prior (pre-play) communication to induce the other player to make a nonmyopic calculation. Whether threat or promise power is the appropriate strategy is context dependent. Threats are not likely to be successful if the opponent has alternative venues for compensation of any losses s/he would incur or, alternatively, is willing and able to endure such losses. Conversely, promises are not likely to be effective if the opponent does not gain some benefits or avoid losses. Both types of prior communication illustrate how each player can alter the other player's calculations and thereby potentially redefine the final outcome.

Figure 2.5 distinguishes between two ways to represent the prisoner's dilemma power game. The first game is a game in which the players choose to "stay" or "move" from cells defined by the exercise of power in the form of deeds (Osgood 1960; Schelling 1960, 1966; Etzioni 1962; George and Simmons 1994). The second game formalizes prior communication as a game in which the players choose to "stay" or "move" from cells defined by the exercise of power in the form of words (Brams 1994, 183–206; Ikle 1964; Zartman, 1978, 2001; Fisher, Ury, and Patton 1991; Zartman and Rubin 2000; Zartman and Faure 2005). Each way of representing this game has its advantages in describing and explaining relations between the players and identifying foreign policy mistakes. The deeds game reflects the actual choices by the players whereas the words game represents attempts in prior (pre-play) communication by one or both players to assess the stability of the power game, that is, whether it is possible to change the game's preference rankings or power distribution by communicating alternative sequences of moves and outcomes via the exercise of threat power and promise power from an initial state of (1,4). As we have seen, it is also possible in the deeds game for Player B to choose "move" unilaterally from (1,4) as a magnanimity strategy without prior communication from Player A in order to avoid (2,2) deadlock (Brams 1994, 67–79).

When players exchange words, they are engaging in prior communication about their willingness to choose "stay" or "move" under different scenarios, thereby also signaling potential movement or stability in the deeds game from an NME. For example, suppose the two players in Figure 2.5 were instead in a prisoner's dilemma game with deadlock (2,2) as the initial state and each has imposed economic sanctions on the other. Each player is unwilling to lift sanctions unless the other reciprocates. The logic of this deeds game precludes either player from lifting sanctions by choosing "move," because the other player may not respond by also lifting sanctions and moving to (3,3). However, it is possible to play this same game symbolically as a words game by exchanging an offer to lift sanctions and a promise to move and stay at (3,3), with both threatening to move to (2,2) in the event either player subsequently defects from (3,3) and resumes negative sanctions.

The introduction of the distinction between words games and deeds games, in which the words game formalizes the exchange of pre-play communication in the form of threats and promises, suggests a generic template of games that operate between players. The words game in the center of the template in Figure 2.6 is a transition game representing the processes of diplomacy (talking), which models the conditions under which it becomes rational to choose "stay" or "move" within the existing deeds game. The symbolic moves within the words game offer clues about the stability of preferences in the existing deeds game and provide a means for influencing each player's future choices to "stay" or "move." The transition game may also act toward altering the dynamics of the deeds game between players on the periphery of the template.

In particular, the symbolic interactions within the words game may lead to a learning or resocialization effect on the two players in a game. The basic idea is that actors, through interaction, can engage in learning processes, and these may lead to a reinforcement or, alternatively, to a change in the initially held preference rankings for settlement, deadlock, domination, and submission. In other words, enemies are not condemned to perpetual enmity, nor are friends necessarily blessed with harmony in perpetuity (Wendt 1999, 170–171, 327; Levy, 1994). There is ample evidence for these possibilities.

FIGURE 2.6   *Words Transition Game Nested in Basic Power Game*

PLAYER B

		Coop (P)		Conf (N)	
		Deeds	Words	Words	Deeds
	Deeds	A & B Settle		A Submits/B Dominates	
Coop (P)					
	Words	*Cell P,P*		*Cell P,N*	
PLAYER A			**WORDS TRANSITION GAME**		
	Words	*Cell N,P*		*Cell N,N*	
Conf (N)					
	Deeds	A Dominates/B Submits		A & B Deadlock	

For example, the end of the cold war between the two superpowers was likely deferred until both Gorbachev and Reagan shifted their prisoner's dilemma conflict game to a no-conflict game. The Soviet leader's diplomatic strategy was guided by his "New Thinking" doctrine, which entailed a strategy of simultaneous cooperative engagement in a words game and a deeds game. Gorbachev's strategy was designed to elicit a cooperative response from President Reagan and convince the Reagan administration that the Soviet Union had changed its strategic preferences to rank settlement rather than domination as its highest outcome (Malici 2006, 2008). This process of graduated reduction in tension (GRIT) suggests that the transition between a conflict and a no-conflict game is often facilitated or impeded by a mixed-motive game, as illustrated in Figure 2.7 (Osgood 1960; Goldstein and Freeman 1990).

A more mundane alternative to change a game and its outcome is to alter the power relations between the two players. Although there is a menu for choice on how this can be achieved, each individual case will dictate what is possible and what is not possible. One player may engage in a significant arms build-up, thereby enhancing its physical power over the other player. Alternatively, one player may form a coalition with a third party and strengthen its power through a military alliance. One way of losing power is to experience a power deflation caused, for example, by a loss of domestic legitimacy and the resulting inability to mobilize the country's armed forces (C. Johnson 1966). Another way is when one player experiences a severe economic crisis incapacitating its industrial and war-making capacities. A third way is for an opponent to detach an ally (Hartmann 1983, 320–337). Any of these occurrences may alter the power relationship between two players and thereby the equilibrium of their game.

As a sequential game theory that incorporates pre-play communication, TOM has the ability to accommodate changing games and outcomes through sequential moves and repeated play by players with two-sided information and the capacity to think ahead. It raises its value compared with more static, conventional game-theoretic analyses with more restrictive rules of play, making it a dynamic model of international politics and an appropriate vehicle for the analysis of foreign policy mistakes (Brams

FIGURE 2.7   *Soviet-U.S. Games at the End of the Cold War*

	Soviet Union		Soviet Union		Soviet Union	
	Coop (P)	Conf (N)	Coop (P)	Conf (N)	Coop (P)	Conf (N)
Coop (P)	3,3	1,4	3,4	1,2	"4,4"	1,2
United States						
Conf (N)	4,1	"2,2"*	4,1	"2,3"*	2,1	3,3*
	Conflict Game (G32)[1]		**Mixed-Motive Game (G27)[2]**		**No-Conflict Game[3]**	
	(Cold War Era)		**(New Thinking Transition Period)**		**(Post–Cold War Era)**	

[1] In the conflict game, the United States (4,1) and the Soviet Union (1,4) each rank domination of the other as the highest outcome.
[2] In the mixed-motive game, the United States ranks domination (4,1) highest while the Soviet Union ranks settlement (3,4) as its highest outcome.
[3] In the no-conflict game, both the United States and the Soviet Union rank settlement (4,4) as the highest outcome. Initial states are in quotation marks, and final outcomes are underlined with Brams nonmyopic equilibria in bold and Nash myopic equilibria asterisked.
Source: Data from Malici (2008, 28, figure 2.1).

2002; see also Brams 2001; R. Stone 2001). The conventions and TOM's solutions to the prisoner's dilemma game assume that both players know the rank order of each player's preferences for the different outcomes to the game and can think ahead to the consequences of the various decisions by each player to "stay" or "move" from each of the cells. Whether the two-sided information assumption and the capacity or inclination to think ahead holds for players in a particular historical situation is really the key question in this book, as failures to do so constitute our formal definition of foreign policy "mistakes" in game-theoretical terms simply as decisions to choose "move" when the rational choice is to choose "stay," or vice versa.

MISTAKES AND COUNTERFACTUAL ANALYSIS

We close this chapter with a famous example of a U.S. president who made these kinds of mistakes by refusing to engage in a serious words game with his political adversaries. Woodrow Wilson's refusal to compromise with the U.S. Senate regarding the Treaty of Versailles after World War I ranks fourth on the list of top ten blunders in the McConnell Center's survey of presidential mistakes. When President Wilson negotiated the Versailles Treaty's terms with the other victors of the Great War, the

Treaty contained the Covenant of the League of Nations organization as a central component. This organization was vital to the success of the peace treaty as the key mechanism for resolving future conflicts between its signatories and thereby avoiding future wars. Its design called for states to negotiate, mediate, or adjudicate their differences and renounce the use of force as a means to resolve any disputes. In the event that a state violated this pledge and resorted to force as an aggressor, the other members of the organization would come to the aid of the victim of aggression (Claude 1962).

This doctrine of collective security thereby institutionalized a favorable balance of power on the side of the state that honored the League's procedures for settling disputes. It also became the focus of objections in the U.S. Senate to joining the League of Nations and thereby committing the United States to permanent involvement in conflicts abroad. Senator Lodge led the opposition to the League Covenant and to ratification of the Versailles Treaty. President Wilson viewed the League as nonnegotiable partly because he had been forced to compromise on many of the substantive terms of the peace treaty ending World War I. He banked on the League as a mechanism for modifying the harsh terms of the peace settlement as the losers recovered from the damages of the war. The conflict between Wilson and Lodge was also personal, as the two leaders had a history of hostility between them (George and George 1964, 1998; Walker 1995).

Rather than seek a compromise that would have the support of the two-thirds majority necessary for ratification by the Senate, Wilson sought to bring the pressure of public opinion on reluctant senators. However, his public campaign of touring twenty-seven cities and giving thirty-seven speeches ended with his physical collapse and the defeat of the treaty. In seeking to alter the balance of power between supporters and opponents in the legislature by the use of negative sanctions (mobilizing public opinion), he instead lost the game (Hartmann 1967). Outside observers and advisors to the president agreed that if Wilson had been willing to compromise on some terms in the treaty, it could have received the necessary votes to ratify it without gutting the League of Nations' organization and its collective security provisions. A coalition of supporters and "mild reservationists" would have voted for the treaty if the latter's reservations had been met with amendments to the treaty. However, Wilson's refusal to negotiate or even to explore the possibility of negotiations led the "mild reservationists" to side with the "strong reservationists" and vote against the treaty (Appleton 1968, 109–121; see also Barck and Blake 1965, 243–263).

This case of a foreign policy mistake made the "top ten" list of presidential blunders, based on a counterfactual analysis. If the United States had ratified the Treaty of Versailles, then U.S. membership in the League of Nations would have made the system of collective security successful in preventing another devastating war. The presence of the United States, committed to the victim of aggression, would have deterred a potential aggressor from using force or would at least have insured a successful defense against such aggression. However, this kind of speculation is suspect on several grounds. As one analyst has put it, "The tape of history runs only once" (Tetlock 1998, 870), that is, a counterfactual argument is not empirically testable because all of the potentially relevant conditions and causes of World War II cannot be reproduced with the sole change being U.S. ratification of the treaty (see also Tetlock and Belkin 1996; Lebow 2010).

Therefore, it is not clear that the logical truth of the causal chain linking the U.S. choice in 1920 to World War II in 1939 is empirically valid. The rise of German, Italian, Russian, and Japanese power in the interwar years may well have offset the logical deterrent effect of U.S. power on the side of the victim in any dispute between these aggressors and their neighbors (Newman 1968; Schweller 1998). The logic of these alternative possibilities is represented in Figure 2.8 in the three collective security games between two disputants. If both players choose conflict as a strategy, their conflict behavior does not always escalate to violence (war). If the balance of power in the collective security game favors the victim of aggression (Vic > Agg), it should logically cause the potential aggressor to move from an initial state of deadlock to a final outcome of settlement. However, if the United States' absence from the League of Nations or an increase in others' capabilities alters the balance of power between the two players either to parity (Vic = Agg) or in favor of the Aggressor

FIGURE 2.8   *Alternative Collective Security Games*

| | Aggressor (G29) | | Aggressor (G27) | | Aggressor (G41) | |
	Coop P	Conf N	Coop P	Conf N	Coop P	Conf N
Coop P	4,3	1,4	4,3	1,4	4,2	2,4
Victim						
Conf N	3,2	2,1	2,1	3,2*	1,1	3,3*

Intentions: Vic, Agg = +,–   Intentions: Vic, Agg = +,–   Intentions: Vic, Agg = +,–
Power: Vic > Agg   Power: Vic = Agg   Power: Vic < Agg

Brams nonmyopic equilibria are in bold. Nash myopic equilibria are asterisked.

(Vic < Agg), then settlement becomes less likely and the probability increases of continued deadlock or domination by the aggressor as the final outcome for the three games in Figure 2.8.

Even if a counterfactual analysis may be logically true, several other conditions must exist in order for it to be empirically valid. The rules of play in game theory simply specify what the players logically ought to do in order to win the game between them. Their actual choices, however, may be at odds with the rules of play for all of the causal reasons outlined in Chapter 1. Human beings are fallible decision makers, as a result of the influence of others or their own foibles. Our theory also assumes that the actions (choices) of the players are jointly necessary and sufficient conditions to produce the stipulated outcome. In fact, the game may not specify the actual historical situation. Either or both players may misdiagnose the actual power situation between them or miscalculate their moves toward a final outcome. Often the game needs to be played repeatedly in order to escalate to the point of war, and other events or actors may intervene in the meantime to prevent war as an outcome by transforming the power relations and intentions that define the game.

Consequently, a relatively modest claim connecting Wilson's choice of strategy with the outcome of the Senate vote on the Treaty of Versailles seems to be more valid than the more ambitious claim that the outcome of Wilson's strategy in 1920 affected decisively the balance of power between the protagonists whose actions started World War II. The use of positive sanctions by granting concessions to the "mild reservationist" group appears to be a strategy superior to the use of negative sanctions by mobilizing public opinion against both "mild" and "strong" reservationists. Since Wilson chose not to play a serious words game to explore the former strategy, however, it is difficult to say for sure. We also do not know whether the latter strategy would have worked, because an intervening event (Wilson's physical collapse) prevented him from continuing to implement it fully to completion.

It is nonetheless possible to make some logical claims about mistakes based on sequential game theory's analysis of Wilson's alternative courses of action and their immediate consequences, as depicted in Figure 2.9. If outside observers were correct and Wilson could have forged a two-thirds majority of supporters and mild reservationists by allowing some minor amendments to the treaty, then it would have logically transformed his game against Lodge and the strong reservationists. The three games are displayed with the outcome of the intervening mixed-motive game between Wilson and the mild reservationists, transforming the power relations that defined the game (G18) between Wilson and the U.S. Senate. An alliance of mild and strong reservationists constituted a coalition with the votes necessary to veto ratification of the treaty and create a (2,4) submission outcome for Wilson in which the Senate rejects the treaty. However, if Wilson and the mild reservationists had decided to play the second mixed-motive game (G27) and reach settlement (3,4) on some minor amendments to the treaty, then the game between Wilson and the

FIGURE 2.9 *Wilson's Alternative Ratification Games in the U.S. Senate*

	U.S. Senate (G18)		Mild Reservationists (G27)		Strong Reservationists (G18)	
	Coop P	Conf N	Coop P	Conf N	Coop P	Conf N
Coop P	3,2	2,4*	3,4	1,2	2,3	1,4
Wilson						
Conf N	4,1	1,3	4,1	2,3*	4,2*	3,1

Intentions: Wil, Sen = –,–   Intentions: Wil, MRs = –,+   Intentions: Wil, SRs = –,–
Power: Wil < Sen   Power: Wil = MRs   Power: Wil > SRs

Brams nonmyopic equilibria are in bold. Nash myopic equilibria are asterisked. Game numbers are Brams's (1994, 215–219). Wil = Wilson; Sen = U.S. Senate; MR = mild reservationists; SR = strong reservationists.

remaining strong reservationists reverses the asymmetrical power relationship in Game 18 between Wilson and the strong reservationists, with the president in a power position to achieve a (4,2) domination outcome and get the amended treaty ratified over the opposition of these irreconcilables.

In conclusion, the case of Woodrow Wilson and the lost peace demonstrates that it is desirable for a putative cause-and-effect relationship to be as intimate and direct as possible in order for a counterfactual analysis to be valid (Lewis 1973; Tetlock and Belkin 1996). We shall be sensitive in the remainder of this book to these cautionary limits in identifying foreign policy mistakes by U.S. presidents in the basic power game via counterfactual analysis by tracing the links in subsequent chapters among intentions, power relations, choices, and outcomes.

PART II

Mismanaged Threats

CHAPTER 3

Fearing Losses Too Little

Deterrence Failures

INTRODUCTION

Realist theorists of international politics paint a rather grim, but perhaps accurate, picture of international life as they reference Thomas Hobbes's notion of a "state of nature." In this environment, the absence of an overarching authority permits vicious human appetites, desires, and inclinations to be pursued without moral restraints. According to realists, international politics is no different than the state of nature. In an anarchical international system, danger and insecurity are prominent features of political life. Implicit in any realist reading of Hobbes's philosophy about the state of nature is a warning against taking prolonged comfort in a country's current safety. It is an appeal to be critical and worry about ubiquitous danger that may await in the future.

In this chapter we examine two cases in which U.S. leaders appeared to have ignored these cautionary warnings. The paradigmatic cases we have chosen are the Japanese attack on Pearl Harbor in December 1941 and the Iraqi invasion of Kuwait in August 1990. In both cases, U.S. presidents recognized that something had gone fundamentally wrong. In the aftermath of the Pearl Harbor attacks, President Franklin Roosevelt described December 7, 1941, as a "date that will live in infamy" (qtd. in Wray 1990, 1). After Iraq invaded Kuwait, President George H.W. Bush described the assault as "a challenge [to the security] of the better world," and the United States found itself in its first post–cold war era conflict (Yetiv 1997, 3).

In both cases, U.S. leaders seemed to have underestimated the threat. However, we should also emphasize that one can also mismanage threats by overestimating them. The former are cases of deterrence failures while the latter are cases of false alarm failures. More specifically, deterrence failures are the result of mistakes of omission that occur when leaders fail to recognize a threat (a diagnostic error of detection) and/or fail to

FIGURE 3.1   *Types and Candidate Cases of Mismanaged Threats*

TYPE OF MISTAKE

	OMISSION (Too Little/Too Late)	**COMMISSION** (Too Much/Too Soon)
THREAT	Pearl Harbor Attack (1940–1941)	Bay of Pigs Invasion (1959–1961)
	(Detection/Hesitation)	(Misperception/Preemption)
CASES	Persian Gulf Conflict (1990–1991)	Vietnam Conflict (1964–1968)
	Deterrence Failures	False Alarm Failures

calculate and take actions to deter it (a prescriptive error of hesitation). False alarm failures are the result of mistakes of commission that occur when leaders anticipate a nonexistent threat (a diagnostic error of misperception) and/or calculate and take actions to overcome it (a prescriptive error of preemption). Both types of mistakes are based on false estimates of each state's intentions to use power or the existing power relationship between them in a dyadic power game and the implications for action that accompany these estimates.

Figure 3.1 shows our framework for the examination of mistakes and the cases we shall examine in this chapter as well as the candidate cases for the next chapter. The typology in this figure illustrates how the cases we have selected are conventionally described and classified. The typology is a heuristic (i.e., it offers a way to think about these historical cases). As our analysis will show, however, it is not always straightforward how to categorize a particular case as involving a mistake of omission or commission, or both. At times it also turns out that a mistake is described in opposite terms from how it is conventionally described and classified by other scholars. The Pearl Harbor attack is a case in point, as we will show in the following pages. It is also not always straightforward how to dissect whether the underlying mistake was diagnostic or prescriptive and whether the latter was necessarily caused by the former.

THE PEARL HARBOR ATTACK

When Japan attacked Pearl Harbor on December 7, 1941, it was widely regarded as an example of successful strategic surprise (Wohlstetter 1962). The Japanese military was able to disguise when, where, and how the attack would occur. Although U.S. leaders did anticipate a possible Japanese attack, the dominant consensus was that it would likely be in the Philippines or elsewhere in the Far East. U.S. leaders also thought they would have more warning if the Japanese were indeed to attack. It would appear with the benefit of hindsight that the U.S. leadership's failure to diagnose when, where, and how the attack would occur was a foreign policy mistake of omission, specifically a failure of detection.

It is well documented that U.S. military and civilian leaders did not recognize the imminence of the attack and failed to prescribe sufficient preventive or mitigating actions. Historians are not unanimous in their conclusions on whether U.S. leaders should have anticipated such a surprise move by Japan. Some analyses fault the interpretation of intelligence while others say that the signal-to-noise ratio and Japan's deceptive tactics of continuing to negotiate up to the time of attack made it hard to detect a warning (Wohlstetter 1962). In any case, there is general agreement on the conclusion that the U.S. leadership committed a mistake of omission as it failed to see the attack coming and did not redeploy the U.S. Navy out of Pearl Harbor to the open sea. In fact, this line of argument has come to be the conventional wisdom about the attack on Pearl Harbor (Hill 1948; Wohlstetter 1962; Mahnken 2002; Borch 2003). We shall revisit this argument through a game-theoretic analysis of the strategic situation between the United States and Japan prior to the attack.

At the outbreak of hostilities between Japan and China in 1937, the formal relations between Japan and the United States were mutually friendly (+,+) between great powers (USA = JAP), which constituted the no-conflict game shown in Figure 3.2.[1] Although the Japanese occupation of Chinese territory affected some relatively minor economic interests of the United States, the initial consensus within the political elite in Washington was that U.S. trade and investment in China was important but not essential (Graebner 1973, 34–35; Utley 1990, 79). Even though

FIGURE 3.2   *Alternative Strategic Situations between the United States and Japan, 1937–1941*

	Japan		Japan		Japan	
	Coop P	Conf N	Coop P	Conf N	Coop P	Conf N
Coop P	4,4*	1,2	3,4	1,2	3,3	1,4
United States						
Conf N	2,1	3,3*	4,1	2,3*	4,1	2,2*
	No-Conflict		Mixed-Motive (G27)		Conflict (G32)	
	Intentions: USA, JAP +,+		Intentions: USA, JAP –,+		Intentions: USA, JAP –,–	
	Power: USA = JAP		Power: USA = JAP		Power: USA = JAP	

Brams nonmyopic equilibria are in bold; Nash myopic equilibria are asterisked.

from the perspective of Washington the invasion may have been morally wrong because it violated international norms and laws concerning the territorial integrity of states, it did not impact the vital interests of the United States, as various Washington officials, including President Roosevelt himself, acknowledged (F. Adams 1971; Tansill 1976; Wray 1990, 5).

However, in subsequent years the United States engaged in a strategic reorientation. This shift was motivated mainly by nostalgic ties of President Roosevelt and some of his close advisors to China, moral presumptions about the sanctity of international law, and the emerging consideration of possible long-term economic benefits in China (Graebner 1973, 34–51; Best 1990, 29; McClain 2002, 471). Furthermore, some high-ranking and influential administration officials abhorred the prospects of Japanese regional hegemony in the Far East. Beginning in 1939, the U.S. leadership decided to impose economic sanctions and to demand Japanese withdrawal from the Asian mainland. This move did impact in very immediate and direct ways the vital interests of Japan, as the country was heavily dependent on the outside world for iron, steel, oil, and other essential raw materials and supplies (Trefousse 1982, 15; Emmerson 1990, 40; McClain 2002, 471).

The U.S. move toward economic sanctions, therefore, changed the relations between the two countries away from the no-conflict game to the mixed-motive strategic game (G27), in which Japan ranked settlement as its highest preference while the United States ranked domination as its highest preference. Some historians have suggested another interpretation of the strategic situation between the United States and Japan prior to December 1941. In this alternative account, it was not only the United States that assumed a conflict posture but also Japan (Davis and Lindley 1942; Feis 1950; Rauch 1950; Langer and Gleason 1953; Heinrichs 1990; Ikuhiko 1990; Wray 1990). Accordingly, the conflict game (G32) in Figure 3.2 depicts a worse-case scenario in which both players shifted to domination as their respective highest-ranked outcomes with the onset of U.S. economic sanctions against Japan. In this conflict game, Japan's negotiations were a diplomatic cover for military preparations to attack Pearl Harbor from a transitory state of U.S. domination (4,1) following the imposition of sanctions. In either case, the U.S. strategic choice of imposing severe economic sanctions created a new strategic situation between the United States and Japan.

The analysis of the mixed-motive game in Figure 3.3 shows that Japan's theoretical strategy in Japanese-U.S. relations after the former's incursion into Manchuria in 1937 is "stay" at (3,4), which should also be the U.S. strategy toward Japan. However, the U.S. decision to impose severe economic sanctions on Japan by 1939 was a move from (3,4) to (4,1). The logic of thinking ahead in Figure 3.3 from an initial state of (3,4) in this game reveals that the U.S. choice was a mistake. The prediction is that Japan would escalate (move) from U.S. domination (4,1) to deadlock (2,3) as a Nash-equilibrium final state unless the United States moved from (4,1) to settlement (3,4) under the influence of Japanese threats or promises during pre-play negotiations at (4,1). A move by Japan to (2,3) would mean a concrete attempt to break the U.S. economic sanctions, which would likely involve military action or at least the threat of military action. When and whether Japan would make this choice would depend on the success of diplomatic negotiations. But if the United States should prove unwilling to retract its economic sanctions, then it is reasonable to expect Japan to escalate. The fact that Japan did not continuously signal a clear threat to attack the United States does not obviate the logic of an impending attack. It is also consistent with Japanese strategic culture and the precedent of Japan's surprise attack on the Russian navy at Port Arthur to begin the 1904 Russo-Japanese War.

FIGURE 3.3   *Strategies of the United States and Japan in 1937–1941*

	Japan Coop P	Conf N		Japan Coop P	Conf N		Japan Coop P	Conf N
Coop P	"3,4" →|	1,2		"3,4" ←	1,2		3,4 |←	1,2
United States	↑	↓		↓	↑		↓	↑
Conf N	4,1 |←	2,3*		4,1 →	2,3*		"4,1" →	2,3*

Japan (1937): Stay Mixed-Motive (G27) Intentions: USA, JAP–,+ Power: USA = JAP	USA (1939): Stay Mixed-Motive (G27) Intentions: USA, JAP–,+ Power: USA = JAP	Japan (1941): Move Mixed-Motive (G27) Intentions: USA, JAP–,– Power: USA = JAP

Brams nonmyopic equilibria are underlined, and Nash myopic equilibria are asterisked. The initial state is in quotation marks, and the final state for a single play of the game with no prior (pre-play) communication is in bold. "Move" is indicated by an arrow (→), and "stay" is indicated by a blocked arrow (→\|) to depict the logic of each player's strategy as s/he "thinks ahead" from the initial state via the method of backward induction.

The same results occur when one assumes the alternative historical interpretation of the strategic situation between the United States and Japan prior to December 1941, that is, when the mixed-motive game (G27) is transformed to the pre–Pearl Harbor conflict game (G32). Both Japan and the United States should have chosen "stay" at (3,3), but the United States chose "move" to (4,1). With Japan having the next move from a state of U.S. domination (4,1) following the imposition of U.S. economic sanctions, Japan has no choice but to move to deadlock (2,2) unless it can convince the United States in pre-play communication that it should be magnanimous and move from (4,1) to (3,3) following a Japanese decision to "stay" at (4,1), in order to avoid a worse outcome for both players.

In fact, there was pre-play communication, and Japan did exercise both threat and promise power, respectively, in the form of offering concessions and warning about the future unpredictability of U.S.-Japanese relations if economic sanctions continued. Ultimately, as this strategy proved unsuccessful, Japan indeed chose to move from U.S. domination (4,1) to deadlock (2,3 in the mixed-motive game and 2,2 in the conflict game), escalating with the attack on Pearl Harbor on December 7, 1941. This analysis leads to the inference that the U.S. decision to shift from cooperation (P) to conflict (N) and impose economic sanctions on Japan was a costly strategic mistake of commission, which precipitated the attack on

Pearl Harbor. President Roosevelt should have been more synoptic regarding the likely Japanese countermove that his move to economic sanctions would encourage.

After the imposition of sanctions and the onset of negotiations, President Roosevelt and his advisors miscalculated again and made an inappropriate strategic choice to "stay" rather than "move" toward settlement as prescribed by the game theoretic analysis above. Such a strategy of magnanimity may have avoided and almost certainly would have deferred a Pacific war in 1941. Mistakes of omission in the interpretation of Japanese negotiating behavior and intelligence reports about Japanese military activities were subsequently made as well, but these "when, where, and how" failures are ultimately relegated to myopic tactical mistakes of detection and hesitation.

We contend that the conventional account about the Pearl Harbor attack is itself myopic, and insofar as it emphasizes the *surprise* aspect of the attack, it is also apologetic. Roosevelt could and should have known that the Japanese leadership would not remain at an inferior state of (4,1), and this knowledge should have weighed heavier in the decision-making process. This inference emerges not only from an objective analysis of the strategic situation between the United States and Japan prior to the Pearl Harbor attack; it is also evident from actual warnings Roosevelt received about the probable consequences of the new U.S. strategy toward Japan. A brief narrative of the main events between 1937 and 1941 supports this argument.

In the prelude to the Pearl Harbor attacks and the subsequent Pacific war, the president found himself under the strong influence of a group of hard-liners in his administration. Inherently hawkish, they rejected sustained considerations of moderation toward Japan. Most prominent among this group of hard-liners were Secretary of State Cordell Hull, his special adviser Stanley Hornbeck, Secretary of War Henry Stimson, Secretary of the Navy Frank Knox, and Secretary of the Treasury Henry Morgenthau (Chihiro 1990, 51). What is notable about this group of hard-liners is that it had little expertise regarding the Japanese policy-making apparatus or its strategic culture and exigencies (Best 1990, 28; Conroy and Wray 1990, xiv; Emmerson 1990, 38).

Despite this lack of knowledge, the group shared two fundamental beliefs about Japan. One was that Japan would seek to avoid war with the United States at all costs. An attack on America was unthinkable. The other assumption followed from the first, namely, that Japan would inevitably submit to unbending U.S. resolve (Graebner 1973, 51; Leopold 1973, 3, 6; Chihiro 1990, 57, 61; Emmerson 1990, 40, 44). Representative of these beliefs was Hornbeck's argument that would be repeated until the Pearl Harbor attacks, namely, that a strong U.S. stand of a "comprehensive and thoroughgoing program of material pressure could prevent military confrontation and lead to a revision in Japanese policy" (Chihiro 1990, 53). This argument was, in effect, on behalf of a strategy of degrading Japanese power, thereby transforming the game with the United States from a symmetrical to an asymmetrical power game favoring Washington and a domination outcome for America.

Opposing this group of hard-liners in the administration was a cohort of moderates. Among them were Assistant Secretaries of State Francis Sayre and Sumner Welles and the director of the State Department's Far Eastern division, Maxwell Hamilton (Graebner 1973, 42). The one person most familiar with the political and strategic context in which decisions were made was Joseph Grew, U.S. ambassador in Japan. Perhaps most important, he understood that the decision-making authority of Japanese Prime Minister Fumimaro Konoe was fragile and that Japanese decisions could easily be influenced by a militarist wing of army and navy generals in the Japanese decision-making elite. It was Ambassador Grew who took the lead among the moderates and engaged in the most sustained criticism of the course the United States was taking toward Japan (Leopold 1973, 6).[2]

The general contentions of Grew and the other moderates were that sanctions were seen simply as a strategy of deterrence or compellence in the United States to enforce international law; however, because its vital interests were at stake, Japan would perceive them as a U.S. effort to dominate Japan and the Pacific region together with Great Britain and the Netherlands (Reynolds 2001, 133). They argued that instead of deterring the Japanese from pursuing an expansionist policy, economic sanctions would exacerbate U.S.-Japanese relations and, in the end, may even provoke the Japanese leadership to go to war with the United States (Chihiro 1990, 51). Ambassador Grew went so far as to warn explicitly that the United States would likely encounter retaliation that might take the form of a "sudden stroke" by the military, and he counseled Washington to face squarely the consequences of whatever action it might take (Emmerson 1990, 39).

The misfortune of the moderates was that they were all lower-ranking officials, and as the crisis with Japan intensified, their warnings were trumped by the group of higher-ranking hard-liners in Roosevelt's cabinet. Under the strong influence of these hard-liners, in January 1939 the president imposed an embargo prohibiting the export of aircraft to Japan. This step was a serious matter. Not only would it affect Japan's status and prestige in the Far East, it would also impair the country's ability to conduct its foreign and security policy (Trefousse 1982, 25–26). Yet, according to Secretary of War Stimson, this measure would entail no risk because Japan was determined to avoid war with the United States (Graebner 1973, 43). Similarly, Secretary of State Hull argued that the U.S. ability to impose economic sanctions thereafter would have a "sobering effect" on Japan because of the latter's economic dependence on the United States (Chihiro 1990, 53; see also Iriye, 1976, 149).[3]

In Washington such sentiments were countered by Assistant Secretary of State Sayre, who argued that sanctions against Japan were highly provocative and posed a serious danger of military conflict (Chihiro 1990, 52). However, President Roosevelt maintained that sanctions were "the constructive thing to do" (qtd. in Graebner 1973, 42). In February, he went further and ordered a cessation of credits to Japan, and finally, he decided to notify Tokyo of his intention in July to abrogate the 1911 commercial treaty that was vital for the Japanese economy. It is notable that Ambassador Grew, even though he was on a home visit at the time of this particular decision, was not consulted by the president. Ignoring the arguments of the moderates, the U.S. leadership gradually extended the list of sanctions and placed the country in a de facto domination posture toward Japan (McClain 2002, 475; Trefousse 1982, 25–26).

Seeing its vital interests threatened by U.S. sanctions policies, the Konoe government proposed a modus vivendi according to which Japan would offer concessions to the United States in China and would, in return, receive a new trade agreement (Graebner 1973, 43; Chihiro 1990, 55). Cognizant of the potential influence of militarists on Prime Minister Konoe and in support of the modus vivendi proposed by Japan, Ambassador Grew communicated to the White House in Washington on December 18, 1939:

The simple fact is that we are here dealing not with a unified Japan but with a Japanese government which is endeavoring courageously, even with only gradual success, to fight against a recalcitrant Japanese Army, a battle which happens to be our own battle. . . . If we now rebuff the Government, we shall not be serving to discredit the Japanese Army but rather to furnish the Army with powerful arguments to be used in its own support. I am convinced that we are in a position either to direct American-Japanese relations into a progressively healthy channel or to accelerate their movement straight down hill. (Chihiro 1990, 55)

This stark warning would once again be overshadowed by the contentions of the hard-liners. Secretary of War Stimson argued, "The only way to treat Japan is not to give her anything" (qtd. in Graebner 1973, 45). Secretary of State Hull, in tandem with his special adviser Hornbeck, was also strongly opposed to any concessions toward Japan and together succeeded in convincing Roosevelt not to negotiate a new commercial treaty until Japan would renounce her aims in China (Chihiro 1990, 55–56; Graebner 1973, 44; Utley 1990, 77–78). This imposition of sanctions was now compounded by the subsequent and ultimate mistake of omission as U.S. leaders failed to calculate the consequences of choosing "stay" at domination rather than choosing "move" toward settlement.

The influence of the hard-liners on the president continued to prevail over that of the moderates in the administration. The former group remained convinced that Japan would ultimately bend to U.S. determination. Secretary of War Stimson, for example, observed that, "[He did] not think . . . the Japanese would attack [American territory] even if [the United States] put an embargo on raw materials for arms. All the evidence . . . indicates that they are more afraid of war with the U.S. than anything else" (qtd. in Ben-Zvi 1976, 385). Thus, after the hard-liners' initial efforts, in June 1940 Congress passed the National Defense Act, authorizing President Roosevelt to restrict or prohibit the exportation of additional strategic materials, such as engines, machinery, iron, steel, and aviation fuel (Trefousse 1982, 25–26; McClain 2002, 475).

U.S. economic sanctions put the Tokyo government under ever-increasing pressure coming also from its domestic realm as these sanctions played into the hands of the militarists in the Japanese government. The militarists had been arguing that the imposition of economic sanctions by the United States necessitated Japanese expansion to ensure vital needs. Now this argument gained in strength (Chihiro 1990, 51). On October 5, 1940, Japanese foreign minister Matsouka summoned Ambassador Grew. He stated that U.S. sanctioning policies "intensely angered the Japanese people" and hinted at severe strategic exigencies that these policies may necessitate. Three days later Ambassador Horinouchi was more explicit, and in a note to Secretary of State Hull, he protested restrictions that he claimed constituted an "unfriendly act" that "may cause future relations between the U.S. and Japan to become unpredictable" (Chihiro 1990, 60).

Secretary Hull remained undeterred. In April of the next year, he handed Ambassador Horinouchi a list of preconditions, which Japan would have to meet before a normalization in its relations with the United States would be possible. The list became known as the infamous "Hull note" and included demands such as the complete Japanese withdrawal from French Indochina and China, the respect for the territorial integrity of other nations, noninterference in the internal affairs of other countries, and no alteration to the status quo except through peaceful means (McClain 2002, 475). These principles were at odds with the United States' own policies in parts of South America and Southeast Asia. What mattered for the Japanese government was that it was being asked to renounce all its gains from the previous ten years and to return to its status of the 1920s, where it would be relegated to a peripheral actor in the Far East (Iriye 1974, 456).

In the meantime, President Roosevelt remained closed to considering warnings of serious consequences resulting from U.S. actions toward Japan. His conviction that Japan would under no circumstances move toward war with the United States reinforced further sanctioning policies during the summer of 1941, and these steps took on unprecedented dimensions (Graebner 1973, 49). In June 1941 the United States required licenses for all oil exports and prohibited all oil shipments from the Atlantic seaboard except to territory in the Western Hemisphere and to Great Britain. This ruling was merely the prelude to the final interdiction of any oil for Japan, which was to come in July (Trefousse 1982, 26).

Facing a complete cessation of oil supplies further stiffened the attitude of the militarist wing in the Japanese government and brought their arguments to bear on Konoe's decisions. They judged that Japan had no course but to secure the raw materials it needed for its survival by force while it still had enough oil. A year prior Japanese forces had occupied northern Indochina. Now Prime Minister Konoe found himself compelled to execute plans for a southern advance, and indeed by the end of July Japanese troops had invaded and occupied French Indochina. Thus, oil sanctions served not to deter Japan from further expansion but promoted, in fact, the exact opposite response (Graebner 1973, 49; Reynolds 2001, 151).

In reaction to Japan's invasion of southern Indochina, on July 26 President Roosevelt ordered the freezing of Japanese funds deposited in U.S. banks (Trefouse 1982, 25–26). This order effectively terminated all U.S. commercial and financial relations with Japan (Graebner 1973, 49). The freezing order underscored the difficulties facing Japan and confirmed, in the perception of the Tokyo government, the U.S. intent together with Great Britain and the Netherlands to dominate the Pacific region and subjugate and dominate Japan (Emmerson 1990, 41). With Roosevelt's decision, Prime Minister Konoe faced the immediate prospect of a fateful choice between the renunciation of the Japanese status as a great power in the Far East and ensuing economic challenges on the one hand and war on the other (Graebner 1973, 49; Iriye 1981, 14; see also Trefousse 1982, 17).

Militarists in the Japanese government argued and pressed for war with the United States. In this escalating situation Prime Minister Konoe sought to ease tensions by proposing a summit meeting with President Roosevelt (Butow 1972; Utley 1990, 80; Reynolds 2001, 141). In Japan Ambassador Grew saw signs of promise, and he urged Secretary Hull to not reject the Japanese proposal "without very prayerful consideration" and to facilitate the summit. He argued that Konoe would not request such a meeting unless he was willing to make concessions (Burns 1976, 95). However, Secretary Hull and his adviser, Hornbeck, disagreed. Although Roosevelt was initially inclined to accept the offer, he was persuaded in the end that no summit meeting should take place until Japan had agreed to renounce all her claims on any foreign territory (Reynolds 2001, 158; Emmerson 1990, 41).

Thus, the crisis deteriorated further, reaching a crucial point at the Japanese Imperial Conference on September 6. The conference called attention to the economic predicament that Japan faced, and government leaders established their diplomatic bottom line. Japan was ready to withdraw from Indochina and commit to no further operations outside the Chinese theater. In return, Tokyo asked for the resumption of trade relations with the United States and the provision of essential resources (Russett 1967, 90; Reynolds 2001, 158). The most important conclusion of the conference was that Japanese leaders made a formal commitment among themselves that either negotiations must bear fruit by October 15 or else Japan would have to go to war with the United States (Russett 1967, 90; Iriye 1981, 32; Trefousse 1982, 30).

The impasse between the United States and Japan extended beyond the Japanese deadline, forcing the resignation of Prime Minister Konoe on October 16. When war minister Hideki Tojo assumed the new premiership, U.S.-Japanese relations were at the brink of war. In a last effort to avert this total escalation, Tojo extended a new offer to withdraw from French Indochina and from most of China except for certain territories in the north, which it wanted to garrison for twenty-five years (McClain 2002, 479). A new deadline of November 29 was set for a U.S. response (Russett 1967, 90). The U.S. leadership, however, made clear that Japan should not expect any such compromise. For Roosevelt, a Japanese commitment to withdraw from all of China had become the sine qua non (McClain 2002, 478; Utley 1990, 80; Graebener 1973, 50).

Being absolutely dependent on foreign resources, such demands were not acceptable to Japan (Russett 1967, 97). Moreover, further concessions would have relegated Japan to a second- or perhaps even third-class power and opened the way for de facto U.S. domination of the region. On December 1, Tojo opened a new imperial conference by stating that his government had "exhausted every means at its disposal to reach a diplomatic settlement," but that in response Roosevelt had "not conceded an inch." He concluded that war had become "inevitable" (qtd. in McClain 2002, 480–481). On the morning of December 7, 1941, Japan attacked Pearl Harbor. The assault killed 2,403 people and destroyed or severely damaged as many as 21 U.S. ships and 339 aircraft (Mueller 1991/92, 174). Had Grew's advice been followed, these outcomes might have been avoided. Grew was prudent, which cannot be said for U.S. hard-liners or the president (Chihiro 1990, 62).

THE PERSIAN GULF WAR

Similar to the Pearl Harbor attack, the Iraqi invasion of Kuwait also came to be labeled as a surprise attack. After several months of negotiations between Iraq and Kuwait over disputed territory and oil extraction rights plus repayment of Kuwait's loans to Iraq during the Iran-Iraq War, Iraqi forces invaded Kuwait on August 1, 1990. This act of aggression was the first challenge to the New World Order of peace and stability heralded enthusiastically by President George H.W. Bush at the conclusion of the cold war (Bush 1990). Indeed, the president described the conflict as a defining moment, for it was shaped by the fundamental changes taking place in global politics, and through the precedent it set, it would influence the emerging character of these politics (Freedman and Karsh 1993, xxx).

However, Saddam Hussein's invasion of Kuwait was significant not only because it threatened the New World Order and the stability of a volatile region; it also affected in very direct ways the vital interests of the United States. Exerting control over Kuwait would allow the Iraqi dictator to be in a very strong position to influence international oil production and pricing. What made the situation even more severe was that Saddam Hussein may also have been preparing to invade Saudi Arabia. In either case, he would then be able to exercise considerable leverage over the United States, which was heavily dependent on imported oil. The same would be true of a number of close U.S. allies who were even

FIGURE 3.4   *Alternative Strategic Situations between the United States and Iraq, 1990–1991*

	Iraq		Iraq		Iraq	
	Coop P	Conf N	Coop P	Conf N	Coop P	Conf N
Coop P	4,4*	1,1	4,3	1,4	2,3	1,4
United States						
Conf N	3,2	2,3*	3,2	2,1	4,2*	3,1

Pre–July 15	July 15–Aug 1	Aug 7–
No-Conflict	Mixed-Motive (G29)	Conflict (G18)
Intentions: USA, IRQ +,+	Intentions: USA, IRQ +,–	Intentions: USA, IRQ –,–
Power: USA > IRQ	Power: USA > IRQ	Power: USA > IRQ

Brams equilibria are in bold; Nash equilibria are asterisked.

more dependent on imported oil as an energy resource. To find itself in such a predicament would be unacceptable to the United States (Renshon 1993, 80–81; Yetiv 1997).

The developing strategic situation between the United States and Iraq is modeled in the game theoretic analysis in Figure 3.4. Before the onset of the crisis, the United States and Iraq were in a no-conflict game. Both players were displaying cooperative actions toward one another, with the United States clearly more powerful than Iraq. However, Saddam Hussein displayed conflict actions on July 15 by mobilizing his armed forces and moving them toward the Kuwaiti border. These steps, in effect, reflected a redefinition of the no-conflict game to a mixed-motive game.

In the mixed-motive game with an initial state of (4,3) mutual cooperation, the stability of this NME depends on the ability of the player who ranks this outcome highest to threaten a move to the other player's worst outcome of deadlock (2,1) if the latter defects from (4,3) to the former's worst outcome of submission (1,4). It is also notable that the possibility of cycling exists in this game: if the two moves from an initial state or (4,3) to (1,4) and (2,1) do occur, the next move by Iraq would be to (3,2) and the final move by the United States would be back to (4,3). The cycle would occur because logically each player would stand to improve by each move, as the rankings in bold show, once the initial move from (4,3) is not deterred by threat power in the form of a credible U.S.

FIGURE 3.5   *Alternative Strategies by the United States and Iraq, 1990–1991*

	Iraq			Iraq			Iraq	
	Coop P	Conf N		Coop P	Conf N		Coop P	Conf N
				(If U.S. deterrent threat fails)				
Coop P	"**4,3**"	←| 1,4		"**4,3**"	→ 1,4		2,3	→ "1,4"
United States	↓	↑		↑	↓		↑	↓
Conf N	**3,2**	→| 2,1*		3,2	← 2,1		**4,2***	← 3,1

U.S. Strategy: Threats Mixed-Motive (G29)	Iraq Strategy: Cycle Mixed-Motive (G29)	U.S. Strategy: Move Conflict (G18)
Intentions: USA, IRQ +,–	Intentions: USA, IRQ +,–	Intentions: USA, IRQ –,–
Power: USA > IRQ	Power: USA > IRQ	Power: USA > IRQ

Initial state is in quotation marks, and final outcomes are underlined. Brams nonmyopic equilibria are in bold. Nash myopic equilibrium is asterisked. The arrows indicate thinking ahead via backward induction by each player about whether to move (→) or not move (→\|).

deterrent threat. A formal demonstration of these strategies appears in Figure 3.5.

In order to avoid an escalatory cycle, the strategy prescribed for the United States by the game analysis is to respond to Iraq's conflict actions with a strong and credible deterrent strategy and to threaten negative consequences. Then Saddam may have demobilized his forces against Kuwait. This reversal would have restored settlement (4,3) as the final state of the mixed-motive game. However, in the period from Saddam Hussein's mobilization of his armed forces on July 15 until his invasion of Kuwait on August 1, the United States made no concerted attempt at deterring Iraq from such actions. Thus, the U.S. failure to make a credible threat from (4,3) encouraged Saddam to continue a cycling strategy in which an invasion of Kuwait eventually moved U.S.-Iraqi relations to (1,4) in Game 18, as shown in Figure 3.5.

The cycling did not continue after President George Bush ordered U.S. troops to Saudi Arabia on August 7, which began the buildup to war unless Iraq withdrew from Kuwait. This belatedly unequivocal action by the United States signaled the transformation of their mixed-motive game to a conflict game (G18, in Figure 3.4) with a new initial state of (1,4). In this game the U.S. strategy called for a move to deadlock (3,1) with the expectation that Iraq would either move voluntarily to a final outcome of submission (4,2) or be forced to do so by a coalition of military forces led by the United States. After several months of diplomatic maneuvering and the buildup of coalition forces in the region, Iraq's army was expelled from Kuwait by a coordinated air, sea, and ground attack led by U.S. forces with their allies.

Why did the United States fail to deter Saddam Hussein's actions against Kuwait? We contend that this failure was due first to a diagnostic mistake of omission, a failure to detect Saddam's intentions even after his decision on July 15 to mobilize along the border with Kuwait. To implement a strategy of deterrence, one must first detect and then, if necessary, alter the prevailing image of the would-be aggressor (Hybel 1993, 7). President Bush and his advisors assumed that Saddam Hussein would not invade Kuwait, because the latter had learned from Iraq's war with Iran how costly another major war would be (Hybel 1993, 7, 51–52; Swansbrough 1994, 264). Hence, in the prelude to the conflict, Iraq appeared only marginally on the foreign policy agenda of the Bush administration and remained there even as the Iraq-Kuwait conflict escalated into a crisis. The National Security Council did not convene even once before the invasion. The second-level Deputies Committee, which is often convened to study major foreign policy issues, had only two meetings about Iraq before the invasion. Secretary of State James Baker's involvement in Iraq policy before the invasion was minimal, and diplomatic interchanges occurred only at the ambassadorial level (Oberdorfer 1991b).

Instead of a comprehensive engagement with the ensuing situation, only a select few of the top officials dealt with it. Among them were President Bush, National Security Advisor Brent Scowcroft, Secretary of Defense Richard Cheney, Chairman of the Joint Chiefs of Staff (JCS) Colin Powell, and the commander of the Central Command, Norman Schwarzkopf. This small group obviated any sustained consideration of alternative interpretations for Saddam Hussein's actions, and this omission allowed for continuous dwelling on false assumptions about the Iraqi dictator. They were convinced that Iraq's war with Iran had made Saddam Hussein a chastened man, aware of the limits of Iraq's power and eager to bind his country to the West (Hybel 1993, 112). They believed further that he would at most try to intimidate Kuwait but would ultimately opt for a settlement. Even though Saddam Hussein sent increasingly clear signs of his aggressive intentions, President Bush and his advisors held fast to this initial belief.

A narrative of Saddam Hussein's actions and the perceptions of U.S. leaders support these points. Evidence of an escalating crisis in the Gulf became available first on May 30, 1990. During the Arab League summit in Baghdad, Saddam Hussein complained to a group of Arab leaders that "economic warfare" was being waged against him by Kuwait (Oberdorfer 1991b; Woodward 1991, 206). He warned that he would not tolerate such behavior and expressed his determination to take action against Kuwait unless its government met his demands for compensation (Hybel 1993, 36). He concluded, "If words do not remedy the situation something effective must be done" (qtd. in Oberdorfer 1991b). Indeed, about two months later the Iraqi dictator unleashed deeds to follow his words. On July 15, a division of the elite Republican Guard began moving from central Iraq southeast toward the Kuwaiti border. The mobilization occurred at a very fast and alarming pace. Within less than twenty-four hours some 10,000 troops and 300 tanks were in place at the border, with a second division about to follow (Freedman and Karsh 1993, 47; Yetiv 1997, 9).

With the onset of the military campaign, Saddam Hussein also continued escalating his hostile rhetoric. In an address to the nation on July 17, he accused Kuwait of "cutting off the livelihood of the Arab nation [Iraq]." He warned yet anew that "if words fail . . . , then we will have no choice but to resort to effective action to put things right and ensure the restitution of our rights" (qtd. in Freedman and Karsh 1993, 48). What is notable about this address is that for the first time Saddam Hussein articulated his warning in public. He thereby committed himself to his objectives in such a way that any compromise with Kuwait would have been seen as capitulation on his part. Thus, there was no room left for bargaining or procrastination. Kuwait had to accept his demands in full or face grave consequences (Ibid., 48).

Indeed, Saddam Hussein made his intentions clearer by the day and set the stage for an invasion of Kuwait. By July 19, 35,000 Iraqi troops from three divisions had been deployed ten to thirty miles from the Kuwaiti border, and the already present tanks had assumed a classic coiled pattern. They were all facing outward thereby allowing for maximum attacking capability and further supply for sustained engagement in an assault against Kuwait (Woodward 1991, 207; Freedman and Karsh 1993, 47; Yetiv 1997, 9).

U.S. intelligence satellites had registered the move of Iraqi troops from the very beginning. The photographs were analyzed by the Pentagon's Defense Intelligence Agency (DIA) and subsequently reviewed by JCS Chairman Colin Powell and by Thomas Kelly, the JCS director of operations. Both men were aware that these new observations posed a dilemma, as they stood in stark contrast to earlier assessments by both the DIA and the CIA. They had come to the conclusion that, although Saddam Hussein wanted to dominate the Gulf region, the costs absorbed by Iraq during its war against Iran would restrain him from using force and engaging in a new war (Woodward 1991, 207; Hybel 1993, 29–30). Powell showed himself troubled by Iraq's actions but not alarmed. Kelly argued that Saddam Hussein was merely attempting to pressure Kuwait to acquiesce to his demands.

Subsequently, the new intelligence was also reviewed by Defense Secretary Richard Cheney and General Norman Schwarzkopf, the commander of the U.S. Central Command. Similar to Powell and Kelly, they concluded that the most Iraq might do was to launch a minor punitive attack (Woodward 1991, 207–209; Hybel 1993, 31). In the end, no substantive significance was attached either to Saddam Hussein's words or deeds. The dominant and prevailing conclusion was that he merely intended to intimidate Kuwait (Freedman and Karsh 1993, 50); however, evidence to the contrary continued to accumulate. On July 24, the *National Intelligence Daily* warned that "Iraq now has ample forces and supplies available for military operations inside Kuwait" (Ibid., 51). One day later the CIA estimated that Baghdad was not bluffing and would probably use force against Kuwait (Oberdorfer 1991b). President Bush was briefed on the danger by CIA Director William Webster, and although the president ordered a naval exercise in the Persian Gulf to demonstrate support for Kuwait, the new information did not alter in fundamental ways his initial assessment of the situation. Like other top officials,

President Bush viewed Saddam Hussein's military mobilization merely as an act of intimidation. He continued to believe that Saddam Hussein would ultimately settle peacefully (Ibid., 51; Hybel 1993, 31).

An occasion to clarify the situation occurred on July 25, when U.S. ambassador April Glaspie met with Saddam Hussein.[4] Regarding Iraq's troop movements on the Kuwaiti border, the ambassador used the occasion to ask Saddam Hussein "in a spirit of friendship, what are your intentions?" Saddam Hussein responded that Kuwait could be assured that "we are not going to do anything until we meet with them. When we meet and we see there is hope, then nothing will happen. But if we are unable to find a solution, then it will be natural that Iraq will not accept death" (qtd. in Stein 1992, 152–53). Because U.S. interests were at stake, Glaspie's subsequent response is surprising, to say the least: "We have no opinion on inter-Arab disputes, like your border dispute with Kuwait" (Sciolino 1991, 280).

In later testimony before the U.S. Senate, Ambassador Glaspie claimed that this text of the conversation released by the Iraqi Foreign Ministry in Arabic had been heavily edited, omitting some of her remarks on the border issue, including her statement "that we insist that you settle your disputes with Kuwait nonviolently . . . not by threats, not by intimidation, and certainly not by aggression" (Sciolino 1991, 270, 283–84). In any case, at the end of her conversation with Saddam Hussein, the ambassador was reassured. She cabled to Washington, "Iraqis are sick of war. . . . His emphasis that he wants peaceful settlement is surely sincere" (Hoffman and Dewar 1991; Oberdorfer 1991b; J. Stein 1992, 153; Freedman and Karsh 1993, 54).

After Glaspie's meeting with the Iraqi dictator, the view in Washington was that the crisis had been abated (Woodward 1991, 212; Freedman and Karsh 1993, 54). President Bush and his advisors continued to rely on Saddam Hussein's words and discounted his deeds even while more evidence to the contrary was accumulating. Satellite photographs kept revealing a rapidly expanding Iraqi military buildup. On July 27, eight divisions of some 100,000 men from the best Iraqi units and 350 tanks were poised on the Kuwaiti border and in formation for extensive operations (Yetiv 1997, 10; Freedman and Karsh 1993, 55). Three days later Walter

Lang, a senior intelligence analyst at the Pentagon's DIA, wrote in his report on Iraqi capabilities and intentions:

[Saddam Hussein] has created the capability to overrun all of Kuwait and all of Eastern Saudi Arabia. . . . I do not believe he is bluffing. I have looked at his personality profile. He doesn't know how to bluff. It is not in his past pattern of behavior. . . . Saddam Hussein has moved a force disproportionate to the task at hand, if it is to bluff. Then there is only one answer: he intends to use it. (Hybel 1993, 31–32)

This stark warning was sent to Secretary of Defense Cheney and JCS Chairman Powell (Freedman and Karsh 1993, 57). Cheney maintained his judgment that Saddam Hussein's actions were intended to intimidate Kuwait rather than prepare for an actual invasion (Ibid., 55). Powell also continued to judge Saddam Hussein's actions as mere "saber-rattling," and he expected the coming month to be quiet. Both Cheney and Powell agreed that DIA intelligence analyst Lang's conclusions about Saddam Hussein's intentions were premature (Hybel 1993, 32). National Security Advisor Brent Scowcroft subsequently also agreed with this assessment and briefed the president accordingly.

As Saddam Hussein's military mobilization was progressing, delegations from Iraq and Kuwait had been engaging in talks in the Saudi Arabian city of Jeddah. However, on July 31, these conversations collapsed without any agreement between the parties (Freedman and Karsh 1993, 59–61; Stein 1992, 157). As the diplomatic track came to a standstill, alarming signs of an impending invasion increased. Yet these signs would be dismissed once again when the Jordanian king Hussein telephoned President Bush and assured him that the Iraqi dictator would not resort to military force. Egyptian president Hosni Mubarak and Saudi Arabian king Fahd also argued to President Bush that the problem was being handled in an Arab way and asked Bush to do nothing to upset the process (Stein 1992, 154; Oberdorfer 1991b; Woodward 1991, 215). These appraisals weighed heavier in Bush's decision-making than the information and the warning from U.S. intelligence agencies (Swansbrough 1994, 264). As a result, the president's fundamental interpretation of Saddam Hussein's intentions remained more or less unchanged. He did not believe that

Iraq would indeed act militarily, and therefore he did not order any additional means aimed at deterring Saddam Hussein.

By the morning of August 1, U.S. satellite photographs showed that Iraq's three armored divisions had moved within just three miles of the Kuwaiti border, with two positioned close to a main four-lane highway leading into the center of Kuwait. The tanks were followed by some eighty helicopters (Freedman and Karsh 1993, 61; Woodward 1991, 219). Even more alarming was that communications equipment, artillery munitions, and supply logistics had been put in place and were fully operational. Lang immediately concluded that Iraq was about to launch an attack. The CIA concurred with the DIA assessment, stating that all indicators pointed to an impending invasion of Kuwait within twenty-four hours (Hybel 1993, 32; Oberdorfer 1991b; Woodward 1991, 219).

On the same day General Schwarzkopf briefed Secretary of Defense Cheney and the Joint Chiefs. Giving a status report on the location of the 100,000 Iraqi troops, Schwarzkopf said that they were positioned in a way to give Saddam lots of options outside of an attack. In his conclusion he did not foresee an Iraqi invasion or a border crossing. It was at this time that Powell, for the first time, disagreed with the prevailing consensus, arguing that with the installations of communications networks and supply logistics an invasion may indeed be imminent. He suggested that Cheney should notify President Bush. However, his urging remained without consequences, as the crisis was transformed into an open conflict (Woodward 1991, 221).

By the evening of August 1, Iraqi tanks had crossed the Kuwaiti border and were moving rapidly toward Kuwait City. Despite plentiful indications of Saddam Hussein's hostile intentions, President Bush and his top advisers had refused to see them as such. Now it was not only the leadership in Washington but the entire nation that had to face the consequences. The United States mobilized 500,000 troops for the forthcoming Persian Gulf War, and Iraq was forced to withdraw from Kuwait. However, this success came at a price. Almost 300 U.S. soldiers lost their lives, and the country spent about $71 billion in the campaign. President Bush's New World Order of peace and stability had failed to deter aggression.

Once again, the dual perspectives of game theory and historical analysis reinforce the conclusion that the president of the United States and his advisors made a major foreign policy mistake. This time it was a categorical diagnostic error in which they failed to detect and misperceived as well the intentions of Iraq's leader, Saddam Hussein. The president and his advisors continued to define the power game between the United States and Iraq as a no-conflict game even after July 15, when Iraq's actions signaled that the Iraq-Kuwait power game was now a mixed- motive game. They failed to consider the implications of this shift in relations between the two Arab states for defining strategic relations between Iraq and the United States. This categorical diagnostic error led to a prescriptive mistake in the form of a deterrence failure to employ threat power against Iraq.

CONCLUSIONS

In the case of Pearl Harbor, the conventional wisdom asserts that the Japanese attack was possible because U.S. leaders committed a diagnostic mistake of omission. Roosevelt and his advisers misinterpreted the tactical intelligence and failed to see the attack coming. Qualifying this explanation, we have argued that it was precipitated by an earlier strategic prescriptive mistake of commission. In the late 1930s, the United States initiated severe economic sanctions against Japan, which affected the latter country's vital interests and threatened to put it in an inferior power position. Roosevelt fundamentally miscalculated the effects of this strategy of compellence on the Japanese response. Our game-theoretic analysis shows that as long as the United States rejected any concessions, Japan was bound to resist and preempt U.S. domination with escalation. At the very least, the Washington leadership should have redeployed the Pacific fleet from Pearl Harbor in anticipation of imminent war action. A "too much, too soon" pattern was followed by a "too little, too late" pattern of foreign policy mistakes.

The Iraqi invasion of Kuwait was a mistake of omission resulting in a deterrence failure. To avoid such an outcome, generally the deterring agent must carefully define unacceptable behavior, signal a commitment to punish transgressors, and demonstrate the resolve to carry through the warning (Lebow and Stein 1987, 8; Russett 1987, 99). To follow these prescriptions, however, the deterring agent must be aware of an ensuing threat in the first place. U.S. leaders failed here. We contend that this prescriptive omission occurred because they committed a diagnostic mistake. After failing initially to detect a threat, they then hesitated to deter it—a pattern of too little, too late. Even though Saddam's intentions were clearly revealed in intelligence reports, President Bush and other top officials held fast to their belief that the Iraqi leader was merely trying to intimidate Kuwait and would opt for a settlement in the end (Hybel 1993, 33).

Foreign policy mistakes are the results of wrong answers to the *kto-kovo* power politics question and the resulting mismanagement in the exercise of positive and negative sanctions. In the Pearl Harbor case, U.S. leaders strongly believed that a strategy of negative sanctions would lead Japanese leaders to revise their policies and retreat from ambitions for great power status. They ignored the logical consequence that the Japanese leadership would instead be compelled to reciprocate. President Roosevelt's hard-line policy toward Japan only served to push the Japanese into conflict with the United States—an outcome that certainly could have been anticipated and perhaps avoided.

Roosevelt and his most influential advisors were incapable of giving proper answers to the *kto-kovo* question, because they were driven by a lack of expertise regarding Japan. Their blindness to reality was demonstrated in an unwillingness or inability to take seriously into account the gravity of Japan's economic plight and the real exigencies of the country's strategic position (Schroeder 1976, 116). Even as late as November 27, 1941, Hornbeck declared that in his opinion, "the Japanese Government does not intend or expect to have forthwith armed conflict with the United States" (qtd. in Graebner 1973, 52). Such calculations were "a product of wishful thinking" as acknowledged by Hornbeck after the attacks (Leopold 1973, 6).

Also in the case of Iraq, U.S. leaders gave misinformed answers to the *kto-kovo* question. President Bush and his advisers did realize that competing inferences could be made from Saddam's deployment of Iraqi troops. However, they all sought to avoid uncertainty and maintain cognitive consistency by rejecting any information that would contradict their initial beliefs (Hybel 1993, 52–55). They failed to consider that Saddam Hussein was determined to assert Iraq's historic claim to Kuwait, establish control over the oil-producing Gulf, and secure for Iraq a commanding voice in the determination of oil pricing and production for the rest of the decade and into the new century (Stein 1992, 156).

If the United States had taken a more cautious and prudent attitude toward Japan, the Pearl Harbor attacks may have been avoided. At the very least, a more prudent approach may have prolonged the crisis and perhaps averted the conflict. As the crisis escalated, the United States engaged in a buildup of military forces in the Philippines, but the completion would have taken until sometime in 1942. Only then would it perhaps have served as a viable deterrent (Masaru 1990, 50). This scenario would also require the United States to accept Japanese concessions short of withdrawal from China during negotiations in 1941. These steps might have bought the time necessary to discourage further Japanese expansion in the Far East by keeping them bogged down in the Chinese interior against Mao's guerrilla forces.

Finally, if the U.S. leadership had come both to recognize Saddam's intentions and to adopt a strategy of deterrence, the Iraqi dictator may have been disabused of his aggressive intentions. The evidence for this counterfactual conjecture comes from Saddam's meeting with U.S. Ambassador Glaspie. After he laid out his grievances and possible intentions regarding Kuwait, Saddam asked, "What is the U.S.'s opinion on this?" Although Saddam was a leader who may have suffered from wishful thinking and megalomania, it is hard to believe that he would have been foolish enough to risk war with the United States, an altercation that he was bound to lose. If Glaspie and other senior U.S. officials had recognized the danger and responded more forcefully instead of declaring that this conflict was an Arab matter, Saddam may have been deterred from attacking Kuwait.

CHAPTER 4

Fearing Losses Too Much

False Alarm Failures

INTRODUCTION

Sir Francis Walsingham is often described as the spymaster for England's Queen Elizabeth I, and he is also often considered to be among the first practitioners of intelligence operations for security purposes. It was his personal experience that led him to say, "There is less danger in fearing too much than too little." Although this statement is intuitively sensible, we will show in this chapter that fearing too much, just like fearing too little, may equally lead to catastrophic consequences. The cases we have chosen for examining exaggerated threats are the Bay of Pigs invasion in 1961 and the escalation of the Vietnam conflict in 1965. The attempted invasion of Cuba and the escalation of the Vietnam conflict under two different presidents are often identified as among the worst U.S. debacles in foreign affairs (Barrett 1988–1989, 637; Khong, 1992, 48; Russo 1998, 19; Stoessinger 1985, 99, 102).

In both cases the presidents also recognized that mistakes were committed. Shortly after the Bay of Pigs failure, President Kennedy described the episode "as the worst experience of my life" (Russo 1998, 19). During the Vietnam War, President Johnson recognized the failing course of the escalation, bemoaning, "I can't get out. I can't finish what I have got. So what the hell do I do?" (L.B. Johnson 1970, 248). The nature of these failures is surprising given the apparent superior power of the United States vis-à-vis smaller opponents. However, a closer examination of both cases reveals the limits of U.S. power and the types of U.S. mistakes of commission associated with fearing losses too much.

THE BAY OF PIGS INVASION

In April 1961, the United States initiated and supported the landing of CIA-trained Cuban exile forces at the Bay of Pigs in Cuba. Scholars called the invasion "the perfect failure" (Higgins 1987; Giglio 2006, 58). The army of Fidel Castro's government met the landing with superior military force and killed or captured the exiles before they could move away from the beach and into the mountains to form a guerilla force. The CIA had included air support as an important part of its invasion plan in case the landing was detected and countered by Castro's forces. However, President Kennedy made the decision to cancel the air cover just shortly before the operation in order to maintain U.S. deniability and to avoid a possible Soviet-U.S. confrontation. In addition to faulty execution and improvisation, the plan suffered from poor intelligence estimates about the probability of success and unrealistic expectations about the loyalty of Cuba's military to Castro and public support for his regime among the Cuban population.

Conventional analyses of the Bay of Pigs episode focus on these and other such factors to explain the mistakes that led to the fiasco (Lynch 1998; Blight and Kornbluth 1998). Our focus is different. We question the assumed necessity of overthrowing Fidel Castro and his regime. Before the Castro-led revolution, Cuban dictator Batista had ruled the country, and in recent years his relationship to Washington had become increasingly contentious. Castro's assumption of power in January 1959—although looked upon critically by the Eisenhower administration—was generally viewed as an opportunity to restore the traditional U.S. relationship to Cuba (Bender 1975, 15, 18; Neustadt and May 1986, 141; R. Smith 1960, 165, 176; Paterson 1994, 244; Pavia 2006, 48). Thus, U.S.-Cuban relations in the initial phase of the Castro regime are depicted through the no-conflict game in Figure 4.1. The game depicts a strategic situation of normal diplomatic relations (+,+) as a no-conflict game between a more powerful and a less powerful state (USA > CUB).

By the summer of 1959, however, it became increasingly evident that Castro intended to redefine economic relations between Cuba and the United States, which in the past had disproportionately benefitted the latter (R. Smith 1960, 177; Russo 1998, 4). The process of nationalizing U.S. private assets in Cuba changed the strategic situation between the two actors to the mixed-motive game (G29), as shown in Figure 4.1. This new game holds U.S. preferences and the asymmetric power relationship constant (USA > CUB) but alters Cuban preferences from a cooperation

FIGURE 4.1   *Alternative Strategic Analyses of Cuban-American Relations, 1959–1961*

	Cuba		Cuba (G29)		Cuba (G18)	
	Coop P	Conf N	Coop P	Conf N	Coop P	Conf N
Coop P	"4,4*" →|	1,1	"4,3" →	1,4	2,3 →	"1,4"
United States	↑	↓	↑	↓	↑	↓
Conf N	3,2 ←	2,3*	3,2 ←	2,1	4,2* ←	3,1
	No-Conflict Game (1959)		Mixed-Motive Game (1960)		Conflict Game (1961)	
	Intentions: USA, CUB +,+		Intentions: USA, CUB +,−		Intentions: USA, CUB −,−	
	Power: USA > CUB		Power: USA > CUB		Power: USA > CUB	
	Cuban Strategy: Stay		Cuban Strategy: Cycle		U.S. Strategy: Move	

Brams nonmyopic equilibria are in bold, and final outcomes are underlined; Nash myopic equilibria are asterisked, and initial states are in quotation marks. Cycling from the initial state in G29 is in bold.

(+) to a conflict (−) strategy. The strategic inference from this game is that as long as the United States does not change its cooperative strategic orientation, a Cuban defection from their relationship of mutual cooperation (4,3) would ultimately cycle back to it, as indicated by the clockwise arrows in G29 of Figure 4.1. The cycle would occur, because logically each player would stand to improve its outcome by each successive move clockwise, as indicated by the payoffs in bold.

Although the United States did respond to a Cuban move from the initial state of mutual cooperation, this was accompanied by a shift in Washington's strategic orientation from a cooperation strategy to a conflict strategy, redefining U.S.-Cuban relations as the conflict game (G18) in Figure 4.1. This shift foreclosed the likelihood of cycling back to settlement as the final outcome and predicted a new NME of U.S. domination (4,2) as the final outcome. The subsequent U.S. decision to engage in covert action rather than engaging in coercive bargaining with Cuba was consistent with this new game. However, the shift in the definition of the strategic situation by the United States also limited the fungibility of U.S. power to the extent that its agents (Cuban exiles) could carry out the principal's plans. Castro possessed considerable military capabilities, as confirmed by experts in the State Department at the time. U.S. leaders believed that Castro was a "weak 'hysteric' leader whose army was ready to defect," but the opposite was actually the case (Janis 1972, 23, 37–38).

FIGURE 4.2   *Cuban Exiles–Castro Regime Power Game*

	Castro Regime	
	Coop P	Conf N
Coop P	3,2	<u>2,4</u>*
Conf N	4,1	1,3

USA/Cuban Exiles (label left of rows)

Intentions: Exiles/USA, Castro Regime –,–
Power: Castro Regime > Exiles/USA

Nash equilibrium is asterisked, and Brams equilibrium is underlined.

Consequently, the U.S. plan failed to alter the domestic power game, shown in Figure 4.2, between the Castro regime and Cuban exiles. Castro's domination (2,4) of the U.S.-supported exiles is both the Nash equilibrium and the Brams NME in this strategic situation, making the Bay of Pigs invasion likely to be a strategic failure in its goal of overthrowing the Castro regime.

Our analysis so far leads to the following inferences: the Bay of Pigs invasion was the product of a dual mistake of commission. On the one hand, the threat posed by the new leader, Fidel Castro, was greatly exaggerated (a diagnostic mistake of misperception). On the other hand, the power of the U.S.-supported exiles to remove the Castro regime as the source of the threat was also overestimated, leading to a prescriptive mistake of preemption and a "too much/too soon" pattern of foreign policy mistakes resulting in a false alarm failure. The botched execution of the invasion in this account is ultimately relegated to a tactical chapter in this larger strategic narrative.

When Fidel Castro, together with his brother Raul, Che Guevara, and their revolutionary cadre overthrew Batista and his regime in January 1959, the new leader was viewed initially neither as a Communist nor as a threat. CIA director Allen Dulles testified to the Senate Foreign Relations committee that Castro did not have "any Communist leanings" and that he was not "working for the Communists." This initial assessment was also shared by the U.S. ambassador to Cuba, Philip Bonsal (Beschloss 1991, 97; Burks 1964, 27–40; Higgins 1987, 42–43; Pavia 2006,

52; Fursenko and Naftali 1997, 51; Schlesinger 1965, 211). Although some top officials in the administration and the president himself were hesitant, for many U.S. policymakers Castro personified a pragmatist who was seeking land reform, profit sharing for farm workers, confiscation of illegal landholdings, and implementation of a liberal constitution (Giglio 2006, 50).

The status quo between Washington and Havana changed when Castro initiated a series of economic reconstruction plans. These conflicted with U.S. interests that were dominating various sectors of the Cuban economy. Among them were Cuba's oil, telephone, mining, electric, and, most important, sugar industries (Giglio 2006, 50; Paterson 1989, 127–128). Through Castro's measures many of these industries were partially or fully nationalized, and although the Cuban regime offered compensation to the affected companies, the act of nationalizing foreign property still constituted an affront. Castro was aware that Washington would perceive his measures as hostile actions, and he hoped initially for a show of Latin American unity to restrain any U.S. reprisals (W. Smith 1984, 9; Giglio 2006, 50).

Growing increasingly wary of Castro, Eisenhower decided in November 1959 to encourage anti-Castro groups within Cuba to "check" or "replace" Castro's regime. The CIA had already developed operational plans toward this end. Until this ultimate goal was reached, the agency recommended that Washington impose a unilateral blockade on Cuba. Indeed, by February of the next year, President Eisenhower had embargoed all arms shipments to Cuba, and he was planning similar measures for other goods (Higgins 1987, 48). In what would be a further escalation, U.S. officials also deliberated the possibility of cutting the Cuban sugar quota. Cuba's economy was generally weak and dependent on foreign countries, but the sugar industry represented its Achilles' heel (Perez 1990, 240).

As the situation deteriorated, Fidel Castro looked toward the Soviet Union as a means to compensate for the economic losses incurred through U.S. sanctions. In the spring of 1960, the Soviet Union agreed to help. It purchased 425,000 tons of sugar immediately and pledged furthermore to purchase one million tons in each of the following four years. In addition, Moscow offered Havana $100 million in the form of low-interest credit and technical assistance toward industrial modernization. The Soviet Union also agreed to sell Cuba crude oil at prices considerably lower than those charged by other foreign oil companies to Cuban refineries, thereby providing immediate savings in foreign exchange for the island (Perez 1990, 241–242; Bender 1975, 20).

It is important to recognize that the economic cooperation between Cuba and the Soviet Union was largely the result of American hard-line policy, which led to a serious economic crisis in Cuba. Castro considered the alliance with the Soviet Union to be one of necessity, and U.S. officials later acknowledged that he was instrumentally but not ideologically committed to it (Perez 1990, 233; Smith 1984, 12–13). In Washington, however, the developing ties between Cuba and the Soviet Union were quickly interpreted as the smaller country becoming a satellite of Moscow. Cuba came to represent the cold war in the U.S. backyard, and as one senator explained, it would become the "target for our national frustration and annoyance with Moscow and the whole communist conspiracy" (Paterson 1989, 125; Etheredge 1985, 2). This misperceived transformation of the Castro regime is well captured in a background memorandum from the State Department and accounts for the exaggeration of the threat attributed to Cuba by the United States:

When the Castro regime came to power in 1959, the United States looked upon it with sympathy, recognized it almost immediately, and welcomed its promises of political freedom and social justice for the Cuban people. . . . Despite our concern at the Cuban regime's mounting hostility toward the United States and its growing communist tendencies, we attempted patiently and consistently from early 1959 until mid-1960 to negotiate differences with the regime.

Elements in the Castro movement engaged in anti-American activities during the revolution against Batista. Soon after it came to power in 1959, the Castro government turned away from its previous promise, permitted communist influence to grow, attacked and persecuted its own supporters in Cuba who expressed opposition to communism, arbitrarily seized U.S. properties, and made a series of baseless charges against the United States. It ignored, rejected or imposed impossible conditions on repeated United States overtures to cooperate and negotiate.

In 1960 Cuba established close political, economic, and military relationships with the Sino-Soviet bloc, while increasing the pace and vehemence of measures and attacks against the United States. We did not take measures in our own behalf to isolate Cuba until July 1960. (qtd. in Etheredge 1985, 1–2)

In May 1960 Castro engaged in an overture to discuss the deteriorating situation. Washington declined and the situation worsened further, with both sides escalating the conflict (Langley 1970, 65). Prior to the summer of 1960, Cuban expropriations had been confined principally to land, mostly sugar estates and cattle ranches. Now the regime ordered the foreign oil companies, Standard Oil, Texaco, and Shell, to refine Soviet petroleum. When these companies refused to do so, reportedly under pressure from Washington, the Cuban government nationalized the refineries (Perez 1990, 242). On July 6, the United States retaliated by cutting Cuban sugar imports by 700,000 tons, the balance of the Cuban quota for the year. Thereafter the quota was fixed at zero, and despite Soviet compensation, this step would have a severe impact on the Cuban economy. Going further, on October 13 the United States began embargoing any exports to the island (Perez 1990, 242–243).

The conflict deepened as the U.S. strategy toward Cuba was not confined to economic sanctions. By March of 1960, the CIA had concretized its plans in a paper titled "A Program of Covert Action against the Castro Regime" (Pavia 2006, 80; Rodriguez 1991, 21). The plan involved covert military action and the forced removal of Castro. The execution of this ambition would be left to President Kennedy. On January 19, 1961, the outgoing Eisenhower told the incoming Kennedy that he must do "whatever is necessary" to overthrow Castro. Kennedy and his administration would indeed continue what had started under the Eisenhower administration and bring the diagnostic mistake of an exaggerated threat to its culmination with a prescriptive mistake of preemption (Beschloss 1991, 104; Giglio 2006, 52).

Kennedy feared Communism. During his presidential campaign, he remarked, "I think there is a danger that history will make a judgment that these were the days when the tide began to run out for the U.S. These were the times the Communist tide began to pour in" (Paterson 1988, 199).

Castro was an immediate priority, as Kennedy considered him "a source of maximum danger" (Higgins 1987, 59). Kennedy believed that although "the Cold War [would] not be won in Latin America, it [might] very well be lost there" (Fursenko and Naftali 1997, 82). Kennedy's anti-Castro feelings were so deep that Secretary of State Dean Rusk commented that the president "had it in for Castro." One observer aptly concluded, "Future positions were frozen. Kennedy became rooted in absolute hostility to Castro" (Patterson 1989, 124; Russo 1998, 11). Kennedy's advisors joined him, and the pathologies of groupthink would henceforth govern the decision-making process (Janis 1972; Wyden 1979).

Almost immediately after his inauguration, Kennedy convened his National Security Council to review the CIA plans for the overthrow of Castro. Involved were Secretary of Defense Robert McNamara, Secretary of State Dean Rusk, CIA Director Allen Dulles, the Chairman of the Joint Chiefs of Staff Lyman Lemnitzer, and Attorney General Robert Kennedy, who also served as the president's personal adviser. A subsequent Joint Chiefs' memorandum summarized the basic consensus that developed:

[The] primary objective of the United States in Cuba should be the speedy overthrow of the Castro government, followed by the establishment of a pro-U.S. government. . . . Unless the United States takes immediate and forceful action, there is a great and present danger that Cuba will become permanently established as a part of the Communist Bloc, with disastrous consequences to the security of the Western Hemisphere. (Higgins 1987, 81)

Kennedy had hostile perceptions of Castro from the beginning, and they would be fostered further in deliberations with his advisors. A central role was played by CIA Director Allen Dulles and Deputy Director Richard Bissell (Wyden 1979, 94; Janis, 1972, 31–32). Already in January 1960, Dulles argued to the then president-elect that Cuba was "being rapidly absorbed into the Sino-Soviet bloc," and he warned that it could soon be a "significant military power that could pose great security problems to the U.S." (Beschloss 1991, 104). Kennedy and his advisors also saw in Castro an ambition to ignite revolutions throughout Latin America and thereby challenge the U.S. hegemony in the Western Hemisphere (Beschloss 1991, 104; Etheredge 1985, 15; Paterson 1994, 257). A State

Department officer summarized the fear: "If we gave in to Castro all along the line, we would get kicked around the hemisphere" (qtd. in Morley 1987, 114).

The Cuban threat was greatly exaggerated. Castro was "an affront to our public pride" and a "mischief maker," Walter Lippmann commented, but he was not a "mortal threat" to the United States (Paterson 1989, 129). Similarly, the chair of the Senate Foreign Relations Committee, J. William Fulbright, stated to the president that Castro would be "a thorn in the flesh, but not a dagger in the heart" (qtd. in Neustadt and May 1986, 149). For the senator, any operation to oust Castro was "wildly out of proportion to the threat" (Giglio 2006, 55). That the threat was exaggerated was later admitted by various administration officials, including Secretary of Defense McNamara, who acknowledged, "We were hysterical about Castro" (Paterson 1988, 205). Similarly, Ambassador Bonsal acknowledged that the attitude of the U.S. leadership toward the Castro regime was unduly influenced by "our largely anti-Castro informers" (Perez 1990, 248).

Kennedy insisted, "We can't go on living with this Castro cancer for ten more years" (Etheredge 1985, 15). He "had it in" for Castro, and so did his main advisors. On March 11, the group gathered anew in a National Security Council meeting. CIA Director Dulles and Deputy Director Bissell explained plans for an invasion at Trinidad. The president criticized the plan for being too noisy—too much like a spectacular World War II landing (Paterson 1989, 130; Russo 1998, 13; Higgins 1987, 93). Subsequently, the CIA was quick to devise a new plan, code-named Operation Zapata, for landings at the Bay of Pigs. After several more high-level meetings and Dulles's assurance that the prospects for Zapata were even greater than they had been for the successful CIA plot in 1954 against Guatemala, Kennedy set April 17 as the day for the covert operation (Paterson 1989, 130).

The plan for Operation Zapata entailed critical changes from the initial plans. Most important, the change of location effectively cut off the contact of the invasion forces with anti-Castro rebels in the Escambray Mountains, who were to form a guerilla force and spur a widening upris-

ing against the Castro regime. In subsequent deliberations, the pathologies of groupthink contributed to the marginalization of this consideration. Dulles and Bissell were so anxious to see the invasion proceed that
they naively believed it would still ignite an uprising. Defense Secretary
McNamara and National Security Adviser Bundy also failed to be critical of the new plan and endorsed the CIA's proposed invasion. Thus, the
inexperienced but driven Kennedy continued in the pursuit of what would
become a disaster (Giglio 2006, 53; Janis 1972).

To be sure, there were critical appraisals of the plans; however, they
did not reach in effective ways the top echelons of the decision-making
process. The Joint Chiefs of Staff considered a substantial popular uprising to be absolutely crucial (Giglio 2006, 53–56), and yet Admiral Burke
placed the new plan's chance of success at less than 50 percent. David
Shoup, commandant of the Marine Corps, was also highly critical (Higgins 1987, 96). Arthur Schlesinger wrote the president on March 15 that
the risks of the operation had been underestimated and that the United
States might be "rushed into something" (Higgins 1987, 99). Similarly,
Assistant Secretary of State Charles Bowles, who was "horrified" at the
principals' complacent acceptance of the plans, submitted a memo to
Dean Rusk on March 31 stating, "We should not . . . proceed with this
adventure because we are wound up and cannot stop" (Janis 1972, 45;
Pavia 2006, 35). Together with long-time presidential advisor John Gal-
braith, Bowles urged the president to pursue restraint. It was a "disastrous idea," as former secretary of state and Johnson advisor Dean Acheson remarked (Giglio 2006, 55–56).

The contingencies for the plan contributed to its failure. The Cuban
exile brigade faced immediate detection on the beaches of the Bay of Pigs
by Castro's troops. The remote location ensured that the invasion went
unnoticed by anti-Castro forces; consequently, it did not come to a popular uprising as forecasted by the CIA and counted on by the principals
(Giglio 2006, 59). What sealed the disaster was Kennedy's decision to
cancel the planned air support for the exiles as the operation was already
under way. The operation was a moral and operational fiasco, and an
administration official described it as "the most screwed up operation

there has ever been" (Etheredge 1985, 1). Kennedy also realized his mistake as he asked, "How could I have been so stupid, to let them go ahead?" (qtd. in Paterson 1989, 132). The immediate consequence was a bloodbath. The long-term consequence was also exactly the opposite of what Kennedy had hoped to achieve, namely, to shut out Soviet influence in the Western Hemisphere. Washington's hostile Cuba policy handed Moscow an opening that was promptly exploited (Langley 1970, 64; Paterson 1989, 129). Instead of driving the Soviets out of Cuba, it drew Havana and Moscow closer together.

A State Department publication after the invasion acknowledged that "It is not clear whether . . . Castro intended from the start to betray his pledges of a free and democratic Cuba, to deliver his country to the Sino-Soviet bloc" (qtd. in Langley 1970, 41). Declassified documents reveal that the U.S. leadership knew that the Cuban-Soviet military linkage, which included the 1962 agreement on nuclear missiles, emanated from Cuba's fear of a U.S. invasion (Paterson 1989, 141–142). Since history runs only once, any claim that better outcomes could have been obtained cannot be made with certainty. The hostile policies of U.S. leaders toward Cuba ensured that one of the worst, if not the worst, outcomes was obtained. It also generated the enduring scholarly conclusion that Kennedy's Bay of Pigs decision was "among the worst fiascoes ever perpetuated by a responsible government" (Janis 1972, 14).

THE ESCALATION OF THE VIETNAM WAR

Cuba's alliance with the Soviet Union and the October 1962 missile crisis were preceded by the fall of China to Mao Zedong's Communist forces and the expulsion of the Nationalist government to the island of Formosa (Taiwan) in 1949 as well as the attack by North Korea on South Korea in 1950 and the First Indochina War (1946–1954). The trajectory of these events led to an ever-increasing threat perception in Washington about the global spread of Communism. The U.S. response in the 1950s was to globalize and militarize the strategy of containment with a series of alliance agreements between the United States in Asia and the Middle East to complement earlier alliances in Western Europe and Latin America.

When France withdrew from Southeast Asia, the United States initiated the Southeast Asian Treaty Organization, whose signatories agreed to act each "in accordance with its constitutional processes" (qtd. in Hartmann 1970, 198) in the event of armed attacks on their security in the treaty area. Included in this jurisdiction was the former French Indochina, consisting of Laos, Cambodia, and Vietnam.

The United States assumed the former role of France as the patron of the government of South Vietnam in Saigon following the 1956 Geneva Accords ending the first Vietnam conflict. The Accords prescribed a temporary partition of Vietnam and called for its ultimate unification with national elections. Ngo Dinh Diem's Saigon government blocked the implementation of the Accords. His rule was repressive, and large parts of the southern population were alienated. The increasing unpopularity of Diem gave an opportunity to the Communist Hanoi regime led by Ho Chi Minh to seize political power through a popular insurrection. On December 12, 1960, Hanoi authorized the creation of the National Front for the Liberation of South Vietnam (NLF), which promised the reunification of Vietnam as well as an end to U.S. influence.

Since 1956, the United States had expanded its assistance to Saigon from economic aid to military training. However, Washington began to conclude by 1963 that Diem was incapable of defeating the NLF and what it perceived as a Communist advance. U.S. officials thus sympathized with the idea of a coup, and indeed, Diem was overthrown and executed in November 1963. After Diem's fall, Hanoi was prepared to discuss the establishment of a neutralist government in Saigon (Schurmann, Scott, and Zelink 1966, 28). Washington rejected such plans and in 1964 began to bomb targets in North Vietnam, which was followed by an intervention with ground forces in July 1965. Hanoi responded over the next three years by sending its own regular army units into South Vietnam to engage American troops. By 1968 the number of U.S. infantry in South Vietnam was approaching 500,000 men.

The largest deployment of U.S. forces since World War II came to be seen as one of the largest blunders in the history of American foreign policy. The Vietnam War has been described as a "mistake of gigantic

FIGURE 4.3   *Domestic and Foreign Vietnam Conflict Games*

	North Vietnam (G18)		Hanoi (G18)		NVN/NLF (G32)	
	Coop P	Conf N	Coop P	Conf N	Coop P	Conf N
Coop P	2,3	1,4	3,2	2,4*	3,3	1,4
United States		Saigon			SVN/USA	
Conf N	**4,2***	3,1	4,1	1,3	4,1	2,2*

Foreign Conflict Game	Domestic Conflict Game	Vietnam Conflict Game
Intentions: USA, NVN –,–	Intentions: SVN, NVN –,–	Intent: SVN/USA, NVN/NLF –,–
Power: USA > NVN	Power: SVN < NVN	Power: SVN/USA = NVN/NLF

Brams nonmyopic equilibria are in bold, and Nash myopic equilibria are asterisked. NVN = North Vietnam; NLF = National Front for the Liberation of South Vietnam; SVN = South Vietnam.

proportions" and a "national catastrophe" (Barrett 1988, 637; Stoessinger 1985, 99, 102). As in the Bay of Pigs case, we contend that the case of Vietnam was a dual false alarm failure of misperception and preemption. U.S. leaders exaggerated the threat and engaged in a strategic mistake of preemption. These diagnostic and prescriptive mistakes were propelled partly by a reliance on faulty historical analogies. In the decision-making process, there were frequent references to the "lessons of Munich." It was argued that Nazism and Fascism would not have swept Europe in the 1930s if decisive action had been taken in 1938 (Khong 1992, 49). The logical prescription was that the spread of Communism had to be halted immediately. Much focus was on this lesson at the expense of a more suitable lesson, namely, the implications that followed from the Bay of Pigs case: U.S. military superiority in the foreign policy domain is not universally fungible. It does not transfer easily or completely into a favorable asymmetric power relationship in the domestic domain of another country. This argument is illustrated in Figure 4.3.

The foreign conflict game on the left side of Figure 4.3 illustrates the strategic situation between the United States and North Vietnam. It is a situation of mutual hostility (–,–), with the United States being more powerful than North Vietnam (USA > NVN). In this game, U.S. domination of North Vietnam (4,2) is a Brams NME as well as a Nash equilibrium. However, this game co-exists with a domestic conflict game depicted in the middle of Figure 4.3. This game shows the hostile relations between the

FIGURE 4.4   *Strategic Analyses for Both Players in Prisoner's Dilemma Game (G32)*

| | NVN/NLF Coalition | | | | NVN/NLF Coalition | |
	Coop P	Conf N			Coop P	Conf N
Coop P	3,3 |←	1,4		Coop P	3,3 →|	1,4
SVN/USA Coalition	↓	↑		SVN/USA Coalition	↑	↓
Conf N	4,1 →	"**2,2**"		Conf N	4,1 |←	"**2,2**"*

SVN/USA Strategy: Stay	NVN/NLF Strategy: Stay
Intentions: SVN/USA,NVN/NLF –,–	Intentions: SVN/USA,NVN/NLF –,–
Power: SVN/USA = NVN/NLF	Power: SVN/USA = NVN/NLF

Initial state is in quotation marks. Final outcome for each player's strategy is underlined. Nash equilibrium is asterisked, and Brams equilibria are in bold.

opposing regimes in Hanoi and Saigon (–,–) and the power superiority of Hanoi (SVN < NVN). In this game, Hanoi's domination of Saigon (2,4) is the Brams NME as well as a Nash equilibrium.

The Vietnam conflict game on the right side of Figure 4.3 illustrates the full complexity of the Vietnam situation. The opponents are the United States and the government of Saigon on the one side and the NLF and Hanoi's government on the other side. The game shows that U.S. power did not reverse the superiority of North Vietnamese power in this strategic situation. Saigon was experiencing a political and military power deflation, and by 1965 it was, in effect, incapacitated without U.S. support. The nature of guerilla warfare and the U.S. military's unpreparedness in such a situation further complicates the matter (Cuddy 2003, 359). For these considerations, the power relationship between the opponents is described best as equal (SVN/USA = NVN/NLF). As a classic prisoner's dilemma situation, this game has mutual settlement and mutual deadlock as Brams NMEs while mutual deadlock is also a Nash equilibrium. According to TOM, if deadlock (2,2) is the initial state of play for the prisoner's dilemma game, then it is also likely to be the final state. The logic leading to this conclusion is shown in Figure 4.4.

One option to overcome the deterministic barrier in prisoner's dilemma logic is to engage in cooperative diplomacy in a words game. The goal for one player is to signal benefits, to induce the other player to

FIGURE 4.5   *Words and Deeds Games in the Vietnam Conflict*

	NVN/NLF			
	P		**N**	
	CO	CO	CF	CF
	Deeds	Words	Words	Deeds
CO Deeds	3,3	$\mid\leftarrow$		1,4
P				
CO Words		**3,4** $\leftarrow$ 1,2		
SVN/USA	$\downarrow$	$\downarrow$	$\uparrow$	$\overline{\uparrow}$
CF Words		4,1 $\rightarrow$ "2,3"*		
N				
CF Deeds	4,1	$\rightarrow$		**"2,2"***

Nested Words/Deeds Power Games

U.S. Strategy: Move	U.S. Strategy: Stay
Words Game	Deeds Game
Intentions: SVN/USA, NVN/NLF –,+	Intentions: SVN/USA, NVN/NLF –,–
Power: SVN/USA = NVN/NLF	Power: SVN/UA = NVN/NLF

Nash myopic equilibria are asterisked, and Brams nonmyopic equilibria are in bold. The initial state for each game is in quotation marks, and final outcome is underlined. P = positive sanctions; N = negative sanctions; CO = cooperation; CF = conflict.

make a nonmyopic calculation and thereby move to mutual settlement in the deeds game. The "lose-lose" determinacy of the prisoner's dilemma logic as well as the possibility for mutual settlement was recognized by Ho Chi Minh when he stated in the spring of 1965, "If the Americans want to make war for twenty years then we shall make war for twenty years. If they want to make peace, we shall make peace and invite them to afternoon tea" (qtd. in Young 1991, 172).

The logic of this analysis is demonstrated below in Figure 4.5 with the NVN/ NLF coalition signaling in pre-play communication a shift in its highest-ranked preference to settlement (P,P) and constructing a mixed-motive words game, thereby opening a possible path for the SVN/USA coalition to move toward settlement as the NME in the deadlocked deeds conflict game of prisoner's dilemma.

The empirical record shows that Hanoi signaled to the United States such situations as "windows of opportunity," leading toward mutual settlement. The prescribed strategy for the United States is to "move" verbally from (2,3) toward the NME (3,4) in the words game by continuing talks or perhaps to deescalate (but not cease) hostile actions in the deeds game. The Johnson administration failed to do either one and instead escalated its conflict actions in 1964 and 1965. Our argument is that U.S. leaders not only made a mistake of commission by exaggerating the threat emanating from the Vietnam situation; they also made a mistake of preemption by escalating military actions and ignoring diplomatic openings from Hanoi, which would have allowed both sides to settle the conflict short of the disaster that befell the United States and Vietnam in the 1960s and 1970s (Schurmann, Scott, and Zelink 1966; W. Thies 1980, 4).

The permissive causes for the Vietnam tragedy can be dated to the mid-1950s. The cold war had reached its first climax with the Berlin blockade crisis a few years earlier, and the strategy of containment had become the dominant U.S. approach toward Soviet Communism and any potential ally of Moscow. On April 7, 1954, Eisenhower for the first time employed the much-cited domino theory to explain the strategic importance of South Vietnam. The theory perpetuated the belief that if South Vietnam fell into the Communist orbit, Laos, Thailand, and Cambodia would follow suit immediately, and they would, in turn, be followed by other countries in the region, leading to an ever-expanding and hostility-driven Communist bloc (Katsiaficas 1992, 33–34; Khong 1992, 83–84; Stavins, Barnet, and Raskin 1971, 104).

The domino theory lacked plausibility (Khong 1992). It resulted from a profound ignorance of Asian history and the vast differences among Asian nations. It was the consequence of a blindness that failed to see that the motivation in much of Asia was primarily from nationalism rather than Communism (Pfeffer 1968, 21; Barrett 1988, 654; Halberstam 1972, 463). Although this difference was crucial and despite the lack of evidence, the theory was passed on from the Eisenhower administration through that of Kennedy and ultimately to the Johnson administration, where it was accepted as an article of faith (Berman 1982, 9). Johnson went even so far as to argue, "If we allow Vietnam to fall, tomorrow we'll be fighting in Hawaii, and next week in San Francisco" (Dallek 1998, 754).

President Johnson was determined not to allow any expansion of the Communist bloc. Early in his presidency, he insisted to White House aides that South Vietnam could not be allowed to "go under"—for Johnson,

Vietnam was the "most critical military area" (Anderson 2005, 42; Kaiser 2000, 288). Indeed, it was just a few days after Kennedy's assassination in November 1963 that Johnson as the new president approved National Security Action Memorandum 273. It restated an earlier U.S. pledge to assist the South Vietnamese "to win their contest against the externally directed and supported communist conspiracy." Its implicit assumption that the Communist centers in Moscow and Beijing were conspiring in the Vietnamese struggle had no bearing in reality (Anderson 2005, 428).

Johnson's fears of Communism and his inclinations against Hanoi would be reinforced by a group of administration hawks. This circle consisted of Secretary of Defense Robert McNamara, Secretary of State Dean Rusk, White House Assistant for National Security Affairs McGeorge Bundy, Assistant Secretary of State for Far Eastern Affairs William Bundy, ambassador to South Vietnam Maxwell Taylor, Chairman of the Joint Chiefs of Staff Earl Wheeler, and General William Westmoreland. The thinking of these principals was rooted in cold war principles and the domino theory, with its flawed implications. The prescription that followed was that Communism, wherever it would appear, would have to be halted militarily (Hoopes 1969; Pfeffer 1968, 56; Janis 1972).

Opposing the hawkish principals was a cohort of moderates. The most prominent figure in this group was Undersecretary of State George Ball, and his dissent is reminiscent to that of Ambassador Joseph Grew in the prelude to Pearl Harbor in 1941. The other moderates were Vice President Hubert Humphrey, Majority Leader Mike Mansfield, Senators Richard Russell and J. William Fulbright, White House aide Bill Moyers, and the so-called Wise Men—former officials such as Dean Acheson and Clark Clifford. These moderates questioned the assumptions of the domino theory as well as Vietnam's strategic value. All of them, and especially Ball, also questioned the efficacy and applicability of U.S. power in the Vietnam theater—in a war that would be unwinnable (Halberstam 1972, 491–495).

Although Johnson would hear the cautionary input from the moderates, the principals maintained the upper hand, and the planning for a military escalation began in January 1964. A memorandum by the Joint

Chiefs of Staff to President Johnson urged him to increase the commitment in order to win the war more quickly: "The United States must be
prepared to put aside many of the self-imposed restrictions which now
limit our efforts, and to undertake bolder actions which may embody
greater risks" (Stoessinger 2005, 102). Specifically, the Joint Chiefs argued
that aerial bombing would bring North Vietnam to its knees and that
Hanoi would have to accept a negotiated settlement on U.S. terms. On
March 1, William Bundy wrote to the president that bombing could indeed
be justified in support of political objectives in Vietnam. It would stop
Hanoi's infiltration of supplies to the NLF, stiffen the resolve of Saigon,
and prove that the United States stood ready to halt the spread of Communism (Berman 1982, 31; W. Thies 1980, 1).

While Washington was planning the escalation of the war, the struggle
within South Vietnam was actually slowing down. The army of South
Vietnam was unable to engage in resistance toward the NLF, but Ho Chi
Minh refrained from sending North Vietnam's troops and delivering a
final blow to the Saigon regime (Kaiser 2000, 294–295). He argued for
negotiations and on June 18 engaged in a concrete overture for a political
settlement. The terms required U.S. withdrawal from Indochina in general
and from Vietnam in particular. Moreover, the sovereignty over any peace
negotiations had to rest with the conflicting parties, including the NLF.
As final points the proposal envisioned eventual reunification of the two
Vietnams and also emphasized that the status of South Vietnam must be
decided by its people. Hanoi also signaled that it was ready and willing to
negotiate on counterproposals from Washington (W. Thies 1980, 37; Schurmann, Scott and Zelink 1966, 29).

This initiative was rejected in Washington. On July 24 Johnson declared in a news conference that "until there is demonstrated upon the
part of those who are ignoring the agreements reached at the conference
table [i.e., the 1954 Geneva Agreements] some desire to carry out their
agreement, we expect to continue our efforts in Vietnam" (W. Thies 1980,
48). At the end of July, Washington dispatched 6,000 additional troops
to Vietnam (Schurmann, Scott, and Zelink 1966, 38). In a second initiative for negotiations, on August 13 Hanoi reacted explicitly to Johnson's

formulated condition, expressing agreement that a solution to the conflict was to be found in a return to the Geneva Agreements. Hanoi also made explicit again that it was willing to negotiate on counterproposals from Washington (W. Thies 1980, 48). Further evidence of North Vietnamese interest in negotiating a political settlement would be forthcoming.

In the meantime, the U.S. ambassador to South Vietnam, Maxwell Taylor, urged the president that "something must be added in the coming months." That something would be aerial bombing (Halberstam 1972, 484). Also in the meantime, the head of the Policy Planning Council, Robert Johnson, and Special Assistant for National Security Affairs Walt Rostow had undertaken a study of the probable effects of a U.S. bombing campaign in Vietnam. It concluded that bombing would not work and predicted that it would imprison U.S. troops in protracted warfare (Stoessinger 2005, 102; W. Thies 1980, 29; Janis 1972, 102). These conclusions were ignored in the top echelons of decision-making, and also ignored was the prediction that there would be no stable and effective government in Saigon, a requirement that the president had previously insisted be met (Halberstam 1972, 509).

The moderates continued in their efforts to balance the influence of the hawks over Johnson. At the heart of their argument was the non-fungibility of U.S. power in the Vietnam theater as well as the strategic irrelevance of Vietnam. Regarding the limits of U.S. power, it was argued that North Vietnam was "impervious" to the type of air bombing Washington was planning and that the U.S. strategy remained on a course that would take the country out "further and further on a sagging limb."[1] The opponents of a bombing campaign also argued that it would almost certainly lead North Vietnam to retaliate by the easiest means at their disposal, namely, the dispatching of increasingly large and eventually massive combat forces to the South to assist the NLF in its fight against the crumbling South Vietnamese enemy (Kattenburg 1980, 126).

Regarding the strategic irrelevance of Vietnam, Senator Mansfield argued to President Johnson that the United States "does not have interests on the Southeast Asian mainland to justify the costs in American lives and resources which would be required."[2] Similarly, Senator Richard Russell declared, "I am inclined to tell the President . . . that if I were President I would . . . load those 23,000 Americans abroad and bring them home" (Barrett 1988–1989, 651). In late 1964, Vice President Humphrey joined the moderates in opposing the bombing plans. In a later memo to the president, dated February 15, he argued his objections to an escalation. His departure from the initial consensus of the principals resulted in his banishment from future foreign policy meetings (Berman 1982, 45).

Despite this criticism, the advocates of an escalation maintained the upper hand (Kattenburg 1980, 128). Indeed, a great deal of "over-optimism" surrounded President Johnson and his principal advisors as they were deliberating about the escalation decisions. Together "they shared a staunch faith that somehow everything would come out right despite all the gloomy predictions in the intelligence reports prepared by their underlings" (Janis 1972, 109–110). Accordingly, the planned air war against North Vietnam, so the principals said, was expected "to last two to six months," and during this time period Hanoi was "expected to yield" (Janis 1972, 126).

The logic behind this expectation represents another way out of a prisoner's dilemma situation, which is to change the power relationship between the players. Instead of shifting to a mixed-motive game with settlement (P,P) as the highest-ranked option for one player, a shift in the power relationship between the players continues the conflict game but shifts the NMEs from (P,P) settlement or (N,N) deadlock to (N,P) domination by the more powerful player and submission by the less powerful player. This analysis is shown formally in Figure 4.6, in which there is a power shift in favor of the United States and a corresponding shift in the preference rankings for both players without changing from a conflict to a mixed-motive game. Unlike the prediction of "stay" at deadlock for both players in the symmetrical conflict game, the prediction is that the weaker player will move from an initial state of (3,1) deadlock to (4,2) domination by the stronger player who will stay at this final outcome, which is both a myopic and a nonmyopic equilibrium in the asymmetrical conflict game.

U.S. decision makers sought the power shift illustrated in the asymmetrical power conflict game (G18) in Figure 4.6. However, it would not be achieved in reality, and the game would not play out as expected. The specific incident that triggered the initial bombing of North Vietnam was

FIGURE 4.6 *Shifts in Equilibria for Symmetrical and Asymmetrical Conflict Games*

	NV/NLF Coalition	
	Coop P	Conf N
Coop P	3,3	1,4
SV/US Coalition		
Conf N	4,1	"2,2"*

Symmetrical Power Conflict (G32)
Intentions: SV/US, NV/NLF –,–
Power: SV/US = NV/NLF

	NV/NLF Coalition		
	Coop P		Conf N
Coop P	2,3	→|	1,4
SV/US Coalition	↑		↓
Conf N	4,2*	←	"3,1"

Asymmetrical Power Conflict (G18)
Intentions: SV/US, NV/NLF –,–
Power: SV/US > NV/NLF

Brams nonmyopic equilibria are in bold. Nash myopic equilibria are asterisked. Initial states are in quotation marks, and final outcomes are underlined.

the encounter and alleged firing on two U.S. warships, the *C. Turner Joy* and the *Maddox*, by North Vietnamese patrol boats in the Gulf of Tonkin at the beginning of August 1964 (Stoessinger 2005, 103). The outcome of the incident was the Gulf of Tonkin Resolution passed by the U.S. Congress on August 7 and used by Johnson as a public and legal justification for escalating U.S. involvement in the Vietnam War. In later years it was revealed that the Gulf of Tonkin incident never occurred, as described by Washington, and that it was a ploy for allowing the president to pursue the bombing of North Vietnam (Alterman 2004).

The air war under the name "Rolling Thunder" began in February 1965. The goal was to force Ho Chi Minh to submit to a settlement on terms dictated by Washington (W. Thies 1980, 3). The decision was fateful as it brought about exactly the opposite of what its authors had hoped for. In April General Earle Wheeler wrote to Secretary McNamara with a dismal appraisal of air strikes against the North between February 7 and April 4, 1965. The general informed the secretary that "the air strikes to date, while damaging, have not curtailed DRV [Democratic Republic of Vietnam] capabilities in any major way" (qtd. in Berman 1982, 52). Ho Chi Minh matched the U.S. air escalation with his own escalation, namely, through infiltration on the ground—a move that the principals thought would not happen (Halberstam 1972, 528). Rather than bringing the opponent to the conference table to negotiate on U.S. terms, U.S. air strikes stiffened North Vietnamese resistance (Kattenburg 1980, 122).

In the meantime, the legitimacy of the Saigon government had declined to an all-time low, with desertion rates from the military forces rising to record highs (Schurmann, Scott, and Zelink 1966, 51). It was only a matter of time until the NLF would be able to claim final victory over Saigon's forces, and in effect the United States would be caught in a vicious dilemma. Withdrawal was unthinkable to Johnson. The only possible response was to meet the NLF challenge directly with U.S. ground troops (Stoessinger 2005, 104). The plan envisioned the deployment of 150,000 U.S. troops, and in effect, as Saigon's capabilities waned, Washington would inherit full responsibility for the war in Vietnam. Confident of the planned commitment, General Westmoreland declared: "I am convinced that U.S. troops with their energy, mobility, and firepower can successfully take the fight to the NLF." He predicted victory by the end of 1967 (U.S. Department of Defense and the House Committee on Armed Services 1971, 4:7, 117–119 and 5:8–12).

As plans for a complete takeover of the war became more concrete, Ambassador Taylor became critical of his initial position, in which he had sided with the hawks. On April 14 he cabled Secretary of State Rusk, "Recent actions relating to the introduction of U.S. ground forces have tended to create an impression of eagerness in some quarters to deploy forces into SVN, which I find difficult to understand. I should think that for both military and political reasons we should all be most reluctant to tie down [military] units in this country" (qtd. in Berman 1982, 60). Around the same time, Clark Clifford, who in 1968 would become Johnson's secretary of defense, also confided his doubts in a letter to the president:

I believe our ground forces in South Vietnam should be kept to a minimum, consistent with the protection of our installations and property in that country. . . . A substantial buildup of U.S. ground troops . . . could be a quagmire. It could turn into an open end [sic] commitment on our part that would take more and more troops, without a realistic hope of ultimate victory. (Clifford 1965)

George Ball warned similarly that "Before we commit an endless flow of forces to South Vietnam we must have more evidence than we now have that our troops will not bog down in the jungles and the rice paddies— while we slowly blow the country to pieces" (Young 1991, 159). Further criticism came from Senator Fulbright, who considered Vietnam to be an "impossible situation" and believed that the United States could not "save" South Vietnam (Barrett 1988, 643; Coffin 1966, 251–252). After discussing his views at length with fellow senator and Johnson mentor Richard Russell, Fulbright sent the president a six-point memo. The first point read: "It would be a disaster for the United States to try to engage in a massive ground and air war in Southeast Asia" (Coffin 1966, 243). Subsequently, on June 15, Fulbright publicized his objection as he declared on the Senate floor:

It is clear to all reasonable Americans that a complete military victory in Vietnam, though theoretically attainable, can in fact be attained only at a cost far exceeding the requirements of our interest and our honor. . . . Escalation would invite the intervention of infiltration on a large scale of North Vietnamese troops. . . . This in turn would probably draw the United States into a bloody and protracted jungle war in which the advantages would be with the other side. (Coffin 1966, 254)

The CIA also shared a pessimistic outlook, declaring, "The arrival of U.S. forces in these numbers (150,000) would not change the communists' basic calculations that their staying power is inherently superior to that of Saigon in Washington" (Berman 1982, 72). As Johnson faced these objections, Hanoi had engaged anew in an initiative toward a settlement. The offer came in the form of "four points," calling for (1) withdrawal of U.S. forces from Vietnam and cancellation of U.S.–South Vietnamese military ties; (2) respect for the military provisions of the 1954 Geneva accords pending Vietnam's reunification; (3) settlement of South Vietnam's internal affairs in accordance with the program of the NLF; and (4) no foreign involvement or interference in the reunification of Vietnam (Kattenburg 1980, 133). It was especially the third point that was unacceptable to Washington.

The rejection of the North Vietnamese initiative lacked a compelling strategic reason. Before the introduction of U.S. and North Vietnamese troops into the theater, the conflict was essentially one between the NLF and the Saigon regime. It was unreasonable to expect one of the two opponents not to be involved in political negotiations for a possible settlement. Johnson's determination to escalate the war also became evident in his rejection to engage in a counterproposal, which Hanoi had invited. Instead, in a speech at Johns Hopkins University, the president repeated the implications of the domino theory and the absolute necessity of defeating Hanoi in order to halt the expansion of Communism (Kattenburg 1980, 132; Berman 1982, 8).

Hanoi went further and agreed to negotiate without the prior withdrawal of U.S. troops. However, President Johnson pushed on with the war course (Schurmann, Scott, and Zelink 1966, 85). By failing to negotiate on this latest offer, he made yet another fateful decision, losing the last chance to settle with the opponents while facing the costs of a ground war (Kattenburg 1980, 133). Accordingly, on July 1, George Ball declared prophetically that the failure to conclude a negotiated settlement would mean "protracted war, involving an open-ended commitment of U.S. forces, mounting U.S. casualties, no assurance of a satisfactory solution, and a serious danger of escalation at the end of the road" (Berman 1982, 89). A little earlier, in a June 18, 1965, memo to the president, Ball had argued that the situation in Vietnam would impose upon the United States an unconventional war in which American power would not be fungible. Specifically, he wrote that "A review of the French experience . . . may be helpful. The French fought a war in Vietnam, and were finally defeated— after seven years of bloody struggle and when they still had 250,000 combat-hardened veterans in the field, supported by an army of 205,000 South Vietnamese" (qtd. in Khong 1992, 152). In Ball's opinion, not even half a million U.S. soldiers would suffice (Young 1991, 159).

The other opponents of an escalation engaged in a last-ditch effort as well. Shortly before the deployment of ground troops, Richard Russell argued to Johnson that Vietnam had no "strategic, tactical, or economic value" to the United States (qtd. in Barrett 1988–1989, 652). Similarly, Russell, Mike Mansfield, and other senators were in "full agreement" that "insofar as Vietnam is concerned we are deeply enmeshed in a place where we ought not to be [and] that the situation is rapidly going out of control" (qtd. in ibid., 652–653).

President Johnson remained on the escalation course. On July 28 he announced that U.S. fighting strength would immediately be increased by 50,000 to 125,000 and that additional U.S forces would be sent as they were requested by General Westmoreland (Berman 1982, xii). Despite three years of Rolling Thunder and the presence of over 500,000 American troops in South Vietnam, the United States was no closer by March 1968 to a satisfactory settlement than it had been at the start of 1965 (Kaiser 2000, 488). The war had become untenable. The president chose then not to run for a second term and signaled his willingness to negotiate with Hanoi. Eventually the war was concluded under a new U.S. president (Nixon) with a U.S.-negotiated withdrawal in 1973. On April 30, 1975, South Vietnam's capital Saigon fell to the forces of North Vietnam after a resurgence of fighting between Saigon and Hanoi. Well over one million people died in the war in the course of the decade from 1965 to 1975.

CONCLUSIONS

In the case of the Bay of Pigs, the focus of historians typically has been on the botched tactical execution of the invasion plans; however, we have focused on the strategic level. We have argued that the assumed necessity for the invasion was ill-founded. It grew from a diagnostic mistake of commission, which was followed by a prescriptive mistake of commission and resulted in a false alarm failure. After Castro's new economic policies, Washington had a choice to continue to rank a settlement outcome highest in an asymmetrical power relationship that favored the United States or to shift to domination as its highest-ranked outcome and escalate from an economic dispute to a military conflict. Fearing danger too much, the Eisenhower administration started with covert escalatory actions in 1960. The Kennedy administration inherited the conflict and made it worse (Paterson 1989, 129). The eventual consequence was a merger of this regional conflict with the cold war conflict between the superpowers and the October 1962 missile crisis, which brought humanity to the brink of nuclear war.

In the case of Vietnam, we have argued that the assumed necessity for U.S. involvement was ill-founded as well. The U.S. escalation reflected diagnostic and prescriptive mistakes of commission, and the consequence was a false alarm failure. The Johnson administration's decision grew out of an obsession with avoiding the mistakes of the 1930s. Just as Nazism expanded in aggressive ways because of inaction, this time it could be Communist expansion. Misguided by false analogies, fearing danger too much, and rejecting opportunities to explore a cessation of the conflict, the Johnson administration maneuvered the country into a costly and unnecessary war.

Both foreign policy fiascoes were the results of improper answers to the *kto-kovo* power politics question and the subsequent mismanagement of power. In the Bay of Pigs case, the United States assumed that this question would be answered in its favor, not realizing the limited fungibility of U.S. power in the Cuban theater. It was the pathology of groupthink in the decision-making process between Kennedy and his main advisors that contributed to this strategic miscalculation (Barrett 1988–1989). According to Kennedy advisor and historian Arthur Schlesinger, the crucial meetings "took place in a *curious atmosphere of consensus*." He notes that "the massed and caparisoned authority of his senior officials in the realm of foreign policy and defense was unanimous for going ahead. . . . Had one senior advisor opposed the adventure, I believe that Kennedy would have canceled it. No one spoke against it" (qtd. in Janis 1972, 39; emphasis Schlesinger's).

In the case of Vietnam, the leaders in Washington miscalculated the efficacy of U.S. air power in a guerilla war. The Pentagon confirmed in a postwar assessment that the idea of bombing Hanoi into submission was a "colossal misjudgement" (Janis 1972, 108–109). Secretary of Defense McNamara also concluded that the achievement of a military victory by U.S. forces in Vietnam was indeed a dangerous illusion (McNamara et al. 1999, 19). Ambassador Taylor acknowledged, "We didn't know ourselves. . . . Until we know the enemy . . . and know ourselves, we'd better keep out" (qtd. in Turner 1975, 102).

The ignorance of Vietnamese realities coupled with a strong fear of Communism were two factors that drove Johnson and his advisers into the Vietnamese quagmire. The Viet Cong were actively assisted by the rural population, and Hanoi was popular while Saigon was not (Barrett 1988–1989, 654; Halberstam 1972, 463). A third factor that kept Washington enmeshed was an "overcommitment to defeating the enemy," which is a decision-making pathology that stands in the way of departing from an erroneous course of action (Janis 1972, 113):

The men in Johnson's inner circle . . . convinced themselves that the Vietnam War was of crucial significance for America's future—a conviction that grew directly out of their own explanations and justifications. It became essential to the policy makers to continue the costly and unpopular war . . . because they had *said* it was essential. Instead of reevaluating their policy in response to clear-cut setbacks, their energetic proselytizing led them to engage in "rhetorical escalation" that matched the military escalation, deepening their commitment to military victory rather than a political solution through negotiation with the government of North Vietnam. (Janis 1972, 117)

There is evidence to suggest that these foreign policy mistakes could have been averted. In the Bay of Pigs case, there was a sufficient amount of warning about the planned strategy, but groupthink and an attitude of hostility toward Cuba prevailed within the top echelons of decision making. Kennedy himself also acknowledged later, "I don't know why we didn't embrace Castro when he was in this country in 1959, pleading for help. . . . Instead of that, we made an enemy of him, and then we get upset because the Russians are giving them money, doing for them what we wouldn't do" (Russo 1998, 10–11; Beschloss 1991, 101).

As a further consequence, the United States from then on had to fight the cold war in its own backyard. Ambassador Bonsal explains in his memoirs that "Russia came to Castro's rescue only after the United States had taken steps designed to overthrow him" (Paterson 1994, 258–259). According to Bonsal, Castro was driven by necessity and fear. As McNamara later acknowledged, "If I had been in Moscow or Havana at that time [1961–1962], I would have believed the Americans were preparing for an invasion" (Paterson 1994, 258–259; Higgins 1987, 55). Had there been no Bay of Pigs and no continuous effort to harass, isolate, and destroy Castro's government, there may have been no missile crisis in 1962, which in the words of former CIA director William Colby pushed the world "as close to an Armageddon as possible" (Wyden 1979, 7; Paterson 1994, 260).

One of the most disturbing insights provided in the analytical narrative of the Vietnam case is the pattern in which Hanoi's moves toward settlement were brought to a close with an intensification of the war by the United States. Indeed, each time the leadership in Washington reacted as though it were faced with a threat rather than with an opportunity (Schurmann, Scott, and Zelink 1966, 23). The disaster could have been averted, but the principals decided to stay on course.

PART III

Mismanaged Opportunities

CHAPTER 5

Seeking Gains Too Late

Reassurance Failures

INTRODUCTION

Generally mistakes are considered to be acts in which the consequence is a loss. They can also be acts in which the consequence is an unrealized gain. Therefore, the Greek sage Pittacus urged, "Know thine opportunity." This advice is sound because, as philosopher and psychologist William James cautioned much later, "He who refuses to embrace a unique opportunity loses the prize as surely as if he had failed." However, opportunities are often difficult for both ordinary people and leaders to recognize. In this chapter, we examine two cases in which U.S. leaders either appear not to have recognized significant opportunities or failed to embrace them. The first case is President Eisenhower's opportunity to reunify Germany and ease superpower relations in 1953–1955 after Joseph Stalin's death. The second is President Reagan's opportunity to pursue an earlier conclusion to the cold war in 1985–1987 after Mikhail Gorbachev's accession to leadership in the Soviet Union.

To be sure, Eisenhower clearly recognized the moment as a potential opportunity, saying after Stalin's death that "the past speaks for itself. I am interested in the future. Both their government and ours now have new men in them. The slate is clean. Now let us begin talking to each other" (Divine 1981, 107). In contrast to Eisenhower, President Reagan only very late perceived his opportunity, as he stuck dogmatically to hostile images of the Soviet Union following the death of Leonid Brezhnev and even with the initial emergence of the Gorbachev phenomenon. As we will show, there were plenty of occasions that he could have recognized as opportunities before finally seizing the moment to help end the cold war.

Like mismanaged threats, mismanaged opportunities are the results of mistakes of omission or commission and may be described as reassurance failures or false hope failures. In this chapter, we consider mistakes

FIGURE 5.1   *Types and Candidate Cases of Mismanaged Opportunities*

TYPE OF MISTAKE

	OMISSION (Too Little/Too Late)	COMMISSION (Too Much/Too Soon)
	German Unification (1953–1955)	Korean Unification (1950–1952)
OPPORTUNITY	(Detection/Hesitation)	(Misperception/Preemption)
CASES	Gorbachev Initiatives (1985–1987)	SALT II Arms Control (1975–1979)
	Reassurance Failures	False Hope Failures

of omission in the form of reassurance failures and focus in the following chapter on mistakes of commission in the form of false hope failures. Figure 5.1 serves to illustrate our general framework in the next two chapters with our selected case studies of mismanaged opportunities by U.S. presidents.

DÉTENTE AND GERMAN REUNIFICATION
AFTER STALIN

After World War II, Britain, France, the United States, and the Soviet Union decided to divide Germany. Division was to be temporary and for local administrative purposes, pending the negotiation of a peace treaty signed by a new German government that would officially end the war. The respective occupation zones reflected the meeting points in June 1945 of the British, American, and Russian armies, which were agreed upon at Yalta in January 1945 and supplemented by splitting the British zone with France. After the Soviet Union refused to cooperate and administer the whole country as a single economic unit, the other great powers unified their zones and adopted a common currency in 1948 (Hartmann 1965). The de facto split of the country prompted a Soviet attempt with the Berlin Blockade to expel the other occupying powers from the capital. An airlift by the Allies thwarted the blockade and stimulated the formation of the NATO alliance (Davison 1958; Shlaim 1983). This event symbolized the onset of the cold war, a process that had begun less dramatically in previous years with disputes over the fates of Poland, Iran, and Czechoslovakia.

After several months of stalemate, Moscow's UN ambassador signaled informally that the Soviet Union would be willing to lift the blockade and restore the status quo ante in return for the resumption of negotiations over German reunification, ending the Berlin crisis (Hartmann 1965). These talks went nowhere until Stalin's death in 1953. With the dictator's passing, however, there did appear to be an opportunity for newly elected U.S. president Eisenhower to work toward reunification and a normalization of the superpower relationship with Stalin's successors, a new collective leadership consisting of Georgi Malenkov, Lavrenti Beria, Nikita Khrushchev, and Vyacheslaw Molotov.

The German question was at the center of the cold war in Europe. Although the escalation of this conflict became entangled with the conflict over the future of Eastern Europe, it was possible in principle for the two sides to begin the resolution of both conflicts by dealing with the German question: should Germany be reunited or remain divided into East and West Germany? Complicating the answer to this question was the answer to another question: should the old German capital city of Berlin remain divided into Western and Eastern zones, or should it be absorbed into the surrounding area of East Germany? To be sure, cold war tensions were not limited to the German question or the conflict over Eastern Europe. By 1953 the two superpowers found themselves in a cold war with hot spots also in Asia—for example, in Korea and French Indochina. The stakes included a general relaxation of cold war tensions, therefore, as well as the issue of German reunification.

Our theoretical analysis of the superpower relations for this time period is shown in Figure 5.2. The figure shows that the power relationship between the two superpowers in Europe was symmetrical (USA = SU), because the local military superiority of Soviet conventional forces was offset by the U.S. nuclear striking force at bases in Western Europe. This power symmetry, along with the symmetrical conflict (−,−) intentions signaled by their behavior during and after the 1948 Berlin crisis, explains their deadlock as the product of a prisoner's dilemma situation (G32) following the end of the crisis up to Stalin's death in March 1953.

FIGURE 5.2   *Strategic Superpower Situations and German Reunification,*
1948–1955

	Soviet Union (G32)		Soviet Union (G27)	
	Coop P	Conf N	Coop P	Conf N
Coop P	3,3	1,4	3,4	1,2
United States				
Conf N	4,1	**"2,2"***	4,1	**"2,3"***

Conflict Game (1948–1953)	Mixed-Motive Game (1953–1955)
Intentions: USA, SU (−,−)	Intentions: USA, SU (−,+)
Power: USA = SU	Power: USA = SU

Brams nonmyopic equilibria are in bold, and Nash myopic equilibria are asterisked. Initial states are in quotation marks.

As a classic prisoner's dilemma situation, this game in Figure 5.2 has mutual settlement (3,3) and mutual deadlock (2,2) as NMEs, while mutual deadlock is also a Nash equilibrium. Theoretically, such a strategic situation forecloses the possibility of rapprochement from an initial state of (2,2). However, during the period of collective Soviet leadership after Stalin's death, the game between the superpowers changed from the conflict game (G32) to the adjacent mixed-motive game (G27), with the Kremlin leaders shifting their highest-ranked preference from (−) domination to (+) settlement. Stalin's successors made general overtures to the Eisenhower administration and also proposed a summit meeting aimed toward a reduction in international tensions. They also hinted that they might be willing to exchange German reunification in return for the country's neutralization (Larson 1997, 39).

In this new situation, a normalization of superpower relations does indeed become theoretically possible. After Moscow signaled settlement as its highest-ranking preference in pre-play communication, it would have been rational for the United States to make a cooperative move from (2,3) deadlock to (1,2), with the expectation that the Soviet Union would reciprocate with a cooperative move toward the game's NME of (3,4) settlement. The formal demonstration of these strategic calculations is shown in Figure 5.3.

The analyses in Figure 5.3 demonstrate a window of opportunity in which both antagonists in the cold war could stand to win by reaching a

FIGURE 5.3   *Superpower Strategies after Stalin's Death*

	Soviet Union			Soviet Union		
	Coop P		Conf N	Coop P		Conf N
Coop P	**3,4**	←	1,2	3,4	→|	1,2
United States	↓		↑	↑		↓
Conf N	4,1	→	"2,3*"	4,1	|←	"**2,3***"

U.S. Strategy (G27): Move	Soviet Strategy (G27): Stay
Intentions: USA, SU (−,+)	Intentions: USA, SU (−,+)
Power: USA = SU	Power: USA = SU

Brams nonmyopic equilibria are in bold. Nash myopic equilibria are asterisked. Final outcomes are underlined for each player from an initial state of (2,3) in quotation marks.

Pareto-superior final state as a NME (see also Larson 1997, 41). However, the United States made a mistake of omission by failing to take advantage of the opportunity. More specifically, it is our contention that the Eisenhower administration misdiagnosed Soviet intentions and ignored Soviet signals on the grounds that they constituted a ploy to divide the West and to derail German rearmament and membership in NATO as well as the establishment of a European Defense Community. To the extent that the shift in Soviet strategy was recognized, the United States failed to make the necessary move to possible settlement. The result was a classic reassurance failure. Ultimately, a rearmed West Germany joined NATO in 1955, and the Soviet Union formed the Warsaw Pact in the same year with East Germany as a rearmed member in the following year. The United States lost the opportunity for a general rapprochement and the possibility of German reunification in particular. In the following narrative, we shall explicate these arguments.

In January 1953 Eisenhower became president, and his administration shared the U.S. consensus of the late 1940s and early 1950s that the Soviet Union was driven by expansionist intentions (Garthoff 1991, 1). Every indication suggested that tensions between the superpowers were about to worsen. In November of the prior year, the United States had tested its first hydrogen bomb. In his subsequent State of the Union speech, Eisenhower added further hostile rhetoric by pledging to "win the Cold War." Adding further fuel to the bellicose line was Secretary of State John

Foster Dulles, as he promised a new "policy of boldness" and a deterrence strategy based on "massive retaliation" (Osgood 2006b, 55–56). The Soviets, for their part, had also just engaged in a massive military buildup, a development that raised serious concerns about Soviet military intentions toward Western Europe (Kramer 2006, xv).

One of the overriding problems in the superpower relationship concerned the future of Germany. "This is the heart of the problem," as U.S. policy planners in the State Department wrote—it was the "Cold War's paramount cause and consequence." The potentials of German power and resources figured crucially in the strategic calculations of the opponents, and both sides feared that added to either side it could be decisive in the balance of power in Europe (Leffler 2007, 127–128; Mastny 2006, 8). Such calculations, combined with the expansion of superpower competition to a global level, as evidenced by the Korean War, made the continuation of the deadlock and an even further escalation of the cold war more likely than not.

A fundamental change occurred on March 6, 1953, when the Kremlin in Moscow announced that Stalin had died (Osgood 2006b, 61). The longtime dictator was succeeded by a collective leadership consisting of Georgi Malenkov, Lavrenti Beria, Nikita Khrushchev, and Vyacheslaw Molotov. These heirs to Soviet rule agreed that Malenkov would be the prime minister and official leader. However, at least in the initial phase, most of the de facto power and authority rested with Beria—he "was the dynamo behind Malenkov" (Leffler 2007, 88; Beria 2001). Formally, Beria assumed the leadership of the Ministry of Internal Affairs. Khrushchev became the secretary of the Central Committee, and Molotov assumed the position of foreign minister.

With this change in the Soviet leadership, new U.S. opportunities emerged. Malenkov had for years favored adopting a more conciliatory foreign policy. Khrushchev recollected, "We had doubts about Stalin's foreign policy," and Beria said it was essential "to end the confrontation with the outside world." The advocacy specifically for German unification among this leadership varied, but faced with a challenging domestic situation, all agreed that cold war tensions needed to be eased (Beria 2001, 252, 262; Talbott 1970, 392–393; Leffler 2007, 89). Indeed, within a few days of Stalin's death, Malenkov made an unexpected appeal. Speaking before the Supreme Soviet on March 16, he announced Moscow's willingness to reach an accord on outstanding East-West issues. He rejected Stalin's "no concessions" principle and declared: "At the present time there is no disputed or unresolved question that cannot be resolved by peaceful means, on the basis of mutual agreement. . . . This applies to our relations with all states, including the United States of America" (Osgood 2006b, 56–61; Ebon 1953, 124–125; Dallin 1961, 125; Divine 1981, 106–107).

The conciliatory signals caught the leadership in Washington by surprise. In a cabinet meeting three days after Stalin's passing, Eisenhower expressed his amazement that the State Department had never devised a plan for this momentous occasion. He exclaimed, "We have no plan. . . . We are not even sure what difference his death makes" (Divine 1981, 106). It seemed that the president was in favor of accepting Malenkov's invitation, but he was not sure that the offer was genuine. "If you could only trust that bastard Malenkov," he stated. However, at the same time he instructed the State Department and the National Security Council (NSC) to "study the problem constantly in an effort to determine whether the Soviets [are] really changing their outlook, and accordingly, whether some kind of modus vivendi might not at long last prove feasible" (Ewald 1981, 226; Kramer 2006, xvi). At a March 19 press conference, Eisenhower stated that any Soviet effort to seek peace would be "just as welcome as it is sincere" (Parmett 1972, 277).

The historical evidence suggests that in the days after Stalin's death, Eisenhower was pragmatic and inclined toward possible rapprochement with the Soviet Union (Larson 1997, 42–46); however, this was not the case for Dulles, who was one of the most influential secretaries of state in U.S. history. He contributed significantly to the continuation of the superpower deadlock. Historians appear to agree that President Eisenhower took a back seat to Dulles in questions of foreign and security policy, and the general consensus is that Dulles designed and executed American diplomacy in the crucial years from 1953 to 1959 (Etheredge 1978; Holsti, 1974–1975; Hughes 1963; S. Adams 1961; Morgenthau 1961). Dulles misdiagnosed the situation as a threat rather than an opportunity, a detection failure based on a misperception that would figure most prominently in the U.S. decision-making process dealing with a Soviet Union without Stalin.

A staunch anti-Communist, Dulles maintained a rigid belief that the Soviets were innately hostile. He was convinced that the Soviet Union wanted to conquer the world and that cooperative agreements would be exploited. Already in 1952 Dulles had declared that the policy of containment formulated under President Truman was bankrupt. He warned that the cold war would be lost if the United States did not go on the offensive, if it did not seek to "roll back" Communism (Dulles 1950, 163; Leffler 2007, 99–100). In an NSC meeting shortly after Malenkov's conciliatory speech of March 16, Dulles talked about ways of "ending the peril represented by the Soviet Union." He suggested that it "could be done by inducing the disintegration of Soviet power. If we keep our pressures on, psychological and otherwise," he urged, "we may either force a collapse of the Kremlin regime or else transform the Soviet orbit from a union of satellites dedicated to aggression into a coalition for defense only, but we must not relax this pressure until the Soviets give promise of ending the struggle" (Garthoff 1991, 16; Kramer 2006, xvi).

A major influence on the president was also C.D. Jackson, head of the Psychological Strategy Board (PSB). The PSB was an autonomous interdepartmental body composed of representatives from the State Department, the Defense Department, the CIA, and the Joint Chiefs of Staff. Its purpose was to act as a coordinating body for all nonmilitary cold war activities, including covert operations (Osgood 2006b, 43). Jackson was convinced that Stalin's death presented the United States with "the greatest opportunity . . . in many years to seize the initiative." On the day the Kremlin announced Stalin's death, Jackson had written to NSC secretary Robert Cutler, "Shouldn't we do everything possible to overload the enemy at the precise moment when he is least capable of bearing even his normal load?" (Osgood 2006a, 29). Jackson and Dulles regarded Soviet moves toward more cooperative and less threatening policies "not only with suspicion, but as an obstacle to American interests rather than steps toward accommodation" (Garthoff 1991, 9; Osgood 2006b, 68). Together they would steer the president away from engaging the Soviet Union in a constructive way.

The new Soviet leadership was doing "surprising things" that the CIA had not expected (Leffler 2007, 104). As if to answer Eisenhower's request for proof of sincerity, the Soviet government made numerous conciliatory gestures. These included an agreement to exchange POWs from the Korean conflict and a proposal for the resumption of the Korean armistice talks. On March 27, the Soviet government apologized to the British government for an air collision over East Germany and proposed talks toward avoiding such incidents in the future. The Soviets also loosened traffic barriers around Berlin, admitted a group of American journalists to Moscow, and withdrew their objections to the new secretary of the United Nations, Dag Hammarskjold. Most significantly, Moscow was calling for a summit to discuss the German question. On March 31, General Vasily Chuikov, chairman of the Soviet Control Commission in Berlin, announced that "reunification of the country" would be "wholly and fully" in accord with Soviet wishes (Osgood 2006b, 62; Leffler 2007, 91; Larson 1997, 49).

Although former director of the State Department's Policy Planning Staff (PPS) George Kennan had been demoted, he was still regarded as one of the country's most eminent Soviet specialists. It was his assessment that "the present Soviet leaders are definitely interested in pursuing with us the effort to solve some of the present international difficulties" (Leffler 2007, 109). The current PPS agreed. Two weeks after Beria's speech, it noted that "there have been more Soviet gestures toward the West than at any other similar period" (Osgood 2006b, 62; Larson 1997, 45, 49; Baring 1972, 23). Shortly afterward, Soviet ambassador to the United States Andrei Vyshinski urged Washington to reciprocate and to "begin to dig the tunnel of friendship from both ends." Moreover, by way of the Norwegian UN representative, Moscow submitted a proposal for a meeting between Eisenhower and Malenkov concerning atomic energy control and disarmament (Larson 1997, 45).

The new Soviet course had no effect on Dulles, who maintained a rigid belief system about the Soviet Union. He had just declared that after evaluating the apparent new course in Soviet foreign policy, there would be no reason for "any great comfort" (Larson 1997, 44). For Dulles, there was "no ground for the belief that there would be change in the basic hostility of the Soviet Union" (Leffler 2007, 105). He was and remained confident that the softer line in Soviet foreign policy was merely a tactical shift intended to divide the Western alliance. Eisenhower took issue with these conclusions. He agreed that "there was no ground to anticipate a basic change in Soviet policy," but he contended that "there was also no ground for believing that no basic changes in Soviet policy were in the offing" (Leffler 2007, 105). Eisenhower and Dulles appeared to disagree on the proper diagnosis of the situation. Ultimately, it would be Dulles's diagnosis that would shape the U.S. response.

After the death of Stalin, Eisenhower had considered addressing a speech to the Soviet Union. To his speechwriter Emmett Hughes he exclaimed, "Look, I am tired . . . of just plain indictments of the Soviet regime" (Divine 1981, 107). He confided, "If Mr. Dulles and all his sophisticated advisers really mean that they can *not* talk peace seriously, then I am in the wrong pew. . . . Now either we cut all of this fooling around and make a serious bid for peace—or we forget the whole thing" (qtd. in Leffler 2007, 103). Eisenhower wanted to "come out straight," without any "double-talk or slick sophisticated propaganda devices" (Larson 1997, 43). He was prepared to say that "recent statements and gestures of Soviet leaders give some evidence that they may recognize this critical moment" (Rostow 1982, 48). Moreover, the president intended to offer new security arrangements for Europe and to propose foreign ministers' negotiations aimed at reunifying Germany and Austria. Dulles and Jackson doubted the strategic timing for the speech, and over the coming weeks they would succeed in eliminating the conciliatory signals in Eisenhower's address (Larson 1997, 42).

On April 8, CIA director Allen Dulles, the brother of the secretary of state, gave a presentation to the NSC. After noting that "the CIA had originally believed that after Stalin's death [the new leaders in Moscow] would play a very cautious game [and] . . . would faithfully adhere to Stalin's policies for a considerable time," he acknowledged that "neither of these estimates had actually proven to be true." He went so far as to describe the changes in Soviet foreign policy as "shattering departures" from Stalin's policies (Kramer 2006, xiv; Ewald 1981, 226). The new trend in Soviet policy was indeed recognized as such. A *New York Times* editorial from April 2, 1953, observed that "since the death of Stalin an unmistakably softer wind has begun to blow out of Moscow" (Larson 1997, 45; see also Rostow 1982, 48). At the same time C.D. Jackson wrote to the president that for a month,

we have given a virtual monopoly to the Soviets over the minds of people all over the world—and in that month, they have moved with vigor and disarming plausibility. . . . They have hammered home the idea that they alone are responsible for peace. They have proposed a Four Power conference on German unification. (Leffler 2007, 103)

In light of the cooperative Soviet gestures, the planned presidential speech assumed more urgency. However, by now its purpose had evolved away from a proposal for constructive engagement toward a means of inspiring caution. A PSB plan that was directed by Jackson argued that in the presidential speech and subsequent propaganda, the United States should "combat any wishful thinking in the free world [and] expose vigorously the motives and pitfalls of any false 'peace' campaigns" (Osgood 2006b, 63). Secretary Dulles also had various suggestions for immediate U.S. concessions and gestures of good will cut from the speech. Among them were Eisenhower's suggestion to meet with Malenkov and a commitment to meet any Soviet cooperative moves "half way" (Larson 1997, 47).

After nearly a month of revision, Eisenhower delivered the speech on April 16 and warned his listeners not to accept Soviet peace overtures too eagerly (Osgood 2006a, 64). The president called upon the Soviets to take "clear and specific steps" to demonstrate sincerity (Divine 1981, 108). These included a truce in Korea, an Austrian treaty and neutralization, the release of World War II POWs, and steps toward disarmament (Garthoff 1991, 6). Because of Dulles's interventions, the speech offered no concessions from the United States and no proposals for negotiation. Two days later, Dulles also delivered a speech that afterward was described as an "acerbic and challenging" cold war speech (Garthoff 1991, 7). His tenor was that the Soviet leaders were engaged in a "peace defensive," not a "peace offensive" (Leffler 2007, 109). He argued that Soviet foreign policy was emanating from deep and enduring sources and that any change in Soviet policy was the result of weakness. The Soviets should be pushed even harder: "I don't know anything better we can do than keep up those pressures right now" (Larson 1997, 46).

The leadership in Moscow was disturbed. Yet despite the secretary's hostility and although divided by a behind-the-scenes struggle for power, it responded with more cooperative deeds. The stalled Korean armistice talks resumed on April 26 after Moscow had pushed the Chinese and the North Koreans on softer negotiating positions. At the same time, the Soviet newspaper *Pravda* advocated a nonaggression pact among the four great powers (Baring 1972, 24). The newspaper also announced that the Soviet Union was prepared to participate in discussions on any issues that were cause of concern. It declared that German reunification might be possible before a peace treaty was concluded. The Soviet leadership thereby distanced its policy from Stalin's insistence that both Germanies take part in such a treaty (Richter 1993, 676). Also of major importance was Moscow's enactment of a series of democratic reforms in East Germany, which may have been designed to facilitate German reunification (Mosley 1953, 21–22; Larson 1997, 49; Richter 1993, 673).

Observing the unfolding events, British Prime Minister Churchill noted that "a new breeze [was] blowing on the tormented world (Osgood 2006a, 56). He emphasized the opportunities that had emerged and wrote, "Great hope has arisen in the world" (Leffler 2007, 106). On May 11, Churchill called for an immediate summit with the Soviets. Whereas the United States had insisted that Germany must be anchored in the Western Alliance, Churchill did not exclude a neutralized reunified Germany as part of a settlement (Steininger 1990, 105). He urged a flexible approach, declaring that "It would be a mistake to assume that nothing could be settled with Soviet Russia unless or until everything is settled" (Divine 1981, 109). Two weeks later Moscow responded favorably to Churchill's suggestion about a summit (Baring 1972, 24). On May 24, *Pravda* announced that Moscow would place the reunification of Germany at the center of its European policy and called for a policy to be "coordinated" by the four powers to resolve the issue (Richter 1993, 676). In what appeared to be a demonstration of sincere intentions, Moscow by the end of May had renounced its territorial claims on the U.S.-NATO partner Turkey and reestablished diplomatic relations with Israel and Yugoslavia.

This period was the time when the window of diplomatic opportunity was open to the widest extent. "Never did negotiations seem so promising," argues German historian Elke Scherstjanoi (1998, 517). However, Secretary of State Dulles continued to maintain his hostile beliefs. He remained convinced that the Soviets had launched a "phony peace campaign," and he tried to halt what he considered an ill-fated rush to the summit. Dulles persuaded Eisenhower to agree to meet only with the British and French in Bermuda to discuss a future summit (Divine 1981, 109). At this time, the administration also initiated the most systematic review of national security policy since the onset of the cold war. Under the direction of Assistant for National Security Affairs Robert Cutler, three task forces were assembled to outline alternative courses of action. What was striking in the presentations of the three task forces was the absence of any emphasis on the chance for peace or the pursuit of détente. Instead, the task forces deliberated the continued viability of containment as well as more aggressive actions to subvert the Soviet bloc and erode Soviet power (Leffler 2007, 124).

It became very evident that the maintenance of East Germany was too costly and that the Soviet leadership was therefore willing to make concessions. In June the Politburo began formulating a directive to the East German Communist Party (SED) that would formalize the "New Course toward the Future of East Germany." It explained that the "grand goal of establishing German unity" required measures from both sides that would "concretely facilitate the rapprochement between both parts of Germany." Significantly, the statement referred to "both parts of Germany" rather than to "two German states." There were also reports that the head of the Soviet High Commission in Germany, Vladimir Semenov, told the SED leaders to prepare themselves for the loss of power that would follow reunification under democratic conditions (Steininger 1990: 110–111; J. Stein 1997, 51).

The question was how much the Soviet Union should concede. The collective leadership was split on this issue. Khrushchev and Molotov were willing to accept a unified neutral Germany without conceding on the building of socialism. The case was different for Beria, who had been the administrator of the Soviet atomic energy program and who understood well the power of nuclear weapons. He was less worried about maintaining strategic positions such as East Germany and shared the view, probably along with Malenkov, that Soviet nuclear weapons were sufficient to deter the United States from an act of aggression. This belief enabled him to favor offering genuine concessions to the West (Richter 1993, 673, 680, 682; Larson 1997, 50). There is indeed considerable evidence that Beria favored a grand bargain that would reunify Germany as a neutral and capitalist government. At a meeting of the Politburo on May 27, he asked, "The GDR? What does it amount to, this GDR? It is not even a real state. It is only kept in being by Soviet troops, even if we do call it GDR" (Harrison 2006, 199).

Although Beria was willing to make considerable concessions to the United States, he simultaneously undertook internal measures that would bolster his power position further among the collective leadership. Fearing that he was planning a coup, Khrushchev orchestrated a plot to have Beria arrested at a Presidium meeting on June 26. Also involved in the plot were Molotov, Minister of Defense Nikolai Bulganin, and Marshal Georgi Zhukov (Leffler 2007, 117; Larson 1997, 51). At the subsequent Central Committee Plenum, Beria was charged with a series of crimes. Advocating the creation of a unified Germany as a "bourgeois, peace-loving state" was only one of them. Although Malenkov had not been siding with Khrushchev, he found himself in a position where he was forced to join in the general condemnation of Beria and his plans to abandon the East German regime (Richter 1993, 681, 684).

After the fall of Beria, the prospects for German unification were reduced significantly, but they may not have been completely eliminated. Certainly, the prospects for a general relaxation of cold war tensions were still alive. As CIA Director Allen Dulles pointed out to his brother, the new course was continued even after Beria's arrest (Larson 1997, 54). Other signs were the signing of the Korean armistice in July as well as the granting of exit visas to Soviet wives of U.S. citizens (Larson 1997, 57). In an important speech on August 8, 1953, Malenkov reaffirmed his goal of negotiating a reduction in tensions. Ambassador Bohlen reported that Malenkov's speech represented a "continuance and emphasis [of the] main line of Soviet foreign policy since Stalin's death which tend to bear out [the] view that these changes stem from sources deeper than simple maneuver" (Larson 1997, 57).

Eisenhower and his advisers settled on a national security policy statement at the end of October 1953. They finally acknowledged that the Kremlin might indeed seek a relaxation of tensions. However, the consensus was that the Soviet leadership had not demonstrated a "readiness to make important concessions to this end." Instead the Soviet rulers were still basing their foreign policy "on the conviction of irreconcilable hostility between the bloc and the non-communist world." In other words, the new Soviet course of the last few months was merely a tactical shift. Therefore, the United States needed to prepare to win the cold war. The work of all three task forces that had been commissioned earlier was integrated together with new Joint Chiefs of Staff concepts into an overall strategy that presumed strategic superiority, deterrence, containment, and a calculated, prudent rollback of Communism (Leffler 2007, 133).

The presumption of American strategic superiority and a rollback of Communism meant that the superpower game was now defined in Washington as a game characterized by a U.S. bully strategy against either an appeasement or a bluffing strategy by the Soviet regime, depending on whether recent Soviet gestures toward détente were taken seriously. These possibilities and their strategic implications are demonstrated in Figure 5.4, in which the assumed U.S. superior power position and its aspiration to roll back Communism make American domination its highest-ranking outcome and conflict its dominant strategy, with a choice of "stay" at deadlock in either game. The analyses of the two Soviet strategies show that from an initial state of deadlock (3,3) a Soviet strategy of appeasement (ranking settlement highest) would simply continue the deadlock as the final outcome. In contrast, a Soviet bluffing strategy (ranking Soviet domination highest) leads to U.S. domination (4,2) as the final outcome from an initial state of deadlock (3,1).

In 1954 the Kremlin was paralyzed to a large extent due to the ongoing internal power struggle. The window of opportunity for President Eisenhower to negotiate with Moscow would eventually close down and lead to the second Berlin crisis. The winner of the power struggle in the Kremlin continued in principle to support the unification of Germany.

FIGURE 5.4   *Alternative Soviet Strategies against a U.S. Bully Strategy*

	Soviet Union			Soviet Union	
	Coop P	Conf N		Coop P	Conf N
Coop P	2,4 →|	1,1		2,3 →|	1,4
USA	↑	↓		↑	↓
Conf N	4,2 |←	"3,3*"		4,2 ←	"3,1*"

Soviet Appeasement Strategy: Stay	Soviet Bluffing Strategy: Move
Intentions: USA, SU (−,+)	Intentions: USA, SU (−,−)
Power: USA > SU	Power: USA > SU
Dominant Strategy: USA (N)	Dominant Strategy: USA (N)

Final outcomes are underlined from an initial state of deadlock, and initial states are in quotation marks. Nash myopic equilibria are asterisked.

Nikita Khrushchev had supported a future for Germany as a reunited, neutral state in central Europe. After signing the Austrian State Treaty in May 1955, Eisenhower was willing to convene for a summit, but it was too little/too late. In the meantime, the momentum of West Germany rearming and joining NATO had become irreversible. In May, Bonn formally joined the Western military alliance. The Soviet Union was unwilling to unite Germany without its disarmament and a reduction of U.S. forces in Europe. This coupling of reunification with European disarmament led to a deadlock and the resumption of a prisoner's dilemma game between the United States and the Soviet Union.

THE GORBACHEV INITIATIVES

Khrushchev's accession to power in the Kremlin would soon be accompanied by an intensified arms race between the superpowers. The United States decided to introduce tactical nuclear weapons into Western Europe, and the Soviet Union decided to expand both its strategic nuclear arsenal and its navy. Dangerous situations developed in the crisis over Berlin in 1961 and the ongoing situation in Cuba following Castro's takeover, culminating in the 1962 Cuban Missile Crisis. This peak in the cold war was followed by a relaxation of tensions initiated by Kennedy and Khrushchev in the aftermath of the confrontation over the introduction of Soviet missiles in Cuba. Their successors expanded and continued détente and peaceful coexistence into the 1970s, slowing the strategic arms race with the Strategic Arms Limitation Talks (SALT) and the SALT I agreement reached by Nixon and Brezhnev in 1972.

Tensions between the two superpowers increased again in the second half of the decade, as SALT II negotiations stalled and the Soviet Union invaded Afghanistan in 1979. By the time Ronald Reagan assumed the presidency in 1981, détente had effectively come to an end and the superpowers found themselves deadlocked again in a prisoner's dilemma game. Following the death of Brezhnev in November 1982, Yuri Andropov and Konstantin Chernenko each served as the leader of the Soviet Union during Reagan's first administration. Although there were short episodes of rapprochement between the superpowers, including proposals for arms reductions talks in this period, overall U.S.-Soviet relations remained conflictual (Malici 2008).

In March 1985, a new leader assumed the position of secretary-general in the Soviet Union. Inheriting a complex political situation both at home and abroad, Mikhail Gorbachev adopted a combination of perestroika and glasnost as domestic reforms and a foreign policy of "new thinking" and "common security" (Lynch 1989; Gorbachev 1987, 1995; Legvold 1988; Thom 1988). The latter pair of concepts reflected his beliefs that the security of the superpowers was inextricably intertwined and that the management of their common security called for a new approach. Gorbachev signaled his intentions with a series of diplomatic proposals and unilateral gestures. His "new thinking" and "common security" doctrines replaced the conflict game shown in Figure 5.5 with the adjacent mixed-motive game. The two superpowers ended up at the end of the decade in the no-conflict game on the right side of Figure 5.5 with an NME of settlement (4,4).

The strategic situation between the superpowers in the mid-1980s is similar to their situation after Stalin's death in 1953. In both cases Moscow transformed the situation between the United States and the Soviet Union by switching away from a conflict (−) strategy to a cooperative (+) strategy. This shift created a mixed-motive game as a new strategic situation with mutual settlement (3,4) as the NME equilibrium solution. The change provided an opportunity for the United States to escape deadlock as an NME. In this situation it was incumbent on Washington to initiate

FIGURE 5.5   *Soviet and U.S. Power Games, 1979–1991*

	Soviet Union		Soviet Union		Soviet Union	
	Coop P	Conf N	Coop P	Conf N	Coop P	Conf N
Coop P	3,3	1,4	**3,4**	1,2	**4,4**	1,2
USA						
Conf N	4,1	2,2*	4,1	2,3*	2,1	3,3*
	Conflict Game 1979–1985 (G32) USA, SU (−,−); USA = SU		Mixed-Motive Game 1985–1986 (G27) USA, SU (−,+); USA = SU		No-Conflict Game 1987–1991 USA, SU (+,+); USA = SU	

Brams nonmyopic equilibria are in bold, and Nash equilibria are asterisked.

a cooperative move from deadlock with the expectation that Moscow would follow suit toward the game's NME settlement.

The formal demonstration of this strategic logic is displayed in Figure 5.6. The United States did not follow this strategy. Like the Eisenhower administration, President Reagan and his advisors made a mistake of omission resulting in a reassurance failure. More specifically, the Reagan administration failed to properly diagnose Soviet intentions regarding arms control and also miscalculated the U.S. response. What distinguishes the episodes in the two administrations from each other is that the latter lasted longer, which proved to be crucial. The extended time period allowed Gorbachev to pursue repeatedly a graduated reduction in tension (GRIT) strategy and permitted Reagan to engage in a process of experiential learning in which he gradually adopted a different image of the Soviet Union (Kramer 2006; J. Stein 1994). Thus, despite Reagan's earlier reassurance failure, the superpowers were able to end the cold war.

We mentioned GRIT in Chapter 2 as a method to alter the payoff matrix of a strategic game. The GRIT strategy employs unilateral cooperative initiatives for "inducing reciprocation" from the opponent. The initiatives should be unexpected surprise moves, should explicitly invite reciprocation, and should be continued over a considerable period of time even if reciprocation is not immediately forthcoming (Osgood 1962, 96–103; see also Osgood 1960 and Etzioni 1962, 84–108). The strategy is irrational, a foreign policy mistake of choosing "move" instead of "stay" at deadlock as shown in Figure 5.6, insofar as the cooperative player runs a

FIGURE 5.6   *U.S. and Soviet Strategies, 1985–1987*

		Soviet Union		Soviet Union	
		Coop P	Conf N	Coop P	Conf N
	Coop P	**3,4** ←	1,2	3,4 →|	1,2
USA		↓	↑	↑	↓
	Conf N	4,1 →	"2,3*"	4,1 |←	"2,3*"

U.S. Strategy (G27): Move   Soviet Strategy (G27): Stay
Intentions: USA, SU (−,+)   Intentions: USA, SU (−,+)
Power: USA = SU   Power: USA = SU

Brams nonmyopic equilibria are in bold, and Nash myopic equilibria are asterisked. Final outcomes are underlined from an initial state of deadlock in quotation marks.

risk of being dominated by the conflictual player until and unless the strategic situation morphs into a no-conflict game (see Figure 5.5). Taking this risk has become known as the "Gorbachev phenomenon" (Crozier 1990; Lewin 1991; Malici 2008).

President Reagan did not know much about the Soviet Union. In fact, U.S. ambassador Jack Matlock (2004, 132) described the president's knowledge as "spotty." Reagan probably stood out as the most anti-Communist of all U.S. presidents. He fervently maintained an image of the Soviet Union as the "evil empire" against which a "crusade" had to be "launched" (Garthoff 1994b, 249; Leffler 2007, 353). At his first press conference after assuming the U.S. presidency, he declared Soviet intentions to be "the promotion of world wide revolution and a one-world socialist or communist state." He denounced the Soviet regime, saying that "the only morality they recognize is what will further their cause, meaning they reserve unto themselves the right to commit any crime, to lie, to cheat" (Leffler 2007, 339; Larson 1997, 190).

Reagan's hostile predilections would not change when Gorbachev assumed the leadership in the Kremlin. Immediately after Gorbachev's accession Reagan declared, "There's a great mutual suspicion between [our] two countries. I think ours is more justified than theirs" (qtd. in Mandelbaum and Talbott 1987, 44). One week later the president reaffirmed an assertive U.S. position, stressed the need for an intensified defense effort, and renewed charges of Soviet violations of political and arms control agreements in the past (Garthoff 1994b, 208). His confrontational stance went even further as he made it a cornerstone of his foreign policy that the United States would "actively, and if necessarily unilaterally, sponsor insurgencies seeking the overthrow of pro-Moscow leftist regimes in the Third World" (Mandelbaum and Talbott 1987, 61).

Among Reagan's influential advisers were Secretary of Defense Caspar Weinberger, CIA Director William Casey, and National Security Adviser Robert McFarlane. These men were "traditional cold warriors," and together with the NSC staff they fundamentally distrusted the Soviet Union and opposed any diplomatic contacts (Leffler 2007, 339; Larson 1997, 191). A different role was taken by Secretary of State George Schultz. Schultz was a conservative pragmatist, and unlike others in this administration, he had negotiated with the Soviets as secretary of the treasury during the Nixon administration. Schultz respected the Soviets as thorough, well-prepared, and able negotiators who would commit to mutually advantageous agreements. His first encounter with Gorbachev at Chernenko's funeral led him to believe that Gorbachev was very different from his predecessors, and he was convinced that change was on the way. President Reagan, in contrast, believed that "Gorbachev will be as tough as any of their leaders" (Schultz 1993, 118–121; Larson 1997, 32, 190–191; Oberdorfer 1991b, 111).

It was Schultz's definition of the situation that would be confirmed rather soon. The first meeting of the Politburo after Gorbachev's accession concluded that the Soviet Union would be ready and willing to concentrate efforts toward détente with the United States. What followed was the beginning of Gorbachev's GRIT strategy and a first wave of conciliatory gestures. On April 7, Gorbachev announced a six-month unilateral moratorium on deployment of intermediate-range missiles (SS-20s) in Europe. On April 17, he went further and proposed a moratorium on all nuclear weapon testing (J. Stein 1994, 179). The shift in Soviet strategy was evident. However, at that time as well as for the next two years, Reagan misdiagnosed the situation and would not recognize these strategic changes (Malici 2006, 137; Malici 2008).

Shortly after Gorbachev's initiatives, Casey wrote to Reagan and reinforced the president's beliefs. According to Casey, Gorbachev and those around him "are not reformers . . . in Soviet . . . foreign policy." He urged Reagan to convince the Soviets that the "original Reagan agenda is here to stay: revived U.S. military power . . . and revived ideological challenge to . . . the Soviet system" (Gates 1996, 332). Instead of reciprocating Gorbachev's moves, Reagan was quoted in a *Washington Post* article from June 15, 1985, declaring that the United States would "demonstrate that communism is not the wave of the future" and instead pushed ahead vigorously with the development of his Strategic Defense Initiative (SDI), a missile shield that would deny the Soviet Union any second-strike capability (qtd. in Goshko 1985). His hostility toward the Soviet Union also led him to consider abandoning the unratified, but so far observed, SALT II Treaty (Garthoff 1994b, 219; Malici 2006, 137–138; Malici 2008).

Gorbachev nevertheless intended to "pave the way by creating a more favorable climate" in U.S.-Soviet relations (Gorbachev 1987, 225). On July 30, he announced a unilateral halt to nuclear testing until January 1. He invited reciprocation, as he promised that "the moratorium would remain in effect beyond that date if the U.S. also refrained from testing" (Goldstein and Freeman 1990, 114). While the Soviet Union indeed halted all tests, the United States remained on a conflictual course. Robert McFarlane labeled the Soviet Union's arguments about arms control a "masterpiece of chutzpah," and subsequently the administration "decided to counter the burgeoning Gorbachev peace offensive by a rebuttal, rather than competition or engagement" (Larson 1997, 202; Garthoff 1994a, 222). On August 17, the United States conducted nuclear tests. At the same time the administration announced that it planned to test an antisatellite weapon in violation of a tacit U.S.-Soviet convention not to target satellites, which were indispensable for arms control verification and the prevention of surprise attack (Larson 1997, 202; Malici 2008, 52–54).

After the announcement of a meeting between President Reagan and Soviet Foreign Minister Eduard Shevardnadze, McFarlane expressed pessimism that "even incremental improvements" could be reached (quoted in Goldstein and Freeman 1990, 117). Similarly, Secretary Weinberger and his assistant secretary for national security policy, Richard Perle, doubted that Gorbachev really wanted change. In the meantime, Schultz came to view Reagan as "a prisoner of his own staff" (Leffler 2007, 354).

Reagan proceeded by stressing his determination to continue SDI and announced that the United States would soon carry out the first live tests of an antisatellite missile. Despite vehement Soviet protests, missile and laser tests began on August 25, continued in September, and culminated in a U.S. announcement regarding the creation of a U.S. space command to coordinate all military systems in space (Malici 2008, 52; Goldstein and Freeman 1990, 118). The only positive development at this time came from Schultz when he instructed all his regional assistants to establish a regular dialogue with their Soviet counterparts (Matlock 2004, 127).

Gorbachev's "peace initiative" continued. In September he proposed reductions of 50 percent in strategic offensive arms to a number of 6,000 nuclear warheads, accompanied by an agreement not to develop, test, or deploy "space-strike weapons" (Garthoff 1994a, 228). Any concession on SDI was out of the question for Reagan. On the same day that Shevardnadze met with Reagan, the United States conducted another nuclear test. Soon afterward, in an unprecedented move, the United States sent the battleship USS *Iowa* (armed with long-range cruise missiles) into the Baltic Sea. Further U.S. moves of escalation followed in November through a unilateral reinterpretation of a key provision of the antiballistic missiles (ABM) treaty. National Security Adviser McFarlane disclosed that the administration was considering a reinterpretation of the ABM treaty. It would permit the development and testing of space-based ABM systems and components—"theretofore believed banned by the treaty" (Garthoff 1994a 230; see also Malici 2008, 53).

The first superpower summit between Reagan and Gorbachev was scheduled in Geneva for November 19–20, 1985. The record at this point was one of Soviet cooperative initiatives and contentious U.S. responses. American officials were pessimistic that agreements could be reached (Matlock 2004, 114; Garthoff 1994a, 223). Secretary Schultz was an exception, and it is interesting to note that he succeeded in excluding Weinberger from the delegation after the latter had been suspected of trying to manipulate the summit (Garthoff 1994b, 237–238). At the summit the Soviets moved closer to the U.S. position on almost every arms control issue; however, it did not come to much (Leffler 2007, 395). In the end, the two leaders agreed in principle on progressing toward the reduction of strategic arms by 50 percent and on negotiations to follow regarding a prospective intermediate nuclear forces (INF) agreement on tactical nuclear weapons. Nothing substantive and immediate was agreed upon, however, and the Geneva summit was therefore a failure (Haslam 1990, 158). U.S. nuclear testing and SDI research continued, and Reagan accused the Soviet Union of various violations of existing arms control agreements in a report to Congress (Malici 2006, 137–142).

Despite this disappointment, Gorbachev continued his GRIT strategy. In January of the new year he proposed a program to eliminate nuclear weapons entirely by the end of the century. Among other things, the plan entailed the elimination of all medium-range missiles and the reduction of strategic arms by 50 percent within five to eight years. Secretary Schultz emphasized to President Reagan that "this is our first indication that the Soviets are interested in a staged program toward zero." In opposition to other advisors, Schultz advised Reagan not to reject the Soviet proposal. The president agreed, and at a subsequent press conference he observed that the plan was "different from the things that we have heard in the past from leaders in the Soviet Union" (Larson 1997, 206–207). Although this was the first time that Reagan would speak favorably of Soviet efforts, the general pattern of contentious U.S. responses would continue.

In March 1986, the U.S. battleships USS *Yorktown* and USS *Caron* entered Soviet waters in the Crimean Sea. Ignoring ongoing talks on regional matters, Reagan on March 21 raised a "continuing horror of the Soviet attempt to subjugate Afghanistan" and authorized over $300 million more in covert military assistance. Ten days later came the disclosure that the United States would supply Stinger antiaircraft missiles to insurgents in Afghanistan and other third world countries led by pro-Moscow regimes (Garthoff 1994b, 272; Malici 2008, 60). When Reagan declared publicly that he would not regret his 1983 labeling of the Soviet Union as the "evil empire," he was joined by Attorney General Edwin Meese, who was quoted in the *New York Times* on March 27 as accusing the Soviet Union of "torture, rape and toxic gas, of famine, of scorched earth and genocide" as "part of a drive to dominate the entire world" (Mandelbaum and Talbott 1987, 45). For Schultz, the rhetoric of the president and other officials was "getting out of hand" (Leffler 2007, 18).

At the end of March, Gorbachev renewed the nuclear testing morato-rium with the provision that the United States would follow suit. Wash-ington defied the invitation and engaged in nuclear weapons tests on April 4. "The picture looked bleak," Garthoff concludes, "but the Soviet leadership was not giving up on prospects for developing relations" (Garthoff 1994a, 275). At the end of April, Gorbachev initiated a devel-opment in Soviet military doctrine toward "defensive principles" and a "balance of military forces at the lowest possible levels," combined with the "reduction of military potentials to the limits necessary for defense" (Garthoff 1994b, 276). More particularly, the proposal called for mutual force reductions of between 100,000 and 150,000 troops within a pe-riod of two years, to be then followed by additional reductions of be-tween 350,000 and 400,000 troops. Gorbachev also proposed reducing "operational-tactical nuclear arms with a range of up to 1,000 km," which posed a major concern to NATO allies such as Great Britain and France (see Malici 2008, 61). These moves of Gorbachev came despite Reagan's confirmation in May of Secretary Weinberger's earlier announcement, quoted in the *Washington Post* on May 28, that SALT II is "dead."

Gorbachev kept pushing. On June 16, he conceded a toleration for "laboratory research" regarding SDI—an unprecedented move on this issue. Another move of this kind followed when he suggested setting INF systems, apart from intercontinental ballistic missiles (ICBMs) and submarine-launched ballistic missiles (SLBMs), at a zero level in Europe for the Soviet Union and the United States but not for other NATO states. By removing an insistence upon compensation for existing British and nuclear forces, Gorbachev broke an important barrier that had hitherto blocked the path to an INF settlement (Haslam 1990, 159; Malici 2008, 61). Although Reagan attributed "a serious effort to the Soviets," he nevertheless advocated the realization of SDI without any signs of com-promise (Oberdorfer 1991a, 169–174). U.S. hostility continued when in September a "naval battle group, for the first time featuring the nuclear-missile-armed battleship USS *New Jersey*, passed through the Kuril Islands into the Sea of Okhotsk for an exercise simulating an attack on Soviet bases" (Garthoff 1994a, 296).

The signs before the Reykjavik summit in October 1986 were not much different from the signs before the Geneva summit (Goldstein and Freeman 1990, 121). Accordingly, Garthoff (1994a, 286) writes that as the Reykjavik summit approached,

it became clear that although Reagan was prepared to negotiate on his own terms, he was not disposed to seek a real compromise. . . . He was prepared for a summit with or without an arms agreement, and he would gain . . . either by showing that the Soviets had accepted his position or that they had not and that he would stand firm until they did.

In Reykjavik, Gorbachev took the initiative and laid out a set of proposals regarding strategic arms, intermediate range missiles, and space weapons. He kept urging a mutual moratorium on nuclear testing although he did not insist on *immediate* implementation, as he had previously. His agenda carried unprecedented concessions, as he accepted an equal 50 percent cut in ICBMs, SLBMs, and heavy bombers (Zemtsov and Farrar 1989, 168; see also Malici 2008, 62). He went further and also agreed to include a cut in the Soviet heavy (SS-18) missiles. He also agreed "to exclude all American forward-based shorter-range systems capable of striking the Soviet Union from the 'strategic forces' to be counted and limited" (Garthoff 1994b, 287). With regards to space weapons and defensive systems, the Soviet side moderated their demand from a fifteen-year nonwithdrawal commitment from the ABM treaty to ten years. Gorbachev reiterated his concession about SDI laboratory research and also his zero-level suggestion regarding INF. He also dropped his earlier demand that French and British weapons should be frozen at existing levels.

In contrast, "Reagan did not have new proposals to advance" (Garthoff 1994a, 286). He accepted the zero-level proposal for Soviet and U.S. INF missiles in Europe. This was not a real concession, because NATO allies were in a position to maintain their missiles, and it disadvantaged the Soviet Union to a much greater extent than it did the United States. Reagan was prepared to consider a ten-year period regarding a nonwithdrawal from the ABM treaty. However, he conditioned it by calling for an agreement with the provision that at the end of the period each side would legitimately be able to deploy ABM defenses (Garthoff 1994b, 228). Regarding SDI, Reagan remained uncompromising. The two super-powers reached near agreements at the end on the elimination of nuclear weapons, an elimination of Soviet and U.S. INF missiles in Europe, and the prospect of elimination of all ballistic missiles. Given that Reagan would make no concession regarding SDI, which was a major concern for the Soviet side, the Soviet hope for a quid pro quo was disappointed (Gates 1996, 409; Malici 2008, 62–63).

Up to this point, Reagan did not recognize the shift in Soviet strategy to be sincere, stating that the "Soviet Union cannot be trusted to keep faith with foreign powers" (Garthoff 1994b, 291). Accordingly, in review-ing U.S. behavior before and after the Reykjavik summit, Mendelsohn (1988, 141) writes that "[a] review of the arms control dialogue during the Reagan administration reveals . . . a remarkable series of retrograde U.S. decisions." Secretary of State for Arms Control Paul Nitze judged the Gorbachev effort as "the best Soviet proposal we have received in twenty-five years." Ultimately, the meeting of Gorbachev and Reagan at Reykja-vik was a missed opportunity for an agreement on comprehensive arms reduction and a possible earlier exit from the cold war with all its burdens (Larson 1997, 212; Garthoff 1994a, 293).

Although Gorbachev's initiatives were not reciprocated by Reagan, his "new thinking" policy "made inroads in American public opinion and among the domestic opponents of Reagan's hard-line foreign policy" (Goldstein and Freeman 1990, 122). It was the mounting pressure from this arena that would soon serve as a stimulus for Reagan to reevaluate his stance. Gorbachev impressed the American public, for example, by receiving an unofficial U.S delegation from the Council on Foreign Rela-tions, which afterward concluded that Gorbachev's efforts to bring about change in Soviet-U.S. relations were sincere and impressive. Other stimuli would emanate from appointment of new advisors. In late 1986, the mod-erate Frank Carlucci became national security adviser. In March 1987, William Casey was replaced as director of the CIA by William Webster. One month later Richard Perle left the administration. In October 1987, Caspar Weinberger resigned as secretary of defense. He was replaced by

Carlucci, and Carlucci's assistant, General Colin Powell, became the new national security adviser (Larson 1997, 219).

From here on things would go in a cooperative direction. During 1987, the Soviet Union had begun disengaging from Afghanistan, and the United States initiated various diplomatic exchanges. In July, Reagan had declared that the U.S. objective would be to "break out of the stalemate of the cold war," and in August he ordered the dismantling of seventy-two Pershing missiles in Europe (Garthoff 1994a, 315). In September, the superpowers committed to the establishment of nuclear risk reduction centers in Washington and Moscow, and at the end of the year the two leaders convened for a summit in Washington and signed the INF treaty. A series of further summits with a focus on arms reductions began, and at the Moscow meeting in July 1990, the superpowers concluded Strategic Arms Reduction Talks (START) with a START I agreement. In the meantime, the Berlin Wall, the very symbol of the cold war, was dismantled, followed by the conclusion of the ongoing "two-plus-four" talks about German reunification. Germany would be officially reunified on October 2, 1990, a momentous event signaling the end of the cold war.

CONCLUSIONS

Stalin's death opened opportunities. The new Soviet leadership had strong incentives to settle cold war tensions, and at least for Beria and possibly also Malenkov, this included German reunification under conditions favored by the United States. A similar situation presented itself in 1985. Upon taking the leadership, Gorbachev made various conciliatory gestures and signaled his willingness to engage in considerable concessions. However, until after the Reykjavik summit, Reagan and his advisors failed to diagnose properly Soviet intentions just as Eisenhower and Dulles had failed a generation earlier. What distinguishes the two cases from each other is that Gorbachev was in a position to keep the window of opportunity open longer. Although Reagan made mistakes, ultimately the cold war did end with a favorable outcome (Malici 2006, 2008).

The failure to respond to a foreign policy opportunity is the result of a wrong answer to the *kto-kovo* question. President Eisenhower seems to have felt that there was a historic moment that could be capitalized on by engaging in the exercise of positive sanctions. However, Dulles was able to influence the decision-making process so that Eisenhower's inclinations never became manifest. Dulles had a fundamentally hostile image of the Soviet Union, and he dogmatically held on to this image even in the face of compelling contradictory signals from the Soviet side. The United States never did engage in the exercise of positive sanctions, an omission that foreclosed the possibility of a constructive engagement with the Soviet Union.

In the case of the Gorbachev initiatives in the 1980s, the *kto-kovo* question was initially answered improperly. President Reagan carried a false image of Gorbachev and was blind to signs of cooperation. What impaired a proper answer to the question was his dogmatic belief system and a closed decision-making group. With the exception of George Schultz, the group regarded the Soviets as invariably malevolent, deceitful, and expansionist (Larson 1997, 239). For more than two years Reagan resisted adjusting his hostile beliefs despite plentiful evidence suggesting that the Soviet overtures were sincere. The United States engaged in negative sanctions instead of positive sanctions that could have brought forth an earlier improvement in Soviet-U.S. relations.

One must acknowledge the scholarly disagreement over whether the Soviets would have withdrawn from East Germany in 1953. By hinting at the possibility of German reunification, the Soviet leadership could have been pursuing the Leninist strategy of offering concessions to divide its opponents (Larson 1997, 41). However, there is good reason to assume otherwise, as we have shown above. "After the death of Stalin," Ambassador Bohlen wrote, "there might have been opportunities for an adjustment of some of the outstanding questions, particularly regarding Germany." He acknowledged, "I think I made a mistake in not taking the initiative and recommending . . . a meeting" (Divine 1981, 110; Larson 1997, 61). An early summit could have probed just how far the Soviets were willing to go, and this diplomatic effort may have put the superpowers as well as the entire world on a different trajectory than what followed over the next several decades.

In the case of Reagan and Gorbachev, the course of events ultimately did come to a good end despite Reagan's reassurance failure. There is little or no doubt that Gorbachev was sincere in his conciliatory signaling and cooperative moves. If Reagan had responded earlier to Gorbachev's peace initiatives, the extraordinary U.S. defense budget could have been relieved, forces in Europe could have been reduced earlier, and huge sums of money might have been saved, releasing the American people from great economic burdens (Larson 1997, 215; Leffler 2007, 127–128).

CHAPTER 6

Seeking Gains Too Soon
False Hope Failures

INTRODUCTION

Intuitively, it is easier to see how mistakes of omission rather than mistakes of commission lead to missed opportunities; however, the latter error can also lead to failure. The classic French playwright Moliere warned, "Unreasonable haste is the direct road to error." In this chapter we examine two cases in which U.S. leaders appeared to have ignored this warning. The first case is President Harry Truman's attempt in 1950 to unify Korea by military force and thereby roll back Communism. The second case is President Jimmy Carter's attempt in 1977 to push for a far-reaching arms control agreement with the Soviet Union and thereby work toward friendlier superpower relations. Truman's mistake in the Korean case became evident as the situation unfolded. According to Secretary of State Acheson, "All the President's advisers knew that something was badly wrong" (qtd. in Wainstock 1999, 84). In the arms control case, President Carter acknowledged his mistake after the failure, saying, "Had I known then what I know now about the Soviet Union, I would have approached [arms reductions] differently, in a little bit slower fashion" (qtd. in Kaufman and Kaufman 2006, 50).

THE ATTEMPT AT KOREAN UNIFICATION

In the late 1940s the cold war saw its first violent manifestations. Escalation was marked with a coup in Czechoslovakia in 1948, the Soviet blockade of Berlin in the same year, and the formation of NATO in 1949. The conflict also expanded from a confrontation between the superpowers in the heart of Europe to a global struggle for power between the "free world" and the "communist bloc." These developments changed the meaning of the U.S. containment strategy from George Kennan's concept of using diplomatic, economic, and political instruments of foreign policy to contain the expansion of Soviet power to the Truman administration's concept of using alliances and military force to contain the expansion of Communist regimes around the globe. While the general strategic posture of the United States remained defensive, temptations would arise to use local power imbalances in favor of the United States for offensive purposes.

One such case was Korea. When Russia entered World War II in the Far East in August 1945, Japanese forces surrendered to Soviet troops above the 38th parallel and to U.S. troops below it on the Korean peninsula. A temporary division of Korea then evolved into a more permanent arrangement in the absence of a peace treaty that would establish a national government for Korea. A Soviet-sponsored government assumed power in North Korea under the leadership of Kim Il Sung while in South Korea a U.S.-sponsored government ruled under President Syngman Rhee. In June 1950, the North Korean army escalated the tensions between the two regimes by crossing the 38th parallel. Because the United States already had troops stationed in the region, the president and his advisors would come to view this situation as an opportunity to use force in order to unify the country under a leadership sympathetic to U.S. interests and, more important, to roll back Communism.

Paradoxically, this opportunity presented itself as a result of a previous U.S. mistake of omission resulting in a deterrence failure. The Truman administration's official declaratory policy in East Asia had been to guarantee Japan's security against external attack, but this commitment did not extend to the Korean peninsula. Nor did it extend to Taiwan, where nationalist forces defeated in China had retreated by October 1949. This stance was consistent with a balance-of-power interpretation of the containment strategy, which assumes that Korea and Formosa were not important in defining the balance of power; however, Japan as a defeated great power was significant, along with the great powers of Western Europe, Russia, and China.

This interpretation left open the possibility that the United States would not resist an attempt to unify Korea by the Pyongyang regime. The game on the left side of Figure 6.1 shows North Korea and South Korea in the interim diplomatic arrangement (3,2) as an initial state, which neither Pyongyang nor Seoul accepted regarding the future of the peninsula.

FIGURE 6.1   *North Korean Strategy in the Korean Power Game*

	N. Korea				N. Korea	
	Coop P	Conf N			Coop P	Conf N
Coop P	"3,2"	2,4*		Coop P	"3,2" →	2,4*
S. Korea				S. Korea	↑	↓
Conf N	4,1	1,3		Conf N	4,1 |←	1,3

Korean Power Game (G18)
Intentions: SK, NK (–,–)
Power: SK < NK

North Korea Strategy: Move
Intentions: SK, NK (–,–)
Power: SK < NK

Brams nonmyopic equilibria are in bold, and Nash myopic equilibria are asterisked. The initial state is in quotation marks, and the final outcome is underlined.

It also shows the conflictual inclinations of both players and the power superiority of North Korea over South Korea. The U.S. failure to extend its umbrella of deterrence to include South Korea led North Korean leader Kim Il Sung to calculate correctly that if there was no likelihood of U.S. military intervention, then he could break the diplomatic status quo with Seoul, move from the initial state of (3,2) to (2,4), and unite Korea by force as shown in the right-hand game of Figure 6.1 (DeRivera 1968; Gaddis 2005, 40–46).

On June 25, 1950, North Korean forces invaded the southern part of the peninsula. The news came as a shock to Washington. President Truman (1965, 339) declared, "The attack upon Korea makes it plain beyond all doubt that communism has passed beyond the use of subversion to conquer independent nations and will now use armed invasion and war." Fearing further Communist expansion, the president and his advisers agreed that the invasion must be repulsed. There was from the beginning, in the president's words, an "almost unspoken acceptance on the part of everyone that whatever had to be done to meet this aggression had to be done" (Truman 1956, 334). The administration renounced its prior exclusion of Korea from the defense umbrella and was prepared to take action (Spanier 1959, 30; Higgins 1960, 22).

Subsequently, at the request of the United States, the UN passed two resolutions. The first resolution on June 25 demanded that North Korean troops withdraw behind the 38th parallel. Two days later the international organization requested its members to help repel the aggression so that "peace and security" could be restored "to the area." Notably, the word "area" was left undefined. The Truman administration would come to use the term as meaning all of Korea, as it recognized the situation as an opportunity to eliminate the Pyongyang regime (LaFeber 1974, 78; I. Stone 1969, 109). In its place the U.S.-sponsored South Korean government would be able to establish control over the entire peninsula (Matray 1979, 322). The destruction of the Pyongyang regime would achieve unification, and the United States would also roll back Communism.

A series of U.S. moves followed. On June 27, President Truman ordered the Seventh Fleet to enter the Taiwan Strait. On September 11, he signed a directive for the invasion of North Korea, and less than a month later, U.S. troops did cross the 38th parallel and moved north toward the Yalu River. These actions complicated the strategic situation, directly threatening Chinese interests, and escalated the local power game between the United States and North Korea into a regional power game between the United States and China. With this shift in power games came changes in the distribution of power from an asymmetrical condition favoring the United States in the local game to a symmetrical condition between the players in the regional game (Jian 1996, 125; Christensen 1992, 136, 148; Halberstam 2007, 341).

The nested games in Figure 6.2 show the complexity of the situation on the Korean peninsula in 1950. The strategic situation cannot simply be reduced to a dyad between the United States and North Korea. The local power game shows them in a conflict game (−,−) with the United States clearly more powerful than North Korea (USA > NK). The game shows further that U.S. domination of North Korea (4,2) is both the Nash and the Brams equilibrium for the game—if the conflict is confined to the local Game 18 between the United States and North Korea. Because U.S. actions in moving to this outcome clearly threatened the vital interests of China, however, moving to this final outcome in Game 18 becomes as well a move away from the initial state of (3,3) for the regional conflict Game 32 of a prisoner's dilemma with mutual conflict (−,−) and relative power symmetry (USA = CH) between the United States and China.

FIGURE 6.2   *U.S. and Chinese Escalation Strategies in the Korean War*

Other

		CO CO Regional Local		CF CF Local Regional	
CO Regional		"3,3"	$\mid\leftarrow$		1,4
CO Local			2,3 $\rightarrow$ "1,4"		
United States		$\downarrow$ $\overline{\uparrow}$		$\downarrow$ $\overline{\uparrow}$	
CF Local		<u>4,2</u>* $\leftarrow$ 3,1			
CF Regional		4,1	$\rightarrow$		<u>2,2</u>*

Nested Local and Regional Power Games

Local Game (G18)	Regional Game (G32)
Intentions: USA, NK (–,–)	Intentions: USA, CH (–,–)
Power: USA > NK	Power: USA = CH
U.S. Strategy: Move	Chinese Strategy: Move

Other is North Korea (NK) in local game and China (CH) in regional game. CO = cooperation; CF = conflict. Brams nonmyopic equilibria are underlined, and Nash myopic equilibria are asterisked. The initial state for each game is in quotation marks, and the final outcome is underlined.

To avoid this development, the United States should have limited its military response in the local game, that is, not move beyond the 38th parallel and be content to restore the status quo ante rather than attempt to unify both parts of Korea. Contrary to the prescription from this analysis, the U.S. choice to move toward local domination in Game 18 was implemented as a move toward domination in regional Game 32. This mistake of commission led the China–North Korea tandem to escalate to mutual deadlock (2,2), as shown in Figure 6.2. Although the possibility that the local and regional games were linked was known to U.S. leaders, they were driven by optimism and unwarrantedly convinced that any conflict would be decided in favor of the United States (Johnson 2004, 32–33; Gaddis 2005, 40–47; De Rivera 1968). The ultimate result was a false hope failure.

Our analysis stands apart from the conventional interpretation of this failure, which we find to be somewhat apologetic. It acknowledges that the Chinese Communists did attempt to deter the American crossing, which is also consistent with TOM's theoretical prediction that China should exercise threat power in pre-play communication to deter the United States from moving beyond local domination (4,2) and away from settlement (3,3) in the regional game. However, it also emphasizes there was a lack of direct communication between Beijing and Washington, making their warnings both too weak and too late to reverse U.S. decisions (Christensen 1992, 129, 131; Lebow 1981). We show below that there were plenty of signs that would have warranted reconsideration of the U.S. decision to move beyond the status quo ante. The literature also tends to attribute major responsibility to U.S. Army General Douglas MacArthur as commander of UN forces for the decision to cross the 38th parallel and for the subsequent disaster (Halberstam 2007). Although it is true that the general's judgment and advice to Truman was severely flawed, a review of the record shows that the executive decisions were made in Washington and not in MacArthur's Far Eastern Command Center in Japan.

By 1950, the consensus in the United States was that Communism posed a major threat to U.S. interests. In April 1950, the National Security Council approved NSC-68 as a response to the Soviet possession of the atomic bomb and the victory of Mao's Communist forces in China. This document emphasized that a "more rapid building up of political, economic, and military strength . . . than is now contemplated is the only course which is consistent with progress toward achieving our fundamental purpose." It requested an unprecedented effort in the countering of Communist expansion and proposed a sharp increase in military expenditures and armed forces (Jian 1996, 113). The North Korean incursion into South Korea was an immediate challenge to this doctrine. At the same time it was an opportunity to translate it into action.

Initially, the officially stated objective of the president was to restore the status quo. At a press conference on July 13, Truman gave a hint to the contrary, though, when a reporter asked whether the United States intended to cross the boundary of the 38th parallel. The president responded that he would "make that decision when it becomes necessary to do it" (Truman 1965, 522–524). Ultimately, he would come to regard the core of the containment doctrine to be falling short. His inclination was toward rollback, and this approach would be encouraged from the Senate ranks, where an increasing number of lawmakers argued for going beyond the limits of the policy of containment, a policy that they labeled "negative, futile, and immoral" (Higgins 1960, 52; Jian 1996, 167).

Despite these inclinations, the president's ultimate strategy was not necessarily a foregone conclusion. He was surrounded by two opposing opinions. Director of the Office of Northeast Asian Affairs John Allison was "convinced that there will be no permanent peace and stability in Korea as long as the artificial division at the 38th parallel continues." According to Allison, the United States possessed a moral obligation to destroy the North Korean army and provide for Korea's reunification. The time had come to "be bold" and to "take even more risks than we have already." He concluded that if "a correct solution of the immediate problem is not reached, a correct long term solution will be impossible" (Higgins 1960, 24; Matray 1979, 319, 324; Halberstam 2007, 328; Wainstock 1999, 60).

As a staunch anti-Communist, Secretary of State Dean Acheson also argued strongly for the opportunity to roll back Communism (Jian 1996, 46). In fact, to garner wider consensus for this position, he replaced dissenting China and Asia specialists at the State Department with more hawkish men. One of the victims of this campaign was George Kennan, who, in his own words, was henceforth "on the sidelines" (Halberstam 2007, 95, 193–194, 324–325). The founder and former chief of the State Department's Policy Planning Staff (PPS) had insisted strongly that the only legitimate objective in Korea should be the restoration of prewar boundaries because an advance northward might trigger Soviet or Chinese intervention (Kennan 1967, 487–488; Kennan 1972, 23–24; Matray 1979, 323). If the United States overreached militarily and applied its power where it was not applicable, the troops would "be distinctly at a disadvantage" (Wainstock 1999, 60).

Paul Nitze was Kennan's successor as director of the PPS, and he agreed with Kennan (Halberstam 2007, 324). Along with staffers Herbert Feis and George Butler, Nitze favored restricting the conflict to areas south of the 38th parallel and restoring the status quo ante. In a memorandum dated July 22, the PPS argued that "the risks of bringing on a major conflict with the USSR or China, if UN military action north of the 38th parallel is employed in an effort to reach a 'final' settlement in Korea, appear to outweigh the political advantages that might be gained from such further military action" (Matray 1979, 323). The fear of Soviet or Chinese action was also reinforced by U.S. ambassador in Moscow Alan Kirk, who warned against an overcommitment of U.S. power (Ibid., 323). Similarly, State Department advisor Charles Bohlen called crossing the 38th parallel "folly," since it would increase the risk of "prodding China or the Soviet Union into a war" (Wainstock 1999, 60).

At least initially, the military leadership voiced support for this position. On July 21, the Joint Chiefs of Staff (JCS) submitted a policy paper that warned against any "excessive commitment of U.S. military forces and resources in those areas of operations which would not be decisive" (Matray 1979, 324). Chairman Omar Bradley stated that it would be "the wrong war, at the wrong place, at the wrong time, and with the wrong enemy." He feared that a forceful reunification of Korea would spread the war beyond the limits of Korea to China (Park 1983, 255). Chief of Naval Operations Admiral Forrest Sherman told Secretary of Defense Louis Johnson that "we should get out of the business of fighting on the Asian mainland" (Higgins 1960, 24). Among the opponents to Truman's plans there was a consensus that U.S. power was not applicable and that the answer to the *kto-kovo* question did not favor the United States.

There was good reason for urging restraint. After World War II the United States had supported the Nationalist government under Chiang Kai-shek. When he lost the civil war against the Communist Party led by Mao Zedong, U.S. support contributed to the antagonism between the two capitals (Jian 1996, 94). The relationship would deteriorate further if the United States invaded the northern part of the Korean peninsula and thereby threatened Chinese interests. The Yalu River's generating plant on the Manchurian border just inside Korean territory supplied electrical power for the Manchurian industrialization program, and it was Beijing's "pilot zone" for a China-wide industrial development program (I. Stone 1969, 127). The U.S. presence in Taiwan and its intervention in Korea would signal that the United States had interests in the region as well, which meant that China would be faced by the unacceptable threat of a two-front war (Christensen 1992, 136, 148). Indeed, because of this threat perception, the Communist leadership started in late 1949 to restructure China's military forces (Jian 1996, 94; Spanier 1959; Whiting 1960).

Despite the existence of these realistic considerations, the hawks, driven by optimism and overconfidence, would win the internal strategy debate (D. Johnson 2004). The influential State Department advisor and later secretary of state John Foster Dulles argued that the "38th parallel was never intended to be, and never ought to be, a political line." If the United States would "have the power to do otherwise, it would be folly to go back to the division of Korea at the 38th parallel" (Halberstam 2007, 99; Jian 1996, 166). He argued further, "Since international communism may not be deterred by moral principles backed by *potential* might we must back those principles with military strength-in-being, and do so quickly" (Matray 1979, 318). Assistant Secretary of State Dean Rusk pointed out that the United States must foster the triumph of national self-determination throughout Asia (Matray 1979, 329). U.S. ambassador to the UN Warren Austin said that Korea could no longer remain "half slave and half free" and that "troops could not be expected to march up to a surveyor's line and stop" (Higgins 1960, 24; Wainstock 1999, 60). All agreed that crossing the parallel and unifying Korea would offer the United States a grand opportunity to roll back Communism.

This advocacy was based on a fundamental miscalculation of the Chinese response. On June 28, one day after Truman had dispatched the Seventh Fleet into the Taiwan Strait, Chinese Premier Zhou Enlai called the move a "violent invasion of Chinese territory," which constituted "an open exposure" of "putting into practice the long-prepared [U.S.] plan to invade China and to dominate Asia" (Jian 1996, 131). Although Beijing did not intervene directly at this point, it did so indirectly, and Washington was aware of it. In a formal report to the Security Council on July 25, General MacArthur declared that "the Chinese Communists have furnished substantial, if not decisive, military assistance to North Korea by releasing a vast pool of combat-seasoned troops of Korean ethnic origin, which provided the means for expansion of the North Korean army" (I. Stone 1969, 97). According to MacArthur, "it is apparent that the North

Korean aggressors have available to them resources far in excess of their internal capabilities" (qtd. in I. Stone 1969, 83).

Despite warnings about direct intervention in the future, the general as well as the civilian leadership in Washington remained optimistic that they would succeed. Because of this optimism, an India-engineered proposal, which would restore the status quo ante, was rejected (Halberstam 2007, 326). The optimism would be fueled by McArthur's success in halting the North Korean military advance in August (Halberstam 2007, 323; Matray 1979, 325, 328). The JCS was now also being swayed, as it received a State Department memorandum that argued that if the United States reunified Korea militarily, "the resultant defeat to the Soviet Union and the Communist world will be of momentous significance" (Reynolds 2000, 50). On September 1, the NSC completed a directive allowing MacArthur to move beyond the 38th parallel in pursuit of forcible reunification. On September 7, 1950, the JCS informed Truman of its support for the NSC recommendations (LaFeber 1974, 84).

Although both Kennan and Nitze continued to warn against military action north of the 38th parallel, President Truman signed the directive on September 11 (Matray 1979, 328). The final decision was based on an evaluation of the possible Soviet reaction. Curiously, less concern was felt about China partly because of the belief that Moscow controlled Chinese movements. Also, the Chinese after a long civil war did not seem capable of effectively fighting the power of the United States (Lafeber 1974, 83). On September 10, Acheson had declared, "I should think it would be sheer madness on the part of the Chinese Communists to intervene and see no advantage to them doing it" (McLellan 1968, 20). U.S. leaders were convinced that military victory would be achieved. It proved to be a serious strategic miscalculation.

On September 15, MacArthur's troops landed behind enemy lines at Incheon. As the North Korean army retreated, MacArthur declared that the war would be over shortly and that September 15, 1950, would stand as "a glorious day in American history" (Wainstock 1999, 47; Christensen 1992, 131). On September 29, the newly appointed Secretary of Defense George Marshall informed MacArthur, "We want you to feel unhampered tactically and strategically to proceed north of [the] 38th parallel" (Jian

1996, 168; LaFeber 1974, 84). Contrary to what some of the literature implies, it was the administration in Washington and not MacArthur who made the decision to cross the 38th parallel. When the general proceeded, he "was not violating policy but putting it into effect" (Matray 1979, 329; see also Spanier 1959, 95).

By late September, Chinese warnings had become more explicit. China's Foreign Office repeated that the Chinese would "always stand on the side of the Korean people," that they would not "tolerate seeing their neighbors being savagely invaded by the imperialist," that they would not "sit back with folded hands and let the U.S. come up to their border" (Wainstock 1999, 63; Spanier 1959, 86). These warnings were taken seriously by the media. At the end of September, the *New York Times* wrote that if the 38th parallel was crossed, "the Chinese Communists might well be provoked to action" (I. Stone 1969, 125). By contrast, MacArthur told Truman that the chances of Chinese intervention were "very little" (Spanier 1959, 91).

Voices of restraint continued to emerge. Kennan argued that it was a serious mistake not to stabilize the front at the 38th parallel in the hope of negotiating a settlement (Higgins 1960, 52–53). U.S. Eighth Army Commander General Walker and South Korean Defense Minister Sin Sen Mo also took the Chinese Communist threat seriously and advocated halting the advance (Higgins 1960, 55). There was again good reason for such cautioning. Prior to the Inchon landing, the main battlefield of the war was in South Korea. Even with the Seventh Fleet moving into the Taiwan Strait and the U.S. military intervention in Korea, the safety of the Chinese mainland was not directly threatened. The Inchon landing led to the rapid shift of the primary combat zone from the South toward the North. If MacArthur's troops reached the Yalu River, China's buffer zone in the northeast would be lost. This advance would constitute a major threat to the country's main source of coal, steel, and water power (Jian 1996, 159, 184; Wainstock 1999).

In reaction to MacArthur's northward advance, Mao Zedong instructed the establishment of a "Northeast Border Defense Army," so that "in case we needed to enter the war we would be prepared" (Jian 1996,

136). Already throughout the summer China had increased its troop strength in Manchuria. By the end of July, four armies, three artillery divisions, four air-defense artillery regiments, three truck transport regiments, one tank regiment, one engineer regiment, and one cavalry regiment, with a total of more than 255,000 troops, had taken position on the Chinese-Korean border (Jian 1996, 137). In September, the UN Command estimated Chinese troop strength at 450,000 (Whiting 1960, 118–122). However, neither MacArthur nor the leaders in Washington gave sufficient weight to these numbers (Wainstock 1999, 63).

On October 1, South Korean troops crossed the 38th parallel (Whiting 1960, 93). On the night of October 2, Premier Zhou Enlai sent through the Indian ambassador K.M. Panikkar a message for Washington: "The American forces are trying to cross the 38th parallel and to expand the war. If they really want to do this, we will not sit still without doing anything. We will be forced to intervene" (Jian 1996, 180, 164; Higgins 1960, 55; Christensen 1992, 129). The Washington leadership remained undeterred. Although it knew that large numbers of Chinese troops were moving quickly toward Manchuria, optimism prevailed and was reinforced. On October 12, the CIA reported to the president that, although the Chinese Communists had the capability of effective intervention, such intervention would not necessarily be decisive (Higgins 1960, 55, 59; Spanier 1959, 98; Christensen 1992, 129).

On October 5, MacArthur notified the UN headquarters of "Chinese Communist military units" in Korea (Whiting 1960, 117). Nevertheless, his troops crossed the 38th parallel two days later. A further extension of MacArthur's discretion was made in a directive on October 9. The general was instructed that even if Chinese intervention occurred, he should continue operations "as long as in your judgment, action by forces now under your control offers a reasonable chance of success" (McLellan 1968, 23). On October 20, MacArthur's troops captured the North Korean capital of Pyongyang. The general remained optimistic, declaring publicly, "the war is very definitely coming to an end shortly" (Higgins 1960, 65). On October 24, he authorized his field commanders to use all ground forces at their command in order to capture all of North Korea (McLellan 1968, 24).

As MacArthur launched his "end-the-war" offensive, he reassured the frontline troops that they would be home for Christmas dinner (Whiting 1960, 117). On November 26, however, they met a massive counteroffensive of Chinese volunteers (Christensen 1992, 132). Within two days the advance that had been launched with such high hopes had become a defeat, and within four days a military disaster was ensuing (McLellan 1968, 35; Higgins 1960, 79). MacArthur acknowledged, "We face an entirely new war" (Lowe 1986, 201). On December 26, the Chinese and North Koreans recrossed the 38th parallel, this time going southward (LaFeber 1974, 85).

The United States failed in its attempt to unify Korea and roll back Communism. When the emerging disaster became obvious, MacArthur argued for the use of tactical nuclear weapons on Chinese targets and a further expansion of the Korean War into a Sino-U.S. war on the mainland of China. When he persisted in this advice publically after being rebuffed by Truman, the president dismissed him as commander of U.S. and UN forces. The ensuing military stalemate on the Korean peninsula between Chinese and American forces lasted until the Eisenhower administration came to power in Washington and signed an armistice in 1953, which created an uneasy peace and a continued source of tensions lasting to the present day.

THE SALT II ARMS CONTROL CASE

Following the Korean War, the cold war reached some of its most dangerous heights, with the threat of nuclear war accompanying the Berlin Wall crisis in 1961 and the Cuban Missile Crisis one year later. In subsequent years the United States and the Soviet Union recognized the need for restraints on nuclear weapons. Neither superpower abandoned domination of the other as its highest preference. Instead, the stability of U.S.-Soviet cooperation rested on the U.S. strategic doctrine of détente and the Soviet doctrine of peaceful coexistence, which recognized the desirability of pursuing negotiated settlements on issues of common concern while competing for domination on others with means short of war. This new relationship and rules of superpower engagement and competition was formalized at the 1972 Moscow summit between President Nixon

FIGURE 6.3　*Alternative Superpower Games, 1972–1979*

| | Soviet Union | | | Soviet Union | |
	Coop P	Conf N		Coop P	Conf N
Coop P	"**3,3**"	1,4	Coop P	"**4,4**"	1,2
United States					
Conf N	4,1	2,2*	Conf N	2,1	3,3*

Détente Conflict Game, 1972–1976	**Ideal No-Conflict Game**
Intentions: USA, SU (−,−)	Intentions: USA, SU (+,+)
Power: USA = SU	Power: USA = SU

Brams nonmyopic equilibria are underlined, and Nash equilibria are asterisked. Initial states are in quotation marks, and final outcomes are underlined.

and Secretary-General Brezhnev. While the summit recognized the continued ideological disagreements, it also established an arms control regime to implement the SALT I treaties and guide future negotiations toward a SALT II agreement. In 1974, President Ford and Brezhnev reached a principled agreement on the terms of a SALT II treaty in Vladivostok. It would go further than the future ceilings established by SALT I for different kinds of weapons systems and actually limit them at particular levels upon ratification by both countries.

However, by the winter of 1975 the (3,3) NME for the superpower détente, as shown in Figure 6.3, began to deteriorate. President Ford toughened his verbal assault on Moscow. The CIA revised its estimates of Soviet defense spending significantly upward, and the Congressional Research Service prepared an alarmist assessment of the "U.S.-Soviet military balance" (Caldwell and Dallin 1979, 201). In April 1976, the Soviets warned against U.S. intervention in Lebanon's civil war. In June, the United States criticized the Soviets for beaming microwaves at the U.S. embassy in Moscow and for Soviet actions in Somalia and Angola. Indeed, by this time the relations between the superpowers were more conflictual than cooperative in the eyes of some observers (Caldwell and Dallin 1979, 202; Hyland 1978, 156; Goldstein and Freeman 1990, 49). The SALT II process came to a halt.

It was in this climate that Jimmy Carter assumed the presidency in January 1977. In his campaign, Carter had positioned himself as running against the Washington establishment. He wanted to be as different as possible in style and approach (Garrison 1996, 111). Also notable was his idealism, especially in his foreign policy approach to two issues. Both issues engaged the problem of easing superpower tensions, renewing détente between the United States and the Soviet Union and reaching the no-conflict game between the superpowers, as shown in Figure 6.3. One issue was nuclear arms control and the stalled SALT II negotiations. A mere conclusion of his predecessors' efforts regarding this issue would not be good enough. In his inauguration speech, Carter promised: "We will move this year a step toward the ultimate goal—the elimination of all nuclear weapons from this Earth."

A second fulcrum of Carter's foreign policy agenda was human rights. It would very quickly collide with the general problem of easing tensions between the superpowers and progress on arms control (Carter 1975, 1982; Skidmore 1993; Melanson 1996). In his idealistic naïveté, Carter assumed he could achieve significant arms reductions with Moscow while launching a campaign against Soviet human rights violations. Carter either ignored or was oblivious to the reality that pursuit of the latter issue was inconsistent with the spirit of the détente principles established at the Moscow summit in 1972, which prohibited interference in the other country's internal affairs. He believed his continued vocal agitation on behalf of human rights should have no effect, as he himself did not link it to other aspects of superpower relations. He would be proven wrong.

Carter inherited from his predecessors a prisoner's dilemma situation, depicted as a détente game in Figure 6.3 because of the initial state of (3,3) mutual cooperation. An initial state of mutual cooperation is a Brams NME and can generally be expected to be stable so long as both superpower players use credible threat power to deter a defection to (1,4) by the Soviet Union or to (4,1) by the United States. In order for threat power to be credible, a move to (2,2) deadlock is theoretically necessary if deterrence fails. When regional clients of the two superpowers became embroiled in crises or military conflicts in the third world without the overt involvement of their respective patrons during the Nixon-Ford years, the ambiguity of these situations permitted Washington and Moscow to maintain general détente and stay at (3,3) while exercising a linkage strategy of punishing each other through passive noncooperation on other issues. The major exception to this indirect strategy was during the 1973 Arab-Israeli war, when each superpower exercised threat power by mobilizing some of their conventional military forces and raising the level of alert in their strategic forces before negotiations in Moscow between Kissinger and Kremlin leaders defused their potential military confrontation in the Middle East (Ambrose 1988, 266–292; Ulam 1983, 83–144).

Although these episodes revealed that détente was fragile during the Nixon and Ford administrations, the state of superpower relations did not deteriorate into (2,2) deadlock in the conflict game depicted in Figure 6.3. They continued to make progress on arms control negotiations. In 1974, they reached a mutual understanding of the terms for a SALT II agreement at a summit in Vladivostok between President Ford and Secretary Brezhnev. The framework laid out a ten-year agreement at the conclusion of which SALT III could be pursued. It included an accord on an equal aggregate level (2,400 launchers and heavy bombers) and an equal sublimit for launchers of missiles with MIRVs (1,320). It did not include compensation for or limitation on U.S. forward-based nuclear delivery systems capable of striking the Soviet Union. The United States also possessed more warheads than the Soviet Union. Agreeing on equal aggregate levels for launchers was a major Soviet concession (Moens 1990, 63). Some other aspects of the limitations had been discussed but not yet formally agreed upon and were left out of the aide-memoire (Garthoff 1994a, 496–497; Talbott 1979, 32–36). Therefore, the two leaders did not sign this agreement as a treaty.

If Carter and Brezhnev could conclude the SALT II agreement, it would be a major step toward reaffirming general superpower détente and halting a potential slide into deadlock, which had characterized the equilibrium of Soviet-U.S. relations for most of the pre-détente period in the cold war. The nested game diagram shown in Figure 6.4 is a useful vehicle for analyzing the situation facing the new Carter administration. The relative volatility of the deeds game between the superpowers can be reduced by using promise power to reassure the Soviet Union in the embedded

FIGURE 6.4   *The Strategic Architecture of Soviet-American Détente*

	Soviet Union			
	CO Deeds	CO Words	CF Words	CF Deeds
CO Deeds	"**3,3**"		1,4	
CO Words		"**3,3**" $\mid\!\leftarrow$	1,4	
United States		$\downarrow$	$\uparrow$	
CF Words		4,1 $\rightarrow$	2,2*	
CF Deeds	4,1			2,2*

Words Game	Deeds Game
Intentions: USA, SU (–,–)	Intentions: USA, SU (–,–)
Power: USA = SU	Power: USA = SU

Brams nonmyopic equilibria are in bold. Nash equilibria are asterisked. Initial states are in quotation marks, and final outcomes are underlined. Arrows specify U.S. "stay" strategy in the words game.

words game shown in the center of Figure 6.4, which represents ongoing SALT talks, to supplement the threat power of the United States in the deeds game. In order to avoid defection from (3,3) and ultimately the Pareto-inferior outcome of deadlock (2,2) in the deeds game, the task in the words game is to signal through friendly words as well as deterrent threats a continued commitment to détente. Eventually, this strategy might even transform the détente game into the no-conflict game that Carter desired (Wendt 1999; Malici 2008; Walker 2004b).

Carter mishandled the situation. In his idealism, he wanted "too much/too soon." Not being satisfied with Vladivostok, the terms of his new arms control proposal were formulated so that they would put the Soviet Union at a distinct disadvantage under American dominance, which were not signals of reassurance or promises of future benefits. Simultaneously, he engaged in a continuous criticism of Soviet human rights violations. These actions left the Soviets suspicious of the real U.S. strategy, and a deadlock ensued over both issues. Brezhnev saw Carter's arms control proposals and his human rights assaults as efforts to dominate the Soviet Union rather than as reassurances that détente should continue (Talbott 1979, 60). These precipitous moves by President Carter in the first few months of his term in office, therefore, violated the prescribed strategy

for the United States within the strategic architecture of Soviet-U.S. détente as shown in Figure 6.4.

Even under the assumptions of Carter's idealistic vision of transforming general Soviet-U.S. relations from a détente game to a no-conflict
game, his initiatives regarding SALT II and human rights were inconsistent with the power games for these issue areas. As shown in Figure 6.5,
the U.S. strategic prescription from an initial state of mutual cooperation
is "stay" in each game, but the actual choice of the Carter administration
in both the arms control and human rights games was "move." This strategy in the arms control game led to a false hope failure and a deadlock
(3,3) outcome in the short run, which would take the remainder of Carter's term to overcome. When he left office in 1980, a renegotiated SALT
II treaty was stalled in the U.S. Senate with dismal prospects for ratification (Talbott 1979). The outcome for the "move" strategy in the human
rights game was also a false hope failure. The asymmetrical power relationship in this issue area favored the Soviet Union, and Moscow did not
relax its posture in dealing with human rights advocates in Russian domestic politics.

The analysis in Figure 6.5 shows the logic that explains this sequence
of events. If the Vladisvostok agreement defined a no-conflict game for
concluding the SALT II negotiations, the less risky prescription is for Carter
to choose "stay" at the initial state of (4,4), by refining, signing, and sub-
mitting a SALT II treaty for ratification. The backward induction analysis
in Figure 6.5 does suggest that if he chooses "move" to (2,1), then the
NME remains settlement (4,4) as a final outcome. However, the risk is
that a U.S. attempt to alter the Vladivostok terms might change the dynamics of the arms control game into a prisoner's dilemma game with (2,2)
deadlock as an NME. More generally, this latter outcome is also consistent with the détente game's prediction in Figure 6.4 of (2,2) deadlock as
an NME if Carter chooses to "move" Soviet-U.S. relations from an initial
state of mutual cooperation.

Therefore, the question is how tightly linked was the general détente
game with the SALT game and the human rights game? If they are not
tightly linked, a repeated play of the no-conflict SALT game from a new

FIGURE 6.5   *U.S. Strategies in Soviet-American Relations in the Carter Administration*

Soviet Union

	CO General	CO SALT	CO Hum. Rts.	CF Hum. Rts.	CF SALT	CF General
CO General	"3,3"		|←			1,4
CO SALT		"4,4"	←		1,2	
CO Hum. Rts.			"3,2" |← 2,4*			
United States	↓	↓	↓	↑	↑	↑
CF Hum. Rts.			4,1 → 1,3			
CF Arms Control		2,1		→	3,3*	
CF General	4,1			→		2,2*

General (G32)
Intentions: USA,SU (−,−)
Power: USA = SU
U.S. Strategy: Stay

Arms Control (No-Conflict)
Intentions: USA, SU (+,+)
Power: USA = SU
U.S. Strategy: Stay

Human Rights (G18)
Intentions: USA, SU (−,−)
Power: USA < SU
U.S. Strategy: Stay

Brams nonmyopic equilibria are underlined, and Nash myopic equilibria are asterisked. The initial state for each game is in quotation marks, and the final outcome is underlined.

initial state of (3,3) generates the theoretical prediction that the players will return to (4,4) settlement as the final outcome. However, the terms of détente at the Moscow summit in 1972 included an understanding that each party would not interfere in the other's domestic affairs. By criticizing the human rights record of the Soviet regime and meeting with Soviet dissidents, Carter chose as well to "move" from (3,2) to (4,1) in the human rights game in Figure 6.5, which leads theoretically to (2,4) as a final outcome. If these two games are tightly linked to the general détente game, a U.S. decision to choose "move" from an initial state of mutual cooperation in one or both of them may lead to deadlock as a final outcome in the general détente game. What is the evidence to support, modify, or refute the results of these alternative theoretical analyses?

Initially, Carter seemed to be fully committed to the Ford-Brezhnev inheritance. During his campaign in 1976, the Democratic Party arms control specialist Averell Harriman had visited Moscow and met with Brezhnev. Carter had instructed Harriman to inform Brezhnev that if elected Carter would move quickly to sign a SALT II agreement based on the Vladivostok accord (Talbott 1979, 39). This would have been welcomed by the Soviets. In a speech on the eve of Carter's inauguration, Brezhnev stressed the Soviets' readiness to go further with arms limitations and reductions but emphasized that first it would be necessary to "consolidate what has already been achieved" on the basis of the Vladivostok accord. In what later turned out to be an anticipatory move, the Secretary-General also warned that new approaches would "only further complicate and delay the solution to the problem" (Garthoff 1994a, 884).

Carter's campaign against Soviet human rights violations began during his time as president-elect. Shortly after his election, he sent a letter of support to Vladimir Slepak, who had been a member of the Moscow Helsinki Group. The group was named after the 1975 Helsinki accord and was charged with monitoring Soviet compliance with the human rights passages of the accords. At the end of the year, the secretary of state designate Cyrus Vance received the exiled Soviet dissident Andrei Amalrik, who urged the incoming administration to do more toward democratization in the Soviet Union (Garthoff 1994a, 629). On January 26, the State Department accused Czechoslovakia, a Soviet satellite state, of violating human rights and harassing advocates. One day later the department praised Soviet dissident Andrei Sakharov and warned that any attempts to intimidate him would "conflict with accepted international standards in the field of human rights" (Garthoff 1994a, 629).

Carter's emphasis on human rights was a departure from the practice of previous administrations. In the realm of arms control, he would also aim at being distinctive. Although he initially displayed a commitment to his predecessors' achievements, by the time he was in the Oval Office it was evident that he found the Vladivostok principles unsatisfactory. As he had hinted in his inauguration, he wanted more. Supportive of his ambitions, although for different motives, was National Security Advisor Zbigniew Brzezinski. Carter was an idealist and Brzezinski a realist. The latter was greatly mistrustful of Soviet motives, and the East-West competition was impossible to resolve in his view (Brzezinski 1983, 146–147; Talbott 1979, 50). Brzezinski saw abandoning the Vladivostok terms and restarting the negotiations completely anew "as an opportunity to halt or reduce the momentum of Soviet buildup" while preserving a U.S. advantage (Brzezinski 1983, 146; Garrison 2001, 776).

Brzezinski's position was also advocated by Secretary of Defense Harold Brown and his associate and deputy director of the NSC, David Aaron. Since the SALT talks affected the programs of the Defense Department more than those of any other government agency, Brown naturally had considerable influence. In the coming weeks, Brzezinski, Brown, and Aaron would represent a cohesive troika. All of them agreed that the United States should maintain and even advance a favorable balance of power for itself. SALT II was the vehicle to do so (Talbott 1979, 50–51; Brzezinski 1983, 146). The counterforce to this troika was Secretary of State Vance. The moderate secretary would find support in Paul Warnke, who was the head of the Arms Control and Disarmament Agency and would very soon be named the chief SALT negotiator. Vance and Warnke believed that the danger to the United States came not so much from the Soviet Union per se. Rather it was situated in the arms race of the superpowers, as this created a cycle of mutual suspicion that could go awry at any time. The task was to build confidence, and a remedy was to be found in an agreement for its own sake, "without excessive concern over which side got the better of the other in the negotiation" (G. Smith 1986, 74–75).

About their common position against Brzezinski, Warnke said that the NSC advisor "did not have the same zeal in pursuing arms control that Vance or I had. . . . Zbig did not like the Russians . . . and I think he was strongly affected by that" (Garrison 1996, 134). Vance and Warnke were more willing to trust Soviet intentions, emphasizing the need to move beyond cold war politics (Garrison 2001, 776). Vance believed that a stable relationship between the United States and the Soviet Union "would pave the way for a wider U.S.-Soviet accommodation" and "help to create an international climate favorable to our other foreign policy objectives" (Brzezinski 1983, 146; Garrison 2001, 787). According to Vance, "We thought it was preferable to go in substantially where the Ford administration had left off." They had, in their own words, "strong doubts that the comprehensive approach could succeed." It was a "long shot" (Vance 1983, 48–49).

In influencing the president toward a more comprehensive approach, Brzezinski had structural and personal advantages. He was the chair of the Special Coordinating Committee (SCC), an interagency cabinet-level body of the NSC working on crisis situations and SALT discussions (Talbott 1979, 54). After the discussions it was Brzezinski's staff that prepared the summaries of the SCC meetings, which together with an attached memo by Brzezinski on his analysis and preferences went to the president (Garrison 1996, 129; Garrison 2001, 780). To Vance, "This meant that the national security advisor had the power to interpret the thrust of discussion or frame the policy recommendations of department principals" (Vance 1983, 37). Brzezinski also shared a personal history with Carter, as he had served previously on the Trilateral Commission with the president and as his campaign advisor. Especially regarding foreign policy, Carter valued how Brzezinski could make complex things seem simple (Garrison 2001, 780).

Carter's inclinations were strengthened further by strong urgings from Congress. The president's choice of Warnke as the chief SALT negotiator was incongruous, because the latter was known to favor only incremental steps in arms control. Warnke's Senate confirmation process had proven to be very daunting, demonstrating the difficulties the administration would face in ratifying an agreement that did not reach far enough (Vance 1983, 51). Also a challenge was Senator Henry Jackson, the chair of the Senate subcommittee on arms control and international security. He spoke for a significant number of like-minded colleagues when he sent the president a memorandum, urging him not to "unnecessarily assume the burden of past mistakes" by simply picking up where Ford and Kissinger had left off. He and other conservative senators opposed Vladivostok and called for deep cuts on the Soviet side (Talbott 1979, 52; Garthoff 1994a, 887; Moens 1990, 68).

Meanwhile, Carter engaged in his first personal correspondence with Brezhnev. In a letter on January 26, he stated that his goal was "to improve relations with the Soviet Union on the basis of reciprocity, mutual respect and benefit." The president expressed hope that early progress in relations could be reached through a quick SALT II accord, but he also pointed to the urgency of proceeding quickly to "additional limitations and reductions in strategic weapons" (Garthoff 1994a, 635, 885; Garrison 1996, 113–114). Brezhnev responded on February 4 to what he perceived as a "constructive and encouraging letter." He insisted on proceeding quickly with the SALT agreement based on the Vladivostok accord and concluded: "Successful completion of this extremely important and necessary matter would allow [us] to directly proceed to more far-reaching measures in this area and would undoubtedly give a new impetus to [the] constructive development of Soviet-American relations on the whole" (Garrison 1996, 113).

Despite Brezhnev's insistence on the Vladivostok principles, on February 14 Carter sent a second letter in which he left open the options of either a quick agreement or a more "comprehensive" one. He provided a few specifications for the latter, such as setting apart the cruise missile and backfire bomber issues. Brezhnev responded on February 25. This time he was significantly less amenable, calling Carter's proposal "lofty," "one-sided," and "deliberately unacceptable." He made clear again that any agreement on SALT had to be based on the terms negotiated at Vladivostok. He denounced Carter's emphasis on human rights as an intrusive interference in Soviet internal affairs with "pseudo-humanitarian slogans." He added, "We would not like to have our patience tested in any matters of international policy, including the question of Soviet-American relations" (Garthoff 1994a, 625, 885; Garrison 2001, 785; Carter 1982, 218; Brzezinski 1983, 155).

The administration's criticism on alleged Soviet human rights violations had indeed been ongoing. On February 7, the State Department protested the arrest of Soviet dissident Aleksandr Ginzburg for channeling monies to a fund for imprisoned dissidents. On February 10, the State Department criticized the arrest of Yury Orlov as the head of the Moscow Helsinki Group. On February 17, Sakharov received a letter of support directly from Carter (Garthoff 1994a, 629). Although Carter seemed sincere in his pursuit of human rights as a fundamental goal, Brzezinski was more instrumental in his support, pressing the issue as a means to an end. He saw an "opportunity to put the Soviet Union on the defensive ideologically" (Dobrynin 1995, 135; Brzezinski 1983, 146–156; Vance 1983, 46). Indeed, Ambassador Dobrynin complained to the State Department that Moscow felt singled out. In the days leading up to Vance's trip to Moscow in March, Carter and his advisors ignored indications that this approach would lead to a confrontation (Garrison 2001, 785).

In early March, the SCC-instructed working groups generated various options for the SALT II negotiations. The principal authors were the director of politico-military affairs of the State Department Leslie Gelb, the NSC aide for the Soviet Union William Hyland, and the deputy assistant secretary for international security affairs at the Defense Department Walter Slocombe. All of the formulated options were in reference to the already existing Vladivostok accords (Talbott 1979, 47). Brzezinski, Harold Brown, and Deputy Director of the NSC David Aaron were not satisfied with the range of options (Moens 1990, 67). Aaron remarked that "the options ginned up by the working level symbolize how rarefied this whole process has become and how we're in danger of losing sight of where we want to go in SALT" (Talbott 1979, 51). Brown considered accepting what had been negotiated by Kissinger to be a "big mistake" (Moens 1990, 68). Together the troika agreed it should be rejected because it did not advance the strategic posture of the United States (Ibid., 68).

Ultimately, this troika was able to frame the proposal in terms that appealed to the president's own motivations (Garrison 2001, 788). Carter decided to disown the 1974 framework agreement and pursue a more ambitious and far-reaching SALT II agreement, dubbed "Deep Cuts" (Dumbrell 1997, 43). Although the proposal carried some creditable arms control purposes, the substantial and deeper reductions were all on the Soviet side. The Soviet Union was to cut its first-line active forces by 400–600 units, its planned ICBMs with MIRVs by 400–500, and its large ICBMs from 308 to 150. The United States would cut only up to 100 of its first-line active forces, none of its ICBMs with MIRVs, and none of its large ICBMs (although it would forgo the development of its future MX

ICBM system). Remarkably, the proposal did not even consider any forward-based-systems (FBS) cuts in Europe, a significant component of U.S. nuclear capabilities (Garthoff 1994a, 889–890).

When the terms of the proposal became known in government circles, Paul Warnke, his deputy Ralph Earle, and his principal technical expert James Timbie were surprised by its starkness. The principal actors on the SSC working group, as well as professional diplomats and other Soviet affairs experts at the State Department, were also skeptical (Talbott 1979, 64). Among them there was widespread agreement that the United States should conclude an agreement based on the Vladivostok accords and then pursue deeper reductions in SALT III (Talbott 1979, 43, 63; Moens 1990, 71). Slocombe thought that the Soviets would not only say "no" but "hell no!" However, nobody vigorously opposed the plan. Vance and Varnke did succeed in getting Carter to agree that a second approach also be offered—one that set aside for the time being the contentious Backfire and cruise missile issues (Garthoff 1994a, 887; Moens 1990, 79; Vance 1983, 49–52).

The administration's human rights campaign continued in the meantime. On March 1, President Carter received dissident exile Vladimir Bukovsky at the White House, telling him that his administration's commitment to human rights was "permanent" (Garthoff 1994a, 629). Brezhnev continued to feel provoked and in a series of speeches strongly protested the internal interference (Talbott 1979, 64). Carter did not realize that his activities in this area had direct negative consequences on the pursuit of his arms control ambitions. On March 4, the president wrote a letter to Brezhnev with a renewed call for deep cuts, noting that "no final agreement was ever reached at Vladivostok." He urged the Soviets to seek with him "a longer-term objective toward which we can progressively move." When Brezhnev responded on March 15, he made clear that any attempt to conclude an agreement on the basis of some "artificially simplified version" would not expedite an arms control agreement (Garrison 1996, 115).

On March 21, Secretary of State Vance arranged to brief Ambassador Dobrynin at the State Department. The ambassador's reaction to Deep Cuts was negative and, according to Vance, reflected "the hardening mood in Moscow" (Vance 1983, 52). Dobrynin complained to Vance that the proposal had little to do with the Vladivostok accords (Talbott 1979, 64–65). Dobrynin also noted the one-sidedness of the proposal favoring the United States. He later recalled, "After I heard what Vance had to say, I told him . . . none of these American proposals give a real basis for achieving a mutually acceptable agreement in Moscow. . . . The fact that [the] American side is striving . . . toward a one-sided advantage, is completely obvious" (Garrison 1996, 117).

A Soviet rejection seemed certain. Nevertheless on March 17, President Carter stated publicly the objectives of his approach on SALT in his address to the UN General Assembly (Garthoff 1994a, 888). This step was a fundamental diplomatic snafu, and government officials were shocked. Until now, both sides in public statements had adhered to the confidentiality of the negotiations. President Carter's "openness" violated that canon of the SALT process and according to Vance (1983, 53) may have heightened Moscow's suspicions of the United States' intentions. The only praise came from Senator Jackson, who publicly lauded Carter's move as "a step in the right direction—away from what he saw as the folly of the Kissinger-Nixon-Ford approach" (Talbott 1979, 66).

On March 27, Vance arrived in Moscow together with Warnke and the U.S. delegation. Perhaps in anticipation of what was to come, just before his departure he lowered expectations as he informed the press that the talks would be merely "exploratory" (Talbott 1979, 68). The talks got off to a bad start. At their very first meeting, Brezhnev objected to the continuing American "interference" in internal Soviet affairs over human rights (Garthoff 1994a, 633). He also made clear that the constructive development of relations would be impossible if the United States did not respect "the principles of equality, noninterference in each other's internal affairs and mutual benefit" on which détente was based (Talbott 1979, 69–70).

To Brezhnev and his advisors as well as to any outside observer, it was very evident that the required reductions fell almost entirely on the Soviet side. Almost all major cutbacks would be in weapons categories in which the Soviets held an edge; there would be few restrictions on systems in which the United States had the advantage (Kaufman and Kaufman 2006, 49–50; G. Smith 1986, 76). Brezhnev called the proposal "unconstructive and one-sided" and "harmful to Soviet security" (Vance 1983, 54; Garthoff 1994a, 890). The Soviets saw the second U.S. proposal—to defer the disputed issues and proceed with an early agreement—also a step back from the U.S. position of early 1976. Nor did they regard it as equitable. Although it would allow Backfire, it would also allow American land- and sea-based cruise missiles—a potentially massive reinforcement of the FBS weaponry. The Soviets rejected the second U.S. proposal as well (Garthoff 1994a, 891).

After the failed meetings, Vance held a press conference, saying that "the Soviets told us that they had examined our two proposals and did not find either acceptable" (Garthoff 1994a, 892; Talbott 1979, 74). Shortly afterward, Soviet Foreign Minister Andrei Gromyko also held a press conference in which he denounced the U.S. position. He accused Carter of abandoning Vladivostok, seeking a public opinion victory, and proposing a deliberately unacceptable set of proposals—in his own strong words, "a cheap and shady maneuver to give the U.S. an edge in nuclear strength" (Garrison 1996, 118). Vance's remarks, followed by Gromyko's denunciation, created gloom and crisis shortly afterward in the relationship between the superpowers (Ibid., 118).

Meanwhile, in the United States Brzezinski also gave a press conference, in which he strongly defended Deep Cuts. Vance disagreed shortly after his return to Washington. He was asked whether the whole venture had been a mistake. He replied, "No one can say that one never makes any miscalculation" (Talbott 1979, 76–77). The American press also described the Carter administration as mistaken. It had tried to change the rules and make sweeping changes. It was "self-indulgent and irresponsible" (Garrison 1996, 119). The failure in Moscow, it seemed, had been inevitable, and there were plenty of indicators for this outcome (Moens 1990, 79–80). President Carter himself eventually also recognized his mistake, saying that the Soviets had rejected his initiative, because "it [was] so substantive and such a radical change from the past" (Talbott 1979, 76).

In 1977 it appeared that there was an opportunity to stabilize arms control relationships and to reaffirm the deteriorating détente relationship between the two superpowers. Carter failed to capitalize on it. A SALT II treaty that was much modified and altered more than Carter had desired was eventually signed by Carter and Brezhnev in Vienna in June 1979. By this time, however, suspicions of Soviet intentions among Republican and conservative Democrats had overtaken those harbored by the administration. Senator Henry Jackson condemned the Vienna agreement as "appeasement in its purest form," comparing it to Neville Chamberlain's 1938 Munich agreement with Hitler. The SALT II agreements stalled in the U.S. Senate, where they would remain for the last year of the Carter administration while the Soviet Union's invasion of Afghanistan torpedoed détente between Washington and Moscow. A new cold war would begin in earnest with the election of President Ronald Reagan, who took office in 1981.

CONCLUSIONS

President Truman made the decision to cross the 38th parallel as he perceived two interconnected opportunities that prevented him from being satisfied with restoration of the status quo ante. One opportunity was reunifying Korea under a government allied with the United States. The second, more important opportunity was a chance to "roll back" Communism (Matray 1979, 314–315, 333). More than three decades later President Carter saw his opportunity to redefine the superpower relationship. The stalled SALT II agreement stood at the center of this opportunity. Concluding the "unfinished business" of the Nixon and Ford administrations would have been a success, but it did not go far enough for Carter (Garthoff 1994a, 886). Both presidents failed.

One of the main assertions in this book is that foreign policy mistakes are the result of false or inaccurate answers to the power politics question of *kto-kovo*. In the cases of Presidents Truman and Carter, we find that it was a certain naïveté, an overambition to make gains and a false sense of optimism in the ability to control outcomes that led to a false answer. These factors were compounded by advisors giving bad advice. Too much optimism hinders giving proper answers to this question, as it mutes critical consideration relating the desired strategic outcomes to the exercise of power necessary to achieve them.

The Chinese leadership warned in word and deed against a northward advance of U.S. troops. Truman and his advisors knew well that the

Chinese had massed 300,000 troops in Manchuria (Spanier 1959, 93). Nevertheless, they were confident that a decisive victory was within easy grasp. The assumption of victory appeared to rest on a belief in the ability and resolve to fight a land war on the mainland of Asia, an assumption that violated the recent lessons learned from Japan's failed attempt to conquer China by invading it in the 1930s. It is a prime example of a U.S. propensity to believe in the omnipotence of its power (Brogan 1952; Fulbright 1966). The decision to cross the 38th parallel was a horrendous miscalculation, and a monumental false-hope failure was visited on the American people.

In the case of President Carter's Deep Cuts approach to arms control, he ignored the cardinal rule of superpower relations as a tit-for-tat pattern of interactions, that is, an equal give and take. Carter's efforts were understood as an attempt to impose new rules on the superpower game. In effect, the Soviet Union would give considerably more than the United States. Moscow's rejection was foreseeable (Moens 1990, 81).

If Truman's decision to cross the 38th parallel and move northward and Carter's pursuit of "deep cuts" were mistakes, it is important to ask what alternative outcomes may have looked like. In the Korean case it is difficult to imagine how any alternative outcome could be worse than the actual one. Truman's decision led to one of the bloodiest wars in modern history. The vast majority of the 54,000 U.S. casualties occurred after crossing the 38th parallel. Overall, more than one million Chinese and Korean troops as well as civilians gave their lives in the ensuing three years of intense fighting (LaFeber 1974, 85, 86). Afterward came an armistice and establishment of a demilitarized zone separating the South from the North. Ironically, this zone remains among the most militarized areas in the world. North Korea has since become an outcast in international life and today is described as a rogue state.

In the case of Carter's Deep Cuts, it is plausible to assume that the conclusion of SALT II based on the Vladivostok accords may have led to a renewal of détente. The consequences of the failure became evident when new issues arose in subsequent years and could not be resolved. Instead of reaching any improvement in relations, President Carter faced an "arc of crisis" stretching from the Horn of Africa into the Middle East in the form of Cuban military assistance in Somalia and Soviet military intervention in Afghanistan. The Carter administration chose economic sanctions and said, via the Carter Doctrine, that the United States would resist any further use of Soviet military force in the Middle East. This stalemate continued through the end of the Carter administration into a new cold war during the first term of the Reagan administration.

PART IV

Maximizing Rationality and Minimizing Mistakes

CHAPTER 7

Foreign Policy Analysis
Maximizing Rationality

INTRODUCTION

A few years ago researchers in computer science at the University of Alberta reported that they had "solved" checkers, a two-person game of strategic interaction (Schaeffer et al. 2007). They developed a program that cannot lose, achieving "at least a draw against any opponent, playing either the black or white pieces," once ten or fewer pieces are left on the board. Starting at the end of a game with only one piece on the board, the researchers examined every possible position from two pieces up to ten pieces on the board. Their computer program, "Chinook," can calculate all 39 trillion positions for the endgame with every combination of ten checkers. Jonathan Schaeffer, chair of the Computer Science Department at the University of Alberta, explained in the *Arizona Daily Sun* on July 20, 2007, "It does not matter how the players make it to 10 checkers left because from that point on, the computer cannot lose. . . . For two players who never make a mistake, every game would be a draw." He goes on to draw a distinction between two approaches, rules of thumb or precise calculations, in solving games and making decisions:

The important thing is the approach. . . . In the past, game-playing programs have used rules of thumb—which are right most of the time—to make decisions. Clearly . . . the world is not going to be revolutionized by this . . . [but] . . . What we've done is show that you can take nontrivial problems, very large problems, and you can do the same kind of reasoning [to make decisions] with perfection. There is no error in the Chinook result. . . . Every decision point is 100 percent.

Schaeffer concludes with some cautionary notes, "Checkers has roughly the square root of the number of positions in chess," pointing out that chess computer programs still rely on rules of thumb because of the computing power necessary to employ such precise calculations. Also, the Chinook checkers solution took eighteen years to achieve and is only a "weak solution," unlike a "strong solution" that would calculate every position from the beginning of a game. There is not currently enough computer power available to calculate either of these precise solutions for the more complex game of chess (Schaeffer et al. 2007, 1522).

In this book we have used the method of backward induction to make calculations and reason backward from the final state of a two-player sequential game of strategic interaction. Steven Brams's (1994) theory of moves (TOM) for such 2×2 games of choosing between two alternating positions (move or stay) by each player exceeds the precision of Chinook's solutions for checkers, specifying strong solutions rather than weak solutions for all seventy-eight possible games that follow TOM's rules of play under the assumption of two-sided information. Brams calculates every position from the beginning to the end of each of these games rather than employing either rules of thumb or relatively weak solutions from intermediate states within a game rather than from its initial state of play. His TOM is also dynamic in the sense that it solves games under the condition of repeated plays of the same game over time (Brams 1994).

In the past few chapters we have explored the diagnostic power of TOM in identifying different types of foreign policy mistakes and inferred what decisions should have been made to avoid them. Such diagnostic and prescriptive knowledge is more than just hindsight, which is often "20/20." However, it does not match the foresight of Chinook, which can anticipate and reproduce the game of checkers in every detail and supply at least weak solutions applicable to that game. Alas, the level of precision offered by TOM for a relatively simple game of only four moves between initial and final states is still not enough to insure that players who apply it to foreign policy decisions in strategic interaction episodes will easily avoid mistakes. Some players will continue to choose "move" when they should have chosen "stay," and vice versa, leading to substantive foreign policy failures following from these procedural errors.

Even a game model like TOM with strong solutions cannot always be applied with the same degree of precision to past, present, or future strategic games in world politics. It can actually be misleading to infer lessons from counterfactual assumptions that accompany TOM's application to the hypothetical world of the future. It is also unrealistic to assume that the rules of play in the artificial world of the theory always apply in the empirical world of the past. There are too many player biases and externalities in the form of actions by other actors playing parallel games in world politics, which can influence the dynamics and outcomes of any single game between two players.

In this chapter we explore the immediate consequences of these troubling possibilities and their implications for making foreign policy decisions and avoiding or reversing procedural mistakes leading to substantive failures. We contend that it is necessary ultimately to rely on rules of thumb as rough approximations to diagnose foreign policy problems and correct or avoid foreign policy mistakes. If this claim is true, then the issue becomes how to select among different rules of thumb as more or less effective solutions. We shall argue that TOM as applied to power games of strategic interaction in world politics is superior to the major alternative rules of thumb, as it can entail the positive features of its competitors plus redress some of their negative attributes. It is a more sophisticated version of older solutions in diagnosing situations and prescribing decisions and raises the likelihood of avoiding or at least minimizing foreign policy failures.

FIXING AND AVOIDING FOREIGN POLICY MISTAKES

How can foreign policy mistakes be mitigated or avoided? We have argued that the minimal standard for diagnosing mistakes is whether a decision is a rational choice, "a choice that leads to a preferred outcome, based on a player's goals" (Brams 1994, 226). If a decision does not meet this criterion, it is a mistake when the decision maker (player) misdiagnoses the context for choice and/or prescribes a choice that does not lead logically to a preferred outcome.[1] We have stipulated that there are only four general political outcomes, settlement, deadlock, domination, and submission, arising from the general definition of politics as a social process of "authoritative allocation of values" (Easton 1953) or the process of determining "who gets what, when, and how" (Lasswell 1958), which reflect the assumptions that politics is about *kto-kovo* or "who (dominates) whom" (Leites 1953) and that "international politics, like all politics, is a struggle for power" (Morgenthau 1985). The four outcomes of settlement, deadlock, domination, or submission refer to the configuration of outcomes between self and other as each exercises power to allocate values between them (Snyder and Diesing 1977). The exercise of power refers to the exercise of positive (appeal, promise, reward) or negative (oppose, threaten, punish) sanctions by self and other in a strategic interaction process leading to one of these four outcomes (Dahl 1957; Baldwin 1971, 1978, 1980; Snyder and Diesing 1977; Lake and Powell 1999).

These perspectives on politics, power, and rationality entail a conceptualization of mistakes as strategic errors. These errors lead to suboptimal outcomes among the four possible outcomes as self and other exercise power toward one another in the form of positive and negative sanctions. This analysis presupposes that self and other can rank the outcomes from most to least preferred as goals, which allows an outside observer to calculate whether the choices they make lead to preferred outcomes for each player. The solution to this calculation inevitably is a function of what each player's choice is as well as how each player ranks the outcomes.

This inevitability leads us to disagree with Baldwin's (2000, 178) dictum regarding foreign policy success and failure: "If strategic interaction affects all techniques equally, it has no relevance to the policy maker trying to choose among them." Here we simply illustrate in Figure 7.1 the truth of our statement about the criterion of strategic rationality with the 2×2 game in which each player (self and other) has two choices: Cooperate P (use positive sanctions in the exercise of power) or Conflict N (use negative sanctions in the exercise of power). The intersection of these choices leads to the four outcomes of domination, submission, deadlock, and settlement, which each player ranks from highest (4) to lowest (1). This game illustrates several points about foreign policy mistakes and the application of purposefulness, mindfulness, and empathy as alternative rules of thumb to meet the rational choice criterion.

First, if self and other are purposeful (i.e., goal oriented) and choose Cooperate P or Conflict N solely on the basis of their most preferred outcome without regard to what choice the other player makes, then self will choose P and other will choose N, and the outcome (1,4) will be the least

FIGURE 7.1 *Different Equilibria as Strategic Rationality Solutions*

	Other			Other	
	Coop P	Conf N		Coop P	Conf N
Coop P	**4,3**	1,4	Coop P	Mutual Settlement	Self Submits/ Other Dominates
Self			Self		
Conf N	2,1	3,2*	Conf N	Self Dominates/ Other Submits	Mutual Deadlock

Nash myopic equilibrium is asterisked, and Pareto-optimal, Brams nonmyopic equilibrium is in bold.

preferred one for self and the most preferred one for other. Clearly, it is a mistake to prescribe a choice based solely on one's highest-ranked preference. Second, if self and other are mindful (i.e., means oriented) and choose P or N on the basis of avoiding one's least preferred outcome, then both self and other will choose N, leading to a (3,2) deadlock outcome in which (a) neither one gets their most preferred outcome, and (b) both are worse off than if both had chosen P for a (4,3) settlement outcome. In order to avoid a suboptimal rational choice and achieve an outcome that is better for both players, therefore, it is desirable for each player to be empathetic (i.e., other oriented) and to take into account the preference rankings of the other player in making an optimal rational choice.[2] However, doing so requires accurate information about the other player's preference rankings. The risk exists of a misdiagnosis and a prescription for choosing Cooperation P or Conflict N, which results in a suboptimal outcome for one or both players.

This requirement has made the criterion of rationality more difficult to implement in practice (Simon 1957; Fiske and Taylor 1991; Geva and Mintz 1997). However, we do not reject it here and instead suggest remedial strategies below for using it in the face of these obstacles. Decision makers are likely to follow the rationality criterion within the external and internal boundaries set by the availability of accurate information and the limitations of the human mind in processing whatever information is available (Mintz 2004; Lake and Powell 1999). Even the "bounded rationality" notion, in which decision makers make choices based on their beliefs and biases, can still be a process employing self and other attributions and inferences about preferences based on beliefs and biases. Although recognizing and acknowledging that beliefs and their implications may not be true is reason for caution, it is not a counsel for despair unless there are no solutions for avoiding or mitigating mistakes based on diagnostic and prescriptive errors. Therefore, we next discuss some general solutions for avoiding foreign policy mistakes, which fall into four basic categories: moral/ethical solutions, generic design solutions, actor-specific solutions, and theoretical solutions.

Moral/ethical solutions involve steps to insure that leaders are held accountable for their decisions, especially if they violate laws or societal norms. Democratic political theory prescribes that leaders who desire to remain in office must stand for election at regular intervals and run on their records. Democratic leaders who have made mistakes are presumably more vulnerable to removal from office and, therefore, may be less likely to make risky or illicit decisions for war leading to foreign policy failures. Empirically, there is some support for this view in the democratic peace literature, although the scope of this generalization does not appear to extend to other kinds of public policy failures (Maoz 1998; Russett and Starr 2000; Bueno de Mesquita et al. 2003). However, it still appears that decision makers who are accountable to others do tend to think more deeply about alternative diagnoses and prescriptions in processing information leading to policy decisions (Tetlock 1983).

Generic design solutions prescribe institutional arrangements that do not emphasize accountability as much as efficiency in processing information and advice within different historical or organizational contexts. For example, students of the U.S. presidency offer solutions in the form of different presidential advisory systems designed to prevent various organizational pathologies, such as the groupthink syndrome or the risky shift syndrome (George 1972; The 9/11 Commission 2004). The precise configuration of these solutions depends on the particular type of regime and the corresponding pathologies associated with it (Roeder 1984; M. Hermann and Hermann 1989; M. Hermann 2001). The distinguishing characteristic of this solution is a focus on the setting in which decisions are made rather than on who makes the decisions.

Actor-specific solutions emphasize the importance of selecting competent and experienced leaders whose expertise raises the likelihood of avoiding mistakes in diagnosis and prescription. However, it is unclear whether experts are really better than novices in diagnosing what is going to happen in politics. Tetlock (2005) has found that experts also make mistakes about diagnosing the future, and the greater the reputation of the experts, the more likely they are to be mistaken. These sobering results suggest that even experts should be cautious and pragmatic rather than ambitious and dogmatic in making diagnoses. Tetlock advocates listening to foxes rather than hedgehogs, the distinction made by Isaiah Berlin between those who know a little about a lot (foxes) and those who know a lot about a little (hedgehogs). The former are more aware of the limitations of their knowledge and less likely to reject new information that does not fit the preconceptions associated with their expertise. Conversely, the effects of experience and expertise may lead to judgments that seem intuitive but are really products of this knowledge base arising from unconscious processes in the mind of the expert (Gladwell 2005).

Theoretical solutions are procedural strategies that all actors (individuals, groups, and organizations) can follow to minimize policy mistakes by either avoiding diagnostic and prescriptive errors or by mitigating the consequences of these errors. Some examples of such rules of thumb for maximizing rationality and minimizing mistakes are as follows (May 1973; White 1984; Fiske and Taylor 1991; Peterson, Maire, and Seligson 1993; Brogan 1952; Jervis 1976; Vertzberger 1990):

- *Think again* to avoid the framing effects of cognitive and motivational biases, such as the fundamental attribution error, egocentric bias, learned helplessness, and the illusion of omnipotence.
- *Think ahead* to see how others see the situation after you make a choice (empathy) and to see whether what you decide depends on what they will do (strategic rationality).
- *Take a time out/sleep on it* to develop the capacity to delay a decision to gain the time necessary to get in touch with feelings, resolve conflicts within the decision-making unit, and to work on the problem with unconscious systems.

- *Identify the nexus of interests and outcomes* (purposefulness) to determine who benefits and how (empathy) from different outcomes and at what costs (mindfulness).
- *Engage in risk assessment* to estimate the cost of doing too much versus the cost of doing too little.
- *Follow the proportionality principle* to tailor a decision proportionate to the stimulus and occasion for decision in order to balance against the risks associated with optimistic versus pessimistic biases of being too cooperative or too conflictual and the weak versus strong biases associated with the *kto-kovo* principle of estimating one's control over events.

We argue that theoretical solutions trump the other solutions by offering a good set of standards against which to judge their efficacy. That is, if the other solutions do not have the effects specified by these theoretical solutions, then these are probably not effective or efficient solutions. While these theoretical solutions considered individually may seem formulaic or even vacuous, we argue that they can be subsumed collectively under the principle of *disjointed incrementalism* as a general decision-making strategy (Braybrooke and Lindblom 1963). The myopic strategy of disjointed incrementalism is to make relatively small, reversible moves away from the status quo under the condition of low information about the consequences and costs of a decision. This strategy is consistent with a proportional response to a decision by others and permits movement away from undesirable conditions in the present while also allowing for corrections and reversals over time in the face of new information following from the decision. It also buys time to think again, to think ahead, and to reestimate benefits and costs, and it averages the costs of doing either too much or too little in the absence of better information. Its authors identify disjointed incrementalism as the optimum *political* strategy, because most decisions by governments occur under the condition of low information and do not require large changes from the status quo. Figure 7.2 contrasts disjointed incrementalism with other strategies of decision making in which the level of information and degree of change varies.

FIGURE 7.2   *Different Strategies of Decision Making*

High
Information

Bureaucratic Strategy	**Utopian Strategy**
(Synoptic Rationality)	(Ideological Thinking)
"Solve the Problem."	"Move toward the good."

Low   High
Change   Change

"Move away from evil."	"Play the odds/Follow your gut."
(Disjointed Incrementalism)	(No Clear Method)
Political Strategy	**Long-Shot Strategy**

Low
Information

Source: Modified from Braybrooke and Lindblom (1963), 78, diagram 2.

Braybrooke and Lindblom (1963) argue that the classical synoptic assumptions of rational choice involving complete and perfect information about the costs and benefits of alternative choices are rarely met in politics except for decisions in bureaucratic settings involving clear problem representation and trivial change—for example, choosing among different brands of office supplies that have clearly marked prices and beneficial features in a steady state environment of demand for these products by the decision unit. They claim that decisions requiring large-scale change under the condition of high information are nonexistent in the political universe. Decision makers who operate under the assumption of high information actually substitute ideology for information and employ a utopian strategy in which risks are not estimated accurately and biases run rampant.

The authors also recognize the possibility of long-shot decisions involving large-scale change under the condition of low information. They do not have a clear strategy for responding to this situation and recommend that decision makers avoid these occasions for decision. Gambling by playing the odds or following one's gut feeling are long-shot strategies to cope with this type of situation in the event that a decision cannot be deferred. Japan's decision in 1941 to attack Pearl Harbor may be an example of such a gamble in which Japan's military leaders elected to gamble that the United States would sue for peace instead of rearming and fighting to the finish in response to the destruction of most of the U.S. Pacific fleet (Levi and Tetlock 1980). President Bush's personal decision to invade Iraq was at least reinforced by gut feelings (Suskind 2006, 308). The Cheney "one percent doctrine" in the Bush administration is one formula for playing the odds, which calculates the risks by weighting a high impact/low probability event (a long shot) as if it were an occasion for decision that cannot be deferred (Suskind 2006; see also Gallhofer and Saris 1979; Taleb 2007).

How does a strategy of disjointed incrementalism avoid mistakes? It avoids the mistakes of omission (detection and hesitation) by easily permitting a move away from the status quo. Only a little information can prompt an incremental change either away from a threat or toward an opportunity depending on the content of the information. It mitigates the mistakes of commission (misperception and preemption) by prescribing a change that is reversible. These characteristics of the strategy address pathologies identified in individual, group, and organizational decision-making processes, such as groupthink, risky shift, and deadlock, by calling for an incremental and gradual rather than an extreme and sudden change in existing policy over time. In short, it is a coping strategy for dealing with complex political problems under conditions of relative uncertainty (low information). It is myopic in its vision and scope and concentrates on reducing costs associated with the present rather than gaining the benefits associated with a nonmyopic vision of the future.

Is there a nonmyopic strategy of decision making that has similar advantages? Classical game theory provides a synoptic strategy that prescribes a simultaneous-move/single-play solution to a strategic interaction problem based on the payoffs assigned by the players to different outcomes. If the payoffs are quantified by cardinal utilities, even games with more than one rational solution can be played with mixed strategies that result in a winning solution on average (Morrow 1994). Ordinal games in which the outcomes are merely ranked present a different problem when there are multiple equilibria (solutions). A Nash equilibrium solution avoids the worst (lowest ranked) outcome for each player and is one in which both players cannot defect without immediately reducing their payoff. There may a better (Pareto-superior) outcome for both players; however, it may not be a stable equilibrium because at least one player may be able to defect to a solution better for one player than the Pareto-optimum solution. In a single-play game, one player may choose a Nash equilibrium strategy while the other chooses a Pareto-optimum strategy. The Pareto player may then get its worst outcome while the Nash player gets its best outcome, which is a possibility in the game presented earlier in Figure 7.1 under single-play rules.

As we have seen in earlier chapters, the sequential game theory developed by Brams (1994) for 2×2 ordinal games addresses these problems by providing nonmyopic solutions to single-play games and specifying solutions to games with multiple equilibria by taking into account the initial state in which the game is played, which player has the next move, and whether the game is repeated between the players over time. TOM reflects more realistic assumptions about strategic interaction in world politics between states who alternate moves; can learn about each other's strategies and preference rankings for the different outcomes of domination, submission, settlement, and deadlock from repeated plays of a game; and do not have to quantify the payoffs or make heroic calculations in their strategic thinking (Brams 2002).[3] It also breaks down a synoptic rational choice of strategy of Cooperation P or Conflict N into a series of incremental choices to "stay" or "move" from one of those strategies.

The logic of this dynamic is illustrated in Figure 7.3 with the same game presented earlier to illustrate the concepts of Nash and Pareto equilibria. Here we show that the Pareto solution is an NME, which both players can discover by thinking ahead in a single play of the game with alternating moves by each player. In this example, the initial state is deadlock (3,2) with a final state (NME) of settlement (4,3). Thinking ahead, self chooses "stay" because other will then choose "stay" if self moves from (3,2) to (1,4). If self chooses "stay" at (3,2), then other will choose "move" from (3,2) because self will then move from (2,1) to (4,3). The NME is (4,3), because it is clear that self has no incentive to choose

FIGURE 7.3   *TOM's Nonmyopic Solution to a Game (G27) with Multiple Equilibria*

	Other	
	Coop P	Conf N
Coop P	4,3 |←	1,4
Self	↓	↑
Conf N	2,1 →	"3,2"*

Self's Strategy: "Stay"

	Other	
	Coop P	Conf N
Coop P	**4,3** →|	1,4
Self	↑	↓
Conf N	2,1 ←	"3,2"*

Other's Strategy: "Move"

Each player can choose "move" (→) or "stay" (→|) from an initial state specified in quotation marks to a final state underlined. The Nash myopic equilibrim is asterisked, and the Pareto-optimal, Brams nonmyopic equilibrium is underlined.

"move" from its highest-ranked outcome and because other realizes that choosing "move" to (1,4) will prompt self to choose "move" away from its lowest ranked outcome to (3,2).

In order to pursue a strategy that is incremental (gradual) and disjointed (reversible) in a sequential game, a player needs only to judge whether it is better to "stay" or "move" from the initial state of play in the game by thinking ahead at least one move and then assessing again whether to "stay" or "move" after the other player responds to the decision. When both players choose "stay" or cycle back to the initial state of play, the game reaches a solution in the form of a final state or equilibrium until or unless a new game is played between the players or the old game is repeated (Brams 1994; Marfleet and Walker 2006). As we have already discussed in Chapter 2, this analysis assumes that each player in the game can diagnose accurately the preference rankings of both players and can think ahead to calculate the consequences of choosing "move" or "stay." Under these assumptions there is a synoptic (nonmyopic) solution to the game that both players will reach under the rules of play in this game. Because the rules of play call for alternating moves, it is also possible for an outside observer to assess whether a player makes a "mistake," that is, wanders in error away from the criterion of rationality (a myopic or nonmyopic solution for the game) by choosing a wrong move.

If a player (self) knows only its own preference rankings and/or does not "think ahead," can a sequential game theory still specify the criterion of strategic rationality so that it is possible to avoid "mistakes," that is, making choices that lead to suboptimal outcomes? So far, we have argued on behalf of a criterion of strategic rationality in which goals, means, and actions of both self and other together provide a superior set of rules for making rational decisions than any one of these rules of thumb as separate decision heuristics. TOM as a sequential game theory incorporates all of them. Here we ask a different but equally significant question: is one of TOM's strategic solutions generally superior to others even in the absence of accurate two-sided information about the preferences of both players (self and other) and their power (*kto-kovo*) relationship? It is possible to assess the relative effectiveness of different strategies by running simulations of strategic interactions between self and other in which one player pursues either the same strategy or a different strategy as the other player under the rules of either single-play or repeated play (Axelrod 1984; Majeski 2004). An expansion of this inquiry to include sequential games allows the players to alternate their choices within a game from different initial states and their roles as ego or alter in different games (Walker 2004b, 2007).

The results of computer simulations of several of these games indicate the success and failure rates of different strategies as roles vis-à-vis each other in terms of the percentage of times a strategic role predicts final outcomes, the percentage of times it achieves its highest-ranked outcome, and the percentage of times it achieves either a settlement (P,P) or domination (N,P) outcome for the player following the strategic role. These criteria measure success by diagnostic accuracy, outcome utility, and a cooperative response from the other player in the final outcome (Marfleet and Walker 2006). The entire repertoire of strategies (roles and counterroles) in these simulations is shown in the seven games in Figure 7.4, in which each player has two possible strategies or roles of Cooperation P or Conflict N ranking settlement (P,P) or domination (N,P) highest under two different power distributions (symmetrical or asymmetrical). A theory of inferences about preferences (TIP) in Figure 7.4 specifies the entire preference rankings of each player for the outcomes of settlement, deadlock, domination, and submission associated with a strategy, and TOM's rules of play prescribe the decision to choose "move" or "stay" for each

FIGURE 7.4   *Strategies for the Exercise of Power in Three Kinds of Games*

	A (+, >)				A (+,=)	
	P	N			P	N
P	4,4*	2,3	**NO-CONFLICT**	P	4,4*	1,2
E(+,<)			**GAMES (+,+)**	E(+,=)		
N	1,1	3,2*			N	2,1	3,3*

	G41			G29			G27	
	A(−,>)			A(−,<)			A(−,=)	
	P	N̲		P	N		P	N̲
P	4,2	2,4	P	4,3	1,4	P	4,3	1,4
E(+,<)			E(+,>)			E(+,=)		
N	1,1	3,3*	N	3,2	2,1	N	2,1	3,2*

MIXED-MOTIVE GAMES (+,−)

	G18				G32	
	A(−,>)				A(−,=)	
	P	N̲			P	N̲
P	3,2	2,4*	**CONFLICT**	P	3,3	1,4
E(−,<)			**GAMES (−,−)**	E(−,=)		
N	4,1	1,3			N̲	4,1	2,2*

ASYMMETRICAL   ←   POWER   →   SYMMETRICAL

Nash myopic equilibria are asterisked, and Brams nonmyopic equilibria are in bold. Dominant strategies are underlined. Outcomes are ranked 4 = highest to 1 = lowest for ego (E) and alter (A) strategies regarding the exercise of positive (P) and negative (N) sanctions. The six TIP propositions are (1) If (+,<), then P,P > N,N > P,N > N,P; (2) If (+,=), then P,P > N,N > N,P > P,N; (3) If (+,>), then P,P > N,P > N,N > P,N; (4) If (−,<), then N,P > P,P > P,N > N,N; (5) If (−,=), then N,P > P,P > N,N > P,N; (6) If (−,>), then N,P > N,N > P,P > P,N.

Sources: TIP is in Marfleet and Walker (2006, 57). Data are from Walker, Malici, and Schafer (2011, 60, figure 3.5). The game numbers for the mixed-motive and conflict games are from Brams (1994, 215–219). The use of ego and alter instead of self and other to identify a player is to indicate that a given player (self or other) in the game may occupy either role defined as a strategy.

player from each of the cells as an initial state (Marfleet and Walker 2006; Brams 1994).

There are three cooperative strategies and three conflict strategies in these games, which are paired with one another under the conditions of power symmetry or asymmetry that define each of them. There is a co-operation strategy (P) for when a player is weaker, equal, or stronger than the other player and also a conflict strategy (N) for each of these power distributions. The design of the simulation provides some answers to two basic *kto-kovo* power questions: which of the different strategies

(P or N) of exercising power is more effective under the different distributions (symmetrical or asymmetrical) of power between the players (Marfleet and Walker 2006)? Before turning to a detailed discussion of the results of the computer simulation, however, it is desirable to be aware of the diversity of the games generated by the different combinations of the exercise of power and the distribution of power.

The two no-conflict games in Figure 7.4 have both myopic and non-myopic equilibria and no dominant strategy for either player. The three mixed-motive games have two NMEs, even though one player has a dominant strategy in two of these games, as does at least one player in the two conflict games. The stronger player with a conflict strategy has a dominant strategy of negative sanctions in the mixed-motive game with an asymmetrical power distribution, as does the player with a conflict strategy in the symmetrical mixed-motive game. Both players have dominant strategies of negative sanctions in the conflict game with a symmetrical power distribution. Settlement (P,P) is a possible NME in five of the seven games, and domination (N,P) is a possible final outcome in the other two games (G41 and G18) for the stronger player who follows a dominant conflict strategy (N) against a weaker player who pursues either a strategy of cooperation (P) or conflict (N). In five of the seven games, there is at least one player who ranks domination first; however, in five of the seven games, deadlock is also at least a myopic equilibrium.

These characteristics are noteworthy because they suggest that it is possible to achieve domination or settlement as normative outcomes of foreign policy success and to avoid the foreign policy failures of submission or deadlock as final outcomes with these strategies. These distinctions are based on the normative judgment regarding the use of power in which ego's eliciting a response of compliance (cooperation) rather than noncompliance (conflict) by other is judged to be a better way to exercise power. This judgment is inferred from the logic of the definition of power as a control relationship in which the agent (ego) elicits a preferred response from the patient (alter) that the latter would not otherwise do.[4] A favorable distribution of power is also neither necessary nor sufficient to achieve our criterion of success, as settlement (P,P) is a possible final outcome in the three symmetrical power games, and deadlock (N,N) is a possible NME in one of the asymmetrical power games as well as in two of the three symmetrical power games.[5]

Collectively, these seven games offer players a menu of strategies for using positive or negative sanctions in three types of *kto-kovo* situations: when ego's power is weaker, equal, or stronger in relationship to alter. Table 7.1 shows the results of play between the strategic dyads of ego and alter when ego chooses to exercise power under TOM's rules of play,[6] with either a cooperative P or a conflictual N strategy under these three conditions vis-à-vis alter, who is also exercising either a cooperative P or a conflictual N strategy. This agent-based simulation of twelve strategies for 2×2 sequential games with ordinal payoffs reveals significant differences in their success rates (Marfleet and Walker 2006). In Table 7.1 is an analysis of the success rates of the strategies employed by the players in the games in Figure 7.4 between ego and alter under two different assumptions (optimist or pessimist) about the opponent. Ego then plays a single game of alternating moves against an opponent (alter) that may or may not define its own subjective game the way ego has done. The results show significant variability in the ability of the strategies embodied in these subjective games to predict outcomes, achieve utilitarian success, and induce cooperation from players who think that they are playing other subjective games.

The cooperation strategies of appease, reward/deter, and exploit are most predictable, useful, and successful in inducing cooperation (87.5 percent) when ego's optimistic expectation is congruent with alter's actual strategy of exercising positive sanctions. Strategies of cooperation generally outperform the conflict strategies of bluff, compel/punish, and bully with only a few exceptions. A bluffing strategy is the most successful strategy for inducing cooperation when alter's strategy is cooperation and the most predictable strategy regarding outcomes when alter's strategy is conflict. When ego's expectation is pessimistic, the predictability of the compel/punish conflict strategy is higher overall than any other strategy. Finally, an appeasement strategy of cooperation has a relatively poor record compared with conflict strategies both for predicting final outcomes

TABLE 7.1 *Outcomes of Intersections of Different Strategies between Ego and Alter*

	ALTER'S STRATEGIES								
	Coop P Sanctions*			All (P+N) Sanctions**			Conf N Sanctions*		
	Pred.	Pay.	Coop.	Pred.	Pay.	Coop.	Pred.	Pay.	Coop.
P Exploit (+,>)									
Optimist (+,<)	**87.5**	**87.5**	**87.5**	66.7	**66.7**	**66.7**	45.8	45.8	45.8
Pessimist (−,<)	62.5	75.0	75.0	54.1	**66.7**	**66.7**	45.8	58.3	58.3
P Reward/Deter (+,=)									
Optimist (+,=)	**87.5**	**87.5**	**87.5**	66.7	**66.7**	**66.7**	45.8	45.8	45.8
Pessimist (−,=)	75.0	75.0	75.0	66.7	**66.7**	**66.7**	58.3	58.3	58.3
P Appease (+,<)									
Optimist (+,>)	**87.5**	**87.5**	**87.5**	66.7	**66.7**	**66.7**	45.8	45.8	45.8
Pessimist (−,>)	16.7	83.3	83.3	25.0	64.6	64.6	33.3	45.8	45.8
EGO'S STRATEGIES*									
N Bluff (−,<)									
Optimist (+,>)	75.0	4.2	**100.0**	45.8	6.3	62.5	16.7	8.3	25.0
Pessimist (−,>)	0.0	4.2	**100.0**	33.3	6.3	62.5	**66.7**	8.3	25.0
N Compel/Punish (−,=)									
Optimist (+,=)	75.0	4.2	75.0	45.8	10.4	54.2	16.7	16.7	33.3
Pessimist (−,=)	83.3	16.7	41.7	**72.9**	22.9	43.8	62.5	29.2	45.8
N Bully (−,>)									
Optimist (+,<)	75.0	33.3	33.3	66.7	37.5	37.5	58.3	41.7	41.7
Pessimist (−,<)	33.3	33.3	33.3	37.5	37.5	37.5	41.6	41.7	41.7

* $n=24$; ** $n=48$; *** Ego's highest-ranked strategies for most predictability, maximum payoff, and cooperation by alter as a final outcome have their percentages in bold.

Source: Data calculated from Walker, Malici, and Schafer (2011), 289, table A.2.

overall (25.0 percent) and especially (16.7 percent) when ego's expectations are pessimistic and not congruent with alter's actual strategy of cooperation.

The variability in results illustrates the strengths and weaknesses associated with Baldwin's (2000) approach to assessing the effectiveness of different foreign policy instruments. The instruments are the different strategies for the agent in Table 7.1, which indicates that against all twelve strategies the overall success of the highest performing cooperation strategies is higher than the highest performing conflict strategies for maximizing utility or inducing cooperation. Baldwin would conclude that, regardless of the opponent's strategy, an agent should choose a cooperation strategy over a conflict strategy as the more effective strategy. However, the results in Table 7.1 also show that the two assumptions regarding (a) ego's diagnosis of alter's strategy as cooperation (+) or conflict (−) and (b) alter's actual strategy both affect the likely success of each strategy. Although the differences within P and N strategies are smaller than the differences between these two strategies, it is not the case for all twelve strategies and especially for differences between conflict (N) strategies. The success rate of cooperative (P) strategies is higher on average than the success rate of conflict strategies in maximizing utilities and inducing cooperation. Since these cooperation strategies are also contingent rather than dominant strategies, it is true that contingent strategies are more successful than dominant strategies in this realist political universe. This last inference is also consistent with our more general argument that disjointed (reversible) strategies are better, as a contingent strategy is more flexible than a dominant strategy.

APPLICATIONS OF DISJOINTED INCREMENTAL PRINCIPLES: THE CUBAN MISSILE CRISIS

To sum up, juxtaposing the strategy of disjointed incrementalism and the results of the computer simulation validates several rules of thumb for avoiding mistakes identified by Braybrooke and Lindblom (1963). A strategy of conditional cooperation as a strategy of disjointed incrementalism fixes and avoids mistakes by being reversible (disjointed), gradual (incremental), and myopic (moving away from evil) rather than synoptic (ideological). More generally, strategic interaction can take on the features of disjointed incremental strategies by pursuing a contingent (reversible) rather than a dominant (irreversible) strategy, remaining gradual in deciding whether to "move" or "stay," by being modestly nonmyopic in thinking ahead to the other player's next move within the parameters set by the 2 × 2 game. These features enhance the likelihood of repeated play and small change, which are the conditions for a successful disjointed incrementalism strategy.

FIGURE 7.5   *Disaggregating Space and Time for Power Games in Long-Shot Situations*

	Alter	
	CO	CF
CO	CO,CO	CO,CF
Ego		
CF	CF,CO	CF,CF

Larger Game Matrix

	Alter			
	CO CO		CF CF	
	Deeds/Words	Words/Deeds		
CO	Deeds			
CO	Words			
Ego				
CF	Words			
CF	Deeds			

Nested Spatial Matrix

	Alter	
	D	E
D	D,D	D,E
Ego		
E	E,D	E,E

Nested Time Matrix

CO = cooperation P sanctions; CF = conflict N sanctions; Moves: D = de-escalatory; E = escalatory.

The "value added" of sequential game theory to disjointed incrementalism is that it can guide the strategic direction and tactical execution of a disjointed incremental strategy for long-shot situations. The results of the computer simulation suggest the following: contingent strategies are better than dominant strategies; cooperative strategies are better than conflict strategies; and incremental strategies are better than radical strategies. In simulations with players who pursue dominant strategies, contingent strategies of cooperation are more adaptable to a broader range of situations. They maximize prediction, utility, and cooperation, thereby reducing the risk of undesirable outcomes. These qualities may be enhanced by a "nested game" (Tsebelis 1990) application depicted in Figure 7.5 of collapsing strategic games of cooperation or conflict into different tracks of words and deeds and tactical games of escalation and de-escalation.

A repertoire of incremental changes and strategic directions in playing power games is shown in Figure 7.6 and illustrated below in its application to the strategic interaction between the United States and the Soviet Union during the Cuban Missile Crisis. The words and deeds rows and columns in Figure 7.5 are extended and transformed in Figure 7.6 so that the variety of words and deeds is increased and movement along this continuum is also refined into a smaller series of steps in either direction. At the same time it is possible to characterize these smaller changes as either de-escalatory or escalatory tactics, depending on the direction of the change, thereby retaining the 2 × 2 configuration of game theory to

FIGURE 7.6 *Expanded and Dynamic Power Continuum for a 2×2 Game*

STRATEGIC DIRECTIONS AND INCREMENTS OF TACTICAL CHANGE

Cooperation (+) ← De-Escalation   (Indeterminate)   Escalation → (−) Conflict
Strategies -- Strategies

DEES	WORDS	STATUS QUO	WORDS	DEEDS
Increase Decrease	Promise Offer	Accept/Reject	Demand Threaten	Decrease Increase
Reward	Influence	Power Continuum	Intimidate	Punish
POSITIVE		SANCTIONS		NEGATIVE

DDE DDD DEE DED	Tactical Sequences	EED EDD EEE EDE
Exploit Reward Deter Appease	Tactics	Bluff Compel Punish Bully
(+, >) (+,=) (+,=) (+,<)	Who-Whom Rules	(−,<) (−,=) (−,=) (−,>)

describe the dynamics of interaction by two players with two choices: "move" (escalate or de-escalate from the status quo) or "stay" (do not escalate or de-escalate from the status quo).

The "who-whom" rules of TIP and "stay-move" rules of TOM govern tactical sequences and strategic solutions to these "smaller" games of escalation and de-escalation as words or deeds games within the "larger" game of conflict and cooperation in Figure 7.5 and permit repeated plays of the same game at different levels of escalation and de-escalation. The optical effects of employing the expanded and dynamic continuum for the exercise of power are to magnify and transform the locations of each player's decisions in the 2×2 game matrix. These effects are illustrated by plotting the locations of four key U.S. and Soviet decisions during the Cuban Missile Crisis in the two game matrices in Figure 7.5, which are reproduced with the locations of these four decisions in Figure 7.7.

The first game matrix depicts each player's decisions in the static game matrix as either conflict or cooperation behavior nested in either the words matrix or the deeds matrix. Since each decision is tagged with a sequence number, it is possible to infer change through time by putting them in numerical order; however, it is relatively difficult to see the pattern because the first two decisions are clustered spatially within the conflict deeds location of this matrix. The historical version of the second game matrix magnifies the locations of these decisions into a more dy-

FIGURE 7.7 *Static and Dynamic Analyses of the Cuban Missile Crisis*

	SU				Sequence of SU and U.S. Decisions
	CO Deeds	CO Words	CF Words	CF Deeds	+0. Status Quo in U.S./SU Relations w. Cuba.
CO Deeds					
CO Words		#4 Final Outcome			#1. SU introduces missiles into Cuba.
U.S.					#2. U.S. embargos Cuba with naval ships.
					#3. SU offers Cuba/Turkey quid pro quo.
CF Words					
CF Deeds		#3		#1, #2 "Status Quo"	#4. U.S. agrees to SU quid pro quo.

Static Game Matrix   **Key Decisions**

* * * * * * * * * * * * * * * *

Detente ↑   SU   ↑D,E   Detente ↑   SU   ↑D,E

←   **D**   E→   ←   **D**   E→

    "Status

    Quo" (I)   (D)

   D   <u>#4</u>   →   #1   **D**   <u>#2</u>   ←   #1b

U.S.   (A) ↑   ↓   (I)   **U.S.**   (D) ↑   ↑ (D)

← **E**   #3   ←   #2 →   ← **E**   #1a   ←   "Status →

E,D   (O)   **E,D**   (D)   Quo"

   ↓   ↓   War   ↓   ↓   War

Dynamic Game Matrix   **Dynamic Game Matrix**
Historical Version   **Counterfactual A/B Versions**

#1. SU introduces missiles into Cuba.   A #1a. SU lowers Cuban economic aid.
#2. U.S. embargos Cuba with naval ships.   A #2. U.S. lowers Cuban economic sanctions.
#3. SU offers Cuba/Turkey quid pro quo.   B #1b. U.S. lowers Cuban economic sanctions.
#4. U.S. agrees to SU quid pro quo offer.   B #2. SU lowers Cuban economic aid.

D = de-escalatory; E = escalatory. Initial state is in quotation marks, and final outcome is underlined. Change increments: I = increase; D = decrease; O = offer; A = accept.

namic field of the exercise of power that transforms the words and deeds categories into escalation or de-escalation. It is possible to locate each decision at a point within these categories and also to measure simultaneously the distance between decisions through time with the expanded and dynamic power continuum in Figure 7.6, which defines the rows and columns of the game matrix.

This transformation from a static to a dynamic game has three effects. The *calculus* effect magnifies the dynamic location of each decision in the second game matrix as a derivative change in its static location in the first game matrix. The *quantum* effect transforms the location of the status quo (E,E) in the first matrix to any of the four possibilities (D,D), (E,D), (D,E), or (E,E) in the second matrix, making its location indeterminate. The *relativity* effect transforms the (E,E) location in the second matrix to these other possibilities relative to its relationship with previous and subsequent decisions over time.[7] For example, its location is (D,D) in the historical version and (E,E) in the counterfactual version of the dynamic matrix even though its location remains the same (CF deeds, CF deeds) in the static version of the game matrix as indicated by existing U.S. economic sanctions against Cuba and Soviet Union economic assistance to Cuba prior to the October 1962 crisis.

The retention of dichotomous values (D or E) to describe these locations allows the application of TOM to analyze the dynamics of the historical and the counterfactual game as it unfolds in two different directions from the same location. The historical version begins with an initial state of (D,D) status quo and escalates toward (D,E) domination by the Soviet Union, then to (E,E) deadlock before moving to (E,D) domination by the United States and a final outcome of (D,D) settlement. The game matrix for two simple counterfactual versions of history from (E,E) status quo moves to (E,D) domination by the United States and on to a final outcome of (D,D) settlement in the "A" version and from (E,E) status quo to (D,E) domination by the Soviet Union and a final outcome of (D,D) settlement in the "B" version. Other counterfactual accounts are possible: possible mutual escalation to war at the lower right corner of the matrix and outcomes of U.S. domination or submission, respectively, in the lower-left and upper-right corners of the matrix. These counterfactuals are less likely than A and B inside the matrix, because their trajectories are not consistent with the postulated U.S. > SU regional distribution of power and would require either a redistribution of power or mistakes as decisions by one or both players that go undetected and/or uncorrected.

Both the historical and counterfactual final outcomes consistent with the U.S. > SU distribution of power are also consistent with the actual historical movement toward détente following the Cuban Missile Crisis. Collectively, they represent the operation of the principle of equifinality in which the same historical outcome may be reached by different paths (George and Bennett 2005). The other counterfactual outcomes than

(D,D) détente represented in the two dynamic matrices by (E,E) war, (D,E) Soviet Union domination, or (E,D) U.S. domination are paths "not taken." As the poet Robert Frost notes, there is more than one path into the future with the one (not) taken making "all the difference."[8] Our explanation for why these alternative paths were not taken instead of the path represented in the historical version by the four key decisions is based on two aspects of the *kto-kovo* (who-whom) question: what is the distribution of power between the United States and the Soviet Union, and how is it exercised during the crisis? The distribution of power is relatively static with U.S. > SU in the Caribbean regional subsystem and U.S.=SU in the global system. We suggest that the exercise of power by each player depended on their choice of strategies (cooperation or conflict) within the constraints of the power distribution for each system and that these choices made "all the difference." The possible U.S. strategies consistent with Soviet conflict strategies and either asymmetric or symmetric power distributions between the players are represented in Figure 7.8 along with their respective equilibrium solutions.

The Cuban Missile Crisis offers an opportunity to assess whether applications of the decision-making heuristics in a disjointed incremental strategy of strategic interaction can make a difference as rules of thumb in detecting, fixing, and avoiding foreign policy mistakes. For both the regional and the global games in Figure 7.8 with the initial state specified as (D,D), the prescription for both players is "stay" at (D,D) with the exception of the U.S. conflict (−) strategy in Game 18. Without the exercise of U.S. threat power in pre-play communication, there is the possibility of cycling by the Soviet Union in those games (G29 and G27) where the United States pursues a cooperation (+) strategy. The actual Soviet decision (#1) to choose "move" from (D,D) was clearly a mistake in G18 and G32, where the United States pursues a conflict (−) strategy, and risky at best in the other two games, where the United States pursues a cooperation (+) strategy. The only player in a position to choose "move" from (D,D) in these games is the one occupying the ego role in G18, which is the United States.

However, the actual U.S. strategy during the Cuban Missile Crisis was consistent with Game 29, in which the United States first escalated

FIGURE 7.8   *Strategic Analyses of Soviet-American Relations in the Caribbean Crisis*

	G29					G27		
		SU (−,<)					SU (−,=)	
		D	E				D	E
	D	"4,3"	1,4	MIXED-MOTIVE		D	"4,3"	1,4
U.S. (+,>)				GAMES (+,−)	U.S. (+,=)			
	E	3,2	2,1			E	2,1	3,2*
	U.S. Strategy: Stay					U.S. Strategy: Stay		
	SU Strategy: Stay/Cycle					SU Strategy: Stay/Cycle		

U.S. Cooperation Strategies in Regional and Global Power Games

	G18					G32		
		SU (−,<)					SU (−,=)	
		D	E				D	E
	D	"2,3"	1,4	CONFLICT		D	"3,3"	1,4
U.S. (−,>)				GAMES (−,−)	U.S. (−,=)			
	E	4,2*	3,1			E	4,1	"2,2"*
	U.S. Strategy: Move					U.S. Strategy: Stay		
	SU Strategy: Stay					SU Strategy: Stay		

U.S. Conflict Strategies in Regional and Global Power Games

ASYMMETRICAL	←	POWER	→	SYMMETRICAL
(Regional Games)				(Global Games)

Nash myopic equilibria are asterisked, and Brams nonmyopic equilibria are in bold. Dominant strategies are underlined. Initial states are in quotation marks, and final outcomes are underlined.

with the embargo (#2) in response to the Soviet attempt to install missiles (#1) and then de-escalated (#4) by accepting the Soviet quid pro quo offer (#3) and stating that Washington did not intend to invade Cuba. The actual Soviet strategy was consistent with the dynamics of both G18 and G29 once Khrushchev took the risk of moving rather than staying at the initial state of (D,D). This strategic analysis is displayed in Figure 7.9 along with a tactical analysis of the sequence of the U.S. and Soviet moves during this game. When the Soviet Union makes a mistake and chooses "move" to (1,4), the ensuing tactical sequence of Soviet moves is a bluff (EED) tactic followed by a U.S. compel (EDD) tactic. The United States "fixes" this mistake by following the prescription for a cooperation (+) strategy by a stronger player against a weaker player pursuing a conflict (−) strategy in a mixed-motive game.

The final outcome of the crisis corresponded to Game 29 rather than the final outcome for Game 18. In both games the Soviet conflict strategy

FIGURE 7.9   *Soviet Strategies and Tactical Sequences for Games 18 and 29*

G18		Tactical Sequences	G29	
SU			**SU**	
D	E	DD 0. Status quo	D	E
		DE 1. SU puts missiles into Cuba.*		
D "2,3"→| 1,4		EE 2. U.S. embargos Cuba.	D "**4,3**"→| 1,4	
		ED 3. SU offers quid pro quo.		
USA $\overline{↑}$ ↓		DD 4. U.S. accepts SU offer.	USA ↑ ↓	
		*Soviet Mistake: Move (E)		
E **4,2*** ← 3,1		SU Tactics: Bluff (EED)	E 3,2 ← 2,1	

SU Strategy: Stay	US Tactics: Compel (EDD)
Intentions: USA, SU (–,–)	
Power: USA > SU	

SU Strategy: Stay/Cycle
Intentions: USA, SU (+,–)
Power: USA > SU

Nash myopic equilibria are asterisked, and Brams nonmyopic equilibria are in bold. The row for the dominant U.S. strategy in G18 is underlined. Initial states are in quotation marks, and the cells with final outcomes are underlined.

involves bluff tactics, but the final outcome for Game 18 is (4,2) domination by the United States instead of (4,3) settlement. Perhaps the Kremlin risked escalation to (1,4) Soviet domination by secretly installing missiles in Cuba, in order to transform the regional game into a symmetrical power game such as the existing superpower global game of the prisoner's dilemma (G32) and to deter a second U.S. invasion of Cuba in the aftermath of the Bay of Pigs fiasco (Allison and Zelikow 1999, 82–88). The risk for Moscow of defining the situation this way is that the United States might be provoked into doing the very thing that the presence of the missiles is intended to deter. If the installation of the missiles could be presented as a fait accompli, then the risk of making this move would be mitigated by the deterrent effects of the shift in the regional balance of power. However, U.S. satellite photos detected the missile sites under construction before the missiles could become operational and prompted a U.S. decision to embargo Cuba in an attempt to prevent the missiles from being armed and placed on their launching pads. The risks of armed confrontation and possible escalation to violence between U.S. naval vessels and Soviet ships as they approached the Cuban blockade led to the Soviet offer to withdraw missiles from Cuba in return for a U.S. pledge not to invade Cuba and to dismantle U.S. missiles in Turkey. The United States accepted the Soviet offer, although the U.S. move was not made public at the time (Ibid.).

It appeared to the outside world that the Kremlin had simply submitted to U.S. domination in Game 18 and agreed to withdraw the missiles for a final outcome of (4,2), which is the NME for this game. Nikita Khrushchev as the Soviet leader had taken a risk that backfired, and it was later used against him when he was ousted from his leadership position a year or so later. Even though he had extracted a commitment from Kennedy that the United States would not invade Cuba, this fig leaf and the secret commitment to dismantle U.S. missiles on the Russian border with Turkey were not sufficient to offset the loss of Soviet prestige and the risk of nuclear war precipitated by his initiative to put missiles in Cuba (Allison and Zelikow 1999; Blight and Welch 1989).

CONCLUSIONS

Previous students of international crises have already employed sequential game theory to reconstruct empirically the dynamics of crisis interactions and explain the outcomes of such military confrontations (Snyder and Diesing 1977; Leng and Walker 1982; Leng 1984; Brams 1994). Other scholars have attempted to identify particular strategies as the most effective ones to "play" such games and to colonize or convert a universe of players to such a strategy (Osgood 1960; Snyder and Diesing 1977; Leng and Walker 1982; Leng 1984, 1993; Axelrod 1984, 1997; Goldstein and Freeman 1990; Wendt 1999). Earlier injunctions to "think ahead," or "identify the nexus of interests and outcomes," or "engage in risk assessment," or "follow the proportionality principle," or "follow the reciprocity principle" in order to balance against the risks associated with optimistic or pessimistic biases of being too cooperative or too conflictual and the weak versus strong biases associated with estimating one's control over events—all of these rules of thumb beg the question of exactly how to carry them out under different conditions specified by different answers to the *kto-kovo* (who-whom) question. The game theory applications in this chapter identify foreign policy mistakes and offer relatively clear guidance in carrying out rules of thumb for avoiding foreign policy mistakes, which are consistent with lessons inferred by these other scholars from their research.

We have argued that TOM as a sequential game theory employed to model the implications of *kto-kovo* (who-whom?) can answer the "how" questions of detecting, fixing, and avoiding foreign policy mistakes. Our approach does not offer exact predictions of the future actions of others and does not make guarantees regarding the exact consequences of different choices. It does offer a modestly nonmyopic approach for "playing the odds" in long-shot situations, such as in crises when information is low and the prospects for change are high. Rather than simply "moving away from the evil" as a myopic "try and see" strategy with a single move, it suggests that a modestly nonmyopic strategy of cooperation (+) with a sequence of tactics that is gradual, incremental, and reversible is both a possible and a feasible strategy of "moving toward the good" even in long-shot situations. A decision maker is generally better off playing a strategy of contingent cooperation rather than a dominant strategy of conflict in strategic interaction situations no matter what the distribution of power is between the players. According to the results of our computer simulations, appeasing is generally better than bluffing by a weaker player against a stronger player; a reward/deter strategy is better than a compel/punish strategy between equal players, and exploiting is better than bullying by a stronger player against a weaker player.

This information is valuable in reducing the indeterminacy of relations between states and in specifying the choices that leaders should make. If a leader knows that contingent cooperation strategies *ceteribus paribus* generally trump either contingent or dominant conflict strategies by being better able to predict final outcomes,[9] achieve highest-ranked preferences, and induce cooperation from the other player, then s/he should choose a cooperation strategy conditioned by estimates of the power distribution between self and other and the strategy of cooperation or conflict pursued by other. These estimates imply a process of *role location* as well as *strategic interaction*, which we argue can explain the occurrence and resolution of international crises as well as episodes of less dramatic or tension-filled encounters between states in world politics (Holsti 1970; Snyder and Diesing 1977; Walker 1979, 1987, 1992, 2004b, 2010; Wendt 1999; Doty 1996; Walker, Malici, and Schafer 2011).

In the case of the Cuban Missile Crisis, the tactical sequences generated by the four key decisions signaled an asymmetrical distribution of
power favoring the United States and the exercise of U.S. power in the
form of tactics reflecting a conditional conflict strategy (−) of compel/
punish. The crisis may have been avoided if the United States had signaled to the Soviet Union in prior communications that it had no intention
of invading Cuba again after the Bay of Pigs fiasco. However, even this
step may not have avoided a Soviet adventure in Cuba to the extent that
Khrushchev linked installation of missiles in Cuba to increased Soviet
bargaining leverage in deciding the fate of Berlin (Allison and Zelikow
1999). The actual enactment of U.S. tactics was a compel (EDD) sequence
also consistent with Game 29 and a (D,D) settlement outcome instead of
a bully (EDE) sequence consistent with Game 18. This tactical sequence
suggests that Kennedy may have shifted the U.S. strategic role during the
crisis from a dominant conflict (−) strategy to a conditional cooperation
(+) strategy that was compatible with both the asymmetrical power distribution in the Caribbean region and the symmetrical power distribution
in the global system. Under both conditions there is a path for the Soviet
Union to reach settlement from deadlock, as shown in Figure 7.10.

This example of role location suggests that this process is approximate
and, depending on the degree of uncertainty in the situation and the skills
of the players, requires a disjointed incremental process in order to be suc-

FIGURE 7.10   *Soviet Strategies for Regional (G29) and Global (G27) Power
Games*

G29 SU		Tactical Sequences	G27 SU	
D	E	DD 0. Status quo	D	E
		DE 1. SU puts missiles into Cuba.*		
D **4,3** →| 1,4		EE 2. U.S. embargos Cuba.	D **4,3** →| 1,4	
		ED 3. SU offers quid pro quo.		
USA ↑	↓	DD 4.U.S. accepts SU offer.	USA ↑	↓
		*Soviet Mistake: Move (E)		
E 3,2 ← "2,1"		SU Tactics: Bluff (EED)	E 2,1 ← "3,2"	
SU Strategy: Move		U.S. Tactics: Compel (EDD)	**SU Strategy: Move**	
Intentions: USA, SU (+,−)			Intentions: USA, SU (+,−)	
Power: USA > SU			Power: USA = SU	

Nash myopic equilibria are asterisked, and Brams nonmyopic equilibria are in bold. Initial states are in
quotation marks, and final outcomes are underlined.

cessful. The exchange of moves by the players provides information to each player about how the other is behaving in the context of the existing distribution of power. Information about alter's move cues what ego's response should be according to the norms in TOM's model of the game associated with ego's strategy of cooperation or conflict. A tactical sequence of such moves signals what strategic role (cooperation or conflict) alter has selected in the context of the existing power distribution. Over time this exchange process constructs at least a partly shared definition of the situation and each player's strategic role along with an equilibrium as a final outcome of the encounter prescribed by TOM's logic and the answer to the *kto-kovo* question (Walker 2010; see also Snyder and Diesing 1977; Leng and Walker 1982). Since different sequential game models may share the same equilibrium and even the same path to that equilibrium for the players, they may not reach exactly the same definition of the situation.

CHAPTER 8

Foreign Policy Analysis
Minimizing Mistakes

INTRODUCTION

If it is impossible always to achieve perfect predictability of outcomes, obtain one's highest-ranked preference, or induce cooperation from others as strategic consequences of our decisions, then what is reasonable to expect from the decision-making efforts of U.S. presidents? What strategy should they apply to the task of keeping the country independent and its people safe, secure, and prosperous? We have argued that the best approach is a disjointed incremental strategy of cooperation informed by an awareness of both the distribution of power and the exercise of power by relevant others in the strategic environment. This strategy may engage others who pursue a strategy of conflict, and the novelty of our approach is to argue that a strategy of cooperation is the most effective one even against them. This position is not based simply on idealism that values peace over war; it entails realism as well about human nature and the human condition, as expressed by Winston Churchill:

Let us learn our lessons. Never, never, never believe any war will be smooth and easy, or that anyone who embarks on that strange voyage can measure the tides and hurricanes he will encounter. The Statesman who yields to war fever must realize that once the signal is given, he is no longer the master of policy but the slave of unforeseeable and un-controllable events. Antiquated War Offices, weak, incompetent, or arrogant Commanders, untrustworthy allies, hostile neutrals, malignant Fortune, ugly surprises, awful miscalculations—all take their seats at the Council Board on the morrow of a declaration of war. (Churchill 1930, qtd. in Sanger 2009, ix)

The wisdom of Churchill's observation captures the dual difficulties of fallible humans making political decisions in a sea of uncertainty as a ship of state, whose efforts to manage risk are compounded in an environment of conflict and war. The cognitive biases, ignoble motivations, bureaucratic politics, and organizational obstacles in one's own country, compounded by the lack of information regarding similar features in other states, interact with the press of time and circumstances to create a sea of uncertainty about the consequences of political decisions. These inherently uncertain features of political decision making are exacerbated by the "fog of war."[1] In other words, the additional stress associated with violence and heightened tension increases ambiguity and uncertainty in the decision-making environment in a time of war. The problem of managing risk also remains present in a noncrisis environment of calmer seas characterized by lowered tensions and lesser stakes. However, crises and wars offer tougher tests for the strategy of disjointed incrementalism as an effective decision-making heuristic for fixing and avoiding mistakes and performing the task of strategic role location, that is, discerning the strategies of others and relating them to one's own.

In this chapter we analyze the process of role location in two wars, the Vietnam War (1969–1972) and the Iraq War (2003–2008), and find that U.S. presidents and their principal advisors followed a relatively weak version of disjointed incrementalism in one war and the opposite of disjointed incrementalism in the other war.[2] In the next chapter we shall examine with laboratory and historical evidence the potential efficacy of selecting strategic roles of cooperation to avoid future mistakes in managing relations with others who may pursue strategies of conflict outside the fog of war. The results will help us in a subsequent chapter to better assess the strengths and weaknesses of disjointed incremental strategic principles compared with other approaches for fixing and avoiding mistakes in dealing with current foreign policy problems facing U.S. decision makers in the Middle East and South Asia.

ROLE LOCATION

Role theory defines the process of role location as identifying the norms appropriate for guiding behavior under different conditions of social interaction in a social dyad and prescribing behaviors consistent with those norms for the role identities of ego and alter as members of the dyad (Walker 1979; Sarbin and Allen 1968). The sources of these norms are both context dependent and agent dependent, insofar as both the features of the social situation and the identities of the occupants of the ego and alter identities in a role dyad affect the content of these norms and the behavior that follows from them. The process of role location is constituted by the processes of role taking and role making, respectively, which refer to the influences of situational features and the expectations of others versus agent characteristics on the behavior that constitutes role enactment. For example, Hamlet's role in Shakespeare's play by the same name is scripted by the author of the play as a set of behaviors in the context of a story with situational demands and expectations, but the role is still enacted in somewhat different ways by the different actors who play the role. The script embodies the norms that constrain the enactment of the role, but the actor both "takes" the role within those constraints as boundaries and "makes" the role his own with the skills and talents he brings to a role.

A final important feature of role theory is the assumption that a role is *social*, that is, a role identity (ego) cannot exist without a counterrole identity (alter) to complete the role dyad. For example, the role of teacher cannot exist without the counterrole of student, the role of parent requires the counterrole of child, and so on (Walker 1992; Wendt 1999). The ensuing social interaction associated with the enactment of role and counterrole by ego and alter under the influence of their respective situational constraints and agent characteristics generates the processes of role taking and role making constituting the general process of role location and culminating in role enactment by ego and alter. So it is with states that enact different roles in the social domain of world politics— for every ego (self's particular role identity), there is an alter (other's particular counterrole identity).

The intersecting strategies of cooperation (+) or conflict (−) identified as strategic interaction patterns in sequential game theory are not just power games. Power distributions and the exercise of positive or negative sanctions by the players also influence the constitution of roles and counterroles and strategic interactions in social encounters, which are constructed by the enactment of roles assigned to ego and alter by the distribution and exercise of power in political games. Role location and its subsidiary processes of role taking and role making precede and accompany role enactment in strategic interaction episodes; they are embedded within game theory models in pre-play communication, in the cues from actual moves of ego and alter within a game, and in the repeated plays of games between them over time.

Violations of the rules of rational choice specified by TOM are also violations of the norms for the roles of ego or alter in those games. Foreign policy mistakes of diagnosis and prescription are the product of errors in role location generated by faulty role-taking or role-making processes on the part of ego and alter. Sequential games of strategic rationality in the broader context of role theory become simply formal models of these processes, in which the power distributions and preference rankings act as role demands and expectations that script the roles for ego and alter. Crises occur between two states (ego and alter) when there is uncertainty about the situational features that define their respective roles toward one another or when one of the roles is occupied by a "bad" actor who does not understand his role. Either it is unclear to ego or alter what the power distribution or strategies are that define the power game between them. Or one of the players does not have the skills or talents to enact the role defined by these features of the situation and makes mistakes that cause uncertainty regarding how to act by the occupant of the counterrole. Resolution of this uncertainty occurs as states exchange behaviors that lead to a climax in the form of a final outcome for the crisis consistent with a shared definition of the situation regarding the distribution and exercise of power between them (Snyder and Diesing 1977; Leng and Walker 1982).

Pre-play communication as well as decisions to "stay" or "move" from an initial state or at intermediate states on the way to a final outcome may facilitate the dual processes of role location and strategic interaction. These processes may take on rather complex forms: states can alter their roles during a crisis as the uncertainty regarding the distribution and exercise of power is resolved and old strategies are replaced with new ones. Over longer periods of strategic interaction, one member of a dyad (ego) may socialize the other member (alter) into a new role through the process of "altercasting," for example, ego's enactment of a cooperation role when alter is expecting the enactment of a conflict role may induce alter to respond with a different counterrole that matches the new cues (Walker 1987, 84–89, 1992, 2004b; Wendt 1999; C. Thies 2001). Enduring rivalries or wars in the domain of world politics may be particularly difficult to transform by altercasting and perhaps require instead an alteration in the power distribution between symmetrical rivals (Malici 2006, 2008; Maoz and Mor 2002). Altercasting is the basis for the process of role transition known as graduated reciprocation in tension reduction (GRIT) and its extensions between members of a dyad over time and across issues (Osgood 1960; Goldstein and Freeman 1990).

The steps in a classic GRIT strategy are for one member of a dyad (ego) to announce a cooperative initiative, invite reciprocity from the other member (alter), and continue the initiative over a sufficient period of time to signal its sincerity even if not immediately reciprocated. If the initiative is successful in eliciting a cooperative response from alter, then it may move forward in de-escalating tensions within the dyad by further sequential, graduated steps by ego and alter (Osgood 1962; Goldstein and Freeman 1990; Etzioni 1962). The graduated, reciprocated features of GRIT make it reversible and also compatible with the strategy of disjointed incrementalism. It may focus on strategic roles that characterize the interactions of a dyad regarding a specific issue, such as arms control, or be extended to include a broader range of issues as in the case of Soviet-U.S. détente relations during the Nixon administration regarding arms control, economic issues, and regional conflicts in the third world (Osgood 1960, 1962; Etzioni1962; Goldstein and Freeman 1990, 14–17).

The process of role location underlying a GRIT strategy of altercasting aims at matching a pair of strategic roles and counterroles, in which the distribution of power acts as a constraint on the selection and enactment of the roles of the respective members in a strategic dyad (Walker 1979, 1987; Wendt 1999, 329–332). All three variables, strategic roles, tactical cues, and power distribution, need to be congruent for a totally coherent role location process to occur and raise the likelihood of a strategic interaction process that is completely rational, that is, free of procedural errors by the players and leading to an NME. The menu of the most credible combinations of strategic roles, tactical cues, and power distributions is shown in Figure 8.1.

FIGURE 8.1   *Congruent Strategies, Tactics, and Power Distributions*

Strategic Role Dyads	Power Distributions and Tactical Cues*		
Ego/Alter	Ego > Alter	Ego = Alter	Ego < Alter
Ego(+)/Alter(+)	Exploit/Appease	Reward/Reward	Appease/Exploit
Ego(+)/Alter(−)	Exploit/Bluff	Deter/Punish	Appease/Bully
Ego(−)/Alter(+)	Bully/Appease	Compel/Reward	Bluff/Exploit
Ego(−)/Alter(−)	Bully/Bluff	Punish/Punish	Bluff/Bully

* Tactical cue sequences to enact a cooperative (+) role are as follows: exploit=DDE; reward=DDD; deter=DEE; appease=DED. Tactical cue sequences to enact a conflict (−) role are as follows: bluff=EED; compel=EDD; punish=EEE; bully=EDE.

The greater the power of ego vis-à-vis alter, the less constrained is ego in the process of role location. If ego > alter, then ego may credibly select either one of the strategic roles of cooperation (+) or conflict (−) and any of their tactical variants in Figure 8.1 because ego has the power to enact all of them. By extension if ego = alter, then ego may credibly select only the strategic roles associated with those roles in which ego = alter or ego < alter. If ego < alter, then Ego may credibly select only the strategic roles associated with that power distribution. These same constraints on role selection also apply to alter. It follows that tactical cues sent by ego and alter in the process of role location are likely to be more or less credible, depending on their congruence with the power distribution between ego and alter and the latitude for role selection it bestows on each member of the dyad.

Social exchange theory models the processes of role taking and role making in role theory between two actors. As the name implies, "exchange" theory focuses on the act of giving or taking one thing in return for another, such as the exchange of cues by ego and alter (Walker 1987, 85–89; Homans 1961; Blau 1964; Baldwin 1978). The behavior exchanged by ego and alter may communicate both the exercise and the distribution of power between them. The valence of their behavior indicates the exercise of power as either positive (+) or negative (−) sanctions while the sequence of tactics signals the distribution of power. Ego(+)/Alter(+) and Ego(−)/Alter(−) strategic role dyads exhibit role taking and mirroring regarding the exercise of power, because their valences are congruent (+,+ or −,−). If ego initiates cooperation (+) or conflict (−), then alter takes the cue and responds with a congruent exercise of power. In contrast, the

Ego(+)/Alter(−) and Ego(−)/Alter(+) role dyads show role making by ego and altercasting by alter, whose response is incongruent with ego's exercise of power in each case.[3]

The combinations of tactical sequences of behavior in Figure 8.1 are displayed in Figure 8.2 as instances of role making or role taking by ego or alter regarding the exercise of power and the distribution of power. The initial pair of escalatory (E) or de-escalatory (D) moves by ego and alter are social acts that define the strategic situation between them as a no-conflict (+,+), mixed-motive (+,− or −,+), or conflict (−,−) situation. The third and fourth moves in the sequence of tactics signal the power distribution as symmetrical (=) or asymmetrical (> or <) between ego and alter and whether the two members of the dyad agree on the power distribution. Four alternating moves between ego and alter are necessary to construct a complete definition of the strategic situation, which can then be modeled with sequential game theory. If the two members of the role dyads in Figure 8.2 agree on both the strategic situation and the power distribution, the two tactical sequences in each role dyad should converge in a definition of the situation that corresponds both to the power distribution and an exercise of power by each actor appropriate for the situation constructed by their respective exchange of cues.

The distribution of power acts as a constraint on the selection of escalatory or de-escalatory tactics by each member of the dyad along with the initial pair of moves between them as cues that define the situation as a no-conflict, mixed-motive, or conflict situation. The possible outcomes of the initial exchange of tactics (**ED, DD, EE, DE**) in the four quadrants assume that ego (in bold) always moves first in the sequence of four moves; however, the logic of possible sequences is exhaustive since the outcomes are the same if the two actors reverse roles and alter initiates the same first move in each quadrant under the same power constraints specified for ego.

It is also instructive to note that ego and alter do not always follow the exact tactics theoretically associated with the power distribution. The power distribution does not affect the outcomes in the upper-left quadrant, because the initial exchange of de-escalatory moves (DD) constructs the situation as a no-conflict (+,+) situation, which both parties can subse-

FIGURE 8.2   *Patterns of Tactical Role Taking and Role Making*

	POS (+)	Alter's Cues	NEG (−)

	ROLE TAKING (+,+)	ROLE MAKING (+,−)
P	IF Ego > Alter: Exploit/Appease (DDDD).	IF Ego > Alter: Exploit/Bluff (DEED).
O	IF Ego = Alter: Reward/Reward (DDDD).	IF Ego = Alter: Deter/Punish (DEEE).
S	IF Ego < Alter: Appease/Exploit (DDDD).	IF Ego < Alter: Appease/Bully (DEDE).
(+)		
	NO-CONFLICT (+,+)	MIXED-MOTIVE (+,−)

Ego's
Cues
_____

	MIXED-MOTIVE (−,+)	CONFLICT (−,−)
N	IF Ego > Alter: Bully/Appease (EDED).	IF Ego > Alter: Bully/Bluff (EEED).
E	IF Ego = Alter: Compel/Reward (EDDD).	IF Ego = Alter:Punish/Punish (EEEE).
G	IF Ego < Alter: Bluff/Exploit (EDDE).	IF Ego < Alter: Bluff/Bully (EEDE).
(−)		
	ROLE MAKING (−,+)	ROLE TAKING (−,−)

E = escalatory (−) move; D = de-escalatory (+) move. Ego and alter make alternate moves in sequences.
POS (+) and NEG (−) are the exercise of power with positive (+) or negative (−) sanctions.

quently reinforce as an equilibrium. Two other exceptions are in the (−,+) and (−,−) quadrants. In the (−,+) case with ego < alter, ego's pursuit of a successful bluff (i.e., bully) (**EDE**) tactic would elicit a deter (**DEE**) tactic by alter in order to achieve alter's second-ranked (E,E) outcome and result in ego's fourth-ranked (E,E) outcome. In the (−,−) case with ego > alter, ego pursues a punish (**EEE**) tactic rather than a bully (**EDE**) tactic in order to avoid a possible fourth-ranked outcome of (**D,E**) and induce a possible first-ranked outcome of (**E,D**) or second-ranked (E,E) outcome consistent with the power distribution.

In these instances a move by one player acts as an additional constraint on the menu of tactics by the other player. It is possible for either ego or alter to choose different moves than the ones specified in Figure 8.2 by these tactical sequences under these power constraints, but they would be mistakes. They would violate a credible path toward an outcome ranked consistently with the power distribution between them and their initial exercise of power toward one another. What constitutes such a violation is within the control of the actors because mistakes are path dependent. With their initial moves, actors choose the paths that define the situation. Although the *distribution* of power may not be immediately susceptible to change, their *exercise* of power defines the situation between them as a no-conflict, mixed-motive, or conflict situation.

Some actors (the stronger one in an asymmetrical power distribution) also have the ability to enact roles in accord with a symmetrical power distribution and thereby empower weaker actors to adopt a counterrole that is consistent with a symmetrical power distribution. A commitment by stronger actors to follow norms and rules or agree to negotiate in addressing and resolving conflicts is an example of such empowerment via altercasting on the part of the stronger member of a role dyad. This kind of commitment leads to the adoption of a strategy of cooperation by the stronger actor and the enactment of positive cues in the form of de-escalatory moves, which risks exploitation by the weaker actor. As we have already noted, if alter as the stronger actor in the lower-left quadrant in Figure 8.2 responds with a cooperation move (D) to a conflict move (E) by ego, there is a risk that ego will be emboldened to choose (E) instead of (D) as the third move in the tactical bluff sequence. Instead of an opportunity for a D,D outcome, which would have avoided both a D,E and an E,D outcome, alter would be constrained to choose "E" and an E,E outcome.

These examples show that the role location process with its constituent role-making and role-taking processes is not exactly predictable, because they are specified by the choices of the actors in the exercise of power as well as constrained by the distribution of power between them. The internal normative logic of strategic rationality dictates that the exercise of power by one actor can both influence and be influenced by the exercise of power by the other actor in a dyad. Therefore, the real issue becomes whether the power distribution permits an actor to pursue a dominant or a contingent strategy and what consequences are associated with each choice in the exercise of power. A dominant strategy is "always choose cooperation (de-escalation)" or "always choose conflict (escalation)" no matter what choice the other actor selects. A contingent strategy is more flexible and can shift between cooperation (de-escalation) and conflict (escalation), depending on the choice that the other actor selects.

The simulation results in Chapter 7 demonstrated generally that contingent strategies of cooperation produced superior outcomes over both dominant and contingent strategies of conflict. In the following two case studies of U.S. foreign policy in Vietnam and Iraq, we shall examine how contingent and dominant strategies have fared in fixing foreign policy mistakes in the fog of war. A case employing a dominant cooperation strategy—that is, "always choose cooperation"—is not tested against the others on the realist theoretical assumptions that "submission" *ceteris paribus* is generally the lowest-ranked outcome for all actors in world politics and an obvious risk associated with a strategy of unconditional cooperation.[4] The normative argument framed in our analysis is that the dual answers to the *kto-kovo* question of who (controls) whom provide the appropriate norm for making political decisions by constraining what is possible, thereby making the conduct of politics "the art of the possible" in Bismarck's words (Knowles 1999, 116).

The distribution of power between actors constrains the selection of credible political tactics, and the exercise of power in the form of positive or negative sanctions shapes the political outcomes of settlement, deadlock, domination, and submission that specify who controls whom and by what means. The processes of role taking and role making model the exercise of power according to the constraints of the distribution of power between actors and their own sequence of choices leading to one of these outcomes as the equilibrium (final outcome). The exchange of cues communicates their respective rankings for these four outcomes and thereby defines what is rational for each actor to choose. Each actor's ranking is a function of the power distribution between them and their operational codes, that is, each actor's choice propensities about whether to enact a cooperation (+) or conflict (−) role and their diagnostic propensities regarding the other actor's propensities to enact a counterrole of cooperation (+) or conflict (−).[5]

Role theory's explanation of role enactment depends most immediately on the power distribution and the cues exchanged between actors. The impact of these situational demands and stimuli are mediated by the skills and talents of ego and alter as they exchange cues and make inferences from them and the power distribution. A skilled politician schooled by experience or blessed with the talent to understand the logic of power politics as the art of the possible will be able to detect whether the cues exchanged by ego and alter are compatible with the power distribution between them (Gelb 2009). As the exchange of moves occurs, a skilled player in the game of power politics learns from the other player's moves and is also sensitive to changes in the distribution of power between them. She will change her operational code from cooperation to conflict at different levels of decision (strategies, tactics, or moves) to reflect these emerging social realities. Failures to detect and adapt to this information and its implications constitute diagnostic and prescriptive foreign policy mistakes.

In order to understand why some political players make mistakes while others avoid them, it is necessary to investigate the sources of their errors. Asking this question is like asking why a baseball player caught or dropped a ball, hit or missed a pitch, threw to the right or the wrong base. Assessments of a player's skill and talent (agent characteristics) along with estimations of the difficulty of the task (situational features) constitute immediate answers to the question of why a player did or did not enact his or her role in any game according to the norms that govern it. Our explanation for the enactment of roles between players in the game of power politics is also couched in terms of each actor's skills and talents and the difficulty of the situation that confronts them. Our application of role theory offers primarily normative rather than empirical generalizations, because it assumes that the norms (rules) of a game should govern the behavior of the players; it does not really address the empirical question of why there are differences in skills and talents or situations that account for errors in following these rules.[6] It is sufficient to point out that these actors have failed to employ whatever skills or talent they possess to meet the challenges of their situations.[7]

In the following case studies of U.S. decisions in the Vietnam and Iraq conflicts, the focus is on whether U.S. leaders followed the rules of rationality in choosing cooperation or conflict as strategies to fix a decision to escalate each conflict into a war that became deadlocked and seemed headed for a U.S. defeat. In both cases U.S. leaders failed to estimate correctly either the dynamics of the local balance of power between the United States and its putative foes or the efficacy and costs of negative sanctions (military force) in reaching the normative goals of diplomatic settlement or military victory as outcomes.

How did these diagnostic and prescriptive mistakes lead to decisions to escalate to war? How were they directly and immediately attributable to deficiencies in the skills and talents of U.S. leaders and to the difficult features of each situation? We have already analyzed the answer for the Vietnam conflict to these questions in Chapter 4. Therefore, our narrative for this case study continues here as U.S. leaders attempted to fix these mistakes and their consequences. Our examination of the Iraq case begins with the mistakes that led to a U.S. escalation of the conflict into a war and then focuses on the ensuing efforts to correct them. In each case study we ask the same questions: Was the strategy pursued by the U.S. consistent with the normative rules of rationality for strategies of cooperation and conflict specified by the dual answers to the *kto-kovo* question? Did U.S. leaders identify correctly the power distribution between the United States and Vietnam or Iraq? And did the United States enact either a role of cooperation or conflict within the constraints created by this power distribution and the exercise of power by the other member of the role dyad? Did the results construct a shared definition of the situation, which led to a stable equilibrium as the final outcome?[8]

ENDING THE VIETNAM WAR

A renewed effort to end the war between U.S. and North Vietnamese forces and their respective allies in South Vietnam accompanied the election of President Richard Nixon and the appointment of Henry Kissinger as the White House assistant for national security affairs. In 1969, the Nixon administration opened negotiations with North Vietnam, which would not end until January 1973 with the signing of the Paris Peace Agreements. The terms of this agreement called for a cease-fire, the withdrawal of U.S. troops, and the return of American POWs. The agreement also called for the creation of a national council of reconciliation and concord in South Vietnam. After the United States withdrew and American POWs came home, Saigon and Hanoi renewed their fighting, and

Vietnam became unified under a Communist regime. The end of the Vietnam conflict came in the form of a mutual peace agreement between Washington and Hanoi plus a subsequent military victory by North Vietnam over South Vietnam (Walker 1977, 2004).

The strategy employed by the Nixon administration toward the achievement of this outcome followed a two-track approach to the negotiations in Paris, which was foreshadowed in an article by Henry Kissinger (1969) published in *Foreign Affairs* before he became President Nixon's assistant for national security affairs. He advocated a two-track approach in which the United States and North Vietnam would negotiate a staged withdrawal of external forces while the contending forces in South Vietnam would work out a political agreement. The first agreement was intended to create a maximum incentive for reaching the second agreement, whose content would be left to the South Vietnamese (Kissinger 1974, 130, 211–234). Kissinger later became the chief U.S. negotiator in key meetings with North Vietnamese officials over the next four years. His approach conflicted with North Vietnam's approach, which called for a one-track negotiations strategy linking a cease-fire and troop withdrawals to the replacement of the Saigon regime with a coalition government that included the National Liberation Front of forces opposed to the South Vietnamese government.

Kissinger would spend three and a half years trying to implement a two-track approach. In the summer of 1970, the U.S. position shifted slightly in an attempt to break the diplomatic deadlock and proposed a cease-fire in place. After Kissinger presented this option secretly to a North Vietnamese negotiator in September, U.S Ambassador David Bruce also officially placed this proposal on the table in October at the Paris talks. North Vietnam's response in both settings was the same—a restatement of their previous one-track negotiating position (Walker 1977, 144).

The exchange of cues between the United States and North Vietnam during 1969 and 1970 is summarized in Figure 8.3. The games constructed by these patterns are next to the sequences of cues and show a total of four games in this period. The bilateral power distribution between the United States and North Vietnam is asymmetrical; however, it was symmetrical at the local level between existing U.S. and North Vietnamese

FIGURE 8.3 *Strategic Interaction Episodes between the United States and North Vietnam, 1969–1970*

Game	State	Move Date	Narrative Description
[BEGIN	E, E	STALEMATE]	
4,3 1,4	D, E	01 U-D 0169	Propose 2-track approach & mutual troop withdrawal.
↑	D, E	02 V-E 0269	Launch fairly large-scale offensive.
"2,2" 3,1	E, E	03 U-E 0369	Begin secret bombing of Cambodia.
(IO)	E, D	04 V-D 0469	State readiness for discussions.
GAME 1 D, D	05 U-D 0569		Call for mutual withdrawal/announce 25,000 troop leave.
4,4 1,2	D, D	06 V-D 0669	NVN units withdraw from SVN/break down to small units.
↑	D, D	07 U-D 0769	Propose serious negotiations—secret talks.
"3,1"→2,3*	D, D	08 V-D 0769	Approve secret meeting.
(IO)	E, D	09 U-E 0869	Meet/exchange well-known views.
	E, E	10 V-E 0869	Meet/exchange well-known views (1-track approach).
GAME 2 D, E	11 U-D 0969		Announce second troop withdrawal (35,000).
4,2←"2,4"	D, E	12 V-E 0969	Dismiss 2nd troop withdrawal/concentrate heavy forces.
	D, E	13 U-D 1269	Announce 3rd troop withdrawal (50,000)/more to come.
1,1 3,3*	D, E	14 V-E 1269	Infiltration rate down Ho trail increases 5–10 times.
(IO)	D, E	15 U-D 1269	Reduce air sorties/reduce search-destroy ground ops.
GAME 3 D, D	16 V-D 0170		Ready for serious negotiations/condemn Vietnamization.
4,3 → 1,4	D, D	17 U-D 0270	Meet/probe on POW treatment issue.
↑ ↓	D, E	18 V-E 0270	Meet/demand Thieu ouster plus troop withdrawal.
"2,2" 3,1	E, E	19 U-E 0470	Promise withdraw/warn NVN/in-out Camb/ready for talks.
(IO)	E, D	20 V-D 0570	Approve talks.
	D, D	21 U-D 0970	Meet/propose new cease-fire plan.
	D, E	22 V-E 0970	Meet/reiterate demand Thieu out/coalition govt.
GAME 4 E, E	23 U-E 0271		Invade-withdraw Laos/meet and propose new peace plan.

Brams nonmyopic equilibria are in bold, and Nash myopic equilibria are asterisked. Initial outcome (IO) states are in quotation marks ,and final outcomes are underlined.

Source: Data are from Walker (2004a), appendix 1, 304–306.

forces inside South Vietnam.[9] Three of the games (G1, G3, and G4) are mixed-motive games in which at least one player signals a preference for settlement (upper-left cell) as the highest-ranked outcome while the other player signals a preference for domination (lower-left or upper-right cell) as the highest-ranked outcome. The fourth game (G2) is a no-conflict game in which both players signal a preference for settlement as their highest-ranked outcome. The tactical sequences of cues employed by both players generally reflect these power distributions and the operational codes selected by each player.[10]

An exception is G3 in which each player's cues are consistent with an asymmetrical power distribution that favors Hanoi over Washington. As the stronger player, the United States ultimately has the discretion to employ any tactical sequence of cues and to enact either a cooperative (+) or a conflictual (–) role. North Vietnam can enact either role within the constraints of a symmetrical power distribution for the conflict in South Vietnam and an asymmetrical power distribution favoring the United States for the conflict between North Vietnam and the United States outside of South Vietnam.[11] However, in these games the two players do not agree on a definition of the power distribution, nor do they agree on the definition of the situation as cooperation or conflict, with the exception of Game 2. So it should not be surprising that the final outcomes of these games are neither myopic nor nonmyopic equilibria.

The role location process leading to the initial outcomes (IOs) of these strategic interaction episodes did not sufficiently reduce the uncertainty in the definition of the situation to reach a stable equilibrium as the final outcome. The United States signaled consistently with its tactical cues that it ranked settlement (upper-left cell) as its highest-ranked (4) outcome while North Vietnam signaled domination (upper-right cell) as its highest-ranked (4) outcome in each game except Game 2. The role-taking process shows that the United States responded to each de-escalatory move by North Vietnam with a de-escalatory move with one exception (Move 09 in G2) while responding to escalatory moves by Hanoi with escalatory moves three times and de-escalatory moves three times. The role-making process in each game shows that the United States pursued cooperation initiatives as the first moves in G1 and G4 while North Vietnam engaged in altercasting as the second moves in both games to define them as mixed-motive games. North Vietnam pursued a cooperation initiative as the first move in G2 and a conflict initiative as the first move in G3. The U.S. response as the second move in G2 mirrored North Vietnam's initiative to define it as a no-conflict game; the United States engaged in altercasting as the second move in G3 to define it as a mixed-motive game.

In the summer of 1971 after the invasion of Laos by South Vietnamese troops, Kissinger met with a member of North Vietnam's Politburo. In a series of six meetings between May 31 and September 13, he continued to advocate the U.S. cease-fire-in-place proposal, and Le Duc Tho responded with a nine-point peace plan that Kissinger adopted as a basis for future negotiations. On August 16, Kissinger presented an eight-point plan that closely paralleled the nine points in Hanoi's plan and attempted to bridge the gap on two points that remained in contention. However,

Hanoi decided to reject the U.S. proposal after considering it for four weeks (Kalb and Kalb 1974, 182–183). The diplomatic deadlock continued throughout the autumn of 1971 and into the spring of 1972. After a massive North Vietnam military offensive across the demilitarized zone (DMZ) and the resumption of U.S. bombing above the DMZ in March and April, Kissinger and Le Duc Tho met again on May 2 in Paris (Walker 1977, 144).

Kissinger proposed a withdrawal of U.S. forces from Indochina within four months in return for a cease-fire agreement and the return of U.S. POWs. Tho rejected this offer and reiterated demands for the ouster of the Saigon government and its replacement with a coalition government, which would be linked to a U.S. military withdrawal. On May 8, President Nixon decided to mine Haiphong and other North Vietnamese ports and accompanied this action with B-52 airstrikes on railroads linking North Vietnam with China (Nixon 1972). Following a Soviet-U.S. summit in June and Sino-Soviet pressure on Hanoi to negotiate seriously with the United States, all major North Vietnamese diplomats returned to Hanoi for consultations (Walker 1977, 145).

On July 19, Washington and Hanoi announced jointly that Kissinger and Tho would resume talks in Paris. By September, North Vietnam had accepted the need for a regime in South Vietnam that was not imposed by one side on the other. These meetings culminated on September 26 when the Hanoi diplomat proposed a "National Council of Reconciliation and Concord" that would lack governmental powers, operate on the unanimity principle, and be composed of the Saigon, NLF, and neutralist segments of South Vietnam's political groups. He also proposed putting in place a cease-fire that would be limited to South Vietnam and did not demand the ouster of the Saigon regime. North Vietnam had finally signaled the end of a one-track approach to the negotiations (Kalb and Kalb 1974, 339–340, 345–346, 349).

On October 8, 1972, Tho met with Kissinger and presented a nine-point proposal that incorporated the two-track approach to the issues of a cease-fire, troop withdrawal, and the Saigon regime's status. Kissinger accepted it, subject to working out some minor revisions, after consultation with President Nixon. The two diplomats then worked out a tentative timetable for completing the revisions, clearing the document with Saigon, initialing the draft document, and signing the final document by October 26, 1972 (Kalb and Kalb 1974, 354–356). However, the United States was unable to meet this timetable, as President Thieu of South Vietnam objected to the terms of the agreement and persuaded President Nixon to support him. He objected to the cease-fire without requiring concomitant withdrawal of North Vietnamese forces and recognition of the DMZ as more than a provisional boundary between North and South Vietnam (Kalb and Kalb 1974, 382–383, 390, 392, 396, 398; Szulc 1974, 54–9; see also Walker 1977).

The exchange of cues between the United States and North Vietnam during 1971 and 1972 is analyzed in Figure 8.4. The bilateral power distribution for the four games constructed by these patterns continues to be stipulated as asymmetrical in favor of the United States between it and North Vietnam and symmetrical at the local level between existing U.S. and North Vietnamese forces in South Vietnam. Three of the games (G5, G6, and G8) are no-conflict games in which both players signal a preference for settlement (upper-left cell) as the highest-ranked outcome. The fourth game (G7) is a conflict game in which both players signal a preference for domination as their highest-ranked outcome.

The tactical sequences of cues employed by both players generally reflect these power distributions and the initial two moves (E or D) selected by each player, with the exception of G6, in which North Vietnam enacts a conflict role consistent with an asymmetrical power distribution in its favor. North Vietnam cannot credibly enact this role with a DDE tactic within the constraints of either a symmetrical power distribution for the localized domestic conflict inside South Vietnam or an unfavorable external power asymmetry between North Vietnam and the United States. The United States as the stronger player ultimately has the discretion to employ any tactical sequence of cues and to enact either a cooperative (+) or a conflictual (–) role. The two players agree on a definition of the power distribution in only one game (G5); however, they agree on the definition of the situation as cooperation (+,+) or conflict (–,–) in all four games. Nevertheless, the final outcomes of these games are neither myopic nor

FIGURE 8.4 *Strategic Interaction Episodes between the United States and North Vietnam, 1971–1972*

Game		State	Move Date	Narrative Description
"4,4"→1,2		E, D	24 V-D 0571	Meet/demand political settlement/propose 9-pt. plan.
		D, D	25 U-D 0671	Meet and accept new plan as basis for settlement.
2,1	3,3*	D, D	26 V-D 0671	Meet/reiterate public demand/private support 9-plan.
(IO)		D, D	27 U-D 0771	Meet/agree on 7 of 9 pts. of NVN plan/propose 2 pts.
GAME 5		D, E	28 V-E 0971	Refuse 2-pt. proposal/stop negotiations 2 mos. later.
4,4	"1,3"	D, E	29 U-D 0172	Propose new try at secret negotiations.
	↓	D, D	30 V-D 0272	Accept proposal/propose postponement until 04-15-72.
2,1	3,2*	D, D	31 U-D 0372	Propose 04-24-72 for new date.
(IO)		D, E	32 V-E 0372	Approve 04-24-72/Attack massively across DMZ.
GAME 6		E, E	33 U-E 0472	Bomb NVN/promise withdrawal/meet/propose cease-fire.
"3,3"	1,4	E, E	34 V-E 0572	Meet/reject cease-fire/demand Thieu out/continue invade.
		E, E	35 U-E 0572	Step up bombing—mine Hanoi & Haiphong.
4,2*	2,1	E, D	36 V-D 0572	NVN troops pause outside Hue to regroup.
GAME 7		D, D	37 U-D 0672	New peace proposal at Moscow summit (Szulc 1974, 43).
4,4	1,2	D, D	38 V-D 0872	Meet/propose unimposed provisional government.
		D, D	39 U-D 0972	Meet/agree to meet again.
"3,1"	2,3	D, D	40 V-D 0972	Meet/propose tripartite interim govt/meet again.
GAME 8		E, D	41 U-E 1072	Announce U.S. won't be stampeded into agreement.

Brams nonmyopic equilibria are in bold, and Nash myopic equilibria are asterisked. Initial outcome (IO) states are in quotation marks, and final outcomes are underlined.
Source: Data are from Walker (2004a), appendix 1, 304–306.

nonmyopic equilibria, with G6 as an exception in which deadlock (3,2) is both the final outcome and a Nash myopic equilibrium.

In the role location process leading to the initial outcomes (IOs) of these strategic interaction episodes, both the United States and North Vietnam signaled consistently with their tactical cues that they ranked settlement (upper-left cell) as the highest-ranked (4) outcome in each game except G7. The role-taking process shows that the United States responded to each de-escalatory move by North Vietnam with a de-escalatory move with one exception (Move 41 in G8), while responding to escalatory move by Hanoi with escalatory moves two times and de-escalatory move one time. The role-making process in each game shows that the United States pursued a cooperation initiative as the first move in G6 and that North Vietnam engaged in mirroring as the second move to define it as a no-conflict game. North Vietnam pursued a cooperation initiative as the first move in two games (G5, G8) and a conflict initiative as the first move in G7. The U.S. response as the second move in G7 mirrored North

Vietnam's initiative to define it as a conflict game, and the United States also engaged in mirroring as the second move in the other two games to define them as no-conflict games.

After the United States airlifted a year's worth of military supplies into South Vietnam, negotiations resumed in November and became deadlocked in December over the Nixon-Thieu demand that the DMZ be recognized as a frontier between the two Vietnams. There was also disagreement over the protocols that would implement the agreement and on the identification of the legitimate political groups in South Vietnam (Kalb and Kalb 1974, 379–385, 411). President Nixon responded with a seventy-two-hour ultimatum to Hanoi that serious negotiations would have to be resumed and a warning to Saigon that any further obstruction on Thieu's part would result in a separate U.S.–North Vietnamese agreement and a cutoff of U.S. aid to Saigon. On December 17, B-52s bombed Hanoi for twelve days, followed by a halt and the president's call for the resumption of negotiations. Le Duc Tho and Kissinger began their last round of talks in Paris in January 1973 and completed a final agreement that was signed on January 27 (Kalb and Kalb 1974, 412–415, 418–422; Kissinger 1973, 162–163; see also Walker 1977, 146–147).

The exchange of cues between the United States and North Vietnam during the three endgames in late 1972 and early 1973 are summarized in Figure 8.5. The general power distribution for these games constructed by these patterns continues to be stipulated as asymmetrical in favor of the United States between Washington and Hanoi but symmetrical at the local level between existing U.S. and North Vietnamese forces in South Vietnam. One game (G9) is a no-conflict game while the other two games are conflict (G10) or mixed-motive (G11) games. The tactical sequences of cues employed by both players reflect these power distributions and the cooperation (+) or conflict roles (–) selected by each player in all three games. North Vietnam can (and did) credibly enact a role within the constraints of a symmetrical power distribution for the conflict and a U.S. role in each game that enacted cues consistent with a symmetrical power distribution. As the stronger player, the United States again had the discretion to credibly enact a tactical sequence of cues consistent with any

FIGURE 8.5   *U.S. and North Vietnamese Endgames, 1972–1973*

Game		State	Move Date	Narrative Description
4,4	1,2	E, D	42 V-D 1072	Meet/old Thieu demand/new 9-pt. plan/agree to 2-trk.
		D, D	43 U-D 1072	Meet/agree on draft/propose military halt/request meet.
"3,1"→2,3*		D, D	44 V-D 1072	Invite early resumption of negotiations.
(IO)		E, D	45 U-E 1172	Lift supplies/withdraw SV bases/meet/new U.S.demands.
GAME 9		E, E	46 V-E 1172	Meet/make Thieu ouster demand after new U.S. demands.
3,3	1,4	E, E	47 U-E 1172	Meet/repeat demands.
		E, E	48 V-E 1172	Meet/repeat demands.
4,1	"2,2*"	E, E	49 U-E 1272	Meet/repeat demands.
GAME 10		E, E	50 V-E 1272	Meet/repeat demands.
"3,4"	1,2	E, E	51 U- E 1272	Ultimatum/bomb/limited bomb halt/total if talks again.
		E, D	52 V-D 1272	Agree to talks.
4,1	2,3	D, D	53 U-D 0173	Meet/reach signed agreement.
GAME 11		D, D	54 V-D 0173	Meet/reach signed agreement.
		D, D	55 U-D 0173	Sign formal agreement.
[END		D, D	SETTLEMENT]	

Brams nonmyopic equilibria are in bold, and Nash myopic equilibria are asterisked. Initial outcome (IO) states are in quotation marks, and final outcomes are underlined.
Source: Data are from Walker (2004a), appendix 1, 304–306.

power distribution and select either a cooperative (+) or a conflictual (–) role. The two players agreed on a definition of the power distribution in all three games and agreed on the definition of the situation as cooperation (+,+) or conflict (–,–) in two of the games (G9, G10). The final outcomes of all three games are either a myopic (G9) or a nonmyopic (G10, G11) equilibrium.

In the role location process leading to the initial outcomes (IOs) of these strategic interaction episodes, the United States signaled with tactical cues that it ranked domination (lower-left cell) as its highest-ranked (4) outcome in the final two games (G10, G11), which is a departure from G9 and seven out of the previous eight games. The role-taking process shows that the United States responded to each de-escalatory move by North Vietnam with a de-escalatory move with one exception (Move 45 in G9) while responding to the three escalatory moves by Hanoi with escalatory moves each time. The role-making process in each game shows that the United States pursued a conflict initiative as the first move in G10 and G11; North Vietnam mirrored the U.S. conflict move to define G10 as a conflict game and engaged in altercasting with a cooperation move to define G11 as a mixed-motive game. North Vietnam pursued a cooperation initiative as the first move in G9, and the U.S. response as the second move in G9 mirrored North Vietnam's initiative to define it as a no-conflict game.

Overall, the United States pursued a strategy of conditional cooperation in eight of the eleven strategic interaction episodes, both initiating and reciprocating cues of cooperation in negotiations with North Vietnam, throughout four years in the midst of the "fog of war." Hanoi's approach was a balanced mix of five conflict and six cooperation strategies in the eleven games in the Vietnam chronology, including ten games with contingent strategies and one game (G4) with a dominant conflict strategy. Although the cues leading to an initial outcome in five of the games signaled that settlement (4,4) was the highest-ranked outcome for both players, they did not reach this final outcome in any of those games and reached settlement as a final outcome only in two (G1, G11) games.

These missed cues and opportunities for settlement could be due to the "fog of war" created by the resort to armed violence, ideological mistrust between the players, bureaucratic communications failures within each government, the exigencies of alliance diplomacy, and stress or fatigue inside each government (Walker 1977, 152–153). Whatever their causes, these outcome patterns underline the difficulty of the role location task and the corresponding desirability of pursuing a disjointed incremental strategy in which it is possible to move away from a bad initial outcome following the exchange of cues. In the eleven games between the United States and North Vietnam, the two players pursued a myopic strategy of disjointed incrementalism in 63 percent of the nineteen opportunities following the initial outcome of these games, either choosing "stay" at the IO or choosing "move" from the IO to an immediately better outcome. In 26 percent of the games, the player with the next move decided to "stay" or "move" consistent with a nonmyopic strategy of disjointed incrementalism. One or the other player made a nonrational choice of "stay" or "move" in 11 percent of these opportunities, passing up an opportunity to improve their IO. These results are summarized in Table 8.1.

TABLE 8.1   *Myopic and Nonmyopic Decisions* by the United States and North Vietnam.*

Actor	G1	G2	G3	G4	G5	G6	G7	G8	G9	G10	G11
USA	Move	**Move**	Stay	Move(2)	**Stay**	Move	n/a	n/a	Stay	Stay	**Stay**
NVN	**Stay**	Move	*Move*	Move	*Move*	Stay	**Stay**	Stay	Move	n/a	n/a

Actor	Myopic	Nonmyopic	Nonrational	Total	Not Applicable
USA	70% (7)	30% (3)	0% (0)	100% (10)	(2)
NVN	56% (5)	22% (2)	22% (2)	100% (9)	(2)
Both	63% (12)	26% (5)	11% (2)	100% (19)	(4)

* Decisions to move or stay at initial outcome: myopic decisions are in roman type; nonmyopic decisions are in bold; nonrational decisions are in italics. Not Applicable (n/a) decisions are instances when the player did not have an opportunity to move first after the initial outcome and the other player chose "stay," making the initial outcome also the final outcome.

STARTING THE IRAQ WAR

The horrific events of 9/11 stand as some of the most defining moments in U.S. history. The attacks in New York and Washington, D.C., killed nearly 3,000 people and altered in fundamental ways the foreign policy of the Bush administration. That night the president noted in his diary, "the Pearl Harbor of the 21st century took place today." He subsequently observed that "night had fallen on a different world" and urged other governments around the world to participate in a "global war on terrorism" (qtd. in Woodward 2004, 24). Soon after the terrorist attacks on the World Trade Center and the Pentagon there emerged the question, "Could they have been averted?"—a question that would also stand at the center of the 9/11 Commission's investigation and report to the U.S. Congress. Our assessment is that mistakes were committed in the prelude to 9/11 and that the possibility of averting an attack of the experienced magnitude was indeed present. Drawing on the accounts of participants and close observers of the policy-making process before 9/11, we have argued in detail elsewhere that it is possible to identify this policy episode as containing diagnostic and prescriptive errors of omission leading to a deterrence failure—that is, the threat was not detected as such and for too long there was no sufficient action undertaken to deter the assault (Walker and Malici 2006).

As the 9/11 Commission noted, there was a massive and pervasive "failure of imagination" inside the highest circles of the U.S. government and most of the nation before the attacks on September 11, 2001. Other mistakes led to a false alarm failure in the U.S. responses to 9/11, leading to the invasion and occupation of Iraq. Prior to 9/11:

> The terrorist danger from Bin Ladin and al Qaeda was not a major topic for policy debate among the public, the media, or in the Congress. Indeed, it barely came up during the 2000 presidential campaign. . . . As late as Sept. 4, 2001, Richard Clarke, the White House staffer long responsible for counterterrorist policy coordination, asserted that the government had not yet made up its mind on how to answer the question "Is al Qaeda a big deal?" (The 9/11 Commission 2004, 9)

Indeed, Secretary of Defense Donald Rumsfeld argued at this September 4 meeting that there were other terrorist concerns such as Iraq. Condoleezza Rice ended the discussions without reaching consensus on any ultimate solution.

A few days later the answer to the question "Is al Qaeda a big deal?" came in the most shocking way. In his analysis of this policy episode, Richard Clarke (2004, 238) concludes that "There were failures in the organizations that we trusted to protect us, failures to get information to the right place at the right time, earlier failures to act boldly to reduce or eliminate the threat." These diagnostic and prescriptive errors of omission resulted in the worst attack on U.S. territory since Pearl Harbor. In the next two years the United States attacked al Qaeda and its Taliban hosts in Afghanistan and adopted a series of domestic and foreign policies in an attempt to prevent another al Qaeda attack on U.S. soil. Many of these decisions were controversial, including a domestic surveillance program and the adoption of enhanced interrogation measures that violated preexisting domestic laws and international treaties (Mayer 2009).

U.S. military forces succeeded in overthrowing the Taliban regime, but the pursuit of crucial al Qaeda leaders failed to prevent their escape into the mountains of western Pakistan. It soon turned out that the war in Afghanistan was only the first phase in the U.S.-declared war on terrorism. The Bush administration turned its attention to Iraq and its leader, Saddam Hussein, as a putative supporter of international terrorism and a potential source of weapons of mass destruction (WMD) for terrorist groups. In a series of steps designed to gain domestic support in Congress and international support in the United Nations, the Bush administration pushed through a congressional resolution at home and forged an international "coalition of the willing" with Britain, Australia, and several smaller states to invade Iraq and overthrow the regime of Saddam Hussein (Marfleet and Miller 2005).

Pre-Invasion Mistakes

The principal foreign policy initiative of the administration in response to the 9/11 attacks was a strategy of preemption in dealing with the threat of terrorist attacks with weapons of mass destruction. In adopting this strategy as a remedy for the "too little/too late" decision-making mistakes of omission that led to 9/11, the United States risked engaging in a pattern of "too much/too soon" mistakes of commission. The shock of underestimating and not responding to the threat of an impending attack on New York City and Washington D.C. created an opportunity to make gradual, incremental, and reversible corrections. The Bush administration instead made hasty, radical, and relatively irreversible adjustments, arguing that the United States had entered a new era post-9/11, in which the old rules, such as domestic wiretapping laws, the Geneva Conventions governing interrogations, and traditional strategic doctrines of deterrence and defense employing the use of force, were either "quaint" as in the case of the Geneva treaties or "outdated" as in the case of strategic doctrine (Mayer 2009).

On March 20, 2003, the United States launched a wave of "shock and awe" air strikes against Iraq and then invaded the country (Gordon and Trainor 2006). The justification provided by Washington was dubious evidence of the Iraqi regime's intent to acquire stockpiles of weapons of mass destruction and an apparent link between al Qaeda and Saddam Hussein. The work of the Iraq Survey Group, which was set up to locate these weapons in the aftermath of the war, as well as various intelligence revelations after the war have demonstrated that these propositions were false (Isikoff and Corn 2006). Was the decision to go to war against Iraq a mistake? Examining again the insights provided by participants and observers of the decision-making process, we can identify this policy episode as fitting the criteria for diagnostic and prescriptive errors of commission leading to a false alarm failure, that is, a misperceived threat of conflict coupled with the initiation of preemptive action that escalated the conflict.

Top officials in the administration were committed to eliminating a latent threat regardless of how unlikely it was to become acute. They focused on any information that exaggerated a threat diagnosis; the events of 9/11 at the minimum permitted and at the maximum encouraged a perception of an almost omnipresent threat. President Bush would later remember that the attacks changed his beliefs about "Saddam Hussein's capacity to create harm," while "all his terrible features became much more threatening." In the president's view, the Iraqi dictator was a "madman." Similarly, he remembered about Vice President Cheney that he "was unwavering in his view that Saddam was a real danger" (qtd. in Woodward 2004, 27, 4). These threat perceptions not only would be perpetuated over time but also would increase in magnitude, resulting ultimately in their exaggeration. The president was aware of the controversial claims regarding Iraqi WMD and the possible lack of international support, stating in private conversations with his advisors that "At some point, we may be the only ones left. That's okay with me. We are America" (qtd. in LaFeber 2002).

In contrast to the top officials in the administration, the intelligence community did not consider Saddam to be an imminent danger. A report of the Brookings Institution in January 2002 concluded that "At present, . . . [Saddam Hussein] appears to be contained every bit as well as the North Korean leadership—and much more tightly than was the Soviet Union during the cold war" (Gordon and O'Hanlon 2001, 7). At the same time the National Intelligence Council had begun to assess the raw intelligence, which to a large extent proved unreliable (Clarke 2004, 267). The most viable answer from this material was that Saddam probably had WMD, but that there was no proof and the case was circumstantial. This conclusion was subsequently supported by a State Department intelligence bureau report, stating the evidence did not add up to "a compelling case" that Iraq has "an integrated and comprehensive approach to acquire nuclear weapons" (Woodward 2004, 199).

Despite the lack of evidence, key officials in the administration remained committed to their beliefs about the Iraqi dictator's intentions, the significant threat he posed, and they continued to build a case for the necessity of war. An important step was made on January 29, 2002, when President Bush delivered his State of the Union address to the U.S. Congress. In that speech Bush branded Iraq along with Iran and North Korea as constituting a tiny but lethal "axis of evil." He argued, "States like these and their terrorist allies are arming to threaten the peace of the world. By seeking weapons of mass destruction, these regimes pose a grave and growing danger." The president concluded, "America would not wait on events while dangers gather."

Being convinced of the Iraqi threat, the focus and commitment was on any information that could potentially support the case for an invasion. The president raised the stakes for war even higher in his State of the Union speech the following year, arguing, "Saddam Hussein recently sought significant quantities of uranium from Africa." The claim was based on Italian intelligence reports from 2001, allegedly indicating that Iraqi agents had attempted to buy uranium yellowcake from government officials in Niger. After the evidence was shared with British and U.S. intelligence services, the CIA sent former State Department official Joseph Wilson to investigate in February 2002. Upon his return, Wilson stated in an oral report to both the CIA and State Department officials that he could not confirm the allegations (J. Wilson 2003). What made the president's assertion more dubious was that the National Intelligence Council, prior to the State of the Union speech, concluded that these allegations were "baseless" (Gellman and Linser 2006, A1).

Any claims of Saddam Hussein's connection to al Qaeda also remained unsubstantiated. Shortly after 9/11, the suspicion was aroused that the Iraqi dictator might have been involved in the attacks (Suskind 2006). Richard Clarke assured top officials that there were no connections between al Qaeda and Saddam Hussein because they were "natural enemies." The British Defense Intelligence reached the same conclusion (Halper and Clarke 2004, 214–215). Vice President Cheney still asserted that Mohammed Atta, one of the 9/11 terrorists, had met in Prague with a senior Iraqi intelligence agent five months before the attack. After further investigation, George Tenet reported to the president, "Our Prague office is skeptical. . . . It just doesn't add up" (qtd. in Suskind 2006, 23). Other instances of alleged collaboration between Saddam Hussein and al Qaeda remained equally unsubstantiated. However, the inflated threat perception prevailed, and worse, the diagnostic mistake was coupled with a prescriptive mistake.

Shortly after 9/11, Vice President Cheney argued to the intelligence community and the National Security Council regarding emerging threats, "It is not about our analysis, or finding a preponderance of evidence. It is about our response" (qtd. in Suskind 2006, 62). Eliminating Saddam was an absolute necessity. Cheney's zeal was seen as a fever by some of his colleagues, even as an obsession (Woodward 2004, 4, 132, 175). His declaration would nevertheless become a "standard of action." This standard, as one observer noted, "would frame events and responses from the administration for years to come. . . . Even if there's just a one percent chance of the unimaginable coming due, act as if it is a certainty" (Suskind 2006, 62). Cheney's reasoning, known as the "Cheney doctrine" inside the administration, would deliver the necessary rationale for an assault until the onset of the war in March 2003.

In a June 1, 2002, speech to the cadets at West Point, President Bush declared that old notions such as containment were no longer valid to ensure the security of the United States. He reasoned that the enemy would now consist of "shadowy terrorist networks with no nation or citizens to defend" and "dictators with weapons of mass destruction [who] can deliver those weapons on missiles or secretly provide them to terrorist allies." Faced with such enemies, the president argued, "If we wait for threats to fully materialize, we will have waited for too long." The president concluded, "Our security will require all Americans to be forward looking and resolute [and] to be ready for preemptive action" (qtd. in Keegan 2004, 100; see also Fallows 2004, 56; and Suskind 2006, 149–150).

At the end of August 2002, Vice President Cheney gave a speech to war veterans in Nashville. Cheney labeled Saddam Hussein a "mortal threat" and said that elimination of the Iraqi dictator was necessary to stop this threat. He asserted that Saddam Hussein possessed WMD and that there was no doubt that the Iraqi leader would amass further weapons and not hesitate to use them. According to Cheney, Saddam Hussein "could be expected to seek domination of the entire Middle East, take control of a great portion of the world's energy supplies, directly threaten America's friends throughout the region, and subject the U.S. or any other nation to nuclear blackmail." He concluded that "wars are never won on the defensive," and as the president had done, he issued a call for preemptive action towards Iraq (Cheney 2002).

Conclusive evidence for these assertions was absent. Such diagnoses and prescriptions as the claims by the president and the vice president are "generally understood to be driven by evidence," but given the logic of Cheney's one percent doctrine, it was not needed (Suskind 2006, 150). The strategy was formalized as official U.S. policy when the White House published *The National Security Strategy of the USA* on September 18, 2002 Preemptive strikes were described as legitimate actions in the conduct of international politics contravening the treaties and customs of international law that had made such historical events as Japan's attack on Pearl Harbor illegal and illegitimate. In a prime time address on October 7, the president raised the stakes once more. He did not acknowledge the lack of "smoking gun" evidence. Instead, he suggested an even larger risk, one that his security adviser Condoleezza Rice had publicly raised some weeks earlier. According to the president, "Facing clear evidence of peril we cannot wait for the final proof, the smoking gun, that could come in the form of a mushroom cloud" (Woodward 2004, 202).

The president and other key officials were aware of this lack of evidence. When George Tenet and Deputy Director of Central Intelligence John McLaughlin went to the Oval Office on December 21 to present the case on WMD, Bush was disappointed. He responded, "I've been told all this intelligence about WMD and this is the best we've got?" (qtd. in Woodward 2004, 249). He remained committed nevertheless. Two weeks later, Bush told Condoleezza Rice in a private meeting, "Time is not on our side here. Probably going to have to, we're going to have to go to war." In Rice's mind this was the president's decision, the point of no return. Everything from here onward was set (Woodward 2004, 254). In the weeks to come, intelligence remained scarce and ambiguous. Just a few days before the onset of the war, the *Washington Post* published a story,

"U.S. Lacks Specifics of Banned Arms" (Pincus 2003). The article was based on a senior administration official who had acknowledged that the intelligence was "pretty thin" (qtd. in Woodward 2004, 355).

This intelligence gap did not matter, as Cheney's one percent doctrine prevailed. "It was not about analysis. It was about our reaction" (Suskind 2006, 79). The inflated threat perception also prevailed on March 20, 2003, when the United States translated diagnostic and prescriptive errors of commission into action and went to war with Iraq. Almost six weeks later, on May 1, 2003, President Bush made a landing on the aircraft carrier USS *Abraham Lincoln*. Addressing the nation from the flight deck, he proclaimed, "Major combat operations in Iraq have ended." While major military operations had indeed terminated, a postwar insurgency would emerge and intensify over the next three years as a desolate postwar situation. Again, the question arises whether the postwar situation in Iraq could have been approached differently.

Post-Invasion Mistakes

What mistakes were committed? Assessing the post-invasion period between 2003 and 2009, we find that a diagnostic error of commission resulted in a false hope mistake, that is, a perceived opportunity for cooperation that did not exist. In turn, this misperceived opportunity was associated with a prescriptive error of omission, a reassurance mistake that took the form of insufficient military and political support for the aftermath of major combat operations. These two mistakes preceded the 2003–2006 time period and the invasion of Iraq. The eventual decision to invade Iraq was controversial from the very beginning of the Bush administration's tenure. Secretary of State Powell was concerned about the lack of international support but even more so about the unviable war and postwar planning within top decision-making circles to oust the Saddam Hussein regime. Even before 9/11, Paul Wolfowitz presented draft plans to the president on how to eliminate Saddam Hussein, which in his assessment would be "relatively easy" (qtd. in Woodward 2004, 21). Powell commented, "This is lunacy" and complained that it was not clear where the off switch was or whether there was an off switch. To the president he argued, "Don't let yourself get pushed into anything until you are ready for it or until you think there is a real reason for it. This is not as easy as it is being presented. . . . Don't let anybody push you into it. . . . You don't have to be bullied into this" (Ibid., 22).

The role of Iraq in the administration's strategy after 9/11 was also controversial, and again Colin Powell figured prominently. In the fall of 2002, he expressed his concerns to the president, arguing that an invasion of Iraq could divert energy from the war on terror and destabilize friendly regimes in Saudi Arabia, Egypt, and Jordan, a perception that was shared by Tommy Franks (Woodward 2004, 257). Critical questions for Powell were how long the deployment into Iraq would last and how success would be defined. According to Powell, no clear answers existed, and he warned the president with the Pottery Barn rule, "You break it, you own it." Similar warnings came from Brent Scowcroft, the national security adviser of the senior President Bush. Scowcroft stressed that the consequences in the region would be dire—it could explode in "outrage." An attack on Iraq could turn the entire Middle East into a "cauldron and thus destroy the war on terrorism" (Halper and Clarke 2004, 227; Woodward 2004, 149).

The president and other top officials remained in a state of false and unwarranted optimism throughout the planning period for the aftermath of the war. Too much credence was given to Ahmed Chalabi, the president of the exiled Iraqi National Congress (INC). As Douglas Feith has explained, "Nobody planned for security because Ahmed Chalabi told us that everything was going to be swell" (qtd. in Fallows 2004, 53). Indeed, just three days before the war began, Cheney confirmed, "I really do believe that we will be greeted as liberators." Similarly, Wolfowitz had argued, "I am reasonably certain that they will greet us as liberators, and that will help us keep requirements down" (qtd. in ibid., 65, 73). Because of the diagnostic and prescriptive errors committed in this policy episode, as one observer commented, "We went in with the minimum force to accomplish the military objectives, which was a straightforward task never really in question. And then we immediately found ourselves shorthanded in the aftermath. We sat there and watched people dismantle and run off with the country basically" (qtd. in ibid., 65–66).

Some months after the onset of the war in Iraq, President Bush in an interview was asked about Secretary of State Colin Powell's "Pottery

Barn" warning before the war. Bush responded, "Basically what he was saying was that if in fact Saddam is toppled by military [invasion], we better have a strong understanding about what it's going to take to rebuild Iraq" (qtd. in Woodward 2004, 152). As Undersecretary of Defense for Policy Douglas Feith acknowledged, it has become "conventional wisdom" that the administration did not have such an understanding (qtd. in Fallows 2004, 53). The mistakes leading to this scenario could have been avoided. An analysis by the Army War College's Strategic Studies Institute concluded that the Iraq War was "a strategic error of the first magnitude" (Clarke 2004, 273).

How did such an error occur? With the shock of the attacks in Manhattan and at the Pentagon, the pre-9/11 draft plans for an invasion of Iraq became more concrete. At the president's request, General Tommy Franks prepared a war plan for Iraq that he presented first to Donald Rumsfeld. The plan called for some 500,000 troops, a figure confirmed by Frank's predecessor as CENTCOM commander, Marine General Anthony Zinni (Fallows 2004, 65). However, in anticipation of congressional resistance to such a large deployment, the Secretary of Defense ordered, "Let's put together a group that can just think outside the box completely. Certainly we have traditional military planning, but let's take away the constraints a little bit and think about what might be a way to solve this problem." Shortly afterward, Franks presented a revised plan that cut down the troop size from 500,000 to 400,000, and he commented, "All of us are going to find a lot of difficulties with this plan."

Indeed, Rumsfeld's idea of the appropriate force size was about 75,000, and to Franks he responded, "I am not sure that that much force is needed given what we've learned coming out of Afghanistan" (qtd. in Woodward 2004, 41; see also Fallows 2004, 64). Rumsfeld's idea was reflective of the administration's false hopes about postwar Iraq, which would continue to be perpetuated. The disagreement between the civilian analysts and top military officials continued until shortly before the actual invasion. On February 25, 2003, Army Chief of Staff General Eric Shinseki testified before the Senate Arms Services Committee. Contrary to Rumsfeld and Cheney's advocacy of a "light hand" for the postwar situation, Shinseki reported that several hundred thousand troops would be needed to sustain security in Iraq in the period after the war and thereby echoed the view of other defense analysts developed months earlier (Woodward 2004, 259; Gordon and O'Hanlon 2001).

The heart of the argument was that "with too few soldiers, the U.S. would win the war only to be trapped in an untenable position during the occupation" (Fallows 2004, 65). However, Rumsfeld and Wolfowitz immediately criticized Shinseki and played down the estimate. At a congressional hearing two days later, Wolfowitz described Shinseki's figure as "widely off the mark" (qtd. in Fallows 2004, 73). When combat operations began, slightly more than 200,000 U.S. soldiers were amassed around Iraq (Ibid., 64, 72). An inadequate estimate leading to a false hope failure had prevailed. It would lead to a short-term success as U.S. forces raced to Baghdad, routing resistance from Saddam Hussein's military forces, and a long-term debacle in the form of communal strife among Shia, Sunnis, and Kurds, an insurgency against the post-Saddam regime by Sunni and Shia dissidents, and al Qaeda terrorist activities (Ricks 2006).

Was it possible to minimize and perhaps avoid these unfortunate consequences? Early on the State Department and seventeen other federal agencies had embarked on an enormous effort called the *Future of Iraq Project*. The project was headed by Thomas Warrick, who was considered by many top officials, such as Cheney and Rumsfeld, to be in the antiwar camp. Indeed, to his associates Warrick explained, "I'm nervous that they're actually going to do it—and the day after they'll turn to us and ask, 'Now what?'" (qtd. in Fallows 2004, 56). The project was structured into seventeen working groups. It involved hundreds of Iraqis from the country's many ethnic and religious factions and analyzed a variety of topics. One of the central conclusions was that "The removal of Saddam's regime will provide a power vacuum and create popular anxieties about the viability of all Iraqi institutions" (Fallows 2004, 58). All of the experts agreed that what came after the fall of Baghdad would be harder for the United States than what came before.

Anticipating many of the problems that eventually beset postconflict Iraq, the participants worked on plans for filling the security vacuum, restoring services, and making the transition to democracy. One of the very important arguments was that contrary to the dominant inclination in the Department of Defense, not all Baath Party members should be considered war criminals and that these people would be an integral part of the reconstruction process (Halper and Clarke 2004, 224–225; Phillips 2003). Similar was the project leaders' concern about the plan to disband the entire army rather than do a selective purge at the top. Warrick and his associates were supported by analysts at the Center for Strategic and International Studies and the Army War College. A report of the latter, for example, argued, "To tear apart the Army in the war's aftermath could lead to the destruction of one of the only forces for unity within the society" (Fallows 2004, 74; see also Clarke 2004, 272).

Despite this intensive planning in the State Department, the authority over postwar Iraq would rest with the Department of Defense. The administration chose General Jay Garner to orchestrate all postwar efforts in Iraq. Upon assuming his post, Garner inquired about documents from the Future of Iraq Project. Rumsfeld responded that he ought not to waste his time reading it. Subsequently, Rumsfeld also requested Garner to excise Warrick from his position, discarding the work of Warrick and drawing instead on the advice of the INC that all Baath Party members should be removed from power and that the military should be disbanded. The INC had assured the administration that they controlled a vast underground network that would rise up in support of coalition forces and support the enforcement of security. Soon after the onset of the war, it became evident that this network had failed to materialize, resulting in the power vacuum that contributed directly to the subsequent fiasco enveloping the Iraqi postwar situation (Halper and Clarke 2004, 225; Ricks 2006).

The false hope failure in postwar Iraq was due to several factors, including bureaucratic obstacles and turf battles, cognitive biases among top leaders such as Defense Secretary Rumsfeld, Vice President Cheney, President Bush, and their advisors, and perhaps even a "broken" policy process in which ideological faith replaced empirical evidence as the basis for making foreign policy decisions (Parker and Stern 2002; Suskind 2004, 2006). However, the most immediate cause was a lack or misapplication of skill and talent in addressing the dual aspects of the *ktokovo* (who-whom) question: what is the distribution of power (symmetrical or asymmetrical) between the United States and its friends or foes in Iraq, and what is the most appropriate exercise of power (positive or negative sanctions) in U.S. foreign policy decisions following the attacks on 9/11?

It would take a tacit revolt by U.S. military officers on the ground in Iraq to alter American military strategy, soon reinforced by parallel developments in Washington, D.C., to generate a belated shift from an enemy-centered strategy in 2003–2006 to a population-centered strategy in 2007–2009 known as the "surge" into Baghdad. The new strategy combined antiterrorist tactics that focused on killing or isolating the enemy irreconcilables with counterinsurgency tactics that centered on detaching the reconcilables from the enemy extremists and protecting the neutral population.[12] The strategic objective was on gaining friends and allies rather than on fighting enemies, with a corresponding shift in the mission of military forces to protect civilians instead of killing terrorists. The U.S. military's activities were to police the city of Baghdad rather than to search out and destroy the Sunni or Shia militias and the al Qaeda jihadists. The phrases to describe this shift in strategic focus were tactics of "persistent patience" in patrolling from posts in Baghdad and its environs rather than "repetitive raiding" into the city from U.S. bases outside the city and "seize, clear, and hold" rather than "search and destroy" territory or people (Ricks 2009).

COMPARING U.S. STRATEGIES IN VIETNAM AND IRAQ

What can we learn by comparing the Vietnam and Iraq cases? A comparison reveals some significant differences as well as some important similarities. In the Vietnam case, the United States pursued a two-track strategy in which the guiding principle for one track was a contingent cooperation strategy directed toward reaching a settlement with North Vietnam regarding a mutual troop withdrawal or cease-fire and the return of POWs. The main principle on the other track was supposed to be a strategy of noninvolvement and delegation to a national council of reconciliation and concord for the resolution of conflict among the factions in Vietnam's civil war. In the Iraq case, the United States applied a principle embodied in the Cheney one percent doctrine, which called for a dominant conflict strategy directed toward reaching a military victory in Iraq. There was no attempt to follow a two-track strategy that would differentiate between others in Iraq besides al Qaeda until after 2006, when the strategic shift to active cooperation with various domestic factions in Iraq occurred. Up to that point, the Iraqi government in Baghdad was supposed to deal with them. These relationships are depicted in Figure 8.6.

The Vietnam games have a global power game of détente with a symmetrical power distribution and a dominant strategy of conflict for the United States with either settlement (3,3) or deadlock (2,2) as an NME. Deadlock was both the initial state and the final outcome regarding the regional Vietnam conflict until Kissinger succeeded in gaining Soviet and Chinese support in the summer of 1972 for the negotiations in Paris. He also changed the local game with a symmetrical power distribution from a conflict game that reflected the global game to a mixed-motive game in which the U.S. strategy shifted from a dominant strategy of conflict to a contingent strategy of cooperation with settlement (4,3) as the NME and final outcome. The logic of this game with its strategy of conditional cooperation was also the power game adopted by the United States in 2007 for the "surge" in Iraq after escalation in the domestic conflict between 2003 and 2006 proved the Cheney doctrine's strategy of unconditional conflict to be insufficient and unsustainable.

The Iraq global game also had a dominant strategy of "always choose conflict" for the United States, according to the principle in the Cheney doctrine discussed in our second case study. This principle calls for preemption against a weaker enemy that is perceived to have the power to hit the United States. This prescription implies symmetrical hostile views and an asymmetrical power relationship between ego (the United States) and alter (other). Cheney's game, derived from these two propositions, has a dominant strategy of conflict for the United States and a predicted final outcome (4,2) of U.S. domination over other. The logic of this game is also consistent with Rumsfeld's pre-9/11 military strategy of dissuasion and the Bush administration's post-9/11 national security doctrine of preemption.[13] This game is based on a correct answer to the *kto-kovo* question regarding the global power game preceding the invasion of Iraq.

FIGURE 8.6 *Nested Games and U.S. Strategies in the Cold War and Post-9/11 Eras*

	Other				Other			
	CO Global	D Local	E Local	CF Global	CO Global	D Local	E Local	CF Global
CO Global	<u>3,3</u>			1,4	2,3			1,4
D Local		<u>4,3</u>	1,4			3,3	1,4	
E Local		2,1	"3,2"*			4,1	"2,<u>2</u>"*	
CF Global	4,1			"2,<u>2</u>"*	<u>4,2</u>			"3,1"

United States (row label for E Local and CF Global section)

	Vietnam Games		Iraq Games	
Game:	Global (G32)	Local (G27)	Global (G18)	Local (G11)
Intentions:	USA, OTH (−,−)	USA, OTH (+,−)	USA, OTH (−,−−)	USA,OTH(−,−)
Power:	USA = OTH	USA = OTH	USA > OTH	USA =OTH
U.S. Strategy:	Stay at (2,2)	Stay at (3,2)	Stay at (3,1)	Stay at (2,2)
Other Strategy:	Stay at (2,2)	Move to (4,3)	Move to (4,2)	Stay at (2,2)

Strategic Path Analysis of Each Game

	Vietnam Games				Iraq Games			
	Global		Local		Global		Local	
	USA	OTH	USA	OTH	USA	OTH	USA	OTH
	<u>3,3</u> ←1,4	<u>3,3</u> →|1,4	<u>4,3</u> ←1,4	<u>4,3</u> →|1,4	2,3 ←1,4	2,3 →|1,4	3,3 ←1,4	3,3 →|1,4
	↓	↑ ↑	↓	↓	↑ ↑	↓	↓	↑ ↑ ↓
	4,1→"2,<u>2</u>"*	4,1|← "2,<u>2</u>"*	2,1→"3,2"*	2,1←"3,2"*	<u>4,2</u>*→|"3,1"	<u>4,2</u>*←"3,1"	4,1→"2,<u>2</u>"*	4,1|← "2,<u>2</u>"*

CO = cooperation; CF = conflict; D = de-escalate; E = escalate. Brams nonmyopic equilibria are underlined, and Nash myopic equilibria are asterisked. Initial states are in quotation marks. The strategic path analysis from initial state to final outcome is indicated by move (→) and stay (→|) arrows.

However, it is not correct regarding the subsequent local power game, which predicts deadlock as the final outcome (2,2) based on a symmetrical power distribution and dominant conflict strategy.

Ironically, the juxtaposition of the two cases reveals that the strengths of one case are also the weaknesses of the other case. The United States did not follow a strategy in either case that was a strong version of the strategy of contingent cooperation toward both the enemy and potential allies. In the first case, a strategy of contingent cooperation in negotiations with North Vietnam did not extend to mediation among domestic factions within Vietnam's civil war and worked only after a successful attempt to get Russia and China to intervene diplomatically with Hanoi. In the second case, a strategy of contingent cooperation was not followed initially toward either al Qaeda or various domestic factions in Iraq's politics and only belatedly followed this principle after 2006 as part of the population-centered military "surge" into Baghdad along with negotiated alliances with the Sunnis and other factions against al Qaeda throughout the country.

The shift in emphasis to a strategy of "gaining friends" instead of "killing enemies" appears to be necessary in order to explain the relative success of U.S. strategies in both cases. In these cases, the local variations in strategy were adopted against a backdrop of a détente-focused, dominant conflict strategy during the cold war era and an enemy-focused, dominant conflict strategy in the post-9/11 era. The Kissinger doctrine of détente does conform more closely at both the global and local levels to the principles of disjointed incrementalism than does the Cheney doctrine. It is also possible that neither strategy is sufficient to fix previous mistakes of diagnosis or prescription that led to two unnecessary wars. The United States did not prevent the imposition of a military solution in Vietnam by Hanoi. It remains an uncertain gamble whether the "surge" strategy resolved the continuation of a deadlock in Iraq and prevented a military victory by one of the factions in Iraqi politics (Ricks 2009). Therefore, it may well be necessary to follow a strategy to adopt contingent cooperation at all levels of world politics—global, regional, and local—prior to the onset of crises and wars in order to avoid military escalation, intractable situations, and precarious attempts to fix rather than avoid foreign policy mistakes. This thesis is the focus of the analysis in the next chapter, in which we will assess laboratory and historical evidence that both supports and qualifies this claim.

PART V

Foreign Policy Mistakes in Complex Adaptive Systems

CHAPTER 9

Avoiding Foreign Policy Mistakes
Extension and Expansion

INTRODUCTION

In the next two chapters we first extend our analysis to situations other than crises and wars and then expand from dyadic to triadic situations the general argument in the previous two chapters for avoiding foreign policy mistakes in dealing with conflict and uncertainty in strategic interactions in world politics. Our general argument is that a disjointed incremental strategy formalized with a strategic game theory model of contingent cooperation is the optimum one for making foreign policy decisions under conditions of uncertainty. If this strategy for minimizing mistakes can cope well with uncertain conditions represented by the stress of international crises such as the Cuban Missile Crisis and the fog of war associated with the Vietnam and Iraq conflicts, it may well be appropriate to extend the disjointed incremental strategy to make dyadic strategic decisions under other conditions short of crisis and war. But is it appropriate as well to expand our contingent cooperation strategy to conditions where the number of actors is a triad or even larger number?

Kenneth Waltz (1979, 192–193) notes, "The three-body problem has yet to be solved by physicists. Can political scientists or policymakers hope to do better charting the courses of three or more interacting states? Cases that lie between the simple interaction of two entities and the statistically predictable interactions of very many are the most difficult to unravel." Such questions raise anew doubts that foreign policy mistakes can be avoided or even corrected, because of two countervailing facts noted by Robert Jervis (1997, 3–4):

We all know that social life and politics constitute systems and that many outcomes are the unintended consequence of complex interactions. . . . [but] . . . Few if any realms of human conduct are completely determined at the systems level. Actors' choices are crucial and . . . are influenced by beliefs about how the system operates.

The collision of these two operating principles, agent and structure, explain the complexity of interactions in social systems and often present "wicked problems"[1] for policymakers to solve. In social systems with only two actors, the complexity of dyadic interactions is a relatively simple matter, and two-person game theory models can model deterministic solutions to a strategic interaction problem. As the number of players expands to three or more, statistical solutions take the place of deterministic solutions, or the game is reduced over time to a series of two-player games that take place sequentially with solutions to earlier games becoming inputs to determine solutions of later games (Brams 1994, 182–206, 213–214). The significance of this increased complexity is that it threatens generalizations about the efficacy of contingent cooperation as a strategy based on generalizations from a two-player model and its corresponding case studies.

Therefore, we proceed cautiously in this chapter first to extend the model's application from the hard cases of dyadic crises and wars to other "two-body" problems, before addressing the challenge posed by more wicked "three-body . . . *n*-body" problems. We shall continue to rely on two-person game theory and role theory as the principal analytical tools in addressing both sets of problems. In Chapter 8, role theory extended the decision-making process *temporally* for two-person games across two stages. These were demarcated by an initial communication stage of four moves by two players to define strategic orientation (+ or −) and power distribution (>=<) prior to a solution stage and final outcome. Social network theory and signed graph theory will supplement game theory and role theory in the next chapter to expand the analysis of interactions *spatially* across triads of two-person games played in two stages.

EXTENSION: TWO-BODY PROBLEMS

The analyses of the Cuban Missile Crisis and the Vietnam and Iraq wars with the sequential game theory model in the last two chapters combine the two operating principles of agency and structure identified by Jervis (1997) as the keys for understanding complex social interactions problems and for solving "wicked" problems. The choices of agents in stage one of the model interact with the power structure created by these choices to define the situation for strategic interaction in stage two of the model. These two stages perform the functions of the prior communication and strategic interaction stages identified by Brams (1994) in TOM and reflect less vividly the escalation and resolution stages of an international crisis identified by Snyder and Diesing (1977).

Although acute international crises often last only a few days or weeks, it is possible to extend the logic of their dynamics to a series of ongoing strategic interaction episodes in political dyads. These episodes may take the form of relationships of estrangement or engagement over more extended periods (Maoz and Mor 2002; Stein 1990; Walker, Malici, and Schafer 2011). The logic of transitional states characterized by rapid, large-scale shifts in the relations between states, such as the shift between war and peace during a military crisis (Brecher, Wilkenfeld, and Moser 1988), may simply be more dramatic manifestations of slower, small-scale shifts in relations within more stable states of peace and war (Walker 2002, 61–65). Dyadic relations of engagement or estrangement may fluctuate within these states without crossing the threshold dividing peace and war. Diplomatic crises as well as military crises may occur as ruptures or turning points within prolonged periods of equilibrium marked by harmony or stalemate (McClelland 1972; Brecher, Wilkenfeld, and Moser 1988; Leng 1993; Walker, Malici, and Schafer 2011).

The implications of the Janus-faced, bidirectional, strategic nature of politics, in which the relations between two political actors can turn in the direction of either conflict or cooperation from any initial state, are perhaps best captured by the prisoner's dilemma game of strategic interaction. In this 2×2 game, the players as prisoners can choose either cooperation or conflict, defined in the anecdote illustrating their dilemma as keeping silent or testifying against one another regarding a crime that they have committed. If they keep silent, their prosecutor has sufficient evidence to send them to prison only for a short jail term. If one testifies against the other, the informant goes free while the other goes to jail for a longer term. If both testify, then both go to jail for the longer term. Neither prisoner is allowed in this game to communicate with the other before making the choice of cooperation (remaining silent) or conflict (informing on the other).

The dilemma for each prisoner emerges as a result of the condition of no prior communication before making their respective choices. The prisoner's dilemma game is what we have labeled in previous chapters as a conflict game "in which the players disagree on the most preferred state" (Brams 1994, 215). It is also a game in which each player has a dominant strategy of choosing conflict (CF) over cooperation (CO) in a single play of the game, such as the situation facing the prisoners. In the absence of pre-play communication or some other mechanism that would convince each player to trust the other one to choose cooperation, there is a risk of a Pareto-inferior outcome. If one player chooses cooperation, the other will choose conflict, thereby gaining his or her most preferred (4) outcome while the other player reaches a least-preferred (1) outcome, instead of both players choosing cooperation and gaining their second-best outcomes (3,3). In order to avoid their worst outcomes with certainty, both players should choose conflict and thereby both receive long jail terms as their second-worst outcome. The logic of the situation and each player's strategy is modeled by two-person game theory in Figure 9.1.

In an extended theoretical and empirical study of this game, Robert Axelrod (1984, 9) argues that "The Prisoner's Dilemma is simply an abstract formulation of some very common and very interesting situations in which what is best for each person individually leads to mutual defection, whereas everyone would have been better off with mutual cooperation." He goes on to explore answers to the question of when a player in such a situation should choose cooperation without changing the nature of the problem. He acknowledges that there is no condition when a single player in a single play of the game should choose cooperation. However, if some of the initial conditions defining the game are altered without changing the rankings of each player's preference order for the outcomes, it is rational to choose cooperation according to the strategic principle of reciprocity.

Axelrod demonstrates this conclusion empirically by means of a pair of computer tournaments in which players were invited to write a computer algorithm specifying when to choose cooperation and when to choose conflict in iterated prisoner's dilemma games. The tournament's winner was a strategy of "tit-for-tat" reciprocity in which a player chooses

FIGURE 9.1   *Prisoner's Dilemma Game Outcomes*

		Prisoner B	
		CO	CF
	CO	3,3 Short Term, Short Term	1,4 Long Term, Freedom
Prisoner A			
	CF	4,1 Freedom, Long Term	2,2* Long Term, Long Term

Nash equilibrium is asterisked, and dominant strategies are underlined. CO = cooperation; CF = conflict. Outcomes are ranked from 4 = highest to 1 = lowest.

cooperation on the first move and does whatever the other player does on each succeeding move (repeated play of the game). This strategy achieved the most success collectively against all other players in each tournament even though the results (the winning strategy) were announced for the first tournament prior to submission of strategies for the second tournament. The only strategy that beat "tit-for-tat" in repeated plays of the game was "always choose conflict," because the initial choice by the "tit-for-tat" player resulted in a win for the "always choose conflict" player in their initial encounter and ties as outcomes in their remaining plays of the game.

However, the "always choose conflict" strategy did not win either tournament. The more important insight from Axelrod's analysis is that an "always choose conflict" strategy does not prevent the emergence of collectively stable relationships of mutual cooperation based on reciprocity in a political universe populated by at least some players whose algorithms specify the choice of cooperation under some conditions and who interact with players who pursue a "tit-for-tat" strategy.[2] Against all other players, whose strategic algorithms at some point specified that they choose cooperation, the "tit-for-tat" player reciprocated with cooperation and continued to do so until the other player chose conflict. The "tit-for-tat" player then reciprocated by choosing conflict but would not continue to punish the other player by choosing conflict if the other player reverted to cooperation. Unlike "always choose conflict," a strategy of cooperative reciprocity avoided missed opportunities for mutual cooperation and minimized extended deadlocks that precluded mutual cooperation. In the end, these features of the "tit-for-tat" strategy meant more success for it than the "always choose conflict" strategy in 200 repeated games against each of the other strategies and an overall victory in both tournaments.[3]

Axelrod's computer simulations based on his tournament results demonstrate that a "tit-for-tat" strategy is usually the most productive overall in a universe of other players with strategies ranging from nice (always choose cooperation) to nasty (always choose conflict), depending on the degree of restrictions in their respective algorithms for choosing cooperation in playing the prisoner's dilemma game (Axelrod 1984, 33; 1997, 14–39). This conclusion depends on two important conditions that supplement the original conditions specified for playing the iterated prisoner's dilemma game. In addition to repeated plays of the game, players are assumed to obey the rules of ecology and evolution in computer simulations based on the results of the two tournaments.

To simulate the processes of natural selection, direct learning from experience, and vicarious learning (imitation of others), the proportion of players with strategies that do not perform well in the tournaments are reduced in future simulations while the proportion of players with more successful strategies are increased.[4] Over time the more successful strategies are increasingly pitted against one another as the less successful strategies decline in the population. According to Axelrod (1984, 55, his capitals), "The results [of the tournament] were a very clear success for TIT FOR TAT. Moreover, the ecological analysis which simulated future rounds of the tournament suggested that TIT FOR TAT would continue to thrive, and that eventually it might be used by virtually everyone."

The explanation for the success of a "tit-for-tat" strategy in a prisoner's dilemma situation rests on three sets of factors: (1) characteristics of the strategy, (2) characteristics of the environment, and (3) characteristics of the agents in the environment. First, in order to be adopted by others and invade the population, the strategy itself must be easily recognizable as well as successful. The rules of "tit-for-tat," that is, initiate cooperation and always reciprocate either conflict or cooperation, are simple and easy to imitate. Second, the strategy requires an environment in which payoffs from future interactions between the same players be sufficiently important to deter a choice of conflict by either player in the present interaction, that is, the sequence of interactions and ensuing payoffs must be long enough and valuable enough to make it more worthwhile to continue to cooperate rather than defect and choose conflict. Third, the agents must either be sophisticated enough to make the calculation about the weight or importance of future moves relative to the present choice of cooperation or conflict in a strategy of "tit-for-tat" reciprocity, or its features must "reflect standard operating procedures, rules of thumb, instincts, habits, or imitations" (Axelrod 1984, 12–15, 19: see also Simon 1955; Cyert and March 1963).[5]

If the necessary environmental characteristics are met and the agents either mutate or stumble by chance on the appropriate strategy, a strategy of cooperative reciprocity may emerge within a population and achieve evolutionary and collective stability even if the agents do not have the cognitive capacity to make the necessary rational calculations. However, a single individual with a "tit-for-tat" strategy in an environment of "meanies" who always choose conflict will not successfully invade the population (Axelrod 1984, 63). This individual's strategy (1) will not be easily recognizable either for its success or its manifest moves, (2) will be employed against opponents that do not weight the payoffs from future interactions against the payoff from the present interaction, and (3) may well be converted instead into the other's strategy over time.

We shall discuss the strategic problem of dealing directly with "meanies" in Chapter 10. Here we report the effects of an indirect strategy of interaction with others in the environment, namely, making friends of others and thereby isolating meanies rather than defeating them directly as enemies. Some environmental characteristics are necessary in order for the "tit-for-tat" strategy to be successful indirectly against an "always choose conflict" strategy, that is, to be able to invade a population of strategies and achieve collective stability. The environment must have players with other strategies and also provide sufficient interaction opportunities for the "tit-for-tat" player to interact with them. Therefore, the success of the "tit-for-tat" strategy depends ultimately on the environment of other strategies in which it operates:

If one imagines a system starting with individuals who cannot be enticed to cooperate, the collective stability of ALL D [always choose defection, i.e., conflict] implies that no single individual can hope to do any better than go along and be uncooperative. A world of "meanies" can resist invasion by anyone using any other strategy—provided that the newcomers arrive one at a time. . . . If the newcomers arrive in small clusters, however, they will have a chance to get cooperation started. (Axelrod 1984, 63)

The good news is that once established, a "tit-for-tat" strategy is also collectively stable. It cannot be invaded by an "always choose conflict" strategy as long as the former continues to be "provocable"—that is, a defection from mutual cooperation is reciprocated with conflict (Axelrod 1984, 66–69).

The significance of Axelrod's analysis of the prisoner's dilemma game is to underscore the bidirectional adaptability of a contingent cooperation strategy of reciprocity in both the easy case of a no-conflict strategy versus the hard case of a conflict strategy and vis-à-vis players with other strategies that range between these two extremes. The winning strategy of "tit-for-tat" in his computer tournaments and simulations both reinforces and qualifies our confidence in the efficacy of our own disjointed incremental strategy of contingent cooperation for reducing uncertainty and maximizing rationality in a Janus-faced political universe of cooperation and conflict. Both strategies prescribe cooperation as an initial move and reciprocity in subsequent moves, which reinforces our confidence in the general robustness of contingent cooperation.

However, it is important to remember that the "tit-for-tat" strategy of reciprocity has its limits. It is not a winner against an unconditional strategy of "always choose conflict" in either a single play or in repeated plays of a prisoner's dilemma situation with the same opponent. It is also not a successful invader of a population of such "meanies" unless the universe of prisoner's dilemma situations also provides the opportunity to interact with players playing strategies other than "always choose conflict." It is not always even the most effective strategy against all other possible strategies, emerging as the overall winner in five out of six simulations. Its success depends as well on how the strategies of those other players fare against one another (Axelrod 1984, 192–205).

Therefore, Axelrod's laboratory analysis of the prisoner's dilemma game is emblematic in many respects regarding the complexities of social decision making in the real world of human affairs. Classical political theorists of the "social contract," such as Hobbes (1996), Locke (1980), and Rousseau (1978), have also grappled with the trade-offs between individual and collective interests represented in the prisoner's dilemma game matrix. The Hobbesian solution rests on the pessimistic assumption that human agents will always choose conflict and that social life will be "nasty, brutish, and short" in the absence of a third-party Leviathan, the state, to whom players agree to surrender the power to enforce a solution of mutual cooperation between them. Whereas the basis of the social contract in Hobbes's theory is the consolidation of coercive power in the hands of the state (if necessary by force of arms), Locke's more balanced solution to the same problem is for individuals to negotiate a social contract to form the state on the basis of laws and to provide it with the power to enforce them while still retaining for the individual a private sphere of personal freedom. Rousseau's more optimistic basis for the social contract is collective voluntary action by individuals reflecting the general will of public opinion, which acts to banish individuals who do not follow its moral imperatives.

These disparate conclusions are generated from theoretical analyses of the "state of nature," a philosophical construct that stipulates a hypothetical set of conditions in which human beings lived originally in isolation or with only intermittent contact with one another rather than in an organized society under the rule of a state. It is the product of counterfactual thought experiments by social contract theorists in which they imagine what life would be like for individuals in the absence of a society governed by a state. Each concludes that the benefits of a social contract, whether it be security (Hobbes), property (Locke), or moral freedom (Rousseau), outweigh the costs of giving up the absolute personal freedom in a state of nature in order to form a society governed by a state.

Although human societies can and do die out (Diamond 2005), the social organization of human life rarely has approached the asocial, zero point postulated by the "state of nature" in philosophy. Neither do states spring into existence fully formed, as Athena did from the head of Zeus in Greek mythology. The actual record of human origins reconstructed by anthropologists and historians suggests that human beings almost always lived in groups in order to reproduce and survive (Diamond 1992; Polk 1997, 24–36). The expansion of human groups in the size and complexity of their social organization is itself a complex historical phenomenon. We contend that the principles governing this development are to be found in systems theory broadly conceived to mean the processes associated with the application of physical and biological laws to human social phenomena.

By laws we do not refer here to the deterministic laws of closed systems, such as a universe of prisoner's dilemma situations populated only by "meanies" who pursue "always choose conflict" strategies against one another. We mean instead contingent generalizations about tendencies in more open systems, with local conditions defined partly by the distribution of situations other than prisoner's dilemma and partly by players with diverse strategies in those situations. We ground our theoretical position within a systems-oriented as well as an agent-centered perspective, because it appears to us that there is no such thing as an isolated agent. Even the smallest biological organism or particle of physical energy seems to be constituted of elements standing in interaction with one another, which is the classic definition of a system (Jervis 1997, 6–10).[6]

With interaction come interdependence and emergent properties of the whole system that cannot be predicated of its parts. Focusing only on those elements without placing them within a systems perspective may not be able to explain complex outcomes. As Jervis (1997, 6) notes, echoing Waltz's earlier observation about three-body problems:

Systems often display nonlinear relationships, outcomes that cannot be understood by adding together the units or their relations, and many of the results of actions are unintended. Complexities can appear even in what would seem to be simple and deterministic solutions. Thus over one hundred years ago the mathematician Henri Poincare showed that the motion of as few as three bodies (such as the sun, the moon, and the earth), although governed by strict scientific laws, defies exact solution.

Citing studies of complex adaptive systems, Jervis (1997, 7) argues that "A systems approach shows how individual actors following simple and uncoordinated strategies can produce aggregate behavior that is complex and ordered, although not necessarily predictable and stable. Similarly, biologists stress that highly complex life-forms are composed of elements that, taken individually, are quite simple." [7]

Any system can also be part of a larger, more complex system, and it is sometimes difficult to tell whether it is better to view a system as autonomous or part of a more inclusive system. This issue is important, because the idea of a system carries within it the emergent property of boundaries, the notion that it is possible to distinguish the system from the environmental setting in which it operates. In the world of physics, boundaries are sometimes difficult to identify, because the distance and time associated with laws governing the interacting parts of a system are immense and not subject to casual observations—take, for example, the laws of motion governing the solar systems and galaxies in the universe (Feynman 1995; Hawking 2005; R. Wright 2000, 258–259).

However, it is also not necessarily the case that large-body systems are more complex than small-body systems. The internal workings of each biological agent may be more complex than the interactions of a two-body social system formed by the pair of agents: is a marriage system more complex than the neural systems in the brains of each partner in the union? It is true that the larger the number of elements in a system, the more complex are its interactions at a given level of analysis—for example, polygamy is a more complex system of marriage than monogamy, even though the inner workings of each subsystem (partner) may be more complex than the interactions among or between them. These observations in theorizing about human behavior underscore the importance of a self-conscious systems perspective that carefully identifies the boundaries of a system and the level of analysis of interest to the observer (Jervis 1997; Wright 2000).

In this book, the primary system of interest is a social system constituted by two actors in world politics. One of those actors in each case is the United States. The boundaries of this system are the territorial frontiers of each actor in a U.S.–*nth* country dyad, with the interactions of power politics in the system modeled with game theory as a two-body strategic interaction problem. As even a cursory look backward to the case studies in earlier chapters reveals, our applications of game theory often expanded into linked or nested relationships with other players, constituting as a result more than a two-player game. Linkages inside each actor expanded from the state level of analysis to encompass domestic interactions between agents as well as interactions between states across local, regional, and global levels of analysis.[8] Therefore, we turn now to a more sustained and self-conscious effort to expand our analysis of foreign policy mistakes beyond the strategic dyad of only two states considered primarily as an isolated and closed social system to an explicit analysis of triads, that is, three-body problems represented as interacting sets of two-body problems.

EXPANSION: N-BODY PROBLEMS

In order to have one, two, three, or *n*-body problems, it is necessary to postulate the existence of bodies. A body may be viewed as a single system constituted by its own elements or as interacting as an element in a system of other bodies.[9] Our primary candidate to analyze the power politics systems of interest in this book is game theory applied as a kind of systems theory to two-body and three-body problems in which the bodies are agents in world politics. We employ game theory as a "complex adaptive systems" approach, which is somewhat different than using it as a theory simply to explain world politics. Scientific explanation implies an attempt to falsify the theory employed in the analysis. We take the explanatory power of game theory for granted here and bracket the task of falsification in favor of using game theory instead to answer a normative question posed by the analysis of complex adaptive systems: "In a world where many players are all adapting to each other and where the emerging future is extremely hard to predict, what actions should you take" (Axelrod and Cohen 1999, xi)?[10]

In order to use game theory to answer this normative question, it is necessary in the remainder of this chapter first to stipulate that game theory is a systems theory and then offer an account of how complex systems of strategic interaction in world politics are generated for normative analysis with game theory. In the next chapter we shall provide a method for expanding game theory to the representation of three-body problems in order to prescribe normative solutions. We shall also illustrate the application of this method to assess future U.S. foreign policy decisions in dealing with the "wicked problems" posed by al Qaeda and the Taliban within the context of selected dyads and triads of agents in the complex regional systems of the Middle East (Israel, Iraq, and Iran) and South Asia (Afghanistan, Pakistan, and India).

Our application of game theory has the following characteristics of a systems theory: (1) elements (players) (2) standing in interaction (making moves) with (3) an emergent structure (the power distribution between the players), which leads to (4) other emergent properties (final outcomes) of the game. These final outcomes are important system effects of the power structure, which determine whether the game of strategic interaction between players continues, transforms, or terminates. However, game theory also models an open system to the extent that players are free to choose moves that lead to unexpected outcomes independent of the power structure. This feature adds an important element of complexity to game theory as a systems theory.

We noted earlier that strategic interaction patterns do not have to be based on agents with the capacity to make rational calculations. Patterns of interaction can arise in nature, based on physical laws of energy, mutation, instinct, or habit, which also conform to the expectations of strategic rationality. Just as the negative and positive charges of electrons and protons, respectively, dispose physical bodies (atoms) toward certain patterns of interaction, so it is possible that certain heritable DNA traits may dispose living bodies (organisms) toward positive interactions with one another or other systems in their environment, which lead to their bio-logical reproduction and also to their social extension and expansion in the form of more complex systems.

Conversely, interactions with others and the environment may be nega-tive and lead to stasis or extinction rather than reproduction or extension for a system of interest.[11] An example of the tendency toward entropy on a small scale of space and time is found in the following observation:

Pour cream in coffee, and the initial distinctions in color, texture, and temperature fade, as does the motion created by the pouring. Generally speaking, Schrodinger observed, systems left alone for very long will become motionless and of uniform temperature; eventually, "the whole system fades away into a dead, inert lump of matter." (Schrodinger 1967, 74, qtd. in Wright 2000, 244)

On the other hand, if the environment of other systems (such as the container in which one pours the coffee) keeps the temperature of the cof-fee high enough, the mixture of elements in the coffee cup may retain their emergent properties and, if replenished with more heated coffee on the stove, may even exhibit enhanced or new properties. The relatively ran-dom quality of such interactions in their initial state is captured by the concept of entropy, which specifies the possible states of a system of inter-acting elements. The impact of stimuli from the system's local environment may reduce the entropy of a system by configuring its interactions into one of its possible states. The same environment may sustain this systemic pattern with positive feedback so that it is reproduced over time and properties emerge from this interaction pattern. These properties may act as an environmental stimulus on systems other than the initial system of interest, reducing the entropy in those systems and leading to emergent properties that may become sources of either positive feedback leading to more complexity (supporting the reduction in entropy) or negative feed-back leading to less complexity (stopping or reversing the reduction of entropy) for the system of interest.

Information in a system is coterminous with a pattern of complexity that reduces entropy; the reduction in entropy (possible states and struc-ture) of the system by the pattern of complexity also represents a reduction in uncertainty and a corresponding gain in information (Wright 2000,

247–249). With information comes the capacity to exercise control, as information is organized energy that may direct action by one element and be received as a signal to respond in one way rather than another by other elements in a system. Thus, the ability to exercise control in a social system with information is an operational definition of political power (Deutch 1966, 146–147; Wright 2000, 247–250). It follows that the capacity of any element to elicit responses from other elements in a system is also an index of its power relative to other elements. In turn, this capacity depends on the kind and degree of organized complexity (reduction of entropy and increase of information) within the subsystem that constitutes any element compared with other elements in the system of interest. In simple terms, the power distribution in a system is either symmetrical and interdependent or asymmetrical and dependent, depending on the ability of elements in a system to exercise control through their own actions over the actions of other elements (Emerson 1972a, 1972b).[12]

In social systems of animals and human beings, the random mutation and evolution of the biological elements in these social systems has led to inherited traits that define their capacity for strategic interaction and the exercise of power based on rational thought processes (Wright 2000, 244–245).[13] The path to this point in human evolution begins theoretically with random interactions among lower (less complex) systems of matter and energy in which entropy is reduced by emerging patterns of complexity that become the organization of a system of interest. This coupling into patterns is what Wright (2000, 252) calls a "non-zero-sum" relationship by which he means that the linked elements of the system in a regular rather than random pattern are now "in the same boat." He notes further (pp. 4–5) that both social scientists and evolutionary biologists divide such patterns in social systems and biological systems into zero-sum and non-zero-sum systems or games. In the artificial world of game theory, a zero-sum game is one in which one player's loss is the other player's gain (thus summing to zero) while a non-zero-sum game has outcomes in which one player's gain is not necessarily the other's loss (thus not summing to zero). Depending on the distribution of information (and therefore the distribution of power) among the players and their information-processing skills, the outcomes of a non-zero-sum game can be win-lose or lose-win as well as win-win or lose-lose.

The classic non-zero-sum game is "the prisoner's dilemma" (R. Wright 2000, 5; Poundstone 1992; Axelrod 1984). The entropy (possible states) of this game includes a win-win outcome as well as the lose-lose, win-lose, and lose-win outcomes depicted earlier in Figure 9.1. Wright (2000, 257) argues that the invasion of non-zero-sum systems of interaction characterizes the history of biological evolution for lower life forms with less complex social systems as well as the biological and cultural evolution of higher life forms with more complex social systems. The mechanisms that generate non-zero-sum systems of interaction are genes in biological systems and memes in cultural systems. Both genes and memes are information about how to organize behavior in an environment. Genes are inherited traits, which specify how a biological system should interact with its environment. They are acquired by mutation and survive or not, depending on positive or negative feedback from the environment. Memes are learned traits, information that is transmitted among elements of a social system by imitation rather than inherited by biological reproduction. The culture of a social system is a collection of memes that may be acquired initially by random interaction with the environment and reinforced by positive feedback from the environment (R. Wright 2000, 87–89).[14]

To connect the artificial mathematical world of game theory to the real physical world of energy, matter, and life, it is not necessary to subscribe to the strong version of Wright's controversial thesis, namely, that the arc of biological and cultural co-evolution bends ultimately toward non-zero-sum relations as the dominant pattern in biological and social systems.[15] However, it is necessary to accept the weaker version of his thesis: (1) human beings as a universal species have the capacity, enhanced under certain conditions by positive feedback from the environment, to recognize and construct social systems whose complexity is characterized by non-zero-sum relations; (2) these social systems are susceptible to analysis by game theory models of strategic interaction. It remains an empirical question whether groups of humans playing non-zero-sum games with a strategy of reciprocal cooperation will invade the general popula-

FIGURE 9.2   *Types of Game Environments and Complexity of Social Systems*

GAME ENVIRONMENTS

	Conflict			Mixed-Motive		No-Conflict

	Game 1		Game 2			Game 3			Game 4	
	CO	CF	CO	CF		CO	CF		CO	CF
CO	3,2	1,4	3,3	1,4	CO	**4,3**	1,4	CO	**4,4***	1,2
CF	4,1	2,3*	4,1	2,2*	CF	2,1	**3,2***	CF	2,1	**3,3***
	Zero-Sum		Non-Zero-Sum			Non-Zero-Sum			Positive-Sum	

Conflict (–,–) _____ Game Environment Continuum _____ (+,+) Cooperation
Games   Games

SOCIAL SYSTEMS

Low   High
Population   Population
Density   Density

Hunter-Gatherer Big Man Chiefdoms City-States Empires Nation-States

Low _____ Social System Continuum _____ High
Complexity   Complexity

Shoshones---EU

Low   High
Resource   Resource
Endowment   Endowment

Nash equilibria are asterisked, and dominant strategies are underlined; Pareto-optimal solutions are in bold.
Source: Data are from R. Wright (2000).

tion of humans who may have either constructed other games or may have been constrained by their local environments to play other games.[16]

To appreciate these real-world limitations, consider the following types of simple (two-body) social systems and their emergent properties represented by the four games in the upper half of Figure 9.2. The first system is a zero-sum conflict game in which each player pursues a dominant strategy of conflict in a single play of the game, leading to a final outcome of deadlock (2,3). The complexity (reduction in entropy) in this system is mapped in the four cells with the possible distribution of resources available to the players represented by their rank-ordered outcomes. If the distribution of information about these outcomes is known to both players, there is a symmetrical power distribution; assuming equal information-processing skills, they can exercise equal power over the final outcome of this game. It is a zero-sum game, because a move by either player from a Nash equilibrium (2,3) will result in a loss for at least one player.[17]

The second system is the classic non-zero-sum conflict game of prisoner's dilemma in which it is still rational for both players to pursue a dominant strategy of conflict in a single play of the game. Again the complexity (reduction of entropy) in the system is mapped in the four cells along with the distributions of resources indicated by the ranked preferences in the cells. It is a non-zero-sum game, because it is possible for both players to improve their gains from a Nash equilibrium (2,2) by choosing mutual cooperation (3,3), which is rational to do under certain conditions that we identified earlier from Axelrod (1984). The third system is a non-zero-sum game and also a mixed-motive game in which one player has a dominant strategy of conflict and the other player has a contingent strategy of co-operation. In a single play of the game both players will choose conflict with deadlock (3,2) as the outcome; however, it is possible for one player (column) to move from deadlock as an initial state to (2,1) with the expectation that row will then move to (4,3) mutual cooperation as a Pareto-superior outcome. The fourth system is a non-zero-sum game and a no-conflict game as well in which both players have a contingent strategy of cooperation and a Pareto-superior outcome of (4,4).

The environmental conditions associated with the emergence of these social systems as different types of games are modeled in the lower half of Figure 9.2. A combination of population density and resource endowment accounts for variation in the complexity of social systems and the movement along the game continuum. As population density and resource endowment change from low to high, the social system of interest in this environment is likely to increase in complexity, and games of strategic interaction in this system are likely to change from zero-sum to non-zero-sum along the game continuum. An extreme case at one end of the complexity continuum is a small hunter-gatherer society with low population density in a scarce resource environment represented by the ancient Shoshone tribe of North America. They were capable of non-zero-sum strategic interactions with one another on a small scale; however, these occurred rarely except within small families (R. Wright 2000, 20–22).

An extreme case at the other end of the complexity continuum is a large civilization,[18] represented by the contemporary European Union with high population density and abundant resources. Non-zero-sum strategic interactions dominate zero-sum interactions in this case, because the combination of demographic and resource conditions in the environment have tended to elicit rapid technological innovation (the acquisition and use of information as power) within the social system to organize complex patterns of cooperation as interactions on a large scale. These patterns are characterized by a non-zero-sum division of labor rather than a zero-sum pattern of competition among its members. In the opposite case where resources are scarce, the carrying capacity of the environment to support population is low. Low population density reduces the rate of technological innovation and the exercise of power, which constrains the patterns of complexity so that the dominant pattern is zero-sum conflict between small groups over scarce resources along with occasional non-zero-sum patterns of cooperation.[19]

The anthropological and historical record of complex cooperation in the real world is mixed with regard to the social systems of world politics. These systems have become more complex in size as the world has grown more connected by technological innovations leading to expansion in trade and investment and communication among local populations in various parts of the world. However, the fact of territoriality remains as a spatial and temporal barrier to establishing cooperation as the dominant pattern of complexity on a global or even a regional scale. With the aid of more advanced technology than possessed by their historical peers, the United States and previous hegemons in world politics have been able to project their capacity to exercise control within regions and around the world; however, they have been unable to decisively overcome two limits on their exercise of power associated with territoriality: these are the uneven territorial distribution of those resources, which does not promote the emergence of non-zero-sum social systems, and the comparative advantage in the exercise of power that accompanies local social systems in their interactions with more remote social systems.

Territoriality refers to a quality of the terrain (area of land) on which humans live, which becomes a territory when it is recognized as under the jurisdiction of those people. Jared Diamond (1992, 227) recalls "that the whole globe is now divided into political states, whose citizens enjoy more or less freedom to travel within the boundaries of their state and to visit other states." He reminds us as well that it is "a modern perspective that we take for granted. Our perspective didn't apply in New Guinea until very recently, and it didn't apply anywhere in the world ten thousand years ago." He continues:

For all but the last ten thousand years of human history, unfettered travel was impossible. . . . Each village or band constituted a political unit, living a perpetually shifting state of wars, truces, alliances, and trade with neighboring groups. Hence New Guinea highlanders spent their entire lives within ten miles of their birthplaces. They might occasionally enter lands bordering their village lands by stealth during a war raid, or by permission during a truce, but they had no social framework for travel beyond immediately neighboring lands. The notion of tolerating unrelated strangers was as unthinkable as the notion that any such stranger would dare appear. . . . *Even today this no-trespassing legacy persists in many parts of the world.*[20] (Diamond 1992, 228; emphasis added)

This common description of social organization by early humans and recent New Guineans is consistent with an environment of scarce resources and low population density accompanied by low technology innovation.

New Guinea highlanders continued longer in this state of nature than other populations, due to geographical terrain barriers that isolated them as a social system from the rest of the world. Their "first contact" with the outside world beyond immediately neighboring lands may have been the last such historical experience of its kind, which other human populations had experienced in earlier times (Diamond 1992, 228–234). Within their social system we would expect to find non-zero-sum complexity based on kinship reciprocity within the limitations set by local population density and resource constraints. After "first contact" with immediate geographical neighbors (non-blood relatives), we would expect a mix of trading and warfare that characterizes a social system based on a dominant pattern of zero-sum interactions with intermittent non-zero-sum interactions based on generalized (not kinship) reciprocity.

Strangers who may intrude from beyond a neighboring territory would be considered enemies. If they were isolated individual nomads banished from their own tribe, they would be killed. If they were larger groups forced by an imbalance between increasing population and decreasing resources to leave their home territory, their numbers might be sufficient to invade and take over some other group's territory, depending on the levels of technology and potential to exercise power distributed between them. In fact, these patterns of contact and expansion have played out around the world on various spatial and temporal scales (Polk 1997; Diamond 1999; R. Wright 2000).

A summary of possible generic patterns in these "first contacts" is found in Figure 9.3. In the upper-left quadrant is the small-scale social system of "friends" with a dominant pattern of non-zero-sum interactions based on kinship reciprocity. The lower-right quadrant is the social system of "enemies" that can occur with "first contact" between strangers, both of whom initiate conflict rather than cooperation as their first interaction. The other two quadrants are the possible mixed patterns of conflict and cooperation between immediate neighbors that can occur, which are relatively unstable and are likely to evolve into either a pattern of friendship or enmity, depending on the interaction of such factors as the local circumstances of scarcity or abundance in resources, population density, the levels of technology, and corresponding cultural sophistication in the acquisition of information (learning) and the exercise of power (control) over the environment (Polk 1997; Diamond 1999; R. Wright 2000). As a result of transportation improvements and the development of possessions rooted in terrain, increases have occurred in the historical pace and the scale of these interactions. As food came to be stored under ground and grown above ground, territory became a possession to be protected and expanded with more mobile armies on horseback and chariot and the construction of more complex fortresses in the form of cities and towns rather than encampments and villages (Polk 1997, 13–75).

FIGURE 9.3   *Possible Patterns of "First Contact" in Social Systems*

	POS (+)	Alter's Cues	NEG (−)

POS (+)   Alter's Cues   NEG (−)

FRIENDS (+,+)   STRANGERS (+,−)

P   IF Ego > Alter: Exploit/Appease (DDDD).   IF Ego > Alter: Exploit/Bluff (DEED).
O   **IF Ego = Alter: Reward/Reward (DDDD).**   **IF Ego = Alter: Deter/Punish (DEEE).**
S   IF Ego < Alter: Appease/Exploit (DDDD).   IF Ego < Alter: Appease/Bully (DEDE).
(+)
        NO-CONFLICT GAMES   MIXED-MOTIVE GAMES
  Ego's _____
  Cues
        MIXED-MOTIVE GAMES   CONFLICT GAMES

N   IF Ego > Alter: Bully/Appease (EDED).   IF Ego > Alter: Bully/Bluff (EEED).
E   **IF Ego = Alter: Compel/Reward (EDDD).**   **IF Ego = Alter: Punish/Punish (EEEE).**
G   IF Ego < Alter: Bluff/Exploit (EDDE).   IF Ego < Alter: Bluff/Bully (EEDE).
(−)

        NEIGHBORS (−,+)   ENEMIES (−,−)

E = escalatory (−) move; D = de-escalatory (+) move; ego's moves are first and third, whereas alter's moves are second and fourth in each sequence. POS (+) and NEG (−) are the exercise of power with positive (+) or negative (−) sanctions. Sequences in bold are strategic interaction patterns in "first contacts" leading to roles of friends, enemies, neighbors, and strangers on the basis of a "tit-for-tat" strategy of reciprocity with symmetrical power relationships held constant.

This expansion dynamic was fueled by the expansion of non-zero-sum patterns of trade and finance as well as by zero-sum patterns of war and conquest. Polk (1997, 129ff) argues that the trader rather than the diplomat or the soldier was the most influential agent of change in the evolution of the size and the interdependence of complex social systems in world politics. Trade initially evolved by friends (kinfolk) sharing a kill as hunter-gatherers, then expanded with immediate neighbors and eventually included complete strangers either directly or indirectly. Transportation improvements connecting societies enabled wondering merchant traders to travel over longer distances by land and water, or immediate neighbors brokered exchanges between nonadjacent societies. Polk highlights the primacy assigned to exchange as follows:

Trade is a peculiarly human activity. Unlike the other aspects of the lives of early man—protecting territory, organizing societies, hunting and gathering, and even practicing rudimentary agriculture—it is unknown among animals. But among people it began early, is practiced in virtually every known society, and is one of mankind's strongest habits. Consequently, as Edward O. Wilson [1975, 551] has observed, "only man has an economy. His high intelligence and symbolizing ability make true barter possible. Intelligence also permits the exchanges to be stretched out in time, converting them into acts of reciprocal altruism." (Polk 1997, 129)

Depending on the operational codes of the leaders and the level of technological innovation, the pattern of "first contact" between societies takes one of the possible patterns in Figure 9.3.[21] If warriors or soldiers lead both societies, the propensity for sequences of escalatory (E) moves leading to an enemy (–,–) relationship is higher, conditioned by the distribution of power between them. If diplomats or traders lead both societies, the propensity for sequences of de-escalatory (D) moves leading to a friends relationship is higher, conditioned once more by the distribution of power between them. In "first contacts" between societies with a heterogeneous pattern of leadership, the imbalanced sequences of moves (ED or DE) lead to strains toward balanced relationships as neighbors (+,+) or strangers (–,–), again conditioned by power distributions.

The sequences leading to outcomes and relations as friends or enemies are more fundamental than neighbors and strangers, as evidenced by the practice in early times of distinguishing friends and enemies on the basis of kinship or nonkinship (Polk 1997, 28–29). However:

Ecology forced on both animals and men another category, between the immediate kindred and aliens: neighbors. The Greeks, as usual, had a word for them: *deme*. Biology explains such groups as being composed of members who are more likely to exhibit histocompatibility—to be able to accept organ transplants—than aliens and more likely to accept those from neighboring demes, nearby aliens, than from those that are more remote. Such affinities arose from the processes of subdivision and migration of groups and intermarriage. . . . On one hand, demes find peaceful interaction possible or normal under certain circumstances, but, on the other, it appears that a high proportion of serious conflict occurs within them rather than among true aliens. . . . [I]n periods of peace . . . rulers addressed one another as "brother" and so, by extension, equated diplomacy to relationships among kindred—as distinct from war, which, by implication occurs among strangers. (Polk 1997, 29–30)[22]

We infer that it is relatively difficult for neighbors and strangers to avoid becoming friends or enemies. There is a strain toward more symmetrical, balanced roles of friends (+,+) or enemies (–,–) between ego and alter in their strategic interaction relationships unless an asymmetrical power relationship makes it feasible either for the stronger to exploit the weaker member of the dyad or for the weaker member to depend on the stronger member. Local conditions associated with territoriality within the dyadic system of interest along with environmental stimuli explain which one of these asymmetrical patterns of exchange is more likely to be the case; it is also possible for an asymmetrical relationship of domination and submission to be based on both possibilities (Emerson 1972a, 1972b).

In this chapter we have extended our analysis of foreign policy mistakes and strategies for fixing and avoiding them from crises and wars to other situations in world politics. Wars and crises tend to be conflict situations with strategic interaction dynamics that are not resolved easily with outcomes of mutual cooperation. In Chapter 8 we examined how decision makers can make choices in those situations to construct a path from deadlock to settlement with a disjointed incremental strategy of conditional cooperation. We have argued in this chapter that the same strategy may be extended to managing other situations in world politics and perhaps expanded from simple dyads to more complex triads of complex adaptive systems. In the next chapter we focus our analysis explicitly on the more complex situations created by increasing the number of actors from two to three and beyond.

CHAPTER 10

Foreign Policy Dynamics
The Middle East and South Asia Systems

INTRODUCTION

This book began with a reference to Plato's (2000) metaphor of the "ship of state" in *The Republic*. We noted that an ocean of relative uncertainty sailed by a ship of human beings with significantly limited capacities for navigation is a recipe for making mistakes. In this chapter we show how complexity theory provides a map for reaching a safe harbor in complex adaptive systems of world politics and how game theory provides a compass for steering clear of foreign policy mistakes.[1] To be sure, the ship of state analogy has limitations. A geographical map of today's world includes borders both linking and separating societies instead of open vistas, which are social facts rather than brute physical facts. They exist as shared information in the minds of humans, but they do not exist independently as physical objects in nature (Searle 1995). Other borders also exist, which may or may not conform to these geographical constructions. Sociocultural systems may be linked or divided by those borders, and social systems may also transcend them. These features suggest that the human condition is marked by both an architectural problem and a navigational problem. Human beings in today's world need information to map and construct a social order as well as steer a course in the conduct of human affairs and world politics.

We contend that game theory and complexity theory can provide these capacities to political decision makers as agents in a complex social system.[2] The value of complexity theory for mapping and game theory for navigating social systems depends on the level of technological innovation and the complexity of the environment in which they operate. The incidence of collisions or wrong turns depends partly on the ability of a map to provide information (reduce entropy) and a compass to organize behavior (exercise power) in the social environment. Where agents are going as well as where they are coming from is also important. It is relatively easy to walk or drive to the local neighborhood grocery store and back. Although today's technology has made it quicker and safer, it is generally more difficult to take a trip to a distant destination and return without mishaps. The reason is that the information and corresponding power to act rationally decreases as one leaves home to travel abroad to deal with strangers rather than neighbors.

In the following examples, we address the three tasks of mapping, constructing, and steering a course for U.S. foreign policy in the regions of the Middle East and South Asia. We shall argue that three kinds of information are needed in order to avoid or minimize foreign policy mistakes. First is the abstract theoretical knowledge provided from complexity theory regarding complex adaptive systems and from game theory regarding strategic interactions. Second is the generic knowledge that is situation specific regarding what kinds of games are operating between agents within a given system of interest. Third is the local or actor-specific knowledge of particular agents as elements in a system of interest (George 1993). We begin below with how to represent complex adaptive systems abstractly so that relevant emergent properties are revealed. Then we enhance these models with generic information about the types of strategic interaction games occurring within them. With the addition of local knowledge about the agents, we conclude with a diagnosis and prescription of the optimum strategy to achieve or at least optimize the chances for mutual cooperation as an emergent property in systems of interest to the United States in the Middle East and South Asia.

MAPPING COMPLEX ADAPTIVE SYSTEMS

The conventions of social network theory and signed graph theory influence the notations that we use here to represent the dynamics of interaction among bodies in complex social systems (Burt 1982, 1992; Burt and Minor 1983; Harary 1961, 1969; Buckley and Harary 1990). Points and the lines connecting them in both theories can represent the elements and interactions of a social system. Positive and negative valences are assigned to represent the connections between elements as relationships of cooperation or conflict. Social network theory emphasizes that it is possible for networks to vary in density, that is, for some or all elements to be connected to each other (Burt 1992). Signed graph theory is a mathematical theory in which the positive and negative signs can symbolize different substantive relationships between a system's elements, which represent cooperation and conflict between agents in the substantive domain of world politics. It specifies that bilateral and trilateral relationships in a network of such elements can be balanced or unbalanced, depending on whether the segments (bilateral connections) have an even or an uneven number of negative valences (Harary 1961). As the analysis expands to triangular cycles (segments connecting three points), it is customary to combine the two lines connecting each segment (pair of points) with a single sign (+ or –) once a balanced (+,+ or –,–) relationship replaces an imbalanced (+,– or –,+) one.

Brief illustrations of applications of these conventions to an *n*-body system in Figure 10.1 are adapted from an application to Middle East networks during the 1956 Suez crisis, which escalated to war between Britain (B), France (F), and Israel (I) versus Arab states led by Egypt (E) and eventually resulted in interventions by both superpowers (Harary 1961). They show that Israeli-Egyptian relations, viewed as an isolated two-body system, are negative and balanced with conflict between them. If the system of interest in the Middle East is expanded to include Britain and France, the *n*-body system has six relationships within a four-body system that has balanced triangular relationships. When the cold war conflict between the United States (U) and the Soviet Union (S) expands into the Middle East, the two conflict systems become connected via Egypt with nine relationships and four triangular relationships in a six-body system.

During the Suez War of 1956, the relationships changed between the United States and Egypt from negative to positive, and a negative relationship emerged between each superpower and the coalition of Britain, France, and Israel (BIF). The emergence of these new relationships included imbalanced triangular relations among the BIF coalition and the two superpowers, which presaged later strains in the NATO alliance over strategic decisions. However, U.S. positive relations with BIF were restored in relatively short order, which eventually balanced the triangular relationship among the United States, Israel, and the Soviet Union regarding

FIGURE 10.1   *Signed Graphs of Middle East and Cold War Conflicts,*
1948–1956

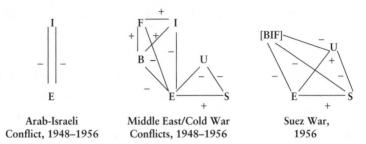

| Arab-Israeli | Middle East/Cold War | Suez War, |
| Conflict, 1948–1956 | Conflicts, 1948–1956 | 1956 |

Countries: Israel (I); Egypt (E); France (F); Britain (B); United States (U); Soviet Union (S). Valences: friendly relations are positive (+), and hostile relations are negative (–).

relations with Egypt (and its Arab allies) for at least the next decade until the 1967 Arab-Israeli Six-Day War.[3]

It is possible to make some generalizations regarding an entire *n*-body system with the logic offered by the mathematical models of social network and signed graph theories. Our use is the more limited one of using these schemes as an accounting system to (1) depict changing relationships over time between pairs of elements in a system of interest; (2) identify triads that link dyads; and (3) analyze the tensions between balancing triadic relationships and managing dyadic relationships that constitute triads. Our interest is primarily a focus on the power relationships and strategic interactions between and among elements in linked two-body and three-body systems. Social network theory and signed graph theory provide some insights into the dynamics of these systems; however, they are not modeled with game theory and do not focus directly on power relationships. Instead, these theories offer analyses that emphasize structural tendencies to move between density and autonomy (defined as frequency and variety of connections) or imbalanced and balanced (defined as consistency) relationships (Burt 1990, 1992; Harary 1961).

Our approach is to focus on density and balance as dependent variables, which are affected by the power distribution as an antecedent structural variable and by intervening variables in the form of decisions to exercise power by agents who are elements in the system of interest. In our analysis we will emphasize systemic causes that are not shown in the diagrams in Figure 10.1 in order to explain more fully as system effects what is represented in those diagrams. Our core theory of systemic interaction patterns and emergent systemic effects of density and balance in n-body systems is a power game theory of strategic interaction conditioned by location.[4] In its application we are guided by the practical interests of complex adaptive systems analysis in answering the basic normative question "What actions should the United States as an element of such a system take in order to avoid foreign policy mistakes?" This approach to problems employs agent-based modeling to explore the effects of increasing complexity among elements in a system:

Whatever name is used, the purpose of agent-based modeling is to understand properties of complex social systems. . . . This method of doing science can be contrasted with the two standard methods of induction and deduction. . . . Like deduction it starts with a set of explicit assumptions. But unlike deduction it does not prove theorems. Instead, an agent-based model generates simulated data that can be analyzed inductively. Unlike typical induction, however, the simulated data come from a rigorously specified set of rules rather than direct measurement of the real world. . . . Agent-based modeling is a way of doing thought experiments. (Axelrod 1997, 3–4)

The goal in this complex adaptive systems approach is to identify solutions to complex problems of engineering or design in which there is an explicit normative standard employed in those solutions (Axelrod and Cohen 1999, 1–11). In our application of this approach, we are interested in identifying strategies that lead over time to cooperation in the interactions among agents in complex systems. To identify such solutions, we shall employ counterfactual thought experiments in the form of constructing different generic zero-sum and non-zero-sum games of strategic interaction between agents in a social system of interest to see what are the emergent properties of cooperation and conflict.[5]

We start with the assumption that the United States is a potential or actual member of a strategic dyad or triad and ask the following questions: What will be the effects of a given U.S. strategy in the system of interest? Is it a foreign policy mistake in the context of existing relations between elements of the system of interest and in light of the U.S. normative goal of increasing cooperation among the elements of this system? Does a U.S. strategy take advantage of existing or potential non-zero-sum games between other agents in the system? These questions address whether U.S. foreign policy should take a direct or an indirect approach in its interactions with other members of a social system. For example, is it less effective to interact directly with two members who have a conflict with one another and more effective to interact indirectly through their respective neighbors? Should interactions in either case be initiated by the United States or by the other agents in the system? Given different generic power distributions as antecedent conditions between agents in the system of interest, what should be the U.S. strategy?

In previous chapters we have answered these questions implicitly by identifying and analyzing U.S. foreign policy mistakes. We identified these mistakes by reducing more complex, three-body problems to simpler, two-body systems of interest and then comparing U.S. decisions with the ones prescribed by sequential game theory models specified by generic power distributions as antecedent conditions. These analyses used a direct approach in the form of emphasizing U.S. interactions with only one other agent in a complex social system of several agents. The initial U.S. strategy tended to be a conflict strategy of dominant or contingent conflict rather than contingent cooperation in these conflict situations. Depending on the evolution of power relations between the United States and its new adversary over time, the conflicts escalated into wars, in which the U.S. outcomes were domination (Japan, Iraq), deadlock (Korea), settlement (Vietnam, Soviet Union), or submission (Cuba).

In one case (Vietnam), a settlement outcome was followed by the renewal of conflict between the local antagonists and a submission outcome for the former U.S. ally (South Vietnam). In another case (Iraq), an initial military victory was followed by an extended guerilla conflict that continued after the cessation of formal hostilities. All but the conflicts with Japan and Iraq occurred during the cold war era and were dominated by competition and conflict between two superpowers, which may provide a structural explanation for the tendency toward an initial U.S. conflict strategy in the majority of the cases (Waltz 1979). However, the Japan and Iraq cases occurred in historical eras with different social systems, and the United States was forced to shift to a strategy of contingent cooperation even during some cold war conflicts (Vietnam, Soviet Union) and accept deadlock (Korea) or submission (Cuba) outcomes in two cases.

This record is not a particularly distinguished one for a direct strategy of conflict in situations where the United States was not a party to the original local conflict. These results provide an incentive to examine alternatives to direct involvement and a conflict strategy in such situations. The first point to notice in such an examination is that the territorial location of the United States has evolved into a relatively simple pattern compared with most other states in the international system.[6] It has only two immediate neighbors (Canada and Mexico), which do not share common borders and therefore are strangers to one another. The logic of territoriality suggests that local patterns of conflict and cooperation would take the passage of time, the development of technological innovations in transportation and communications, and the expansion of trade to link all three of these states as a three-body system. In fact, the local relations between each of these dyads evolved into a three-body system only recently, with the formation of the North American Free Trade Agreement (NAFTA). The leading agents in this evolution were businessmen rather than diplomats or warriors. Technological innovations in transportation and communications gave momentum in their interactions to the evolution of direct strategies of cooperation in non-zero-sum games rather than strategies of conflict in zero-sum games.[7]

The evolution of U.S. relations with more distant strangers in the rest of the world has been more complex. Relations between other states preceded relations with the United States and often involved local conflicts between neighbors with common borders. The four different patterns in Figure 10.2 of evolving relations represent historical patterns in U.S. foreign relations in North America, Europe, and Asia in the twentieth century. The antecedent relations, (+) or (−), are followed by subsequent relations, (+) or (−), in a pattern predicted by signed graph theory in three of the four cases. The first pattern is the simple and direct pair of dyadic relations between the United States and its immediate neighbors in North America for most of the twentieth century followed by the triadic pattern of NAFTA in 1992. The other three patterns are historical examples of

FIGURE 10.2   *Signed Graph Theory's Structural Explanations of U.S. Foreign Relations*

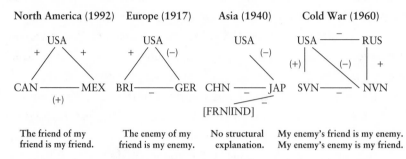

North America (1992)   Europe (1917)   Asia (1940)   Cold War (1960)

| The friend of my friend is my friend. | The enemy of my friend is my enemy. | No structural explanation. | My enemy's friend is my enemy. My enemy's enemy is my friend. |

Prior relations are not in parentheses, and subsequent relations are in parentheses. Countries: United States (USA); Canada (CAN); Mexico (MEX); Britain (BRI); Germany (GER); China (CHN); Japan (JAP); France (FRN); Indochina (IND); Russia (RUS); South Vietnam (SVN); North Vietnam (NVN). Relations are friendly (+) or hostile (−).

some variations in the more complex patterns of U.S. relations with distant strangers outside of North America in the twentieth century.

The structural explanations of U.S. foreign relations below each example in Figure 10.2 are based on signed graph theory's mathematical proposition that imbalanced relations tend toward balanced relations over time and the old Arab proverb quoted by Jervis (1997, 211): "The friend of my friend is my friend; the enemy of my friend is my enemy; the enemy of my enemy is my friend." He also notes that:

The elements in a social system often form a configuration that is consistent or balanced (using these terms as synonyms). . . . [It] . . . has been described by psychologists, sociologists, and political scientists . . . [and] . . . also appears in animal behavior. . . . Consistency, then, can be thought of as the "natural order" of a system. That is, a system will become consistent if nothing stops it. Because many other forces can intervene, imbalance is not surprising in a statistical sense, but it does need to be explained. . . . *Much of the explanation comes from the preferences and strategies of the actors. Although it is their behavior that drives some configurations to balance, actors often seek imbalance and under some conditions can achieve it.* (Jervis 1997, 210; emphasis added)

The example of U.S. foreign relations in Asia prior to World War II is likely one such deviant case identified in italics. The United States imposed economic sanctions on Japan in 1940 for invading French Indochina during the Sino-Japanese War, although its antecedent relations with all of the other bodies were not close. America was neither a neighbor of Japan nor an ally of either China or France. The other examples follow one or more of the Arab proverbs, as Mexico and Canada eventually joined with the United States in a balanced triangle of cooperation based on their prior friendly relations with a mutual neighbor. The United States eventually entered World War I in 1917 on the side of its British trading partner after an unsuccessful attempt to remain neutral between Britain and Germany (Walker and Schafer 2007). During the cold war between the superpowers as enemies, the United States became the friend and even the military ally of an enemy (South Vietnam) of a Soviet friend (North Vietnam).

In the North American case, the United States occupies a primary role as the common direct link in both of the two strategic dyads that constitute the antecedent relations in the system of interest. In the European case, the United States occupies a secondary role as a member of one of the strategic dyads that is the system of interest. In the Asia and cold war cases, the United States occupies a tertiary role in the system of interest. These primary, secondary, and tertiary roles are defined temporally in terms of whether they are antecedent conditions or subsequent effects in the analysis of the system's complexity. U.S. relations with Canada preceded its relations with Mexico as neighbors, and both relationships were antecedent structural conditions for a subsequent relationship between Canada and Mexico. The U.S. trading relationship with Britain and the outbreak of World War I between Britain and Germany preceded U.S. entry into the war, as did the history of the American "special relationship" with England as the latter's former colonies. The cold war relationship between the superpowers, Russian support for Communist revolutionaries in former European colonies such as Vietnam, and domestic violence between North and South Vietnam preceded the U.S. decision to replace France as the patron of South Vietnam and the adversary of North Vietnam.

Depending on its location in a triangle and within the larger system of interest, it is possible in triangular relations for a state "to gain a pivotal position, i.e., the ability to align with either of the other two who lack this flexibility" (Jervis 1997, 181). Factors that enhance or reduce this ability include the density of relations versus structural holes between a given element and other elements in the system. In the North American and European cases, the antecedent positions of the United States and Britain are denser than the other elements in their respective systems, because they connect directly with those other elements, whereas there is a structural hole (no direct connection) between Canada and Mexico and between Germany and the United States in their respective systems. Social network theory specifies that the denser position of the former states constrains their behavior compared with the latter states who are more structurally autonomous (fewer direct ties with others) than the former (Burt 1992). The actor with the most structural autonomy in the antecedent condition is the United States in the third and fourth cases. In the Asia case, the United States has no direct previous ties with China, Japan, or Indochina and only one direct tie (with Russia) in the cold war case.

Jervis (1997, 182) argues both theoretically and with historical examples that it is sometimes worthwhile to seek the pivot, noting, "A state in the pivot can make gains that are out of proportion to its economic and military resources." The determinants of a pivotal position in the system of world politics include location, technology, and a pragmatic ideology. He also argues that it is possible to act either as an external (less dense) or internal (more dense) pivot within a system. The classic example of a state that sought and played a role as an internal pivot in European politics is Germany between 1870 and 1890. Bismarck as the German leader constructed a dense system of alliances that isolated France, which was Germany's principal enemy following a German victory in the 1870 Franco-Prussian war of German unification. According to social network theory's density proposition, France's structural autonomy (isolation) should empower it to be an external (less dense) pivot as the state with the most flexibility to align itself with others.[8]

However, the density proposition from social network theory regarding the number of ties does not take into account the nature of those ties, which constrained the ability of other states with lower density ties in the system to align with France. Also, the composition of Germany's social network was really a series of links with neighbors and strangers, with Germany as an external pivot in a tertiary role that made Berlin initially autonomous from the others prior to reaching either an alliance or an understanding with one or both parties in conflict with one another.[9] It is our contention that the United States in the post–cold war era is in a unique location to play a similar pivotal role in the international system (Joffe 1995). A superpower in a relatively autonomous geographical location with technological superiority has a unique set of traits to play a tertiary role as an external pivot to enhance cooperation and reduce conflict between local enemies outside North America. The main missing ingredient has been a pragmatic ideology, which reduces the acceptability of the United States as an honest broker in regions such as the Middle East and South Asia. This absence was particularly striking with the rise of neoconservative ideology, amplified by the tragedy of 9/11, in the Bush administration (Mann 2004; Robison 2006). The new Obama administration's more pragmatic leadership style offers an opportunity to remedy this shortcoming in dealing with U.S. relations in these regions, which we shall illustrate below.

The two main generic features of strategic interaction situations within systems of world politics are the distribution and the exercise of power. We have emphasized in our previous dyadic analyses the importance of correctly identifying the answer to the dual aspects of the *kto-kovo* (who controls whom?) power question, respectively, which identify the distribution of power as symmetrical or asymmetrical and whether the exercise of power is positive sanctions (+), negative sanctions (−), or a mix (±) of the two strategies. With this information about possible features of the situation, we can construct the game of strategic interaction occurring between members of a dyad that is defined by the rank order of preferences for the settlement, deadlock, domination, and submission outcomes associated with these generic features. These possibilities are illustrated in Figure 10.3, which shows the possible segments that can make up a power triad of ABC agents with the possible preference rankings for each player in a strategic segment of the triad specified by the theory of preferences about inferences (TIP) from the possible types of power distributions between the players.

FIGURE 10.3   *Constructing Generic Interaction Situations*

Dyadic Interactions	ABC Segments and Distributions			Outcome Cells	
	Symmetric	Segment	Asymmetric		
A|B No-Conflict Game	$A^{+,=} \mid B^{+,=}$	A ——— B	$A^{+,>} \mid B^{+,<}$	Settle (0)	Submit/ Dominate (1)
B|C Mixed-Motive Game	$B^{-,=} \mid C^{+,=}$	B ——— C	$B^{-,>} \mid C^{+,<}$		
A|C Conflict Game	$A^{-,=} \mid C^{-,=}$	A ——— C	$A^{-,>} \mid C^{-,<}$	Dominate/ Submit (3)	Deadlock (2)

The six TIP propositions for constructing the outcome cells of each game are (1) If $(+,<)$, then $0 > 2 > 1 > 3$; (2) If $(+,=)$, then $0 > 2 > 3 > 1$; (3) If $(+,>)$, then $0 > 3 > 2 > 1$; (4) If $(-,<)$, then $3 > 0 > 1 > 2$; (5) If $(-,=)$, then $3 > 0 > 2 > 1$; (6) If $(-,>)$, then $3 > 2 > 0 > 1$.
Sources: Marfleet and Walker (2006), 57 for TIP; Walker, Malici, and Schafer (2011), 263, figure 14.5 for segments and valences.

The ABC symmetrical and asymmetrical triads from the segments in Figure 10.3 are constructed and analyzed for the emergent properties of equilibrium stability and valence stability in Figure 10.4. In the symmetrical power triad all three players are equal in power and pursue different strategies in different segments of the triad. The combination of symmetrical power distributions and positive sanctions between the players in segment A|B make their strategic equilibrium stable at (4,4) along with balanced valence stability in the form of a mutually positive (+,+) relationship between them. The other two symmetric segments, B|C and A|C, have more than one equilibrium in their respective games and a relatively unstable, imbalanced (+/−) relationship between the agents in these segments. The indeterminate nature of the final states in these two segments, which depend on which member of the dyad has the next move from different initial states, makes the triad an open system in which the triadic relationships can range in valence stability represented by the triadic outcomes menu in Figure 10.4. The same statements are true regarding the strategic and valence equilibria for the three segments, {A|B B|C A|C}, in the asymmetrical power triad.

With the information from Figure 10.4 for a particular power triad, we can address the following questions about its emergent properties: Is the triad of interest relatively stable or unstable under the antecedent conditions specified by the generic features of the strategic situations between the agents in the triad? What are some possible U.S. pivot strategies regarding the triad of interest? What are the consequences of pursu-

FIGURE 10.4   *Power Triads with Dyadic Strategies for the Actors in Each Segment*

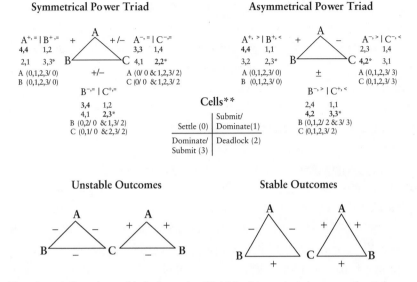

The valences indicate the possible final states (equilibria) for the game in each segment of a triad as balanced (+ or −) or imbalanced (+) (domination/submission). *Nash equilibria are asterisked, and Brams equilibria are in bold for each game. **Cells below each game are numbered o to 3 (upper left clockwise to lower left) as initial states with corresponding final states separated by a slash mark when each player has the next move (Marfleet and Walker 2006, 58–62). The row player is listed first, and the column player is listed second below each game. The final states of each triad are more or less balanced (stable) according to the menu of triadic outcomes (Harary 1961).
Source: Data are from Walker, Malici, and Schafer (2011), 263, figure 14.5.

ing a pivot strategy of conditional cooperation toward different segments of a particular dyad or triad? In the following analyses that address these questions, we shall illustrate answers with examples from U.S. foreign policy options regarding key strategic triads in the Middle East and South Asia. These examples are not historical case studies that necessarily explain past or present U.S. decisions. They are counterfactual case studies designed as thought experiments and intended to be decision heuristics for policy makers and for strategists as they make future decisions in these regions. In addition to *kto-kovo* dyadic power relations, our analysis of triadic situations created by linked power dyads in these two regions will also emphasize spatial location as an important generic feature. Are the dyads that constitute the segments in a triad of strategic interactions between neighbors or strangers?

STEERING U.S. FOREIGN POLICY DECISIONS IN THE
MIDDLE EAST AND SOUTH ASIA

The Middle East and South Asia regions are the sites of several "wicked problems" facing past and present U.S. presidents and their administrations. The *wicked problem* phrase is popular among policy analysts and planners as a description of what we have identified more generally as a particularly difficult form of *n*-body problems and what psychologists have also termed "ill-structured" problems.[10] Two of the latest and most prominent of these problems are ones identified in the popular discourse of U.S. foreign policy as nuclear proliferation and terrorism. Nuclear proliferation and terrorism are linked as problems by journalists and policy analysts concerned with the possibility of terrorists obtaining and using WMD such as nuclear weapons (Suskind 2006, 2009; Sanger 2009; Kilcullen 2009). We focus on these problems because they are common features in our two regional systems of interest and because of their global significance as wicked problems for states outside these regions.

What decisions and actions should the United States or other states choose to solve these problems and to prevent nuclear weapons from becoming linked to terrorists? The administration of George W. Bush chose a dominant conflict strategy as a direct solution via the Bush-Cheney doctrine of strategic military preemption in the form of military attacks on suspected terrorist locations, especially Iraq and Afghanistan, in the Middle East and South Asia. The Obama administration has repudiated this doctrine both in Iraq and Afghanistan and reviewed its strategic approach to both regions. Two key components of this strategic review are the declarations by the Obama administration (1) to take an explicitly regional perspective and (2) to redress an imbalance in the use of military and diplomatic means to deal with these problems.

The declaration of these principles means that the U.S. strategy in Iraq needs to be part of a broader regional strategy encompassing other key players in the Middle East, including Turkey, Iran, Syria, Lebanon, Jordan, Israel, and Egypt. The expansion to a regional perspective in South Asia means that ongoing conflicts in Afghanistan and Pakistan are now called the AFPAK problem in Washington with both Iran and India entering into the strategic calculations regarding the national security of these larger states and the smaller ones in the region. It is also possible to extend the number of key players among the larger states to include Russia and China in both regions. The reason that these problems take on a regional scope is because of the principle of territoriality that binds the various states together as complex adaptive systems of strategic interaction. The one country that does not share borders with any other states in these two regions is the United States.[11]

This external location along with the technological ability to project American power makes the United States a candidate to play the tertiary role of external or internal pivot in the conflicts among neighbors and strangers in the region. Before examining these possibilities, however, it is important to recognize and acknowledge three caveats.

- Other countries inside as well as outside these regions may also be situated to play a *tertius gaudens* role. They may have stronger economic and cultural ties than the United States with some of the protagonists in the Middle East and South Asia. It is therefore possible for the United States to play a role either as a third-party member in a regional dyad or as a party linked to one or more members of a triad with an existing pivot.

- Although others may have situational and historical advantages, they may not have the U.S. ability to exercise political power effectively in dealing with regional problems. The imbalance between opportunity and capability may explain the tendency to turn to Washington for involvement in regional problems and the U.S. record of direct rather than indirect intervention.

- It is possible to argue that the problems of nuclear proliferation and terrorism plus their potential conjunction in the future makes these local and regional problems global and existential for states around the world. This position was the basis for the Bush administration's military interventions in Iraq and Afghanistan and the Obama administration's preoccupation, respectively, with Iran and Pakistan as potential or actual nuclear powers.

These caveats reflect the complexities of the geographical and histori-cal situations in the two regions of interest, which point to the need to qualify any theoretical generalizations that emerge from the following counterfactual analyses. Depending on the regional system and triad of interest, more than one state may be appropriate to play this role (Kinzer 2010). Therefore, in our analysis we set aside the question of who should seek and maintain the pivot role and focus instead on the actions and consequences of alternative strategies for the *tertius gaudens* actor, defer-ring until the end of this chapter an assessment of whether it should be the United States.

The Middle East

The issue of a possible nuclear proliferation and terrorist nexus in this region revolves around the three "I"s: Israel, Iraq, and Iran.[12] Israel al-ready has nuclear weapons and the means to use them against its imme-diate neighbors as well as peripheral states in the region, which gives Is-rael a second-strike deterrent against an all-out conventional invasion or a nuclear strike on Israel. The Israelis do not presently have the conven-tional capability to strike and destroy actual or potential nuclear weapons sites located beyond its immediate neighbors. They also lack the capacity of direct retaliation against terrorists who may acquire and use nuclear weapons against Israel from hidden and dispersed locations. To preempt this possibility, Israel has threatened retaliation against potential suppliers of such weapons terrorists and even launched preemptive strikes against those who tried to acquire this capability.[13] Iraq did not have nuclear weapons at the time that the United States invaded and occupied the coun-try in 2003; however, the Bush-Cheney administration shared the Israeli fear that Iraq would develop and possibly share them (or the technology to build them) with terrorist groups such as al Qaeda and its allies.

Iran potentially poses the same general threats of developing nuclear weapons and possibly sharing them with others who may use them against the United States or Israel. The former inference is based on the reluctance of Iran to cooperate with the International Atomic Energy Agency in in-spections of its peaceful nuclear energy program while the latter inference

FIGURE 10.5   *Strategic Triads among Major States in the Middle East*

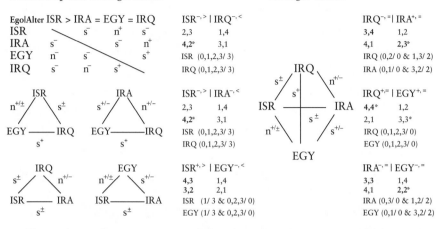

Nash equilibria are asterisked, and Brams equilibria are in bold. Valence outcomes are mutual cooperation (+); mutual conflict (–); cooperation or conflict (+/–); submission/domination (±). Countries are Israel (ISR); Iran (IRA); Egypt (EGY); and Iraq (IRQ). Locations are neighbors (n) with a common border or strangers (s) with no common border.

rests on current Iranian support for enemies of Israel with regional and global reach, such as Hezbollah in neighboring Lebanon, who are considered terrorists by Israel and the United States. Israel, Iraq, and Iran are also parties in the relationships of major tension among states in the region, which makes their actual or potential nuclear capabilities and relations of amity or enmity with terrorist groups even more significant (Hartmann 1982).

In order to map the relations of major tension and the emerging strategic dyads and triads that constitute them, the first step is to create a matrix or grid that locates these agents according to their power and role relationships. Figure 10.5 provides this information with columns and rows arranging the players in descending distribution-of-power relationships (>=<), cells designating their locations as neighbors (n) or strangers (s), and exercise-of-power valences toward each other as positive (+) or negative (–). With this map it is possible to construct and analyze the dyads and triads as complex adaptive systems and assess strategies for altering the initial states of conflict in these systems toward balanced relationships of mutual cooperation. We are also interested in whether and how the United States might seek a tertiary role of external pivot within these systems and exercise its power toward this end.

The strategic triads in Figure 10.5 for the three "I"s" plus Egypt show only one dyad as a no-conflict game with a relationship of cooperation (+). Iraq and Egypt are strangers rather than neighbors and do not have a relationship of tension between them in this figure. If the Baghdad regime aligns with Iran and/or persecutes Sunnis in Iraq after the United States withdraws from Iraq, however, then this relationship is likely to change from cooperation (+) to conflict (−). The same can be said of the game between Egypt and Iran, which already has two equilibria (mutual cooperation or mutual conflict): if Iraq tilts toward Iran along with the domestic persecution of Sunnis in Iraq, then there is likely to be a shift from an initial state of mutual cooperation to a new equilibrium of mutual conflict between Egypt and Iran. This shift may also occur if Iran acquires nuclear weapons. The dyad between Iran and Iraq also has two equilibria (mutual cooperation and mutual conflict); the stability of mutual cooperation as an equilibrium in both dyads depends on the ability and resolve of one or both players to exercise threat power in order to prevent defection and a shift to mutual conflict as an equilibrium. These three dyads are all non-zero-sum games, which have mutual cooperation as a possible stable equilibrium.

The other three segments within the strategic triads in Figure 10.5 are less stable for three reasons. One is that some of these are relations between neighbors, as in the ISR | EGY case, which means that the possibility of war is higher in the absence of buffer states between them. Or the power distribution is asymmetrical rather than symmetrical, as in the ISR | IRQ case, which means the stronger power can impose a domination/submission (±) equilibrium. The third reason is that the dyadic relations may be a zero-sum game, as in the ISR | IRA case, with only a Nash equilibrium instead of a non-zero-sum game with a Pareto-superior outcome.

Combining these dyads into triads and assessing their valence stability, we first ask: what is the composition of each triad in terms of zero-sum and non-zero-sum segments? Two of the strategic triads in Figure 10.5 are non-zero-sum triads, that is, each of their segments is a non-zero-sum dyad. The relatively less stable exceptions are the {ISR, IRQ, IRA} strategic triad with two zero-sum segments and the {ISR, EGY, IRQ} triad with one zero-sum segment. The two triads share a zero-sum ISR | IRQ segment, plus there is a zero-sum ISR | IRA segment in one of the triads. We next ask: what are the implications for a player who contemplates a *tertius gaudens* role in each of these less stable systems of interest? If the goal is to convert zero-sum to non-zero-sum relations as a first step toward constructing a system of mutual cooperation, then a state contemplating a tertiary pivot role of conditional cooperation as a strategy should ideally be willing and able to enact it toward Israel and both Iran and Iraq.

The possible system effects of such a third-party intervention are shown in the top half of Figure 10.6. The immediate effect of the pivot intervention of conditional cooperation is to make the previously stable (balanced) relationship in the {ISR, IRQ, IRA} triad coexist with an unstable (imbalanced) relationship in the {ISR, Pivot, IRA} triad and a stable (balanced) relationship in the {IRQ, Pivot, IRA} triad. If the IRQ | IRA segment shifts from a mixed-motive to a no-conflict game and this segment thereby combines into a single coalition as an agent, then the problem in an intermediate state reduces to an unstable (imbalanced) triad with four possible outcomes. The best outcome is for the pivot's intervention to change the negative valences in the antecedent condition to all positive valences, which is a stable (balanced) triad of non-zero-sum games.

A second-best outcome is for the pivot's intervention to create an unstable (imbalanced) triad with two non-zero-sum segments between the pivot and the agents in the ISR | [IRQ | IRA] segment, creating the intermediate condition for a shift in the ISR | [IRQ | IRA] segment from a zero-sum (−) to a non-zero-sum (+) game.[14] It is better than the third outcome, which is for a non-zero-sum game to be created in only one of the two new segments, shown as the Pivot | ISR segment in Figure 10.6. The result is a triad between the pivot and the problematic segment that resembles structurally the stable (balanced) {ISR,IRQ,IRA} triad that is the antecedent condition: there is no net gain in non-zero-sum segments in the system. The final outcome is for an unstable (imbalanced) triad of three zero-sum games to replace the antecedent condition: there is both a net loss in non-zero-sum games and a shift from a stable to an unstable triad.

FIGURE 10.6   Tertius Gaudens *Strategies and Outcomes for Middle East Triads*

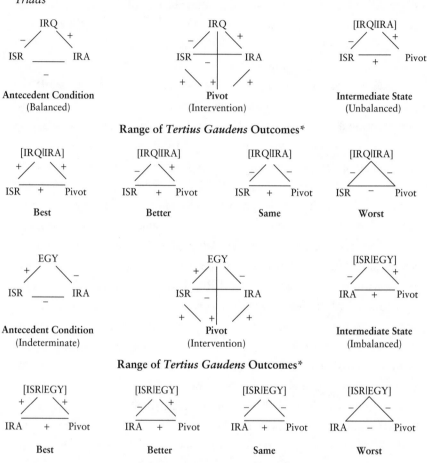

Range of *Tertius Gaudens* Outcomes*

Range of *Tertius Gaudens* Outcomes*

* Range from worst to best outcomes compared with antecedent condition as baseline. Positive (+) valence indicates a non-zero-sum game, and negative (−) valence indicates a zero-sum game for each segment of a triad. Countries are Israel (ISR); Egypt (EGY); Iran (IRA).

What are the strategic interaction dynamics between the segments in this triad that can account for these outcomes, and how can the less desirable outcomes be avoided? The answers to these questions are linked and depend on the strategies of each player in a particular segment of interest. As Axelrod (1984, 1997) demonstrated, some strategies are better than others for inducing cooperation in the non-zero-sum game of prisoner's dilemma. In turn, we demonstrate that some strategies are better for constructing a non-zero-sum game in which Axelrod's strategies can work to induce a mutual cooperation outcome as a stable equilibrium. Depending on the distributions of power between the players, however, there are limits to the success of even the more successful strategy of conditional cooperation compared with its alternatives of conditional conflict, containment, or preemption.

The limits of a conditional cooperation strategy under the condition of a symmetrical (=) power distribution are demonstrated in Figure 10.7. A conditional cooperation strategy opens a path to mutual cooperation in a game against a strategy of conditional conflict or soft containment; however, it is unsuccessful against a strategy of hard containment or preemption. These strategies present more difficult, "wicked" problems for the pivot, which require as a solution that the other player change its preference rankings either to soft containment or conditional conflict in order to construct a non-zero-sum game with a Pareto-superior outcome. Other's hard containment and preemption strategies construct zero-sum games and are anomalies from the normative theoretical perspective of TIP's rational choice assumptions regarding the *kto-kovo* question. If the players are equal in power, a hard containment strategy of deadlock > domination > settlement > submission is not sustainable over the long term unless the player is satisfied with deadlock over settlement or domination as a permanent outcome. The same is true for a preemption strategy of domination > deadlock > settlement > submission.

The equilibria for strategic interaction games derived from the intersection of these preference rankings and any of the other strategies in Figure 10.7 does not lead to domination or settlement as final outcomes unless the power distribution shifts in favor of the player with one of these strategies.[15] If the pivot persists in implementing a strategy of conditional cooperation with sufficient skill, it is often possible to induce a strategic shift by the other player. In order to effect this change, the pivot needs to induce either learning or structural adaptation by the other player. Learning may occur either vicariously by other's observation of pivot's strategic interaction with the alternate member of the triad or directly through the pivot's efforts to communicate its strategy in prior communication and by repeated plays of the existing game.[16] Structural

FIGURE 10.7   *Conditional Cooperation Strategy versus Alternative Strategies by Others*

	Other			Other			Other			Other	
(G27) CO	CO	CF	(G51) CO	CO	CF	(G15) CO	CO	CF	(G24) CO	CO	CF
CO	4,3→|	1,4	CO	4,3*←	1,2	CO	4,2	1,3	CO	4,2	1,4
Pivot	↑	↓	Pivot	↓	↑	Pivot			Pivot		
CF	2,1←	"3,2"*	CF	2,1 →	"3,4"*	CF	2,1	"3,4"*	CF	2,1	"3,3"*

Conditional Conflict	**Soft Containment**	**Hard Containment**	**Preemption**
Intentions: Piv, Oth (+,−)	Intentions: Piv, Oth (+,−)	Intentions: Piv, Oth (+,−)	Intentions: Piv, Oth (+,−)
Power: Pivot = Other	Power: Pivot = Other	Power: Pivot = Other	Power: Pivot = Other

Nash equilibria are asterisked, and Brams equilibria are in bold. Initial state is in quotation marks. Arrows indicate "move" (→) while blocked arrows (→|) indicate "stay."

adaptation may occur in the form of changes in the power distribution between the players whereby other's power position shifts from a symmetrical to an asymmetrical relationship favoring the pivot or the alternate member of the triad.

The optimal strategy for the pivot to induce either learning or structural adaptation by other is conditional cooperation toward other's neighbors and any strangers on the periphery of the regional system of interest, especially those who have significant relations with other. This approach creates more than one strategic triad with structural pressures toward a balanced pattern of mutual cooperation. One example in the Middle East would be for the pivot to initiate and maintain non-zero-sum games with the EGY | IRA and EGY | ISR segments of the system, as attributed to the United States in the bottom half of Figure 10.6. On the basis of the games in Figure 10.5, the antecedent conditions in this triad are a mixed-motive game between ISR | EGY and a conflict game between EGY | IRA, both of which have multiple equilibria (+ or −), whereas the ISR | IRA game is a zero-sum conflict game. If the pivot intervenes with a conditional cooperation strategy directed at all three members of the {ISR,EGY,IRA} triad, the two neighbors (ISR and EGY) may become a coalition and create an imbalanced triad as an intermediate state. The range of possible final outcomes from this intermediate state is also shown in Figure 10.6. The first two represent a net increase in the number of non-zero-sum games in the triad while the last two outcomes show no improvement or a net decrease in such games. Theoretically, the likelihood of each outcome depends on the strategies of the other members of the triad in response to the pivot's strategy of conditional cooperation.

The preceding counterfactual analyses of the most powerful agents that constitute strategic triads in the Middle East regional system have operated at the state level of analysis without considering agents within the domestic subsystems within these states. Nor have we considered other agents in the Middle East regional system, such as Jordan, Lebanon, and Syria, who are less powerful neighbors of these states. A more complex analysis would take them into account. The argument for starting with the most powerful states is that they have leverage over the less powerful states, including domestic factions within them. For example, Iran has friendly relations with Syria, and both have influence with Hezbollah in Lebanon. Israel and Egypt have friendly relations with Jordan, and all three of them have influence over Hamas and the Palestinian Authority in the West Bank and Gaza. If the more powerful states can reduce their mutual tensions, then the next step is to exercise power jointly over the smaller actors who present threats to the region's stability.

South Asia

Although a top-down strategy of conditional cooperation may work in the Middle East because of the vertical ties between the more powerful and less powerful actors in this region, this approach may be less applicable in South Asia. The major states in the regional system of South Asia include Iran, Pakistan, Afghanistan, and India. All of these states are neighbors of at least one other state in this set, which binds them together into strategic triads similar to the states of Israel, Iraq, Egypt, and Iran in the Middle East. They also face the common problems of nuclear proliferation and terrorism, which are linked by the possibility of terrorists obtaining and using WMD such as nuclear weapons (Coll 2004; L. Wright 2006; Sanger 2009; Kilcullen 2009; Rashid 2009). The main difference between the two regional systems is that two key actors (Afghanistan and Pakistan) face entrenched domestic terrorist threats from local insurgents in relatively inaccessible areas within each country, exacerbated by the long-term presence of foreign terrorists represented by al Qaeda.[17]

The intrusion of al Qaeda has created a stronger "accidental guerilla syndrome" in these societies than in Iraq, and the pursuit of al Qaeda by outside forces into remote tribal areas in the two countries following the 9/11 attacks has led the local populations there to ally with al Qaeda against outside intervention. This alliance decision is based on a previous history of local grievances against a weak central government and al Qaeda's relative ideological affinity as fellow Muslims compared with Western forces. In contrast to Iraq, al Qaeda in Afghanistan and Pakistan already had an established local presence as guests of the Taliban regime in Afghanistan prior to 9/11 and a regional presence as clients of the Pakistan government dating back to the Afghan war with the Soviet Union (Coll 2004; Kilcullen 2009).[18]

These features of the regional system in South Asia lead us to construct in Figure 10.8 a power map of the region that does not represent Afghanistan as a single actor. We instead distinguish between the Afghanistan government of northern war lords and Pashtuns in the central government and the Taliban forces of southern/eastern Pashtuns and al Qaeda foreign fighters. The latter extend into Pakistan's tribal territories and are united by membership in the Pashtun ethnic group, which is almost 50 percent of the Afghan population but a much smaller minority inside Pakistan.[19] The Pashtun regions in the two countries are geographic neighbors that separate most of the rest of their respective countries from one another. The Pashtun location as a buffer zone between Pakistan and Afghanistan makes the pair geographic strangers rather than neighbors even though a political map of South Asia makes them appear to be neighbors. In effect, the Pashtun region spanning the two countries is the location of a Taliban/al Qaeda agent acting separately from either of its constituent parts of Afghanistan and Pakistan.[20] Finally, the inhospitable terrain and difficult traveling conditions in particular make local tribal differences from village to village very important throughout Afghanistan and the Pashtun area of Pakistan in the absence of modern roads and means of transportation to the capital cities and other large population centers in Afghanistan and Pakistan.[21]

Inspection of the strategic triads in Figure 10.8 reveals a strategic triad of cooperation among Iran, India, and Afghanistan, {IRA, IND, AFG},

FIGURE 10.8 *Strategic Triads among Major States in South Asia*

Power Map

Ego|Alter IND = PAK > IRA > AFG = [TAL|AQ]

IND	n⁻	s⁺	n⁺	s⁻
PAK	n⁻	n⁻	n⁻	n⁺
IRA	s⁺	n⁻	n⁺	n⁻
AFG	n⁺	n⁻	n⁺	n⁻
TAL|AQ	s⁻	n⁺	n⁻	n⁻

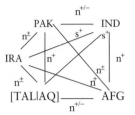

Strategic Triads   **Strategic Games**

IRA⁻ᐠ	PAK⁻ᐳ		IRA⁻ᐟᐳ	TAL⁻ᐸ		IRA⁺ᐸ	IND⁺ᐳ
3,2	2,4*	2,3	1,4	4,4*	2,3
4,1	1,3	4,2*	3,1	1,1	3,2*
IRA (0,1,2,3/ 3)		IRA (0,1,2,3/ 3)		IRA (0,1,2,3/ 0)	
PAK (0,1,2,3/ 3)		TAL (0,1,2,3/ 3)		IND (0,1, 2,3/ 0)	

PAK⁺ᐳ	TAL⁺ᐸ		PAK⁻ᐳ	AFG⁻ᐸ		PAK⁻ᐟ⁼	IND⁻ᐟ⁼
4,4*	1,1	2,3	1,4	3,3	1,4
3,2	2,3*	4,2*	3,1	4,1	2,2*
PAK (0,1,2,3/ 0)		PAK (0,1,2,3/ 3)		PAK (0,3/ 0 & 1,2/ 2)	
TAL (0,1,2,3/ 0)		AFG (0,1,2,3/ 3)		IND (0,1/ 0 & 3,2/ 2)	

IND⁻ᐳ	TAL⁻ᐸ		IND⁺ᐳ	AFG⁺ᐸ		AFG⁻ᐟ⁼	TAL⁻ᐟ⁼
2,3	1,4	4,4*	1,1	3,3	1,4
4,2*	3,1	3,2	2,3*	4,1	2,2*
IND (0,1,2,3/ 3)		IND (0,1,2,3/ 0)		AFG (0,3/ 0 & 1,2/ 2)	
TAL (0,1,2,3/ 3)		AFG (0,1, 2,3/ 0)		TAL (0,1/ 0 & 3,2/ 2)	

AFG⁺ᐸ	IRA⁺ᐳ
4,4	2,3
1,1	3,2
AFG (0,1,2,3/0)	
IRA (0,1,2,3/0)	

Nash equilibria are asterisked, and Brams equilibria are in bold. Valence outcomes are mutual cooperation (+); mutual conflict (−); cooperation or conflict (+/−); and submission/domination (±). Actors are India (IND), Iran (IRA), Pakistan (PAK), Afghanistan (AFG), Taliban (TAL), and al Qaeda (ALQ). Locations are neighbor (n) and stranger (s).

and a strategic dyad of cooperation between Pakistan and the Taliban–al Qaeda alliance [PAK | TALAQ]. The remaining segments of the strategic triads in Figure 10.8 are symmetric or asymmetric conflict dyads. These two clusters form single nodes, which we expand in the latter case back into a triad of {PAK, TAL, AQ} to incorporate analysis of the relationship between an [IRA, IND, AFG] coalition versus the Taliban movement plus al Qaeda in the "Federally Administered Tribal Areas" of Pakistan and in rural Afghanistan.

The strategic situations created by this new configuration of agents are shown in Figure 10.9 and analyzed as a series of intermediate states in chronological order with final outcomes from antecedent conditions and strategic pivot interventions. The results indicate that if the pivot pursues an intervention strategy of conditional cooperation toward Pakistan and [IRA, IND, AFG] as the major states in South Asia first and if these interventions produce the consequences predicted by signed graph theory, then the ensuing results are consistent (1) as intermediate states with strategic triads balanced with cooperation between these states and the pivot; and (2) as final outcomes in the form of eventual joint conflict toward the Taliban and al Qaeda by Pakistan and the IIA coalition.

This top-down approach to constructing non-zero-sum games between Pakistan and the [IIA] coalition specifies that if the pivot pursues a successful strategy of conditional cooperation toward each of these actors in Model (1), the predictions are that (1) the relations between PAK and IIA will shift from conflict (–) to cooperation (+); (2) relations between PAK and TAL will shift from cooperation (+) to conflict (–); and (3) relations between the pivot and TAL will be conflict (–). These predictions are consistent with the initial conditions for each dyad specified in their strategic games as relations in each triad, a pivot strategy of conditional cooperation, and the Arab proverb applying the theorems of signed graph theory to political triads under these initial conditions. The {PIV, IIA, PAK} triad becomes stable (balanced) after the shift in IIA | PAK relations occurs in accord with the "friend of my friend is my friend" proposition. The {IIA, PAK, TAL} triad becomes stable (balanced) after the shift in relations in PAK | TAL relations occurs in accord with the "enemy of my enemy is my enemy" proposition. The same proposition holds for PIV | TAL relations in the {PIV, IIA TAL} triad.

In Model (2), the antecedent conditions are specified by the conflict relations between PAK and TAL from the shift in relations between PAK and TAL in Model (1) and the pivot's intervention strategy in Model (1). The predictions are that relations between ALQ and PIV will be conflict (–) as will relations between PAK and ALQ. The same prediction for PAK | IIA in Model (1) and ALQ | PIV in Model (2) are evident in Model (3) and Model (4), respectively, when relations with the Taliban are not consid-

FIGURE 10.9 *Pivot Models of Strategic Triads among Major States in South Asia*

Power Map

Ego\Alter	[IIA] = PAK > TAL = ALQ		
[IIA]		$n^{+/-}$ $\quad$ $n^{\pm}$ $\quad$ s^{-}	
PAK	$n^{+/-}$	n^{+} $\quad$ $s^{\pm}$	
TAL	$n^{\pm}$ $\quad$ n^{+}	s^{+}	
ALQ	s^{-} $\quad$ $s^{\pm}$ $\quad$ s^{+}		

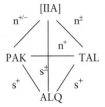

Strategic Triads $\qquad\qquad\qquad\qquad$ **Strategic Games***

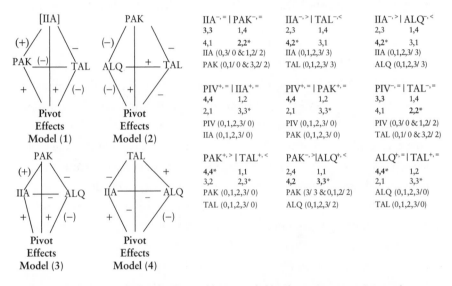

Nash equilibria are asterisked, and Brams equilibria are in bold. Valence outcomes are in parentheses, and antecedent valence conditions are not. Strategic valences are: mutual cooperation (+); mutual conflict (−); cooperation or conflict (+/−); and submission/domination (±). Actors are India, Iran, Afghanistan (IIA), Pakistan (PAK), Taliban (TAL), al Qaeda (ALQ), and pivot (PIV). Locations are neighbors (n) and strangers (s).

ered within the triads of interest in Model (3) and when relations with Pakistan are omitted from the triads of interest in Model (4). All four models in Figure 10.9 assume as an initial condition that the {IRA, IND, AFG} strategic triad is cohesive—that is, it constitutes a stable (balanced) triad of mutual cooperation as indicated earlier in Figure 10.8.

This assumption implies that a top-down approach to South Asia similar to the one applied in the Middle East case study should begin with the pivot's attempt to formalize this coalition with a conditional cooperation strategy. The pivot's relations with Pakistan in Figure 10.9 may either precede or follow this step. It is also the pivot's role to facilitate the shift in relations from (–) to (+) between [IIA] and PAK. Pivot and [IIA] would then together encourage a shift in relations between PAK and TAL in Model (1) corresponding to their own relations with TAL. The pivot's role in Model (2) would be to establish cooperation with PAK and then balance the {PIV, PAK, ALQ} triad by establishing conflict relations with ALQ if they did not already exist. The sequence of steps for the incumbent of the pivot role is generally the same in Model (3) and Model (4).

CONCLUSION

Can and should the United States enact the pivot role in the Middle East and South Asia? According to Jervis (1997, 177–209), the determinants of a pivotal position in the system of world politics include location, technology, and a pragmatic ideology. These factors affect the type of pivot role available to a state as well as the prospects for enacting the role with success. He also argues that it is possible to act either as an external (less dense) or internal (more dense) pivot within a system, depending on whether the state's location is deeply enmeshed within a system of interest or is relatively autonomous in a structural hole (see also Burt 1992; Joffe 1995). A fourth determinant of success is the strategy that the potential pivot enacts. Strategy is crucial in establishing the criteria for success by specifying preference rankings for the possible outcomes that partly define the strategy, which we have identified as settlement, deadlock, domination, or submission. In turn, the determinants of power distribution and the exercise of power include location and technology, plus the ideologies and strategies of actors other than the pivot (Jervis 1997).

The United States has the geographic location to occupy an external pivot role in both regions. It also has the technology in terms of military and economic resources to project its power into each region. The question is whether its ideology and the density of its historical relations in each region provide the United States with sufficient flexibility and autonomy to enact the role of an external pivot with a strategy of conditional cooperation. The U.S. cultural bias toward democracy and the doctrines of

American omnipotence and exceptionalism has made U.S. strategy relatively dogmatic, inflexible, and arrogant toward foreign cultures and conflicts (Brogan 1952; Fulbright 1966; Kennan 1984; Hunt 1987; Becevitch
2008). We have argued in our historical case studies of U.S. foreign policy mistakes that these tendencies have made the United States prone to
the pursuit of strategies of conditional or unconditional conflict, beginning with its strategic choices leading to Japan's attack on Pearl Harbor,
continuing with the strategy of containment and coercion throughout the
cold war era, and culminating with a strategy of preemption after 9/11.

The United States is also deeply enmeshed in relations with key states
in the Middle East and South Asia, which call into question its structural
autonomy and corresponding capacity to play the role of external pivot.
Historical roles that have painted it as the patron of Israel and the Great
Satan of Iran make it relatively difficult to broker the necessary non-zero-
sum relations between Egypt and Iran or between Iran and Israel, which
may facilitate and lead to the resolution of the conflict between Israel, the
Palestinians, and its other Arab neighbors in the Middle East (Parsi 2007;
Slavin 2007; R. Wright 2008). Historical blowback from U.S. support for
the Mujahideen in Afghanistan, historical entanglements during the post–
cold war era in Saudi Arabia, Iraq, and the Persian Gulf, and the resulting al Qaeda attacks on the United States on 9/11 have further hampered
the U.S. ability to play a pivot role in both South Asia and the Middle
East. The location of al Qaeda in Afghanistan with funds from sympa-
thizers in Saudi Arabia and logistical support from elements in Pakistan's
military-intelligence complex prompted the United States to seek allies in
South Asia following the 9/11 attacks and to intervene with military
force in both Iraq and Afghanistan.

In spite of these structural impediments, we believe that it is possible for
the United States to play a pivotal role in each regional system. The choice
of U.S. strategy is a crucial intervening variable in determining the success
of either an external or an internal pivot. If the United States selects a
strategy of conditional cooperation and enacts it with the skills of pragmatic rather than dogmatic leadership, it is possible for U.S. leaders to
avoid or minimize foreign policy mistakes. If a first approximation of
foreign policy success is the number of non-zero-sum relations compared

with zero-sum relations within a social system, the choice of strategy and a pragmatic style of leadership are likely to be necessary to maximize this goal.

Skillful implementation of the strategy as a compass is the next step, which requires a map of the dynamics in the system of interest in order to operate. It is important to remember that part of the navigation of social relations is their construction—compasses are used to make maps as well as to follow them. In both instances, the goal is the reduction of uncertainty and the management of risk associated with bad outcomes. In this book we have argued for the use of game theory, role theory, social network theory, and complex adaptive systems analysis as analytical tools to map the terrain of world politics and steer leaders toward a safe harbor. Together they offer navigational aids and architectural plans for constructing networks of non-zero-sum relations, which are necessary but not sufficient for sustainable cooperation in world politics. There are also some rules of diagnosis and prescription, which are keys to eliciting and constructing cooperation from non-zero-sum strategic situations. We shall present them in our concluding chapter as some final thoughts for leaders and strategists in the policy community who want to avoid foreign policy mistakes of omission and commission in the exercise of political power.

CHAPTER 11

Some Final Thoughts
Exploring the Rationality Frontier

INTRODUCTION

A recent study of the social behavior of ants showed that ants are more rational in making collective decisions than humans (Edwards and Pratt 2009). In an interview the authors explained, "This is not the case of humans being 'stupider' than ants. Humans and animals simply often make irrational choices when faced with very challenging decisions. . . . This paradoxical outcome is based on apparent constraint: most individual ants know of only a single option, and the colony's collective choice self-organizes them from interactions among many poorly-informed ants" (qtd. in Coulombe 2009). The authors of the study define irrational choices as those based on other criteria than the net utility (benefit) of an option measured by its intrinsic attributes. In the case of the ants, the options were alternative nest sites possessing the attributes of light strength and entrance size, which varied in terms of brighter or darker light and a bigger or smaller entrance (Edwards and Pratt 2009).

The task at hand for the ant colony was to find a new nest, which involved choosing between two sites (A and B) with very similar net advantages ($A \approx B$). The authors conducted three experiments in which they observed no strong preference for A versus B. Then they introduced a third option as a decoy (D) site that was clearly dominated by (less attractive than) just one of the original pair ($D_A < A$) in Experiment 2 and then by just the other one of the original pair ($D_B < B$) in Experiment 3. They looked for evidence of "irrational" behavior in the form of defections to the clearly superior option, that is, from B to A in Experiment 2 and from A to B in Experiment 3, and found no statistically significant pattern of defection in either the number or the proportion of ants who chose A versus B or D in either of these experiments. The results contradicted significant patterns of defections in the presence of D between A and B in experiments with other animals and with humans (Edwards and Pratt 2009).

The authors speculate that decentralized features of decision making among ants explains the lack of irrationality in reaching a collective decision to prefer one option over others. Ants do not rely on equal information about the options and instead rely on the reports of individual scouts who also do not visit all of the sites. A scout instead makes an absolute judgment of the utility (net benefit), based on the fit of intrinsic attributes at its visitation site with an ideal site defined by these attributes.[1] Scouts do not make a comparative evaluation of one site's attributes with another site's attributes, based on visits to all sites. Non-scouts also learn only absolute information about a site and are not distracted or confused by the more complex task of making multiple observations and comparisons of all sites. Scouts then compete to recruit non-scouts to their site, by sending signals regarding degree of absolute fit, and a quorum effect further reinforces the actual choice of one site over another site by a colony (Edwards and Pratt 2009).

Animals and humans with centralized decision-making processes, who can make comparative evaluations among options rather than judge each one's utility solely on its intrinsic attributes, introduce more opportunity for making mistakes in consistently ranking and choosing among options. The complexity of the ranking task, time or stress constraints, and cognitive or motivational biases regarding extraneous attributes associated with comparing different options may account for errors in rationality. The introduction of a third decoy option in addition to two original options in the experiments with ants simply suggests that these possibilities are not present when the decision makers do not engage in comparative evaluations of options. These experiments do not rule out the possibility that the absence of the conditions that cause errors is relatively rare, especially among solitary animals and humans. So are ants really more rational than humans in making collective decisions to accomplish a task by choosing among different options? It would appear to depend on how the collective decision-making process is organized among humans as well as variations in external and internal constraints, such as the complexity of the task and the computational capacities of the decision maker (Edwards and Pratt 2009, 3660).

More broadly, the ant experiments raise anew the question of what it means to be rational and thereby avoid mistakes. Edwards and Pratt

(2009, 3655–3656) identify three sources as explanations for errors in rationality. One is the *experimental or the natural setting*, which may make it harder for subjects to be rational or bias the process toward or away from comparative evaluations, as in the case of the ant experiments and decentralized decision-making organization. A second is the *complexity of the problem*, which may be intrinsically hard to solve because of the number of attributes and the prohibitive costs of information necessary to solve it. A third is the *computational resources of the agent*, who may not have the cognitive capacities to make a rational choice, depending on the problem's complexity and the available information. Whereas the second explanation emphasizes information scarcity, the third explanation emphasizes information richness that is too much for the subject to process. The ant colony in the experiments addresses the rationality problem facing a ship of state in a sea of uncertainty by sending out scouts equipped by evolution with clear criteria of fitness, which act as a map and a compass to steer the ship to a safe harbor.

EXPANDING THE FRONTIERS OF RATIONALITY
IN AN UNCERTAIN WORLD

In Part I of this book we identified clear criteria of fitness and the tools to serve the dual functions of a map and a compass for making foreign policy choices by a human colony in an uncertain world. We also acted as scouts and used these tools in Parts II and III to explore the spatial and temporal alternatives to the status quo by looking backward at the history of U.S. foreign policy as one colony of humans. Then we expanded our perspective in Parts IV and V to examine the entire evolutionary history of world politics and end by looking forward with counterfactual analyses to locate alternative U.S. future roles in complex adaptive systems of the Middle East and South Asia. In this chapter we summarize our experience as scouts and conclude with some final thoughts about the criteria of fitness for avoiding foreign policy mistakes.

Cognitive errors in processing information and behavioral errors by leaders in making strategic choices in these cases convey several lessons. Foreign policy mistakes (like other mistakes) are often more complex than one might think. In the first chapter of our book we developed typologies of foreign policy mistakes for the purpose of categorizing and analyzing them. The next four chapters distinguished between mistakes of omission and mistakes of commission and diagnostic and prescriptive mistakes. On the basis of whether the decision makers faced a threat or an opportunity situation, we argued that mistakes lead to deterrence failures and false alarm failures or to reassurance failures and false hope failures. In these analyses we emphasized that mistakes are different from failures. Mistakes are procedural errors whereas failures are the ultimate consequences or outcomes, which may or may not follow from errors of omission or commission. Among other things, final outcomes depend on whether players in a strategic interaction episode make subsequent choices that cancel out their previous mistakes.

We also found that our typologies, like any typologies in the social sciences, are ideal types and that actual cases may not neatly fit one type over another. U.S. mistakes in the case study of Japan's attack on Pearl Harbor are good examples. Depending on the focus of the analysis, one may come to different conclusions. If the analytical focus ranges widely and encompasses an extended period before the attack on December 7, 1941, U.S. leaders seem to have engaged in a prescriptive mistake of commission. However, if the focus is narrower, focusing on only a few months before the attack, then the U.S. mistake seems to have been one of omission on the diagnostic level. Thus, just how much the analyst decides to zoom in temporally and spatially may make a difference when categorizing a particular case. The intricacies of an actual case may also be important. There was rarely evidence that supported an exclusive categorization of one kind of mistake over the other in a particular case. Although there may have been supporting evidence for different categories of mistakes, one kind usually received more voluminous and/or compelling support than another. In each case we attempted to focus on what seemed to be the crucial moments, that is, those moments that steered subsequent events in one direction rather than the other.

Ultimately, we must acknowledge that such judgment calls are to some extent in the eye of the beholder, and in the end every conclusion is still somewhat contestable. We believe that it is important to acknowledge these challenges and the limitations of our typologies. However, we contend that the intricate details of political interactions are what make heuristic simplifications necessary in order to gain a better understanding of the phenomenon under investigation. Theorizing a problem necessarily requires simplification, which allows entry into the problem space of a particular case. A categorical typology of foreign policy mistakes allows analysts to study them more systematically from a comparative perspective and mitigates against committing "the fallacy of misplaced concreteness" identified by Whitehead (1948).[2]

Analyzing mistakes is also problematic even when these mistakes are theorized. At the beginning of our book, we provided a brief survey of factors that may contribute to the different kinds of mistakes in our typologies. Among scholars and analysts, cognitive biases and group dynamics are certainly among the most prominent and widely discussed factors. In our analysis, we found these and many other concepts at work, but we also found that it is rarely a single factor to which the mistake can ultimately be traced. Therefore, we have confined ourselves theoretically to a primary focus on the immediate antecedents of decisions: the distributions of power and preference rankings between players in a strategic interaction episode formalized as a game. Across all of our cases, we noted that there was almost always a faction of hard-liners opposed by moderate voices seeking to influence the president. We captured this pattern theoretically with our distinctions between the use of negative and positive sanctions in the exercise of power and the differences in preference rankings and distributions of power associated with them.

It would be virtually impossible to list or identify all of the other factors that contributed to the individual mistakes we have examined in this book.[3] It is exactly this limitation that motivated us to develop a framework identifying the immediate antecedent conditions for making or avoiding foreign policy mistakes. Nevertheless all of the factors we noted in our case studies, the organizational setting for decisions, the complexity of the strategic problem, and the information processing and computational capacities of the decision makers, helped us understand how and why there were procedural errors of diagnosis or prescription in answering the power politics question *kto-kovo*? They also pointed to the following remedies that we identified in Part IV of our book:

- *Moral/ethical solutions* involving steps to insure that leaders are held accountable for their decisions, especially if they violate laws or societal norms;
- *Generic design solutions* prescribing institutional arrangements that do not emphasize accountability as much as efficiency in processing information and advice within different historical or organizational contexts;
- *Actor-specific solutions* emphasizing the importance of selecting capable and experienced leaders whose expertise raises the likelihood of avoiding mistakes in diagnosis and prescription;
- *Theoretical solutions* specifying procedural strategies that all actors (individuals, groups, and organizations) can follow to minimize policy mistakes by avoiding diagnostic and prescriptive errors or mitigating the consequences of mistakes.

These solutions address different sources of foreign policy mistakes. Moral/ethical solutions and generic design solutions examine the setting for making decisions. The theoretical and actor-specific solutions focus on the complexity of the problem and the human and technical resources employed to diagnose and solve it. We have focused on the complexity of the problem and theoretical solutions based on the assumption that theoretical solutions trump the other solutions by offering a good set of standards against which to judge their efficacy. If the other solutions do not have the effects specified by the theoretical solutions, then they are probably not effective or efficient solutions in their own right. To sum up our effort, we end our book with ten precepts for carrying out an intervention strategy and avoiding foreign policy mistakes in the exercise of power.

TEN PRECEPTS FOR AVOIDING AND FIXING
FOREIGN POLICY MISTAKES

1. *Correct answers to the kto-kovo question are the basis for diagnosing and prescribing political action and for avoiding, minimizing, or correcting foreign policy mistakes.* Game theory in this book is employed simply as

a tool to formalize these answers so as to enable decision makers to reduce the uncertainty in the political universe and manage the risk of undesirable outcomes. Our normative political assumptions are that (1) it is better to settle than to reach deadlock and better to dominate than submit; (2) Pareto-superior outcomes are better than outcomes that favor one player at the expense of the other, so settlement is better than domination. With these assumptions and the information from answers to the *kto-kovo* question of who (controls) whom, we have identified games of strategic interaction with Pareto-superior (non-zero-sum) outcomes and the strategies that can reach these outcomes.

2. *The empirical answer to the kto-kovo question is not always clear, which leads us to recommend conditional cooperation as an optimum strategy implemented with the principles of disjointed incrementalism.* Since it is not always clear what the power distribution is in a strategic situation and how each player ranks the outcomes of settlement, deadlock, domination, and submission, it is better to pursue a conditional strategy that is contingent on the other player's strategy rather than a dominant strategy of "always choose cooperation" or "always choose conflict."

3. *A conditional strategy should be reversible (disjointed) and an incremental (small change) strategy is more easily reversible than a radical (large change) strategy.* This realization leads us to recommend a disjointed incremental strategy of implementation and gradual rather than radical escalation or de-escalation away from the status quo. Take more time and smaller steps and honor the principles of reciprocity and proportionality.[4]

4. *The players in a strategic situation have the power to change preferences and power distributions as well as behaviors.* One player can affect the other's behavior by choosing and signaling different strategies. There are two sets of preferences that are consistent with each of the distributions of power (symmetrical or asymmetrical) between players. Although the power distribution between players may be relatively transparent and fixed, the intersection of their preferences for settlement, deadlock, domination, and submission may not be equally clear and stable. Even though one or both players may not be able to alter the distribution of power, if they can change their own preferences and communicate the shift to other players, they can alter the strategic equilibria in their respective power games.

5. *It is possible to affect behavior, preferences, and even the distribution of power between two players by interacting with third parties in a system of interest.* This principle opens up a range of pivot strategies in which intervention by a third player can affect the behavior, preferences, and power distribution between two other players. The effectiveness of such a *tertius gaudens* strategy depends on the location of the players in a social system in which location has three dimensions: as a spatial position defined as territoriality; as the complexity of social organization along a temporal evolutionary continuum of social systems identified in terms of population density and technology (the development of resource endowments); and defined dynamically as structural holes of relative autonomy in an *n*-body social system.

6. *Location in each of these senses significantly qualifies the answer to the kto-kovo question.* The home team has a definite advantage in the strategic interaction games of world politics as well as in athletics. Military power must be projected to a location in order to be effective on the ground and degrades away from home by becoming more costly and difficult to deploy. The terrain constrains the exercise of military power by a stranger and empowers the local player who knows both the territory and the neighbors. Resolve or the willingness to exercise power is greater when the game is on your territory and the stakes are yours rather than someone else's possessions. These maxims are familiar to students of war and politics and account for the success of weaker parties in zero-sum games of asymmetric warfare (Kilcullen 2009).

7. *An indirect cooperation strategy of winning friends rather than a direct conflict strategy of defeating enemies qualifies the negative impact of location on the power of strangers by pooling and coordinating the power of local neighbors and foreign strangers within a regional system of interest.* A stranger may be able to enact an external pivot role by intervening and supplying what U.S. Secretary of State Dean Acheson (1969) called the "missing ingredient" in determining neighborhood dynamics in a regional or domestic system.

8. *The "missing ingredient" is usually not the exercise of military power or the adoption of a dominant conflict strategy.* Strategies of conditional conflict, hard containment, and preemption are not as effective as condi-

tional cooperation or soft containment strategies, because they do not create non-zero-sum situations that are the real missing ingredients for reaching outcomes of mutual cooperation.

9. *In some situations it is not possible to directly construct a non-zero-sum game that has mutual cooperation as a strategic equilibrium.* Each player must have preference rankings that permit a conditional strategy of either cooperation or conflict to generate mutual cooperation as a stable equilibrium. When facing a player with preference rankings and a local power distribution that neutralizes enactment of the latter strategies, the only alternative is either to withdraw from interaction or to adopt an indirect strategy of winning friends rather than killing enemies and thereby "invade" the population and the strategic environment surrounding a player with a "meanie" strategy (Axelrod 1984, 1997; Skyrms 2004; Kilcullen 2009).

10. *The diplomatic exercise of soft power, constructing non-zero-sum games with Pareto-superior outcomes between strategic dyads surrounding a player with a dominant conflict strategy, may eventually by the power of example cause a shift away from a "meanie" strategy of dominant conflict* (Axelrod 1984, 1997; Skyrms 2004; Nye 1990; Gelb 2009). The passage of time may lead to the creation of non-zero-sum relations within the player's subsystem that create opportunities for non-zero-sum relations with the outside world (Kennan 1947; R. Wright 2000, 65–77). Isolation in the form of denying friends with a strategy of soft containment toward a recalcitrant foe and a conditional cooperation strategy toward its neighbors may also degrade an enemy's power. This outcome is likely to depend ultimately on the internal population density and resource endowment of that player. If these factors are low, zero-sum relations within the player's subsystem may continue to be a dominant strategy until the subsystem itself disintegrates, with entropy as a final outcome (R. Wright 2000).

The fitness criteria of rationality that govern these rules are that a foreign policy must keep the people of the United States secure while not threatening the security of others. An intervention strategy of conditional cooperation in which the United States initiates cooperation but resists exploitation by others meets these criteria. The agent-centered and structure-oriented analyses in this book offer theoretical reasons plus empirical evidence from experimental and natural settings to support the inference that this strategy of intervention is efficient and effective in managing uncertainty and fostering cooperation among agents in the complex adaptive systems of world politics (Walker, Malici, and Schafer 2011). Similar to the destruction of the nest in the ant colony experiment, the 9/11 attacks on the United States have created an incentive for scouts in our human colony to identify and construct a site with an optimum domestic living climate and external security environment in the twenty-first century; these criteria of fitness are analogues to optimum light and safe entrance criteria in the ant colony experiment. We hope that our report to readers will have a "quorum" effect in U.S. academic and policy communities similar to the one generated by a report from scouts in an ant colony. We believe that following these rules will help U.S. presidents in the conduct of American foreign policy to avoid mistakes and navigate a course toward a safe harbor in the uncertain world of the twenty-first century.

Appendix

FIGURE A.1   *Logical Proofs of Outcomes for Different Pivot Strategies*

A. Conditional Cooperation by Pivot vs. Alternative Strategies by Others

	Other			Other			Other			Other	
(G27)	CO	CF	(G51)	CO	CF	(G15)	CO	CF	(G24)	CO	CF
	CO 4,3 →|1,4			CO 4,3* ← 1,2			CO 4,2 1,3			CO 4,2 1,4	
Pivot	↑	↓	Pivot	↓	↑	Pivot			Pivot		
	CF 2,1← "3,2"*			CF 2,1 → "3,4"*			CF 2,1 "3,4"*			CF 2,1 "3,3"*	

Conditional Conflict	Soft Containment	Hard Containment	Preemption
Intentions: Piv, Oth (+,−)	Intentions: Piv, Oth (+,−)	Intentions: Piv, Oth (+,−)	Intentions: Piv, Oth (+,−)
Power: Pivot = Other	Power: Pivot = Other	Power: Pivot = Other	Power: Pivot = Other

B. Conditional Conflict by Pivot vs. Alternative Strategies by Others

	Other			Other			Other			Other	
(G32)	CO	CF	(G49)	CO	CF	(G6)	CO	CF	(G11)	CO	CF
	CO 3,3 1,4			CO 3,3 ← 1,2			CO 3,2 1,3			CO 3,2 1,4	
Pivot			Pivot	↓	↑	Pivot			Pivot		
	CF 4,1 "2,2"*			CF 4,1 → "2,4"*			CF 4,1 "2,4"*			CF 4,1 "2,3"*	

Conditional Conflict	Soft Containment	Hard Containment	Preemption
Intentions: Piv, Oth (−,−)	Intentions: Piv, Oth (−,−)	Intentions: Piv, Oth (−,−)	Intentions: Piv, Oth (−,−)
Power: Pivot = Other	Power: Pivot = Other	Power: Pivot = Other	Power: Pivot = Other

C. Soft Containment by Pivot vs. Alternative Strategies by Others

	Other			Other			Other			Other	
(G49)	CO	CF	(NC)	CO	CF	(NC)	CO	CF	(G13)	CO	CF
	CO 3,3 1,4			CO 3,3* 1,2			CO 3,2 1,3			CO 3,2 1,4	
Pivot			Pivot			Pivot			Pivot		
	CF 2,1 "4,2"*			CF 2,1 "4,4"*			CF 2,1 "4,4"*			CF 2,1 "4,3"*	

Conditional Conflict	Soft Containment	Hard Containment	Preemption
Intentions: Piv, Oth (−,−)	Intentions: Piv, Oth (−,−)	Intentions: Piv, Oth (−,−)	Intentions: Piv, Oth (−,−)
Power: Pivot = Other	Power: Pivot = Other	Power: Pivot = Other	Power: Pivot = Other

D. Hard Containment by Pivot vs. Alternative Strategies by Others

	Other			Other			Other			Other	
(G6)	CO	CF	(NC)	CO	CF	(NC)	CO	CF	(G4)	CO	CF
	CO 2,3 1,4			CO 2,3* 1,2			CO 2,2 1,3			CO 2,2 1,4	
Pivot			Pivot			Pivot			Pivot		
	CF 3,1 "4,2"*			CF 3,1 "4,4"*			CF 3,1 "4,4"*			CF 3,1 "4,3"*	

Conditional Conflict	Soft Containment	Hard Containment	Preemption
Intentions: Piv, Oth (−,−)	Intentions: Piv, Oth (−,−)	Intentions: Piv, Oth (−,−)	Intentions: Piv, Oth (−,−)
Power: Pivot = Other	Power: Pivot = Other	Power: Pivot = Other	Power: Pivot = Other

(*continued*)

FIGURE A.I *(continued)*

E. Preemption by Pivot vs. Alternative Strategies by Others

	Other			Other			Other			Other	
(G11)	CO	CF	(G13)	CO	CF	(G4)	CO	CF	(G9)	CO	CF
CO	2,3	1,4	CO	2,3	1,2	CO	2,2	1,3	CO	2,2	1,4
Pivot			Pivot			Pivot			Pivot		
CF	4,1	"3,2"*	CF	4,1	"3,4"*	CF	4,1	"3,4"*	CF	4,1	"3,3"*

Conditional Conflict	**Soft Containment**	**Hard Containment**	**Preemption**
Intentions: Piv, Oth (–,–)	Intentions: Piv, Oth (–,–)	Intentions: Piv, Oth (–,–)	Intentions: Piv, Oth (–,–)
Power: Pivot = Other	Power: Pivot = Other	Power: Pivot = Other	Power: Pivot = Other

These games are numbered as (G number) according to the numbered taxonomy in Brams (1994, 215–219) and specified by the symmetrical or asymmetrical power relations and intentions expressed as preference rankings by pivot and other as the row and column players in Walker (2007). Nash equilibria are asterisked, and Brams equilibria are in bold. Initial state is in quotation marks. Arrows indicate "move" (→) while blocked arrows (→|) indicate "stay" given the initial state. There is no movement from an initial state of deadlock in those games where the Pivot strategy is (D) Hard Containment or (E) Preemption. Dominant strategies are underlined.

Notes

1. Brams assigns game numbers only to the fifty-seven games where the players do not agree on a most-preferred state and power matters in specifying the outcomes. The remaining games "are no-conflict games with a mutually best (4,4) state . . . no kind of power—moving, order, or threat—is needed by either player to implement them as outcomes" (Brams 1994, 215).

2. For similar game-theoretic frameworks, see Elster (1982); Axelrod (1984); Raub (1990); Becker (1996); Clark (1998); and Maoz and Mor (2002).

3. Brams (1994, 225) defines a Pareto-optimal/superior state as "one that is not Pareto-inferior. A state is Pareto-superior to a (Pareto-inferior) state if it is better for all players, or better for at least one player and not worse for any other players."

4. TOM has been criticized for the "arbitrary assignment of a starting point" (R. Stone 2001, 224), but we do not find this criticism compelling. According to Brams, "the choice of the initial state, and what constitutes future states and eventually an outcome, depends on what the analyst seeks to explain" (Brams 1994, 26). Games have a history, and the task is to be sensitive "to issues of time, place, and the circumstances of the players to model accurately the strategic situation at hand" (Brams 2001, 247). We agree with Brams that it is by such considerations that the initial state in a game can be determined.

5. Brams (1994, 220) defines backward induction as "a reasoning process in which players, working backward from the last possible move in a game, anticipate each other's rational choices." For example, it is the reasoning process governing the game of checkers when one player decides to move one piece rather than another on the board, depending on what the other player's rational move is likely to be in response under the rules of play governing this game. TOM's rules of play for 2×2 sequential games are more complex than the ones for checkers, but the reasoning process of backward induction is the same for both games (Brams 2002, 395; Aumann 1995). We return in Chapter 7 to a discussion of this process and whether or how it is applicable in order to avoid mistakes in complex political situations.

6. Brams (1994, 225) defines prior communication as follows: "Prior communication occurs when a player with threat power, in making a compellent or deterrent threat, communicates its willingness and ability to stay, if necessary, at a Pareto-inferior state." Repeated play of the game makes the threat credible.

CHAPTER 3

1. For a broad survey of U.S.-Japanese relations during the period preceding the Pearl Harbor attacks see Iriye (1967).

2. Good insights into Grew's thinking about restraint and how this view collided with the dominant thinking of the hard-liners can be found in his memoirs (1952). See also Grew (1942, 1944), Heinrichs (1966), and Iriye (1973).

3. Hull's (1948) memoirs provide good and revealing insights into the mistaken thinking of the U.S. government in the run-up to the Pearl Harbor attack.

4. For a good overview of the context in which this meeting occurred, see Freedman and Karsh (1993, 52–54).

CHAPTER 4

1. Mansfield, Letter to the president, December 9, 1964, National Security File, Name File: Mansfield, box 6, LBJ Library.

2. Mansfield, Letter to the president, March 24, 1965, National Security File, Memos to the president from M. Bundy, vol. 9, box 3, LBJ Library. See also Barrett 1988–1989, 649.

CHAPTER 7

1. It is worth noting again that it is possible for mistakes to lead to success as well as to failure. As Baldwin (2000) has pointed out, goals may be achieved in spite of mistakes, in the form of diagnostic or prescriptive errors that raise the cost of achieving a preferred outcome. By extension it is also possible for success or failure to depend on the decisions of others in a strategic interaction situation. The other player's mistakes can lead to one's goals just as another player's resources and actions can thwart one's goals even though one makes no mistakes.

2. Recall that an outcome that is better for all players or at least better for one player without being worse for the other player is called a Pareto-optimal solution or outcome in the parlance of game theory (see Brams 1994, 324–325; Morrow 1994).

3. Even repeated plays of a simultaneous-move game demonstrate that players can adopt strategies that vary in their rates of success and the predictability of avoiding failure (Rapoport and Chammah 1965; Axelrod 1984; Majeski 2004).

4. This normative judgment may have to be modified in particular cases if the intention of the agent is to elicit a conflict response, for example, if the goal in the exercise of power is for the agent to manipulate the patient by acting as an agent provocateur (McClelland 1966; Wilkinson 1969).

5. It is important to remember that this menu does not exhaust all possible strategies or games (Brams 1994; see also Rapoport and Guyer 1966; Rapoport, Guyer, and Gordon 1976). The strategies are consistent primarily with a realist political universe in which power matters more than identities or interests in shaping preference rankings for the outcomes of settlement, deadlock, domination, and submission. It is possible to expand the menu and incorporate constructivist identity and liberal interest variables; however, both the distribution and the exercise of power remain influential in these games, too (Walker 2007).

6. It is more accurate to say "TOM-inspired" rules of play since ego does not actually know alter's actual preferences and calculates decisions to "move" or "stay" based on the possible alternative ranking of preferences stipulated by TIP for different combinations of positive and negative sanctions and symmetric or asymmetric distributions of power between ego and alter. Infinite cycling back to an initial state as a final state is also contrary to the simplest version of TOM's termination rule for determining a final state, which says that players would anticipate and avoid cycling by not moving from an initial state if doing so would lead back to it. Although the process of termination differs from a pure TOM solu-

tion, "the end result is the same—cycling problems result in termination of the game at the starting quadrant" (Marfleet and Walker 2006, 63).

7. The names for these effects are metaphors rather than strict analogies to their counterparts in physics. The calculus is the mathematics developed by Newton and Leibnitz to describe rates of change rather than static relationships between variables. Quantum mechanics in physics is the study of movements by minute physical particles that do not have a determinate (fixed) location because they are constantly in motion. The relativity effect is Einstein's insight that the location of a physical object in time and space depends on the frame of reference used to locate it (Feynman 1995; Hawking 2005; Adler 2002).

8. Frost (1969, 105) wrote, "Two roads diverged in a wood, and I—I took the one less traveled by, and that has made all the difference."

9. Of course other things are not always equal. In addition to qualifications to this generalization based on the other player's strategy and the power distribution between them, there are case-specific characteristics in its application that make this generalization a contingent instead of a universal. We shall explore the limits of generalizability regarding the strategy of conditional cooperation at some length in the next two chapters.

CHAPTER 8

1. The phrase is attributed to von Clausewitz (1984, 140), who wrote, "Finally, the general reliability of all information presents a special problem in war: all action takes place, so to speak, in a kind of twilight, which, like fog or moonlight, often tends to make things seem grotesque and larger than they really are."

2. Tracing the role-making and role-taking processes in U.S. decision making for these two cases and selecting them according to their variation in the independent variable of decision-making strategy (disjointed incrementalism and its opposite) with decision outcome (success or failure) as the dependent variable are "process-tracing" and "structured-focused" extensions of Eckstein's "crucial-case" study design, in which a single case is examined to accept or refute rival normative theories of decision making. The normative theories are the sequential game theory solutions from the simulations in Chapter 7 that take the form of contingent versus dominant decision-making strategies: a contingent strategy specifies gradual, incremental, reversible decision-making principles while a dominant strategy specifies more rapid, radical, and irreversible decision making. The use of the process-tracing method and the selection of an additional case help overcome weaknesses in a single-case design by increasing the number and variation of observations within and across the cases. The earlier examples in this book are "disciplined-configurative" and "heuristic" case studies in which each case is interpreted and evaluated with a single sequential game theory (TOM) as the normative criterion for making the interpretations and finding general solutions to building a theory of foreign policy mistakes (Eckstein 1975; King, Keohane, and Verba 1994; George and Bennett 2005; see also Walker 2004a).

3. Role making occurs when one member of a role dyad initiates interaction by enacting a cue (+ or −) toward the other member. Role-taking occurs when the other member of a role dyad responds by mirroring (+,+ or −,−) the cue from the other member, which corresponds to the congruence proposition in role theory, in which balance, that is, the same valences or signs, is a special case of congruence (Walker 1979, 1987; Sarbin and Allen 1968). Altercasting is a form of role making that occurs when one member of a role dyad responds by not matching (+,− or −,+) the cues and corresponding expectations of the other member,

which may result in one of the following corollaries of the altercasting proposition identified by exchange theory: the aggression proposition when the cue giver (+) subsequently matches the unexpected response (–) by shifting from (+,–) to (–,–); the approval proposition when the cue giver (–) subsequently matches the unexpected response (+) by shifting from (–,+) to (+,+). These propositions from exchange theory are also consistent with the logic of a GRIT strategy. See Walker (1987, 86–89) and Goldstein and Freeman (1990, 14–17).

4. Submission is considered the lowest-ranked outcome by realists either because of the substantive losses associated with it or because of the loss of prestige, that is, an actor's reputation for resolve in the exercise of power (Morganthau 1985; Snyder and Diesing 1977; Mercer 1996). In the case of both a vast power asymmetry between actors or the absence of substantive interests worth a conflict with another actor, an unconditional strategy by the weaker actor of "bandwagoning"—that is, "always choose either cooperation or submission"—may be sufficiently rational to override prestige considerations (Walker 2007; Schweller, 1994). Such cases are very rare in the history of U.S. foreign policy since World War II, when the United States became a superpower and therefore very unlikely to be the weaker power in a strategic dyad.

5. By "operational code" we mean here simply the diagnostic and choice propensities regarding cooperation and conflict attributed to ego and alter that define an actor's role and counterrole within a role dyad. The sources of these propensities may be situational, cultural, or idiosyncratic, respectively, which can be expressed as beliefs by the actor. However, we are not concerned here with these sources and focus only on their surface manifestations as answers to the dual answers to the *kto-kovo* question regarding the distribution and exercise of power between members of a strategic role dyad. See Schafer and Walker (2006) for discussions of the sources of an actor's operational code and the beliefs that constitute its propensities for cooperation and conflict.

6. It is of course possible to analyze the sources of a role with "role" as a dependent variable and examine such factors as societal or idiosyncratic attributes of the occupant of the role as independent variables. See Schafer and Walker (2006), Feng (2007), and Malici (2008) for operational code analysis as an approach to sources. For other related approaches to this question, see Walker (1987, 1992) and Walker, Malici, and Schafer (2011).

7. The difference between a normative and an empirical theory is not so great as some assume. Although the focus is invoked in normative theory on the "ought" rather than the "is" in empirical theory to distinguish them, both theories can take the logical form of universal generalizations. These generalizations function as "covering laws" in both kinds of theories, but these laws are justifications for behavior in normative theories and explanations for behavior in empirical theories. It is also possible for the laws in both theories to exercise causal power over human behavior (Ball 1987; Snyder 2003; Glaser 2010).

8. These two case studies address the same questions but employ different methods. The Vietnam case study employs the process-tracing method by comparing the sequence of moves by the United States and North Vietnam over time on the battlefield and at the conference table with the sequence of moves predicted by TOM. The Iraq case study employs the congruence method of matching the predicted final outcome of a power game, deduced from the answers to the *kto-kovo* question and the general exercise of negative or positive sanctions as a strategy by the United States and Iraq, with the actual outcome of their strategic interactions in two time periods: pre-invasion and post-invasion. See George and Bennett (2005) for a discussion of process-tracing and congruence methods of case study design.

9. These power distributions are based on the observations of outside observers (the authors) and do not necessarily reflect the real-time perceptions and beliefs of the players, which makes the analysis of these games primarily a normative exercise executed against the frame of reference provided by these judgments.

10. Each game in the chronology begins when one or the other player chooses to escalate (E) or de-escalate (D) from the status quo and ends after at least four moves (the initial outcome) when the player with the next move chooses "stay" rather than "move" or if the next move would return the game to the initial outcome. This termination rule is consistent with the rules of play for TOM (Brams 1994, 27–29; see also Walker 2004a, 289–291).

11. Although the bilateral distribution of power between the United States and North Vietnam favored the former, this assessment assumes that neither China nor the Soviet Union would intervene if the United States should decide to invade North Vietnam. Such an expansion of the war would risk a change in the local distribution of power from asymmetrical to symmetrical, merging it in effect with the regional power distribution in Asia and the global power distribution between the two superpowers.

12. There are two accounts of the strategic shift, emphasizing different perspectives on its dynamics. Ricks (2009) reports that the shift to a "surge" strategy began with the appointment of General Raymond Odierno in 2007 as a new commander of U.S. Army III Corps in Iraq. He adopted lessons learned in his previous tour of duty and the opportunity to reflect on new doctrine emerging inside U.S. Army circles to redirect tactics away from killing the enemy and gaining the allegiance of the population. Woodward (2008) reports that the shift began with a battle over strategy in Washington, D.C. that culminated in the decision to adopt a surge strategy. The two accounts converge with an emphasis on the appointment in 2007 of General David Petraeus as the top U.S. commander in Iraq. He reinforced the new local initiatives by Odierno in day-to-day tactical operations and provided legitimacy for the winners of the battle over strategy back in Washington, D.C.

13. Rumsfeld had argued in a memo prior to 9/11 that the United States should use "our existing force structure to dissuade nations abroad from challenging our interests while we transform our armed forces to meet 21st Century conditions" (qtd. in Suskind 2004, 82). Former Treasury Secretary Paul O'Neill attributed the Bush administration's pre-9/11 fixation on Saddam Hussein's regime to this notion of dissuasion: "A weak but increasingly obstreperous Saddam might be useful as a demonstration model of America's new, unilateral resolve. If it could be effectively shown that he possessed, or was trying to build, weapons of mass destruction—creating an 'asymmetric threat,' in the neoconservative parlance, to U.S. power in the region—his overthrow would help 'dissuade' other countries from doing the same" (Suskind 2004, 86).

CHAPTER 9

1. "Wicked problems" are "a class of problems that has no single solution and no 'stopping rule' that indicates when it is solved, and where the very act of trying to solve it changes its nature, so that attempts to solve it are not repeatable and there is no possibility of success through trial and error" (Kilcullen 2009, 153; see also Rittel and Webber 1973).

2. We shall defer to Chapter 10 an extended discussion of what to do when faced with another player who pursues a dominant strategy of "always choose conflict." The concept of collective stability assumes a population of individuals employing a certain strategy and a single individual who then employs a mutant strategy discovered by conscious deliberation,

trial and error, or blind luck. If the mutant strategy gets a higher payoff than the strategy of the typical member of the population, then it can invade the population in interactions with the native strategy. If no other strategy can invade it, then the mutant strategy is said to have achieved evolutionary and collective stability, that is, "survival of the fittest," through the process of natural selection. In computer simulations based on the results of Axelrod's two computer tournaments, the features of a "tit-for-tat" strategy proved to have evolutionary and collective stability against other likely strategies in an iterated prisoner's dilemma simulation (Axelrod 1984, 55–57 and appendix B; 1997, 14–39; see also Poundstone 1992; Mitchell 2009, 214–224, for extensions and qualifications).

3. Axelrod (1984, 8) makes interval or cardinal assumptions about the values for each outcome in the four cells of the prisoner's dilemma game and assigns points of 5, 3, 1, and 0 to the outcomes ranked highest (4) to lowest (1) in Figure 9.1. His results are also consistent generally with the tournament among the strategies represented in the ordinal power games in Chapter 7 of this book (see also Marfleet and Walker, 2006).

4. Axelrod (1984, 50) justifies this assumption with the following argument: "In human terms, a rule which was not scoring well might be less likely to appear in the future for several different reasons. One possibility is that a player will try different strategies over time, and then stick with what seems to work best. Another possibility is that a person using a rule sees that other strategies are successful and therefore switches to one of those strategies. Still another possibility is that a person occupying a key role . . . [in politics or business] . . . would be removed from that role if the strategy being followed was not very successful. Thus, learning, imitation, and selection can all operate in human affairs to produce a process which makes relatively unsuccessful strategies less likely to appear later."

5. "There is no need to assume that the players are rational. They need not be trying to maximize their rewards" (Axelrod 1984, 19). This point implies the applicability of strategic interaction between nonrational organisms such as bacteria or higher-level animals without the cognitive capacities to reason at the level of humans. For extended examples of this phenomenon, see Axelrod (1984, 88–108) and R. Wright (2000, 243–300).

6. Jervis (1997, 6) states, "We are dealing with a system when (a) a set of units or elements is interconnected so that changes in some elements or their relations produce changes in other parts of the system, and (b) the entire system exhibits properties and behaviors that are different from those of the parts." He cites Bertalanffy and Rapoport (1956) and Ashby (1960) among others as the founders of general systems theory. Early applications to world politics are Kaplan (1957) and Rosecrance (1963); see also Waltz (1979).

7. Complex adaptive systems are systems with certain characteristics, which are summarized by Axelrod and Cohen (1999, 7) as follows: "When a system contains agents or populations that seek to adapt, we will use the term complex adaptive system" (italics, capitals, and bold from the original are removed). An agent is an element in a system that can act "more or less purposefully" as a strategy that can vary and copy other strategies in interactions with other agents in a process of selection (changing strategies) that results in adaptation, that is, "improvement according to some measure of success" (Axelrod and Cohen 1999, 4–7).

8. In our case studies of U.S. foreign policy mistakes, we have focused on U.S. relations with Japan, North Korea, Cuba, Vietnam, Iraq, and the Soviet Union. In all of these cases, there were initially two players in the social system with local conflicts between them that stimulated U.S. involvement. The U.S. response tended to be intervention on the side of one player, which had the systemic effect of converting the local conflict into a conflict between the United States and the other player.

9. At each level of organization there is a body that is considered elemental, that is, bracketed as irreducible within the system of interest. The constituent parts of bodies in physical systems are electrons and protons that constitute the atom and are the elemental bodies in subatomic physics. By extension, individuals may be considered the elemental body in social systems with genetic personality traits as constituent parts of the individual as a biological system.

10. The optimum use of game theory is still somewhat contested in political science although accepted widely in both the social and biological sciences. An example of the more skeptical position, that it is good for normative rather than explanatory analyses of foreign policy decisions, is J. Stein (2007); see also the earlier exchanges between rational choice and cognitive schools of International Relations theorists in Geva and Mintz (1997) and Downs (1989). Schelling (1978, 1984), Axelrod (1984, 1997), and Wright (2000) are examples of scholars who exemplify the uses of game theory for the study of complex adaptive systems in the social and biological sciences. Prominent examples of scholars using game theory to explain international relations include Snyder and Diesing (1997), Oye (1986), A. Stein (1990), Bueno de Mesquita and Lalman (1992), Brams (1994), Snyder (1977), Powell (1999), Lake and Powell (1999), and Majeski (2004).

11. The positive and negative outcomes of interactions represent what systems theorists label positive or negative feedback, respectively, which refer to whether the effects of interaction are to arrest and reverse the tendency of all systems toward entropy in accord with the second law of thermodynamics, that is, for a system to lose the patterns of organized complexity that makes it a system and revert to random or no interactions among its elements and eventual extinction or conversion of those bodies into other forms of matter or energy (R. Wright 2000, 244). See also Jervis (1997, 125–176) for applications of positive and negative feedback to systems of world politics.

12. This analysis specifies the answer to the question of *kto-kovo* (who [controls] whom), which is the core question posed in earlier chapters of this book. See also Walker, Malici, and Schafer (2011) for an extended exploration of the theoretical implications of this insight in the study of foreign policy and world politics.

13. R. Wright (2000, 291) identifies the following heritable traits as the mix leading to the capacity for rational thought and social cooperation: "learning, learning by imitation, teaching, some use of tools, along with elementary grasping abilities, a mildly robust means of symbolic communication, and a rich social existence featuring, in particular, hierarchy and reciprocal altruism (a combination that, in turn, brings Darwinian logic that can turn a mildly robust means of communication into a full-fledged language)." He concludes (pp. 296–297) that these traits are found individually in other animals, but humans were the first species to evolve them collectively via the biological principle of natural selection. Together they account for the unique human capacity for advanced cultural evolution in which technological innovation and other forms of culture (information) reinforce the biological traits in a pattern of co-evolution toward mutual cooperation.

14. R. Wright (2000, 257) maintains "that non-zero-sumness tends, via both biological and cultural evolution, to *emerge*. And it has often emerged among entities—villages, cities, states—whose relationship had once been overwhelmingly zero-sum. . . . The underlying reason that non-zero-sum games wind up being played well is the same in biological evolution as cultural evolution. Whether you are a bunch of genes or a bunch of memes, if you're all in the same boat you'll tend to perish unless you are conducive to productive coordination. For genes, the boat tends to be a cell or a multi-celled organism or occasionally . . . a looser

group such as a family; for memes, the boat is often a larger social group—a village, a chiefdom, a state, a religious denomination. . . . Genetic evolution thus tends to create smoothly integrated organisms, and cultural evolution tends to create smoothly integrated groups of organisms."

15. There is a long-standing and intense controversy about whether this directional pattern exists and, if so, whether it is by chance or by necessity (R. Wright 2000, 265–281; E. Wilson 1975, 1978; Gould 1996).

16. R. Wright (2000, 5, 27) admits that "Back in the real world, things are not usually so clear-cut. A merchant and a customer, two members of a legislature, two childhood friends sometimes—but not always—find their interests overlapping. To the extent that their interests do overlap, their relationship is non-zero-sum. . . . For now the point is that human nature itself, unadorned by technology, carries mutual benefit and thus social structure, beyond the confines of family. . . . We instinctively play both non-zero-sum and zero-sum games. The interplay of these two dynamics throughout history takes some time to tell."

17. This kind of conflict game is the closest one can get to a strict zero-sum game with ordinal rather than cardinal preferences. Ordinal preferences cannot be summed to zero; however, they can be compared to see whether they are Pareto-superior (both players gain) or Pareto-inferior (at least one player loses) compared with other solutions.

18. "Civilization" is used here simply in the sense employed by anthropologists to indicate a level of social complexity characterized by farming and writing as cultural features (see R. Wright 2000, 107–123). Using these technological developments as cultural markers of civilization does imply that the higher the level of technology, the more "civilized" is the social system—that is, a society with more information (higher complexity and reduced entropy as a system) has a greater capacity to exercise control over its environment. According to Wright (2000, 337–347), this increased capacity brings with it the quality of "non-zero-sumness," which is the basis for the emergence of sustained cooperation in more complex social systems.

19. See Wright (2000, 20–22) for an extended discussion of the Shoshone example of a hunter-gatherer people who lived apart in a scarce environment except for occasional cooperation in hunting rabbits together when the rabbit population became abundant. In a pattern somewhat reminiscent of Rousseau's story about a stag hunt in the state of nature, the Shoshone cooperated occasionally in larger numbers under the leadership of an ad hoc "rabbit boss" to surround rabbits instead of deer and share the spoils of their joint kills. The "rabbit boss" is likely the source of a technological innovation in the form of a large woven net held by the beaters who surrounded the bushes in which the rabbits resided. The net promoted cooperation by removing the temptation of individuals to calculate that a "bird in the hand is worth two in the bush," which plagued the attempt to cooperate in Rousseau's stag hunt example (see Waltz 1959, 167–168). For a discussion of Rousseau's stag hunt with game theory applications to world politics, see Jervis (1978); a more general social analysis with game theory is Skyrms (2004). Wright (2002, 29–242) also revisits the anthropological and historical records of the last several millennia to analyze cooperation in human societies with more advanced positions on the complexity continuum for social systems. He ends his historical survey with a discussion of large-scale systems in world politics and the impact of globalization on the complexity of such systems in the twenty-first century.

20. Polk (1997, 30–31) comments regarding territoriality that when human groups were small (approximately twenty-five to fifty members) and based on kinship, they were the basis for all action and sentiment and the source of food and defense. Moreover, it remains

so today, "though softened by cultural and technological improvements," especially in parts of Asia and Africa. "Where resources were scarce and the margin between life and death was thin, each group would naturally have been driven by its absolute need to defend the means it had to feed itself. The 'fit' in Darwin's sense were those who defended it effectively. What they fed themselves on was, of course, a territory, so 'territoriality,' identification with a discrete piece of the earth, is deeply implanted in the human experience. This, along with kinship, can be observed at every level of experience, from the workings of our bodies through studies of animals and primitive societies up to and including our own attitudes and actions toward the world in which we live. Territoriality is the ancestor of nationalism, which is still today the most powerful political sentiment."

21. It is possible to think of the operational codes of social systems as the sequences of D and E strategies in Figure 9.3 and as analogous to the sequences of DNA strategies in the genetic codes of biological systems (Hoagland and Walker 1979; Walker 1982; Walker, Schafer, and Young 2003). The former are constituted as memes by the beliefs of leaders, and the latter are constituted by the genes in the chromosomes of cells. Both contain information about the exercise of power in their respective environments and are subject to various sources of change—learning in leaders and mutation in cells—from interaction with their respective environments. A cultural argument that suggests that operational codes reflect such cultural norms is found in Leites (1953); see also Lebow (2008).

22. Polk (1997, 30) characterizes these practices as "more articulate, more sophisticated manifestations of what appears to have been a common substratum" with earlier, less complex forms of social systems. He comments, "So consider what that basis was. Given their level of technology, kindred groups of early peoples were defined by fairly precise margins: they had to be large enough to accomplish the minimum chores of a seminomadic scavenging, hunting, and gathering economy and to defend themselves but small enough to keep in contact with one another and to keep themselves in proportion to the accessible supply of food."

CHAPTER 10

1. We refer to both game theory and complexity theory to emphasize that the former is a theory of agency while the latter is a theory of systems. They both focus on human interactions but from different analytical vantage points defined by the distinction between parts and wholes, respectively, which is a relative rather than an absolute distinction. A "whole" system of elements standing in interaction with one another may also be a "part" (element) of a larger system. It is an analytical decision to treat the same object as one or the other. Complexity is an emergent property of a system, whereas actions are properties of agents in a system that may generate complexity in space and time as an emergent property of their spatial positions and their collective interactions over time (Mitchell 2009).

2. Together these tools operate metaphorically in a way similar to the electronic GPS satellites linked to today's automobiles and cell phones. They also constitute a global positioning system, which assists users in reaching their desired political destinations in world politics. However, electronic global positioning systems are truly global in scope, with satellites in space connecting to people on the ground and informing them of their position.

3. The details of each conflict that support the relationships in Figure 10.1 are briefly that between 1948 and 1956 Egypt and the Arab states objected to the formation by the United Nations of two states, Israel and Palestine, from the former League of Nations mandate of

Palestine. Britain and France supported Israel in this conflict, because of separate conflicts with Egypt, respectively, over the latter's nationalization of the Suez Canal and the support of nationalists in French colonies in North Africa. The United States' conflict with Egypt was over the latter's decision to accept funding from the Soviet Union instead of the United States for the Aswan Dam, which brought the cold war conflict to the Middle East. However, when the Anglo-French-Israeli coalition invaded Egypt to liberate the Suez Canal in 1956, the United States implemented economic sanctions against Britain, and the Soviet Union threatened to use military force against the Europeans unless the coalition's forces withdrew from Egypt (Thomas 1967). Later strains in the NATO alliance over European security issues are covered by Kissinger (1965) and Neustadt (1970).

4. Location refers to three sets of phenomena that collectively specify location dynamically in terms of both space and time: location as a *spatial* position defined earlier in this book by Polk (1997) as territoriality; location as complexity of organization along a *temporal* evolutionary continuum of social systems identified in the last chapter by Wright (2000); location conceptualized *dynamically* as structural holes or pivot roles identified later in this chapter by social network theory as a *tertius gaudens* role in a three-body social system (Burt 1992, 30–31; Jervis 1997, 177–204). The Latin phrase *tertius gaudens* translates roughly as the "third (who) benefits" and refers to the advantages of occupying a third party role in a situation characterized by conflict between two other parties (Burt 1992; Merton 1957; Simmel 1955). Schweller (1998) offers an analysis of triadic world politics among the great powers limited to the 1930s; treatments of system dynamics and strategies in other historical periods can be found in Jervis and Snyder (1991); the problem of complexity in international systems is explored in Snyder and Jervis (1993). Jervis (1997) also provides a general analysis of system effects in world politics, including an assessment of disadvantages as well as advantages of occupying a pivotal role in relationships with other agents in world politics.

5. Axelrod (1984, 1997) and others have employed agent-based computer simulations to conduct such thought experiments, which have the advantages of analyzing larger and more complex social systems than dyads and triads. We show here the dynamics of smaller and less complex social systems with the architecture of social network and signed graph theory instead of resorting to machine simulations. Our results are consistent with machine simulations of strategic dyads in the systems of interest reported earlier in Chapter 7 (see also Marfleet and Walker 2006).

6. This simple pattern was not always the case. The early history of the United States was marked by a more complex pattern of borders with territorial extensions of European powers. However, the Louisiana Purchase and other territorial acquisitions reduced this complexity by the end of the nineteenth century (Elman 2004, 2005)

7. Even though the asymmetrical power distribution favors the United States in these cases, leading to some U.S. exploitation of the others, the normal pattern of recent relations is a pattern of cooperation governed by treaties and institutional rules (Stevenson 2006).

8. Jervis also emphasizes that one of the keys to Bismarck's success in a pivotal role was his satisfaction with the status quo, which meant that Germany did not pose a threat to others, compared with revisionist states who are likely to make enemies of several states rather than conserving the number of enemies (Jervis 1997, 184; see also Hartmann 1982). States who share fewer common borders with others are more likely to have structural autonomy and a pivotal position to maneuver with fewer constraints. Technology provides the information to project power beyond neighbors to enact a pivotal role in conflicts with strangers. A pragmatic ideology may raise a state's acceptability as either a mediator or ally

in conflict situations between two or more other states, especially in a system characterized by ideological disputes. All of these characteristics reduce constraints and increase the ability to be flexible. Other scholars of world politics who emphasize the effects of location (defined primarily as spatial position) on international security or international political economy include Richardson (1960); Hartmann (1982); Siverson and Starr (1991); Vasquez (1993); Senese and Vasquez (2008); Modelski (1987); and Thompson (1983).

9. For example, Germany's alignments with Austria and Russia insured both states against the possibility that Germany would not be an ally of one against the other in their conflict. This step also reduced the incentive of either country to seek an alliance with France against its enemy. Bismarck combined this defensive tertiary role with diplomacy as an "honest broker" in mediating conflicts between other states outside Europe. His assurances that he did not seek a colonial empire reduced the likelihood that England's competition with France in Africa and Russia in the Middle East would be resolved in favor of mutual cooperation in the face of competition from Germany outside Europe (Jervis 1997; Hartmann, 1982). There are some parallels between Germany's shift to a rigid two-bloc system after 1890 and the Bush administration's rigid strategic declaration after 9/11 to other states in the global system that they were either "with us or against us" (see Woodward 2002, 30–31, 47, 90).

10. Rittel and Webber (1973) distinguish between "wicked" and "tame" problems, while Newell and Simon (1972) distinguish between "ill-structured" and "well-structured" problems (see also Sylvan and Voss 1998). Tame and well-structured problems are like two-body problems in that they have well-defined problems and solutions. Ill-structured and wicked problems resemble three-body and n-body problems in that they lack deterministic solutions. Riddel and Webber (1973) suggest that wicked problems differ from tame problems in that the former lack boundaries. The latter mostly arise in the social sciences (rather than in traditional science and engineering), where "the aim is not to find the truth, but to improve some characteristics of the world where people live" (qtd. in Fitzpatrick 2003). They share the characteristics of "ill-structured" problems, which have no clear definition and no internal stopping rules; the problem and solution co-evolve so that it is not possible to exhaustively enumerate the set of solutions; there is no test of a solution that is conclusive across time and space because a wicked problem and its solution are unique; the process of solution is nonlinear (see Fitzpatrick 2003, 4). Some analysts distinguish as well between "wicked" and "super wicked" problems, in which the latter has the characteristics of the former plus the following features: time is running out; there is no central authority; those solving the problem are also causing the problem. Global climate change is an example of a "super wicked" problem (Lazarus 2009).

11. Such clusters of countries form regional security complexes, defined by Buzan and Waever (2003, 291) as "a set of units whose major processes of securitization, desecuritization, or both are so interlinked that their security problems cannot be reasonably analyzed or resolved apart from one another." The boundaries of a security complex do not have to coincide exactly with the requirement of common borders, but shared borders are a common feature of security complexes (Walker 2007).

12. A final nuclear threat may be Syria, whose attempt to build a nuclear reactor with North Korea's assistance was destroyed by Israel (Sanger 2009, 276–279). If Iran develops them, there is also an incentive for other countries, including Egypt, Saudi Arabia, and the Persian Gulf states, to acquire nuclear weapons in the region (Sanger 2009; Parsi 2007).

13. According to Parsi (2007, 270), Israel has a second-strike nuclear capability in the form of 200 nuclear warheads and three nuclear-equipped Dolphin submarines and has

launched preemptive strikes with conventional weapons against Iraq in 1980 and Syria in 2007 (Parsi 2007; Sanger 2009).

14. The postulated pressure is based on the premise from signed graph theory and the corresponding Arab political proverb, "My friend's friend is my friend."

15. These conclusions are demonstrated in the Appendix.

16. See the discussion in Chapter 2 about GRIT as an implementation strategy and, in Chapter 7, about the features of implementing a disjointed incremental strategy in either the direction of cooperation or conflict.

17. Local comparisons of social organization and terrain between Iraq and Afghanistan and the intrusion of al Qaeda from the neighboring states of Syria and Pakistan, respectively, are in Stewart (2004, 2006) and Kilcullen (2009). The terrain is less accessible and the presence of al Qaeda is more long-term in the Afghanistan case, and the degree of intrusion is greater into the domestic affairs of Afghanistan by the intelligence and military services of their respective neighbors of Iran and Pakistan (see R. Wright 2008; Coll 2004; Rashid 2000, 2009).

18. While the local tribes in each country consider both al Qaeda Arabs and Westerners as strangers, the smaller social distance between them and a common enemy in the central governments of Afghanistan and Pakistan, respectively, make it easier for the local guerillas to ally with al Qaeda (Kilcullen 2009, 35–38). Theoretically, the relations between local tribes and their respective states are also marked more by zero-sum than non-zero-sum relations, because the lower population density and resources in their remote areas have retarded the development of non-zero-sum relationships that would integrate them into their respective nations (see R. Wright 2000 and the earlier theoretical analysis in Chapter 9 of this book).

19. Pashtuns are also a significant group within the central government in Kabul and have allied with the northern war lords. Historically, Pashtuns dominated Afghanistan's central government before the civil war that began in 1978, which continues to the present. One of the side effects of the war was the emergence of the Taliban faction of rural religious extremists within the Pashtun ethnic group in Afghanistan, who were dissatisfied with the corruption of Pashtun leaders and the violence of northern war lords who ruled from Kabul (Rashid 2000). According to Rashid (2009, xviii), Pashtuns are 42 percent of the population in Afghanistan. Pashtuns are only 15 percent of the population in Pakistan, which also has a Punjabi (44 percent), (Sindhi (14 percent), Baloch (4 percent) and other (2 percent) distribution of minorities in its ethnic profile.

20. The Pashtun area of Afghanistan is in the southern and eastern regions of Afghanistan and abuts the Pashtun area of southern and western Pakistan. The Pashtun areas in Pakistan are administered by the Pakistan central government as "Federally Administered Tribal Areas" and do not have the status of provinces within Pakistan's federal system of government. There are also significant numbers of Pashtuns in western and northern Afghanistan, but they are a minority in those areas. Tajik (27 percent), Hazara (9 percent), Uzbek (8 percent), and smaller concentrations of other minorities (14 percent) dominate parts of the area north of the Hindu Kush mountain range, which divides much of the country geographically along a northeast to southwest axis (Rashid 2009, xviii).

21. The Duran line, drawn by British colonial administrators to demarcate the border between Afghanistan and Pakistan, separates the Pashtun areas of Afghanistan and Pakistan; however, it is not recognized by the Pakistan government nor is it honored by local Pashtuns as the final border between Afghanistan and Pakistan (Rashid 2009).

CHAPTER 11

1. The ideal site attributes are size of entrance and strength of light. This ant species (*Temnothoraz curvispinosus*) prefers a small entrance and weak light. The original new sites A and B varied in Experiment 1 by one (A) having a larger entrance and weaker light and by the other (B) having a smaller entrance and stronger light. The two decoys varied in Experiment 2 by D_A having the same strength of light and a larger entrance than A and in Experiment 3 by D_B having the same entrance size and a stronger light than B (Edwards and Pratt 2009).

2. The fallacy is to mistake one interpretation of a case as correct and the only possible one. "A concrete representation of a case is just one of an infinite number of possible representations, which only an abstract formulation of the interpretation susceptible to counterfactual reasoning can reveal" (Post and Walker 2003, 403). They cite Hedstrom and Swedberg (1998, 15) as the source of the phrase "fallacy of misplaced concreteness" who in turn cite Whitehead (1948, 52).

3. An inventory and very useful discussion of the various kinds of sources of diagnostic and prescriptive mistakes is the recent study of U.S. intelligence failures in Iran and Iraq by Jervis (2010).

4. These steps and principles are consistent with Axelrod's (1984, 1997) rules for playing the quintessential non-zero-sum game of prisoner's dilemma: enlarge the shadow of the future, be "provocable" in responding to conflict with conflict, and be forgiving rather than punitive—that is, beyond an immediate response to conflict, be willing to initiate cooperation.

Bibliography

Acheson, D. 1969. *Present at the creation*. New York: W.W. Norton.

Adams, F. 1971. The road to Pearl Harbor. *Journal of American History* 58: 73–92.

Adams, S. 1961. *Firsthand report*. New York: Harper

Adler, R. 2002. *Science firsts*. New York: John Wiley and Sons.

Allison, G. 1971. *Essence of decision*. Boston: Little, Brown.

Allison, G. and P. Zelikow. 1999. *Essence of decision*. 2nd ed. New York: Longman.

Alterman, E. 2004. *When presidents lie*. New York: Penguin Books.

Ambrose, S. 1988. *Rise to globalism*. New York: Penguin Books.

American Heritage Dictionary. 1994. 3rd ed. New York: Dell.

Anderson, D. 2005. *The Vietnam War*. New York: Palgrave Macmillan.

Appleton, S. 1968. *United States foreign policy*. Boston: Little, Brown.

Ashby, R. 1960. *Design for a brain*. New York: John Wiley.

Aumann, R. 1995. Backward induction and common knowledge of rationality. *Games and Economic Behavior* 8: 6–19.

Axelrod, R. 1976. *Structure of decision*. Princeton, NJ: Princeton University Press.

Axelrod, R. 1984. *The evolution of cooperation*. New York: Basic Books.

Axelrod, R. 1997. *The complexity of cooperation*. Princeton, NJ: Princeton University Press.

Axelrod, R. and M. Cohen. 1999. *Harnessing complexity*. New York: Free Press.

Bachrach, P. and M. Baratz. 1962. The two faces of power. *American Political Science Review* 56: 947–952.

Baldwin, D. 1971. The power of positive sanctions. *World Politics* 24: 19–38.

Baldwin, D. 1978. Power and social exchange. *American Political Science Review* 72: 1229–1242.

Baldwin, D. 1979. Power analysis and world politics. *World Politics* 31: 471–506.

Baldwin, D. 1980. Interdependence and power. *International Organization* 34: 471–506.

Baldwin, D. 2000. Success and failure in foreign policy. *Annual Review of Political Science* 3: 167–182.

Ball, T. 1987. Is there progress in political science? In *Idioms of inquiry*, ed. T. Ball. Albany, NY: SUNY Press.

Barck, O. and N. Blake. 1965. *Since 1900*. Rev. ed. New York: Macmillan.

Baring, A. 1972. *Uprising in East Germany*. Ithaca, NY: Cornell University Press.

Barrett, D. 1988–1989. The mythology surrounding Lyndon Johnson, his advisers, and the 1965 decision to escalate the Vietnam War. *Political Science Quarterly* 103: 637–663.

Beach, L.R. and T. Mitchell. 1978. A contingency model for the selection of decision strategies. *Academy of Management Review* 3: 439–449.

Becevitch, A. 2008. *The limits of power*. New York: Metropolitan Books.

Becker, G. 1996. *Accounting for tastes*. Cambridge, MA: Harvard University Press.

Bell, D., H. Raiffa, and A. Tversky, eds. 1988. *Decision making*. New York: Cambridge University Press.

Ben-Zvi, A. 1976. Hindsight and foresight. *World Politics* 28: 381–395.

Bender, L. 1975. *The politics of hostility*. Hato Rey, Puerto Rico: Inter American University Press.

Bennett, A. 1999. *Condemned to repetition?* Cambridge, MA: MIT Press.

Beria, S. 2001. *Beria, my father*. London: Gerald Duckworth.

Berlin, I. 1996. Political judgment. In *The sense of reality*, ed. H. Hardy. New York: Farrar, Straus & Giroux.

Berman, L. 1982. *Planning a tragedy*. New York: Norton.

Bertalanffy, L. von and A. Rapoport. 1956. *Yearbook of the Society for the Advancement of General Systems Theory*, vol. 1. Ann Arbor: University of Michigan Mental Health Research Institute.

Beschloss, M. 1991. *The crisis years*. New York: HarperCollins Publishers.

Best, G. 1990. Franklin Delano Roosevelt, the New Deal, and Japan. In *Pearl Harbor re-examined*, ed. H. Conroy and H. Wray. Honolulu: University of Hawaii Press.

Betts, R. 1978. Analysis, war, and decision. *World Politics* 31: 61–89.

Blau, P. 1964. *Power and exchange in social life*. New York: John Wiley & Sons.

Blight, J. and P. Kornbluth, eds. 1998. *Politics of illusion*. Boulder, CO: Lynne Rienner.

Blight, J. and D. Welch. 1989. *On the brink*. New York: Hill and Wang.

Boettcher, W. 2005. *Presidential risk behavior in foreign policy*. New York: Palgrave Macmillan.

Borch, F. 2003. Comparing Pearl Harbor and "9/11": Intelligence failure. *Journal of Military History* 67: 845–860.

Brams, S. 1994. *Theory of moves*. Cambridge: Cambridge University Press.

Brams, S. 2001. Response to Stone. *Journal of Conflict Resolution* 45: 245–254.

Brams, S. 2002. Game theory in practice. In *Millennial reflections on international studies*, ed. M. Brecher and F. Harvey. Ann Arbor: University of Michigan Press.

Braybrooke, D. and C. Lindblom. 1963. *A strategy of decision*. New York: Free Press.

Brecher, M., B. Steinberg, and J. Stein. 1969. A framework for research on foreign policy behavior. *Journal of Conflict Resolution* 13: 75–101.

Brecher, M., J. Wilkenfeld, and S. Moser. 1988. *Crises in the twentieth century*. New York: Pergamon.

Brogan, D. 1952. The illusion of American omnipotence. *Harper's Magazine* 205: 21–28.

Brzezinski, Z. 1983. *Power and principle*. New York: Farrar, Straus & Giroux.

Buckley, F. and F. Harary. 1990. *Distance in graphs*. Reading, MA: Addison-Wesley.

Bueno de Mesquita, B. 1981. *The war trap*. New Haven, CT: Yale University Press.

Bueno de Mesquita, B. and D. Lalman. 1992. *War and reason*. New Haven, CT: Yale University Press.

Bueno de Mesquita, B., A. Smith, R. Siverson, and J. Morrow. 2003. *The logic of political survival*. Cambridge, MA: MIT Press.

Burks, D. 1964. *Cuba under Castro*. New York: Foreign Policy Association.

Burns, J. 1976. Showdown in the Pacific. In *Pearl Harbor*, 3rd ed., ed. G. Waller. Lexington, MA: D.C. Heath and Company.

Burt, R. 1982. *Toward a structural theory of action*. New York: Academic Press.

Burt, R. 1992. *Structural holes*. Cambridge, MA: Harvard University Press.

Burt, R. and M. Minor. 1983. *Applied network analysis*. Beverly Hills, CA: Sage.

Bush, G. 1990. *Toward a new world order*. Washington, DC: U.S. Department of State, Bureau of Public Affairs, Office of Public Communication.

Butow, R. 1972. Backdoor diplomacy in the Pacific. *Journal of American History* 59: 48–72.

Buzan, B. and O. Waever. 2003. *Regions and powers*. Cambridge: Cambridge University Press.

Caldwell, L. and A. Dallin. 1979. U.S. policy toward the Soviet Union. In *Eagle entangled: U.S. foreign policy in a complex world*, ed. K. Oye, D. Rothchild, and R. Lieber. New York: Longman.

Carter, J. 1975. *Why not the best?* Nashville: Broadman.

Carter, J. 1982. *Keeping faith*. New York: Bantam.

Cheney, R. 2002. Speech to Veterans of Foreign Wars, Nashville. *The Guardian*, August 27. Available at: http://www.guardian.co.uk/world/2002/aug/27/usa.iraq.

Chihiro, H. 1990. Miscalculations in deterrent policy: U.S-Japanese relations, 1938–1941. In *Pearl Harbor reexamined*, ed. H. Conroy and H. Wray. Honolulu: University of Hawaii Press.

Christensen, T. 1992. Threats, assurances, and the last chance for peace. *International Security* 17: 122–154

Churchill, W. 1930. *My early life*. New York: Scribner.

Clark, W. 1998. Agents and structures. *International Studies Quarterly* 42: 245–270.

Clarke, R. 2004. *Against all enemies*. New York: Free Press.

Claude, I. 1962. *Power and international relations*. New York: Random House.

Clausewitz, C. von. 1984. *On war*. Ed and trans. M. Howard and P. Paret. Princeton, NJ: Princeton University Press.

Clifford, C. 1965. Letter to the president, May 17. National Security File, deployment of major troops, Box 41, LBJ Library.

Coffin, T. 1966. *Senator Fulbright*. New York: E.P. Dutton.

Coll, S. 2004. *Ghost wars*. New York: Penguin Press.

Colvin, I. 1971. *The Chamberlain cabinet*. London: Gollancz.

Conroy, H. and H. Wray, eds. 1990. *Pearl Harbor reexamined*. Honolulu: University of Hawaii Press.

Coulombe, M. 2009. Ants more rational than humans, study says. Arizona State University, *ASU News*. Available at: http://asunews.asu.edu/20090724_rationalants.

Crozier, B. 1990. *The Gorbachev phenomenon*. Lexington, GA: Claridge Press.

Cuddy, E. 2003. Vietnam: Mr. Johnson's war—or Mr. Eisenhower's? *Review of Politics* 65: 351–374.

Cyert, R. and J. March.1963. *A behavioral theory of the firm*. Englewood Cliffs, NJ: Prentice-Hall.

Dahl, R. 1957. The concept of power. *Behavioral Science* 2: 201–215.

Dahl, R. and C. Lindblom. 1953. *Politics, economics, and welfare*. New York: Harper and Row.

Dallek, R. 1998. *Flawed giant*. Oxford: Oxford University Press.

Dallin, D. 1961. *Soviet foreign policy after Stalin*. Philadelphia: J.B. Lippincott.

Davis, F. and E. Lindley. 1942. *How war came*. New York: Simon and Schuster.

Davison, P. 1958. *The Berlin blockade*. Princeton, NJ: Princeton University Press.

Dawes, R. 1976. Shallow psychology. In *Cognition and social behavior*, ed. J. Carroll and J. Payne. Hillsdale, NJ: Erlbaum.

DeRivera, J. 1968. *The psychological dimension of foreign policy*. Columbus, OH: Charles E. Merrill.

Deutch, K. 1966. *The nerves of government*. London: Free Press

Diamond, J. 1992. *The third chimpanzee*. New York: HarperCollins.

Diamond, J. 1999. *Guns, germs, and steel*. New York: W.W. Norton.

Diamond, J. 2005. *Collapse*. New York: Penguin Press.

Divine, R. 1981. *Eisenhower and the cold war*. New York: Oxford University Press.

Dobrynin, A. 1995. *In confidence*. New York: Times Books.

Doty, R. 1996. *Imperial encounters*. Minneapolis: University of Minnesota Press.

Downs, G. 1989. The rational deterrence debate. *World Politics* 41: 143–238.

Dulles, J. 1950. *War or peace*. New York: Macmillan.

Dumbrell, J. 1997. *American foreign policy*. London: Macmillan.

Easton, D. 1953. *The political system*. New York: Alfred Knopf.

Ebon, M. 1953. *Malenkov*. New York: McGraw-Hill.

Eckstein, H. 1975. Case study and theory in political science. In *Handbook of Political Science*, vol. 7, ed. F. Greenstein and N. Polsby. Reading, MA: Addison-Wesley.

Edwards, S. and S. Pratt. 2009. Rationality in collective decision making by ant colonies. *Biological Sciences* 276: 3655–3661.

Eisenhower, D. 1965. *Waging peace*. Garden City, NY: Doubleday.

Elman, C. 2004. Extending offensive realism. *American Political Science Review* 98: 563–576.

Elman, C. 2005. Explanatory typologies in qualitative studies of international politics. *International Organization* 59: 293–326.

Elster, J. 1982. Sour grapes. In *Utilitarianism and beyond*, ed. A. Sen and B. Williams. Cambridge: Cambridge University Press.

Emerson, R. 1962. Power-dependence relations. *American Sociological Review* 27: 31–41.

Emerson, R. 1972a. Exchange theory, part I. In *Sociological Theories in Progress*, vol. 1, ed. J. Berger, M. Zelditch, and B. Anderson. Boston: Houghton-Mifflin.

Emerson, R. 1972b. Exchange theory, part II. In *Sociological Theories in Progress*, vol. 1, ed. J. Berger, M. Zelditch, and B. Anderson. Boston: Houghton-Mifflin.

Emerson, R. 1976. Social exchange theory. *Annual Review of Sociology* 2: 335–362.

Emmerson, J. 1990. Principles versus realties. In *Pearl Harbor reexamined*, ed. H. Conroy and H. Wray. Honolulu: University of Hawaii Press.

Etheredge, L. 1978. *A world of men*. Cambridge, MA: MIT Press.

Etheredge, L. 1985. *Can governments learn?* New York: Pergamon Press.

Etzioni, A. 1962. *The hard way to peace*. New York: Collier Books.

Ewald, W. 1981. *Eisenhower the president*. Englewood Cliffs, NJ: Prentice-Hall.

Fallows, J. 2004. Blind into Baghdad. *Atlantic Monthly* (January/February): 52–74.

Feis, H. 1950. *The road to Pearl Harbor*. Princeton, NJ: Princeton University Press.

Feng, H. 2007. *Chinese strategic culture and foreign policy decision-making*. London: Routledge.

Feynman, R. 1995. *Six easy pieces*. Reading, MA: Addison-Wesley.

Fisher, R., W. Ury, and B. Patton. 1991. *Getting to yes*. Boston: Nathan and Tyler

Fiske, S. and S. Taylor. 1991. *Social cognition*. New York: McGraw-Hill.

Fitzpatrick, G. 2003. *The locales framework*. Boston: Kluwer Academic Publishers.

Freedman, L. and E. Karsh. 1993. *The Gulf conflict, 1990–1991*. Princeton, NJ: Princeton University Press.

French, J. and B. Raven. 1959. Bases of social power. In *Studies in Social Power*, ed. D. Cartwright. Ann Arbor: University of Michigan Press.

Frost, R. 1969. The road not taken. In *The poetry of Robert Frost*, ed. C. Lathem. New York: Holt, Rinehart, and Winston.

Fulbright, J.W. 1966. *The arrogance of power*. New York: Random House.

Fursenko, A. and T. Naftali. 1997. *One hell of a gamble*. New York: W.W. Norton.

Gaddis, J. 2005. *The cold war*. New York: Penguin.

Gallhofer, I. and W. Saris. 1979. Strategy choices of foreign policy makers. *Journal of Conflict Resolution* 23: 425–455.

Garrison, J. 1996. *The games advisors play*. Doctoral dissertation, Department of Political Science, University of South Carolina.

Garrison, J. 2001. Framing foreign policy alternatives in the inner circle. *Political Psychology* 22: 775–807.

Garthoff, R. 1991. *Assessing the adversary*. Washington, DC: Brookings Institution.

Garthoff, R. 1994a. *Détente and confrontation*. Washington, DC: Brookings Institution.

Garthoff, R. 1994b. *The great transition*. Washington, DC: Brookings Institution.

Gates, R. 1996. *From the shadows*. New York: Simon and Schuster.

Gelb, L. 2009. *Power rules*. New York: Harper.

Gellman, B. and D. Linser. 2006. A "concerted effort" to discredit Bush critic. *Washington Post*, April 9, A1.

George, A. 1969. The operational code. *International Studies Quarterly* 13: 190–222.

George, A. 1972. The case for multiple advocacy in making foreign policy. *American Political Science Review* 663: 751–785.

George, A. 1980. *Presidential decisionmaking in foreign policy*. Boulder, CO: Westview Press.

George, A. 1993. *Bridging the gap*. Washington, DC: United States Institute for Peace.

George, A. and A. Bennett. 2005. *Case studies and theory development*. Cambridge, MA: MIT Press.

George, A. and J. George. 1964. *Woodrow Wilson and Colonel House*. New York: Dover Publications.

George, A. and J. George. 1998. *Presidential personality and performance*. Boulder, CO: Westview Press.

George, A. and W. Simmons. 1994. *The limits of coercive diplomacy*. Boulder, CO: Westview Press.

Geva, N. and A. Mintz. 1997. *Decisionmaking on war and peace*. Boulder, CO: Lynne Rienner.

Giglio, J. 2006. *The presidency of John F. Kennedy*. Lawrence: University Press of Kansas.

Gladwell, M. 2005. *Blink*. New York: Little, Brown.

Glaser, C. 2010. *Rational theory of international politics*. Princeton, NJ: Princeton University Press.

Goldstein, J. and J. Freeman. 1990. *Three-way street*. Chicago: University of Chicago Press.

Gorbachev, M. 1987. *Perestroika*. New York: Harper and Row.

Gorbachev, M. 1995. *Memoirs*. New York: Doubleday

Gordon, M. and B. Trainor. 2006. *Cobra II*. New York: Pantheon Books.

Gordon, P. and M. O'Hanlon. 2001. A tougher target. *Washington Post*, December 26, A31.

Goshko, J. 1985. Reagan lashes communism. *Washington Post*, June 15, A17.

Gould, J. 1996. *Full house*. New York: Harmony Books.

Graebner, N. 1973. Hoover, Roosevelt, and the Japanese. In *Pearl Harbor as history*, ed. D. Borg and S. Okamoto. New York: Columbia University Press.

Grew, J. 1942. *Report from Tokyo.* New York: Simon and Schuster.

Grew, J. 1944. *Ten years in Japan.* New York: Simon and Schuster.

Grew, J. 1952. *Turbulent era.* Boston: Houghton Mifflin.

Haas, E. 1953. The balance of power as a guide to policy-making. *Journal of Politics* 15: 370–298.

Halberstam, D. 1972. *The best and the brightest.* New York: Random House.

Halberstam, D. 2007. *The coldest winter.* New York: Hyperion.

Halper, S. and J. Clarke. 2004. *America alone.* Cambridge: Cambridge University Press.

Halperin, M. 1974. *Bureaucratic politics and foreign policy.* Washington, DC: Brookings Institution.

Harary, F. 1961. A structural analysis of the situation in the Middle East in 1956. *Journal of Conflict Resolution* 5: 167–178.

Harary, F. 1969. *Graph theory.* Reading, MA: Addison-Wesley.

Hartmann, F. 1965. *Germany between east and west.* Englewood Cliffs, NJ: Prentice-Hall.

Hartmann, F. 1967. *The relations of nations.* New York: Macmillan.

Hartmann, F. 1970. *The new age of American foreign policy.* London: Macmillan.

Hartmann, F. 1982. *The conservation of enemies.* Westport, CT: Greenwood Press.

Hartmann, F. 1983. *The relations of nations.* 6th ed. New York: Macmillan.

Harrison, H. 2006. The new course. In *The cold war after Stalin's death,* ed. K. Larres and K. Osgood. Lanham, MD: Rowman and Littlefield.

Haslam, J. 1990. *The Soviet Union and the politics of nuclear weapons in Europe, 1969–1987.* Ithaca, NY: Cornell University Press.

Hawking, S. with L. Mlodinow. 2005. *A briefer history of time.* New York: Bantam.

Hedstrom, P. and R. Swedberg. 1998. *Social mechanisms.* Cambridge: Cambridge University Press.

Heinrichs, W. 1966. *American Ambassador Joseph Grew and the development of the United States diplomatic tradition.* Boston: Little, Brown.

Heinrichs, W. 1990. The Russian factor in Japanese-American relations, 1941. In *Pearl Harbor reexamined,* ed. H. Conroy and H. Wray. Honolulu: University of Hawaii Press.

Hermann, M. 1980. Explaining foreign policy behavior using the personal characteristics of leaders. *International Studies Quarterly* 24: 7–46.

Hermann, M. 2001. How decision units shape foreign policy. *International Studies Review* 3: 47–81.

Hermann, M. 2003. Assessing leadership style. In *The Psychological Assessment of Political Leaders,* ed. J. Post. Ann Arbor: University of Michigan Press.

Hermann, M. and C. Hermann. 1989. Who makes foreign policy decisions and how. *International Studies Quarterly* 33: 361–387.

Herrmann, R. 1988. The empirical challenge of the cognitive revolution. *International Studies Quarterly* 32: 175–203.

Herrmann, R. 1991. The Middle East and the new world order. *International Security* 16: 42–75.

Herz, M. 1966. *Beginnings of the cold war.* Bloomington: Indiana University Press.

Hewitt, J. 1994. *Self and society.* Boston: Allyn and Bacon.

Higgins, T. 1960. *Korea and the fall of MacArthur.* New York: Oxford University Press.

Higgins, T. 1987. *The perfect failure.* New York: W.W. Norton.

Hill, N. 1948. Was there an ultimatum before Pearl Harbor? *American Journal of International Law* 42: 355–367.

Hoagland, S. and S. Walker. 1979. Operational codes and crisis outcomes. In *Psychological models in international politics*, ed. L. Falkowski. Boulder, CO: Westview Press.

Hobbes, T. 1996. *Leviathan*. New York: Cambridge University Press.

Hoffman, D. and H. Dewar. 1991. State Department, panel, spar over envoy. *Washington Post*, July 13, 1, 14.

Holsti, K.J. 1970. National role conceptions in the study of foreign policy. *International Studies Quarterly* 14: 233–309.

Holsti, O. 1974–1975. Will the real Dulles please stand up? *International Journal* 30: 34–44.

Holsti, O., R. Brody, and R. North. 1964. Measuring affect and action in international reaction models. *Journal of Peace Research* 1: 170–189.

Homans, G. 1961. *Social behavior*. New York: Harcourt, Brace, and Jovanovich.

Hoopes, T. 1969. *The limits of intervention*. New York: David McKay Company.

Hosenball, M. and E. Thomas. 2001. Danger: Terror ahead. *Newsweek*, February 19.

Hughes, E. 1963. *The ordeal of power*. New York: Atheneum.

Hull, C. 1948. *The memoirs of Cordell Hull*. New York: Macmillan.

Hunt, M. 1987. *Ideology and U.S. foreign policy*. New Haven, CT: Yale University Press.

Hunt, M. 1996. *Lyndon Johnson's war*. New York: Hill and Wang.

Hurst, S. 1999. *The foreign policy of the Bush administration*. New York: Cassell.

Hybel, A. 1993. *Power over rationality*. Albany, NY: SUNY Press.

Hyland, W. 1978. SALT and Soviet-American relations. *International Security* 2: 156–162.

Ikle, F. 1964. *How nations negotiate*. New York: Harper and Row.

Ikuhiko, H. 1990. The road to the Pacific war. In *Pearl Harbor reexamined*, ed. H. Conroy and H. Wray. Honolulu: University of Hawaii Press.

Iriye, A. 1967. *Across the Pacific*. New York: Harcourt, Brace, and World.

Iriye, A. 1973. The role of the United States embassy in Tokyo. In *Pearl Harbor as history*, ed. D. Borg and S. Okamoto. New York: Columbia University Press.

Iriye, A. 1974. Japan's policies toward the United States. In *Japan's foreign policy, 1968–1941*, ed. J. Morley. New York: Columbia University Press.

Iriye, A. 1976. Toward Pearl Harbor. In *Pearl Harbor*, 3rd ed., ed. G. Waller. Lexington, MA: D.C. Heath and Company.

Iriye, A. 1981. *Power and culture*. Cambridge, MA: Harvard University Press.

Isikoff, M. and D. Corn. 2006. *Hubris*. New York: Crown Publishers.

Janis, I. 1972. *Victims of groupthink*. Boston: Houghton Mifflin.

Janis, I. 1982. *Groupthink*. Boston: Houghton Mifflin.

Janis, I. 1989. *Crucial decisions*. New York: Free Press.

Janis, I. and L. Mann. 1977. *Decision making*. New York: Free Press.

Jervis, R. 1976. *Perception and misperception in international politics*. Princeton, NJ: Princeton University Press

Jervis, R. 1978. Cooperation under the security dilemma. *World Politics* 30: 167–214.

Jervis, R. 1997. *System effects*. Princeton, NJ: Princeton University Press.

Jervis, R. 2010. *Why intelligence fails*. Ithaca, NY: Cornell University Press.

Jervis, R. and J. Snyder, eds. 1991. *Dominos and bandwagons*. New York: Oxford University Press.

Jian, C. 1996. *China's road to the Korean War*. New York: Columbia University Press.

Joffe, J. 1995. Bismarck or Britain? *International Security* 19: 94–117.

Johnson, C. 1966. *Revolutionary change*. Boston: Little, Brown.

Johnson, D. 2004. *Overconfidence and war*. Cambridge, MA: Harvard University Press.

Johnson, L. B. 1970. *A White House diary*. New York: Holt, Rinehart, and Winston.

Johnson, R. 1974. *Managing the White House*. New York: Harper and Row.

Kahneman, D., P. Slovic, and A. Tversky, eds. 1982. *Judgment under uncertainty*. New York: Cambridge University Press.

Kahneman, D. and A. Tversky. 1979. Prospect theory. *Econometrica* 47: 263–292.

Kaiser, D. 2000. *American tragedy*. Cambridge, MA: Harvard University Press.

Kalb, M. and B. Kalb. 1974. *Kissinger*. Boston: Little, Brown.

Kaplan, M. 1957. *System and process in international politics*. New York: John Wiley.

Katsiaficas, G., ed. 1992. *Vietnam documents*. Armonk, NY: M.E. Sharpe.

Kattenburg, P. 1980. *The Vietnam trauma in American foreign policy, 1948–1975*. New Brunswick, NJ: Transaction Books.

Kaufman, B. and S. Kaufman. 2006. *The presidency of James Earl Carter*. Lawrence: University Press of Kansas.

Keegan, J. 2004. *The Iraq war*. New York: Alfred Knopf.

[Kennan, G.] "X." 1947. The sources of Soviet conduct. *Foreign Affairs* 25: 566–582.

Kennan, G. 1967. *Memoirs, 1925–1950*. Boston: Little, Brown.

Kennan, G. 1972. *Memoirs, 1950–1963*. Boston: Little, Brown.

Kennan, G. 1984. *American diplomacy, 1900–1950*. Chicago: University of Chicago Press.

Khong, Y. F. 1992. *Analogies at war*. Princeton, NJ: Princeton University Press.

Kilcullen, D. 2009. *The accidental guerilla*. New York: Oxford University Press.

King, G., R. Keohane, and S. Verba.1994. *Designing social inquiry*. Princeton, NJ: Princeton University Press.

Kinzer, S. 2010. *Reset*. New York: Henry Holt.

Kissinger, H. 1965. *The troubled partnership*. New York: McGraw-Hill.

Kissinger, H. 1969. The Vietnam negotiations. *Foreign Affairs* 47: 211–234.

Kissinger, H. 1973. Dr. Kissinger's news conference, January 24. *Department of State Bulletin* 68: 155–169.

Kissinger, H. 1974. *American foreign policy*. New York: W.W. Norton.

Knowles, E. 1999. *The Oxford dictionary of quotations*. 5th ed. New York: Oxford University Press.

Kowert, P. 2002. *Groupthink or deadlock?* Albany, NY: SUNY Press.

Kowert, P. and M. Hermann. 1997. Who takes risks? *Journal of Conflict Resolution* 41: 611–637.

Kramer, M. 2006. International politics in the early post-Stalin era. In *The cold war after Stalin's death*, ed. K. Larres and K. Osgood. Lanham, MD: Rowman and Littlefield.

LaFeber, W. 1974. Crossing the 38th. In *Reflections on the cold war*, ed. L. Miller and R. Pruessen. Philadelphia: Temple University Press.

LaFeber, W. 2002. The Bush doctrine. *Diplomatic History* 26(4): 543–558.

Lake, D. and R. Powell. 1999. International relations. In *Strategic Choice and International Relations*, ed. D. Lake and R. Powell. Princeton, NJ: Princeton University Press.

Langer, W. and S. E. Gleason. 1953. *The undeclared war, 1940–1941*. New York: Harper.

Langley, L., ed. 1970. *The United States, Cuba, and the cold war*. Lexington, MA: D.C. Heath and Company.

Larres, K. and K. Osgood, eds. 2006. *The cold war after Stalin's death*. Lanham, MD: Rowman and Littlefield.

Larson, D. 1997. *Anatomy of mistrust*. Ithaca, NY: Cornell University Press.

Lasswell, H. 1958. *Politics: Who gets what, when, and how*. New York: Meridian Books.

Lazarus, R. 2009. Super wicked problems and climate change. *Cornell University Law Review* 94: 1153–1233.

Lebow, R. 1981. *Between war and peace*. Baltimore: Johns Hopkins University Press.

Lebow, R. 2008. *A cultural theory of international relations*. Cambridge: Cambridge University Press.

Lebow, R. 2010. *Forbidden fruit*. Princeton, NJ: Princeton University Press.

Lebow, R. and J. Stein. 1987. Beyond deterrence. *Journal of Social Issues* 43: 5–71.

Leffler, M. 2007. *For the soul of mankind*. New York: Hill and Wang.

Legvold, R. 1988. *Gorbachev's foreign policy*. New York: Foreign Policy Association.

Leites, N. 1953. *A study of Bolshevism*. New York: Free Press.

Leng, R. 1984. Reagan and the Russians. *American Political Science Review* 78: 338–355.

Leng, R. 1993. *Interstate crisis behavior, 1815–1980*. New York: Cambridge University Press.

Leng, R. and S. Walker. 1982. Comparing two studies of crisis bargaining. *Journal of Conflict Resolution* 26: 571–591.

Leopold, R. 1973. Historiographical reflections. In *Pearl Harbor as history*, ed. D. Borg and S. Okamoto, 1–23. New York: Columbia University Press.

Levi, A. and P. Tetlock. 1980. A cognitive analysis of Japan's 1941 decision for war. *Journal of Conflict Resolution* 24: 195–211.

Levy, J. 1994. Learning and foreign policy. *International Organization* 48: 279–312.

Levy, J. 1997. Prospect theory, rational choice, and international relations. *International Studies Quarterly* 41: 87–112.

Lewin, M. 1991. *The Gorbachev phenomenon*. Berkeley: University of California Press.

Lewis, D. 1973. *Counterfactuals*. Cambridge, MA: Harvard University Press.

Locke, J. 1980. *Second treatise on government*. Indianapolis: Hackett Publishing.

Lowe, P. 1986. *The origins of the Korean War*. New York: Longman Publishing.

Lukes, S. 1974. *Power*. London: Macmillan.

Lynch, A. 1989. *Gorbachev's international outlook*. New York: Institute for East-West Security Studies.

Lynch, G. 1998. *Decision for disaster*. Washington, DC: Brassey's.

MacDougall, J. 1991. A decision-making approach to understanding American policymakers. In *The Vietnam War*, ed. M. Gilbert. Westport, CT: Greenwood Press.

Mahnken, T. 2002. *Uncovering ways of war*. Ithaca, NY: Cornell University Press.

Majeski, S. 2004. Asymmetric power among agents and the generation and maintenance of cooperation in international relations. *International Studies Quarterly* 48: 455–470.

Mandelbaum, M. and S. Talbott. 1987. *Reagan and Gorbachev*. New York: Vintage Books.

Malici, A. 2006. Reagan and Gorbachev. In *Beliefs and leadership in world politics*, ed. S. Walker and M. Schafer, 127–150. New York: Palgrave Macmillan.

Malici, A. 2008. *When leaders learn and when they don't*. Albany, NY: SUNY Press.

Mann, J. 2004. *Rise of the vulcans*. New York: Penguin.

Maoz, Z. 1990. Framing the national interest. *World Politics* 43: 77–110.

Maoz, Z. 1998. Realist and cultural critiques of the democratic peace. *International Interactions* 24: 3–89.

Maoz, Z. and B. Mor. 2002. *Bound by struggle*. Ann Arbor: University of Michigan Press.

March, J. and J. Olsen. 1989. *Rediscovering institutions*. New York: Free Press.

Marfleet, B.G. and C. Miller. 2005. Failure after 1441. *Foreign Policy Analysis* 1: 333–359.

Marfleet, B.G. and S. Walker. 2006. A world of beliefs. In *Beliefs and leadership in world politics*, ed. M. Schafer and S. Walker. New York: Palgrave Macmillan.

Masaru, I. 1990. Examples of mismanagement in U.S. policy toward Japan before World War II. In *Pearl Harbor re-examined*, ed. H. Conroy and H. Wray. Honolulu: University of Hawaii Press.

Mastny, V. 2006. The elusive détente. In *The cold war after Stalin's death,* ed. K. Larres and K. Osgood. Lanham, MD: Rowman and Littlefield.

Matlock, J. 2004. *Reagan and Gorbachev.* New York: Random House.

Matray, J. 1979. Truman's plan for victory. *Journal of American History* 66: 314–333.

May, E. 1973. *"Lessons" of the past.* New York: Oxford University Press.

Mayer, J. 2009. *The dark side.* New York: Random House.

McClain, J. 2002. *Japan.* New York: W.W. Norton.

McClelland, C. 1966. *Theory and the international system.* New York: Macmillan

McClelland, C. 1972. The beginning, duration, and abatement of international crises. In *International crises*, ed. C. Hermann. New York: Free Press.

McLellan, D. 1968. Dean Acheson and the Korean War. *Political Science Quarterly* 83: 16–39.

McNamara, R., J. Blight, R. Brigham, T. Biersteker, and H. Schandler. 1999. *Argument without end.* New York: Public Affairs.

Melanson, R. 1996. *American foreign policy since the Vietnam War.* Armonk, NY: M.E. Sharpe.

Mendelsohn, J. 1988. The Soviet-American arms control dialogue before and after Reykjavik. In *Soviet-American relations*, ed. D. Nelson and R. Anderson. Wilmington, DE: SR Books.

Mercer, J. 1996. *Reputation and international politics.* Ithaca, NY: Cornell University Press.

Merton, R. 1957. *Social theory and social structure.* New York: Free Press.

Middlemas, K. 1972. *Diplomacy of illusion.* London: Weidenfeld and Nicholson.

Milner, H. 1991. The assumption of anarchy in international relations theory. *Review of International Studies* 17: 67–85.

Mintz, A. 2004. How do individuals make decisions? *Journal of Conflict Resolution* 48: 3–13.

Mitchell, M. 2009. *Complexity.* New York: Oxford University Press.

Modelski, G. 1987. *Long cycles in world politics.* Seattle: University of Washington Press.

Moens, A. 1990. *Foreign policy under Carter.* Boulder, CO: Westview Press.

Morgenthau, H. 1961. John Foster Dulles. In *An uncertain tradition,* ed. N. Graebner. New York: McGraw-Hill.

Morgenthau, H. 1985. *Politics among nations.* 6th ed. New York: Alfred Knopf.

Morley, M. 1987. *Imperial state and revolution.* New York: Cambridge University Press.

Morrow, J. 1994. *Game theory for political scientists.* Princeton, NJ: Princeton University Press.

Moscovici, S. and M. Zavalloni. 1969. The group as a polarizer of attitudes. *Journal of Social Psychology* 12: 125–135.

Mosley, P. 1953. The Kremlin's foreign policy since Stalin. *Foreign Affairs* 32: 20–33.

Mueller, J. 1991/1992. Pearl Harbor. *International Security* 16: 172–203.

Neustadt, R. 1970. *Alliance politics.* New York: Columbia University Press.

Neustadt, R. and E. May. 1986. *Thinking in time.* New York: Free Press.

Newell, A. and H. Simon. 1972. *Human problem solving*. Englewood Cliffs, NJ: Prentice-Hall.

Newman, W. 1968. *The balance of power in the interwar years, 1919–1939*. New York: Random House.

Nisbett, R. and L. Ross. 1980. *Human inference*. Englewood Cliffs, NJ: Prentice-Hall.

Nixon, R. 1972. Denying Hanoi the means to continue aggression. *Department of State Bulletin* 68 (February 29): 747–750.

Nye, J. 1990. *Bound to lead*. New York: Basic Books.

Oberdorfer, D. 1991a. *From the cold war to a new era*. Baltimore: Johns Hopkins University Press.

Oberdorfer, D. 1991b. Missed signals in the Middle East. *Washington Post Magazine*, March 17, 19–41.

Olson, M. 1965. *The logic of collective action*. Cambridge, MA: Harvard University Press.

Osgood, C. 1960. *Graduate reciprocation in tension reduction*. Urbana: University of Illinois Press.

Osgood, C. 1962. *An alternative to war and surrender*. Chicago: University of Illinois Press.

Osgood, K. 2006a. The perils of coexistence. In *The cold war after Stalin's death*, ed. K. Larres and K. Osgood. Lanham, MD: Rowman and Littlefield.

Osgood, K. 2006b. *Total cold war*. Lawrence: University Press of Kansas.

Oye, K. 1986. *Cooperation under anarchy*. Princeton, NJ: Princeton University Press.

Park, H.K. 1983. American involvement in the Korean War. *The History Teacher* 16: 249–263.

Parker, C. and E. Stern. 2002. Blindsided? *Political Psychology* 23: 601–628.

Parmett, H. 1972. *Eisenhower and the American crusades*. New York: Macmillan.

Parsi, T. 2007. *Treacherous alliance*. New Haven, CT: Yale University Press.

Paterson, T. 1988. *Meeting the Communist threat*. New York: Oxford University Press.

Paterson, T. 1989. Fixation with Cuba. In *Kennedy's quest for victory*, ed. T. Paterson. New York: Oxford University Press.

Paterson, T. 1994. *Contesting Castro*. New York: Oxford University Press.

Pavia, P. 2006. *The Cuba project*. New York: Palgrave Macmillan.

Perez, L. 1990. *Cuba and the United States*. Athens: University of Georgia Press.

Peterson, C., S. Maire, and M. Seligman. 1993. *Learned helplessness*. New York: Oxford University Press.

Pfeffer, R., ed. 1968. *No more Vietnams?* New York: Harper and Row.

Phillips, D. 2003. Listening to the wrong Iraqi. *New York Times*, September 20, A13.

Pincus, W. 2003. U.S. lacks specifics of banned arms. *Washington Post*, March 16, A17.

Plato. 1892. *The dialogues of Plato*. Trans. Benjamin Jowett. Oxford: Clarendon Press.

Plato. 2000. *The Republic*. Ed. G.R.F. Ferrari. Trans. Tom Griffith. Cambridge: Cambridge University Press.

Polk, W.1997. *Neighbors and strangers*. Chicago: University of Chicago Press.

Post, J. and S. Walker. 2003. Assessing leaders in theory and practice. In *The psychological assessment of political leaders*, ed. J. Post. Ann Arbor: University of Michigan Press.

Poundstone, W. 1992. *Prisoner's dilemma*. New York: Anchor Books.

Powell, R. 1999. *In the shadow of power*. Princeton, NJ: Princeton University Press.

Preston, T. 2001. *The president and his inner circle*. New York: Columbia University Press.

Rapoport, A. and A. Chammah. 1965. *Prisoner's dilemma*. Ann Arbor: University of Michigan Press.

Rapoport, A. and M. Guyer. 1966. A taxonomy of 2×2 games. *General Systems: Yearbook for the Society of General Systems Research* 11: 203–214.

Rapoport, A., M. Guyer, and D. Gordon. 1976. *The 2×2 game*. Ann Arbor: University of Michigan Press.

Rashid, A. 2000. *Taliban*. New Haven, CT: Yale University Press.

Rashid, A. 2009. *Descent into chaos*. New York: Penguin.

Raub, W. 1990. A general game-theoretic model of preference adaptations in problematic social situations. *Rationality and Society* 2: 67–93.

Rauch, B. 1950. *Roosevelt*. New York: Creative Age Press.

Renshon, S. 1993. Good judgment and the lack thereof during the Gulf War. In *The political psychology of the Gulf War*, ed. S. Renshon and D. Larson. Pittsburgh: University of Pittsburgh Press.

Renshon, S. and D. Larson. 2003. *Good judgment in foreign policy*. New York: Rowman and Littlefield.

Reynolds, D. 2000. *One world divisible*. New York: W.W. Norton.

Reynolds, D. 2001. *From Munich to Pearl Harbor*. Chicago: Ivan R. Dee.

Richardson, L. 1960. *Statistics of deadly quarrels*. Chicago: Quadrangle.

Richter, J. 1993. Re-examining Soviet Policy towards Germany in 1953. *Europe-Asia Studies* 45: 671–691.

Ricks, T. 2006. *Fiasco*. New York: Penguin Press.

Ricks, T. 2009. *The gamble*. New York: Penguin Press.

Rittel, H. and M. Webber. 1973. Dilemmas in a general theory of planning. *Policy Sciences* 4: 155–169.

Rodriguez, J. 1999. *The Bay of Pigs and the CIA*. New York: Ocean Press.

Roeder, P. 1984. Soviet policies and Kremlin politics. *International Studies Quarterly* 28: 171–193.

Robison, S. 2006. George W. Bush and the Vulcans. In *Beliefs and leadership in world politics*, ed. M. Schafer and S. Walker. New York: Palgrave.

Rosecrance, R. 1963. *Action and reaction in world politics*. Boston: Little, Brown.

Rousseau, J. 1978. *The social contract and discourses*. Trans. G.D.H. Cole. New York: Dutton.

Russett, B. 1967. Pearl Harbor. *Journal of Peace Research* 4: 89–106.

Russett, B. 1987. Further beyond deterrence. *Journal of Social Issues* 43: 99–104.

Russett, B. and H. Starr. 2000. From democratic peace to Kantian peace. In *Handbook of war studies II*, ed. M. Midlarsky. Ann Arbor: University of Michigan Press.

Russo, G. 1998. *Live by the sword*. Baltimore: Bancroft Press.

Sanger, D. 2009. *The inheritance*. New York: Harmony Books.

Sarbin, Th. and V. Allen. 1968. Role theory. In *The handbook of social psychology*, vol. 1, ed. G. Lindzey and E. Aronson. Reading, MA: Addison-Wesley.

Schafer, M. and S. Crichlow. 1996. Antecedents of groupthink. *Journal of Conflict Resolution* 40: 415–435.

Schafer, M. and S. Crichlow. 2010. *Groupthink vs. high quality decision making in international relations*. New York: Columbia University Press.

Schafer, M. and S. Walker, eds. 2006. *Beliefs and leadership in world politics*. New York: Palgrave Macmillan.

Schaeffer, J., et al. 2007. Checkers is solved. *Science* 317: 1518–1522.

Schelling, T. 1960. *The strategy of conflict*. Cambridge, MA: Harvard University Press.

Schelling, T. 1966. *Arms and influence*. New Haven, CT: Yale University Press.

Schelling, T. 1978. *Micromotives and macrobehavior*. New York: W.W. Norton.

Schelling, T. 1984. *Choice and consequences*. Cambridge, MA: Harvard University Press.

Scherstjanoi, E. 1998. Die sowjetische Deutschlandpolitik nach Stalins Tod 1953. *Vierteljahreshefte fuer Zeitgeschichte* 46: 503–517.

Schlesinger, A. 1965. *A thousand days*. Boston: Houghton Mifflin.

Schrodinger, E. 1967. *What is life? The physical aspect of the living cell and mind and matter*. New York: Cambridge University Press.

Schroeder, P. 1976. An appraisal. In *Pearl Harbor*, 3rd ed., ed. G. Waller. Lexington, MA: D.C. Heath and Company.

Schultz, G. 1993. *Turmoil and triumph*. New York: Charles Scribner's Sons.

Schurmann, F., D. Scott, and R. Zelink. 1966. *The politics of escalation in Vietnam*. Boston: Beacon Press.

Schweller, R. 1994. Bandwagoning for profit. *International Security* 19: 72–107.

Schweller, R. 1998. *Deadly imbalances*. New York: Columbia University Press.

Sciolino, E. 1991. *The outlaw state*. New York: John Wiley and Sons.

Searle, J. 1995. *The social construction of reality*. New York: Free Press.

Senese, P. and J. Vasquez. 2008. *The steps to war*. Princeton, NJ: Princeton University Press.

Shawcross, W. 2004. *Allies*. New York: Public Affairs.

Shlaim, A. 1983. *The United States and the Berlin blockade*. Berkeley: University of California Press.

Silvert, K. 1967. A hemispheric perspective. In *Cuba and the United States*, ed. J. Plank. Washington, DC: Brookings Institution.

Simmel, G. 1955. *Conflict and web of group affiliations*. Trans. K. Wolff and R. Bendix. New York: Free Press.

Simon, H. 1955. A behavioral model of rational choice. *Quarterly Journal of Economics* 69: 99–118.

Simon, H. 1957. *Models of man*. New York: John Wiley.

Simon, H. 1976. *Administrative behavior*. New York: Free Press.

Simon, H. 1985. Human nature in politics. *American Political Science Review* 79: 293–304.

Siverson, R. and Starr, H. 1991. *The diffusion of war*. Ann Arbor: University of Michigan Press.

Skidmore, D. 1993. Carter and the failure of foreign policy reform. *Political Science Quarterly* 108: 699–729.

Skyrms, B. 2004. *The stag hunt and the evolution of social structure*. New York: Cambridge University Press.

Slavin, B. 2007. *Bitter friends, bosom enemies*. New York: St. Martin's Press.

Slovic, P., B. Fischoff, and S. Lichtenstein. 1977. Behavioral decision theory. *Annual Review of Psychology* 28: 1–39.

Smith, E. 1975. *The presidency of James Buchanan*. Lawrence: University Press of Kansas.

Smith, E. and M. Schecter. 1994. *The United Nations in a new world order*. Claremont, CA: Keck Center for International and Strategic Studies.

Smith, G. 1986. *Morality, reason, and power*. New York: Hill and Wang.

Smith, R. 1960. The *United States and Cuba*. New York: Bookman Associates.

Smith, W. 1984. *Castro's Cuba*. Washington, DC: Woodrow Wilson International Center for Scholars.

Snyder, G. 1997. *Alliance politics*. Ithaca, NY: Cornell University Press.

Snyder, G. and P. Diesing. 1977. *Nations in conflict*. Princeton, NJ: Princeton University Press.

Snyder, J. 2003. Is and ought. In *Progress in international relations theory*, ed. Colin Elman and Miriam Elman. Cambridge, MA: MIT Press.

Snyder, J. and R. Jervis. 1993. *Coping with complexity in the international system*. Boulder, CO: Westview Press.

Snyder, R., H. Bruck, and B. Sapin. 1962. *Foreign policy decision making*. New York: Free Press.

Spanier, J. 1959. *The Truman-MacArthur controversy and the Korean War*. Cambridge, MA: Harvard University Press.

Sprout, H. and M. Sprout. 1956. *Man-milieu relationship hypotheses in the context of international politics*. Princeton, NJ: Center of International Studies, Princeton University.

Sprout, H. and M. Sprout. 1965. *The ecological perspective in human affairs*. Princeton, NJ: Princeton University Press

Stavins, R., R.. Barnet, and M. Raskin. 1971. *Washington plans an aggressive war*. New York: Random House.

Stein, A. 1990. *Why nations cooperate*. Ithaca, NY: Cornell University Press.

Stein, J. 1992. Deterrence and compellence in the Gulf, 1990–1991. *International Security* 17: 147–179.

Stein, J. 1994. Political learning by doing. *International Organization* 48: 155–183.

Stein, J. 2007. Foreign policy decision-making. In *Foreign policy*, ed. S. Smith, A. Hadfield, and T. Dunne. Oxford: Oxford University Press.

Steinbrunner, J. 1974. *A cybernetic theory of decision*. Princeton, NJ: Princeton University Press.

Steininger, R. 1990. *The German question*. New York: Columbia University Press.

Stevenson, M. 2006. Economic liberalism and the operational code beliefs of U.S. presidents. In *Beliefs and leadership in world politics*, ed. M. Schafer and S. Walker. New York: Palgrave.

Stewart, R. 2004. *The places in between*. New York: Harcourt.

Stewart, R. 2006. *The prince of the marshes*. New York: Harcourt.

Stoessinger, J. 1985. *Why nations go to war*. 4th ed. New York: St. Martin's Press.

Stoessinger, J. 2005. *Why nations go to war*. 9th ed. Belmont, CA: Wadsworth/Thomson Learning.

Stone, I. 1969. *The hidden history of the Korean War*. New York: Monthly Review Press.

Stone, R. 2001. The use and abuse of game theory in international relations. *Journal of Conflict Resolution* 45: 216–244.

Strong, R. 2005. *Decisions and dilemmas*. Armonk, NY: M.E. Sharpe.

Suskind, R. 2004. *The price of loyalty*. New York: Simon and Schuster.

Suskind, R. 2006. *The one percent doctrine*. New York: Simon and Schuster.

Suskind, R. 2009. *The way of the world*. New York: HarperCollins.

Swansbrough, R. 1994. A Kohutian analysis of President Bush's personality and style in the Persian Gulf crisis. *Political Psychology* 15: 227–276.

Sylvan, D. and J. Voss. 1998. *Problem representation in foreign policy decision making*. New York: Cambridge University Press.

Szulc, T. 1974. Behind the Vietnam cease-fire. *Foreign Policy* 15: 21–69.

Talbott, S., ed. 1970. *Khrushchev remembers*. Boston: Little, Brown.

Talbott, S. 1979. *Endgame*. New York: Harper and Row.

Taleb, N. 2007. *The black swan*. New York: Random House.

Tansill, C. 1976. Back door to war. In *Pearl Harbor*, 3rd ed., ed. G. Waller. Lexington, MA: D.C. Heath and Company.

Taylor, A.J.P. 1962. *The origins of the second world war*. New York: Atheneum.

Tetlock, P. 1983. Accountability and the complexity of thought. *Journal of Personality and Social Psychology* 41: 74–83.

Tetlock, P. 1991. Learning in U.S. and Soviet foreign policy. In *Learning in U.S. and Soviet foreign policy*, ed. G. Breslauer and P. Tetlock, 20–59. Boulder, CO: Westview Press.

Tetlock, P. 1998. Social psychology and world politics. In *The handbook of social psychology*, vol. 2, ed. D. Gilbert, S. Fiske, and G. Lindzey. New York: McGraw-Hill.

Tetlock, P. 2005. *Expert political judgment*. Princeton, NJ: Princeton University Press.

Tetlock, P. and A. Belkin, eds. 1996. *Counterfactual thought experiments in world politics*. Princeton, NJ: Princeton University Press.

The 9/11 Commission. 2004. *Final report of the national commission on terrorist attacks upon the United States*. Washington, DC: U.S. Government Printing Office.

Thies, C. 2001. A social psychological approach to enduring rivalries. *Political Psychology* 22: 693–725.

Thies, W. 1980. *When governments collide*. Berkeley: University of California Press.

Thom, F. 1988. *Glasnost, Gorbachev and Lenin*. London: Policy Research Publications.

Thomas, H. 1967. *Suez*. New York: Harper and Row.

Thompson, W. 1983. *Contending approaches to world system analysis*. Beverly Hills, CA: Sage.

Trefousse, H. 1982. *Pearl Harbor*. Malabar, FL: Robert E. Krieger.

Truman, H. 1956. *Memoirs by Harry S. Truman*, vol. 2. New York: Doubleday.

Truman, H. 1965. The president's news conference of July 13, 1950. Available at: http://www.trumanlibrary.org/publicpapers/

Tsebelis, G. 1990. *Nested games*. Berkeley: University of California Press.

Tuchman, B. 1984. *The march of folly*. New York: Knopf.

Turner, R. 1975. *Vietnamese Communism*. Stanford, CA: Hoover Institution Press.

Tversky, A. and D. Kahnemann. 1986. Rational choice and the framing of decisions. *Journal of Business* 59: S251–S278.

Tversky, A. and D. Kahneman. 1991. Loss aversion in riskless choice. *Quarterly Journal of Economics* 41: 1039–1061.

Tversky, A. and D. Kahneman. 1992. Advances in prospect theory. *Journal of Risk and Uncertainty* 5: 297–323.

Ulam, A. 1983. *Dangerous relations*. New York: Oxford University Press.

United States Department of Defense and the House Committee on Armed Services. 1971. *U.S.-Vietnam relations, 1945–1967*. Washington, DC: Department of Defense and the House Committee on Armed Services.

Utley, J. 1990. Cordell Hull and the diplomacy of inflexibility. In *Pearl Harbor re-examined*, ed. H. Conroy and H. Wray. Honolulu: University of Hawaii Press.

Vance, C. 1983. *Hard choices*. New York: Simon and Schuster.

Vasquez, J. 1993. *The war puzzle*. Cambridge: Cambridge University Press.

Vertzberger, Y. 1990. *The world in their minds*. Stanford, CA: Stanford University Press.

Vertzberger, Y. 1998. *Risk taking and decisionmaking*. Stanford, CA: Stanford University Press.

Von Neumann, J. and O. Morgenstern. 1953. *Theory of games and economic behavior.* Princeton, NJ: Princeton University Press.

Voss, J. and T. Post. 1988. On the solving of ill-structured problems. In *The nature of expertise,* ed. M. Chi, R. Glaser, and M. Farr. Hillsdale, NJ: Erlbaum.

Wainstock, D.. 1999. *Truman, MacArthur, and the Korean War.* Westport, CT: Greenwood Press.

Walker, S. 1977. The interface between beliefs and behavior: Henry Kissinger's operational code and the Vietnam War. *Journal of Conflict Resolution* 21: 129–167.

Walker, S. 1979. National role conceptions and systemic outcomes. In *Psychological models in international politics,* ed. L. Falkowski. Boulder, CO: Westview Press.

Walker, S. 1982. Bargaining over Berlin. *Journal of Politics* 44: 152–164.

Walker, S. 1987. *Role theory and foreign policy analysis.* Durham, NC: Duke University Press.

Walker, S. 1992. Symbolic interactionism and international politics. In *Contending dramas,* ed. Martha Cottam and Chic-yu Shih. New York: Praeger.

Walker, S. 1995. Psychodynamic processes and framing effects in foreign policy decision-making. *Political Psychology* 16: 697–717.

Walker, S. 2002. Beliefs and foreign policy analysis in the new millennium. In *Millennial reflections on international studies,* ed. M. Brecher and F. Harvey. Ann Arbor: University of Michigan Press.

Walker, S. 2004a. The management and resolution of conflict in a "single" case. In *Multiple paths to knowledge in international relations,* ed. Z. Maoz, A. Mintz, T. C. Morgan, G. Palmer, and R. Stoll. Lanham, MD: Lexington Books.

Walker, S. 2004b. Role identities and the operational codes of political leaders. In *Advances in political psychology,* ed. Margaret Hermann. Amsterdam: Elsevier.

Walker, S. 2007. Generalizing about security strategies in the Baltic Sea region. In *Security strategies, power disparity, and identity,* ed. Olav Knudsen. Burlington, VT: Ashgate.

Walker, S. 2010. Binary role theory and foreign policy analysis. Presented in the Foreign Policy Analysis workshop, "Integrating foreign policy analysis and international relations through role theory," at the Annual Meeting of the International Studies Association, New Orleans, February 16–20.

Walker, S. and A. Malici. 2006. U.S. presidents and foreign policy mistakes in the exercise of power. Presented at the annual meeting of the American Political Science Association, Philadelphia, August 31–September 3.

Walker, S., A. Malici, and M. Schafer. 2011. *Rethinking foreign policy analysis.* New York: Routledge.

Walker, S. and M. Schafer. 2007. Theodore Roosevelt and Woodrow Wilson as cultural icons of U.S. foreign policy. *Political Psychology* 28: 747–776.

Walker, S., M. Schafer, and M. Young. 2003. Profiling the operational codes of political leaders. In *The psychological assessment of political leaders,* ed. J. Post. Ann Arbor: University of Michigan Press.

Waltz, K. 1959. *Man, the state, and war.* New York: Columbia University Press.

Waltz, K. 1979. *Theory of international politics.* Reading, MA: Addison-Wesley.

Wendt, A. 1999. *Social theory of international politics.* New York: Cambridge University Press.

White, R. 1984. *Fearful warriors.* New York: Free Press.

Whitehead, A. [1925] 1948. *Science and the modern world*. New York: New American Library.

Whiting, A.. 1960. *China crosses the Yalu*. Stanford, CA: Stanford University Press.

Wilkinson, D.1969. *Comparative foreign relations*. Belmont, CA: Dickenson.

Wilson, E. 1975. *Sociobiology*. Cambridge, MA: Harvard University Press.

Wilson, E. 1978. *On human nature*. Cambridge, MA: Harvard University Press.

Wilson, J. 2003. What I didn't find in Africa. *New York Times*, July 6, 9.

Winter, D. 2003a. Assessing leaders' personalities. In *The psychological assessment of leaders*, ed. J. Post. Ann Arbor: University of Michigan Press.

Winter, D. 2003b. Measuring the motives of political actors at a distance. In *The psychological assessment of leaders*, ed. J. Post. Ann Arbor: University of Michigan Press.

Wohlstetter, R. 1962. *Pearl Harbor*. Stanford, CA: Stanford University Press.

Woodward, B. 1991. *The commanders*. New York: Simon and Schuster.

Woodward, B. 2002. *Bush at war*. New York: Alfred Knopf.

Woodward, B. 2004. *Plan of attack*. New York: Simon and Schuster.

Woodward, B. 2008. *The war within*. New York: Simon and Schuster.

Wray, H. 1990. Japanese-American relations and perceptions, 1900–1940. In *Pearl Harbor re-examined*, ed. H. Conroy and H. Wray. Honolulu: University of Hawaii Press.

Wriggins, W. H. 1969. *The ruler's imperative*. New York: Columbia University Press.

Wright, L. 2006. *The looming tower*. New York: Alfred Knopf.

Wright, R. 2000. *Nonzero*. New York: Vintage Books.

Wright, R. 2008. *Dreams and shadows*. New York: Penguin.

Wyden, P. 1979. *Bay of Pigs*. New York: Simon and Schuster.

Yetiv, S. 1997. *The Persian Gulf crisis*. Westport, CT: Greenwood Press.

Young, M. 1991. *The Vietnam wars, 1945–1990*. New York: HarperCollins.

Zartman, W., ed. 1978. *The negotiation process*. Beverly Hills, CA: Sage Publications.

Zartman, W. 2001. *Preventive negotiation*. Lanham, MD: Rowman and Littlefield.

Zartman, W. and G. Olivier Faure, eds. 2005. *Escalation and negotiation in international conflicts*. Cambridge: Cambridge University Press.

Zartman, W. and J. Rubin, eds. 2000. *Power and negotiation*. Ann Arbor: University of Michigan Press

Zemtsov, Ilya and John Farrar. 1989. *Gorbachev*. New Brunswick, NJ: Transaction Publishers.

Index

Note: Page numbers followed by *f* and *t* indicate figures and tables.